The Velvet Underground

The Velvet Underground

What Goes On

Edited by
Sean Albiez and David Pattie

BLOOMSBURY ACADEMIC
NEW YORK • LONDON • OXFORD • NEW DELHI • SYDNEY

BLOOMSBURY ACADEMIC
Bloomsbury Publishing Inc
1385 Broadway, New York, NY 10018, USA
50 Bedford Square, London, WC1B 3DP, UK
29 Earlsfort Terrace, Dublin 2, Ireland

BLOOMSBURY, BLOOMSBURY ACADEMIC and the Diana logo
are trademarks of Bloomsbury Publishing Plc

First published in the United States of America 2023
This paperback edition published 2024

Copyright © Sean Albiez and David Pattie, 2023

Each chapter copyright © by the contributor, 2023

For legal purposes the constitute an extension of this copyright page.

Cover design: Louise Dugdale
Cover image ©: GAB Archive / Redferns / Getty Images

All rights reserved. No part of this publication may be reproduced or transmitted in any form or by any means, electronic or mechanical, including photocopying, recording, or any information storage or retrieval system, without prior permission in writing from the publishers.

Bloomsbury Publishing Inc does not have any control over, or responsibility for, any third-party websites referred to or in this book. All internet addresses given in this book were correct at the time of going to press. The author and publisher regret any inconvenience caused if addresses have changed or sites have ceased to exist, but can accept no responsibility for any such changes.

Library of Congress Cataloguing-in-Publication Data
Names: Albiez, Sean, editor. | Pattie, David, 1963- editor.
Title: The Velvet Underground: what goes on/edited by Sean Albiez and David Pattie.
Description: [1st.] | New York, NY: Bloomsbury Academic, 2022. | Includes bibliographical references and index. | Summary: "An academic collection that explores and examines The Velvet Underground in the 1960s and the solo activities of band members up to the present"– Provided by publisher.
Identifiers: LCCN 2022009573 (print) | LCCN 2022009574 (ebook) |
ISBN 9781501338410 (hardback) | ISBN 9781501393907 (paperback) |
ISBN 9781501338427 (epub) | ISBN 9781501338434 (pdf) | ISBN 9781501338441
Subjects: LCSH: Velvet Underground (Musical group) | Reed, Lou. |
Warhol, Andy, 1928-1987. | Nico, 1938-1988. | Rock musicians–United States–Biography. |
Rock music–1961-1970–History and criticism. | Rock music–1971–1980–History and criticism. |
Avant-garde (Aesthetics)–History–20th century.
Classification: LCC ML421.V44 V48 2022 (print) | LCC ML421.V44 (ebook) |
DDC 782.42166092/2–dc23
LC record available at https://lccn.loc.gov/2022009573
LC ebook record available at https://lccn.loc.gov/2022009574

ISBN:	HB:	978-1-5013-3841-0
	PB:	978-1-5013-9390-7
	ePDF:	978-1-5013-3843-4
	eBook:	978-1-5013-3842-7

Typeset by Integra Software Services Pvt. Ltd.

To find out more about our authors and books visit www.bloomsbury.com and sign up for our newsletters.

For Celie, Joe, Jacqui and Cameron

Contents

Contributors — viii

Introduction – The Velvet Underground: What went on
Sean Albiez and David Pattie — 1

1. Saved by rock and roll: The Velvet Underground in and out of history *Jeffrey Roessner* — 17
2. The Velvet Underground and the networks of sound, vision and words of the fertile transatlantic crescent 1965–7 *Johnny Hopkins and Martin James* — 31
3. Andy Warhol films the Velvet Underground and Nico *Glyn Davis* — 53
4. 'The riskiest kind of writing available': Lou Reed, Grove Press and the literary underground *Thom Robinson* — 67
5. The Velvet Underground and musical archetypes *Julijana Papazova* — 83
6. Lou Reed's Great American Novel *Peter Griffiths* — 97
7. Nico, captain of her own ship: Cultural accreditation and mid-1960s experimental rock *Mimi Haddon* — 113
8. European Son: 'Europe' in Nico, Cale and Reed's long-1970s solo work *Toby Manning* — 131
9. 'I'll be your mirror': The Velvet Underground as the legacy of Ziggy Stardust *Martin James and Johnny Hopkins* — 145
10. What Caroline says: Berlin, 1973 and 2006 *David Pattie* — 161
11. Unfrozen borderlines: Nico, John Cale and Brian Eno at the Berlin Nationalgalerie *Sean Albiez and Timor Kaul* — 173
12. Noise annoys: Lou Reed's *Metal Machine Music* *Mark Goodall* — 197
13. The Velvet Underground is a Jonathan Richman song *Cibrán Tenreiro Uzal* — 209
14. 'It's not that I don't want to play your favourites': Lou Reed, improvisation and performance *David Pattie* — 223
15. Portrait of the artist as Andy Warhol: Lou Reed and John Cale's *Songs for Drella* *Elizabeth Ann Lindau* — 237
16. The late musical voice: John Cale and Lou Reed in the twenty-first century *Sean Albiez* — 253

Discography – The Velvet Underground and Solo Works — 277
Index — 289

Contributors

Sean Albiez is an independent scholar and a musician. He has published on electronic music, music technology, punk and post-punk. He is currently researching topics in electronic music history and has thirty years' experience lecturing in popular music at UK universities and colleges. He is the co-editor of *Kraftwerk: Music Non Stop* (2011) and *Brian Eno: Oblique Music* (2016), and contributing editor (Music Technology) for the *Bloomsbury Encyclopaedia of Popular Music of the World*. He produces electronic music as ghost elektron and – with Martin James – as Nostalgia Deathstar.

Glyn Davis is Professor of Film Studies at the University of St Andrews, UK. He is a theorist and historian of queer visual culture, with a particular interest in experimental and avant-garde cinema. Recent publications include a special issue of *Third Text*, 'Imagining Queer Europe' (2021, co-edited with Fiona Anderson and Nat Raha), and *Queer Print in Europe* (2022, co-edited with Laura Guy).

Mark Goodall is Senior Lecturer in Film at the University of Bradford, UK. He has published books on the Beatles *(The Beatles, or 'The White Album'* 2018), music and the occult (*Gathering of the Tribe: Music and Heavy Conscious Creation* [2013] 2022) and shock cinema of the 1960s (*Sweet and Savage: The World, Through the Mondo Film Lens* 2018). He co-edited *New Media Archaeology* (2018) and edited a special edition of *Film International* (2019). He has written for *The Guardian, The Independent, The New European* and *Shindig!* and plays with the group Rudolf Rocker.

Peter Griffiths is a writer based in the East Midlands, UK. His fiction has appeared in various anthologies published by Inkermen Press, and he has written widely on creative writing theory. He is currently seeking a publisher for his first novel, and is at work on a book attempting to bridge the gap between creative writing theory and literary criticism. His other interests include the intersection of literature and other art forms, science fiction and British avant-garde literature of the 1960s.

Mimi Haddon is Senior Lecturer in Music at the University of Sussex, UK. She is a musicologist whose work focuses on popular music, primarily on the genres of punk, post-punk, alternative, folk, jazz, blues, rock and the avant-garde. Her research has appeared in the journals *Twentieth-Century Music, Popular Music, Women & Music: A Journal of Gender and Culture* and the *Journal of British Cinema and Television*. She is the author of *What Is Post-Punk? Genre and Identity in Avant-Garde Popular Music, 1977–82* (2020).

Johnny Hopkins is Senior Lecturer in Music and Media Industries at Solent University, Southampton, UK. His research interests include music, national identity and nationalism, John and Alice Coltrane, and the representation of Native Americans in popular music. He has published research on music marketing and PR, Elvis Presley, The Who, Swinging London and the rebranding of post-colonial Britain. He has thirty years' experience as a PR, live promoter and DJ. He was Head of Press at Creation Records and has worked with artists including Oasis, Lee 'Scratch' Perry, Adrian Sherwood, Primal Scream, Jesus and Mary Chain, Maureen Tucker, MC5 and the Sonics.

Martin James is Professor of Creative and Cultural Industries at Solent University, Southampton, UK. His research interests include music journalism, the UK and US music press and late twentieth-century alternative musics – specifically punk, post-punk, electronic music and hip hop. He is the author of *French Connections: From Discotheque to Discovery* (2003, 2021), *State of Bass: Jungle – The Story So Far* (1997, 2020), co-author of *Understanding the Music Industries* (2103) and co-editor of *Media Narratives in Popular Music* (2021). He is a musician, vocalist with Nostalgia Deathstar and heads the record label and book publisher State of Bass.

Timor Kaul is a teacher of music, history, religion and ethics and a former semi-professional musician. He lectured at the Universität der Künste, Bochum, on Kraftwerk, the subcultural techno-video productions of 29nov films and popular music semiotics. He is undertaking ethnomusicological research on 'Lebenswelt House/Techno: DJs und ihre Musik' at the Institut für Europäische Musikethnologie, Universität zu Köln, Germany. He has written articles on electronic music history, including 'Kraftwerk: Die anderem >Krauts<', in Lücke, M. and Näumann, K. (eds) (2017), *Reflexionen zum Progressive Rock*, and on electronic body music and techno in Hecken, T. and Kleiner, M.S. (eds) (2017), *Handbuch Popkultur*.

Elizabeth Ann Lindau is Assistant Professor of Music History at California State University, Long Beach, USA. Her research explores intersections between avant-gardism and rock music since the 1960s, particularly in the output of the Velvet Underground, Yoko Ono, Brian Eno and Sonic Youth. She has published articles and chapters in *Women and Music*, the *Journal of Popular Music Studies*, the *Journal of the Society for American Music* and the volumes *Tomorrow Is the Question: New Directions in Experimental Music Studies* (2014) and *Brian Eno: Oblique Music* (2016).

Toby Manning teaches and writes on popular culture of the post-war period. A former music journalist for *The Word*, *Q*, *Mojo*, *NME* and *Select*, his books include *The Dead Straight Guide to Pink Floyd* (2015) and *John le Carré and the Cold War* (2018). Based in London, his *'Mixing Pop and Politics': A Marxist History of Popular Music* will be published by Repeater in 2023. He is also working on a study, *Cold War Culture*.

Julijana Papazova is a postdoctoral researcher at the European Scientific Institute-ESI at the University of La Laguna, Spain. Her research is dedicated to popular music studies and the history of alternative rock and indie music club scenes. Her recent research publications include the chapter 'The Yugoslav and Post-Yugoslav Alternative Rock Canon' in *Eastern European Music Industries and Policies after the Fall of Communism. From State Control to Free Market* (2021). She is the author of the book *Alternative Rock in Yugoslavia in the Period 1980–1991* (2017).

David Pattie is Senior Lecturer in Drama and Theatre Arts at the University of Birmingham, UK. He researches and publishes in a number of areas: popular music performance and culture, contemporary British and Scottish theatre, and the work of Samuel Beckett. He is the author of *Rock Music in Performance* (2007) and the co-editor of the books *Kraftwerk: Music Non Stop* (2011) and *Brian Eno: Oblique Music* (2016).

Thom Robinson teaches English literature at Newcastle University, UK. He has a research specialism in the work of William S. Burroughs, with articles on Burroughs published in *Comparative American Studies* and the *Times Literary Supplement*, as well as online at RealityStudio. He is currently writing a book about Burroughs and nostalgia.

Jeffrey Roessner is Associate Dean of the Hafenmaier College of Humanities, Arts and Social Sciences and Full Professor of English at Mercyhurst University, USA, where he leads classes in contemporary literature, popular music and creative writing. He is the co-editor of *Write in Tune: Contemporary Music in Fiction* (2014). Recent publications include essays on the Beatles, along with articles on Roddy Doyle, Robert Johnson, rock mockumentaries, the post-confessional lyricism of R.E.M., and satellite radio and the re-conception of musical genres. Along with his academic writing, he has authored a book on songwriting, *Creative Guitar: Writing and Playing Rock Songs with Originality* (2009).

Cibrán Tenreiro Uzal is an interim lecturer at the Faculty of Communication Sciences, Universidade de Santiago de Compostela, Spain. His research interests focus on the relations between music and cinema, particularly in fandom and amateur creativity and local scenes. His recent publications include articles on scene films in punk and post-punk, and a study of amateur concert videos in the Galician underground scene in *Popular Music, Technology, and the Changing Media Ecosystem: From Cassettes to Stream* (2020). He also works as a journalist, and as a musician in the bands Esposa and Ataque Escampe.

Introduction – The Velvet Underground: What went on

Sean Albiez and David Pattie

Lou Reed died in 2013. To mark the occasion, the *Guardian* reprinted a 2003 Simon Hattenstone interview. Generally, the period after an artist's death is a time for social reverence; even the most uncomfortable truths about the artist's life are covered over or retrospectively downplayed. Not so with Reed; the interview chosen showed him at his most recalcitrant:

> 'You can't ask me to explain the lyrics because I won't do it. You understand that, right.' … Anyway, he says, this is just the character talking. Yes, but has he ever considered what his older self could teach his younger self, and vice versa? 'I can't answer questions like that. What is it you really wanna know, because if it's personal stuff, you won't get it.' … I ask him if he thinks of Lou Reed as a person or a persona. 'I don't answer questions like that.'
>
> (qtd. in Hattenstone 2003)

The interview degenerates from there, in a manner familiar to many interviewers over the years. Reed gives short answers, snaps at Hattenstone over the nature and scope of the questions and only seems – momentarily – to be more forthcoming when he is asked a detailed question about music. Throughout his life it is possible to find examples of Reed responding (or not responding) to interviewers in this way. In Australia in 1975 he answered standard questions ('What will you play?' and 'What's it like singing to Japanese people?') with short, sarcastic or deflecting replies. For example, the recently blonde Reed had let his hair revert to its natural colour, so a journalist asked him, 'Are you happier as a brunette?' Reed's deadpan response: 'Are you happier as a schmuck?'

It is easy to conflate attitudes expressed in interviews with the music Reed produced, and then, by extension, with the music produced by the Velvet Underground and those musicians associated with the band. The Velvet Underground, like Reed, are held to be the avatars of a particularly insouciant version of New York cool – a band whose influence was undeniable, but whose music frequently seemed designed to discourage the casual listener. Familiarity with the band's first album has perhaps dulled the impact of the music, but the transition, for example, between the conventionally sweet cadences and melody of 'Sunday Morning' and the jarringly aggressive 'I'm Waiting for the Man' is still shockingly abrupt. The band's music could be confrontational (in Martin Amis' first novel, *The Rachel Papers* (1973), the callow protagonist tries to intimidate a pair of hippie girls by playing 'the most violent and tuneless of all my American LPs, *Heroin* [sic] by the Velvet Underground' (55)); this seemed of a piece with the band's attitude, which appeared designed to intimidate not only their peers but the culture those peers promoted. Asked for the band's opinion of the music and culture of the 1960s West Coast, Reed was characteristically acerbic:

> We had vast objections to the whole San Francisco scene ... We used to be quiet, but I don't care any more about not wanting to say negative things, 'cause somebody really should say something. Frank Zappa is the most untalented bore who ever lived. You know, people like Jefferson Airplane, Grateful Dead, all those people are just the most untalented bores that ever came up. Just look at them physically. I mean, can you take Grace Slick seriously? It's a joke.
>
> (Bockris 2014: 136–7)

It is worth looking at both the content and tone of this dismissal. It is a sweeping assertion of difference which conceals complexity (it is hard, for example, to imagine an artist as critical of the 1960s West Coast as Frank Zappa, and The Mothers of Invention album *We're Only in It for the Money* [1968] is a point by point refutation of the hippie dream). However, it would be difficult to characterize the statement as vitriolic. Rather, it is cool; the artists are 'bores', and Reed is speaking not out of anger but because 'someone really should say something'. The quote reads as though drafted by Andy Warhol and has the artist's wearily unemphatic tone, the condemnations delivered without qualifiers but also without any sense of wasted emotional heat. The counterculture was characterized by colour, carnival, community and overt passion; the New York scene as personified by the Velvets was cool, monochromatic, alienated but culturally assured – at least in its judgement of the rest of the nation.

This is one of the narratives that have been woven around the band in the years since their dissolution. It is, however, not the only possible one. Matthew Bannister (2010) pointed out that the band were capable of engendering any number of stories, and without their later resuscitation by enthused musicians and critics, they may have remained 'a footnote in rock history'. Lester Bangs and Brian Eno celebrated their freedom from musical constraint and their deconstruction of musical convention, and Jeremy Gilbert (1999) outlined their challenges to gender norms in a queering of rock. Bannister remarks that '[a]ccording to these critics ... it was the Velvets, not the counterculture, that were the true "revolution"'. They were more than the incarnation of a peculiarly urban approach to popular music; the Velvets simultaneously demolished the form and content of pop, and established the artist's right to freely express experiences and modes of being that were taboo, even for the rest of the counterculture. This reading bears testament to a key part of the band's story; it was created, by and large, retrospectively, as part of what might be called a revisionist history of the 1960s – one that places the Velvets and New York, rather than the Grateful Dead and San Francisco, at the heart of this history (Gilbert 1999). The band were lucky in their followers; in the mid-1970s having a cultural tastemaker like Bowie on their side meant that they found themselves possessing a substantial cultural cachet almost overnight. They were also lucky in that the cultural scene they were part of has itself proved to be one of the most influential in post–Second World War Western culture.

Pop Art – an artistic movement that developed in both the UK and the United States in the later 1950s – concerned itself with the proliferation of images in the mass-media culture of the time. Pop artists favoured clear, banal everyday images; in doing so, they implicitly collapsed the distinction between art and craft, and between the avant-garde and those images produced as an adjunct to the practices of capitalism. Warhol, it could be argued, took the idea of Pop to its logical conclusion; his work both described and was bound up in the processes of mass production that provided the raw material for Pop Art. The scene that coalesced around him in the early 1960s formed a cultural counterweight to the developing scenes in Los Angeles and San Francisco. The Factory – which opened in 1962 on East 47th Street in Manhattan, before moving in 1967 to Union Square – combined behaviour as louche and extreme as anything to be found on the West Coast, and a commitment to the idea of Art as an industrial process. As Simon Warner (2012) argues, this apparent contradiction meant that Warhol's Factory was both a part of and apart from the cultural trends of the mid and late 1960s. The artist and those who congregated around him might have embraced the idea of sexual freedom, of drugs as a necessary lifestyle adjunct, of the hallucinatory power of popular cultural forms such as music and cinema, but they did so dispassionately, without heat, rather than with the evangelical zeal of the hippie movement. Warner portrays the 'almost Brechtian alienation' Warhol adopted in distancing himself from the 'trash aesthetic' of his artwork: 'if the blandly mundane is transposed or the darkly dangerous is depicted, it is barely engaged with, nor commented upon, a kind of degradation through banality. If there is ambivalence in the piece on show, there is also an equivocal morality behind its construction' (Warner 2012). From this characterization, one can see the appeal that Reed's lyrics and the Velvets' music would have had for Warhol; the affectless narrator of 'Heroin', the protagonists in 'Sister Ray', worried that a sailor's bleeding body will stain the carpet, placed against music that seems stuck on a perpetual loop, going nowhere.

As the Factory house band, the Velvet Underground would have earned a small place in the cultural history of the twentieth century, but the band themselves contained not just skilled songwriters but also musicians who were influenced by what might be regarded as competing strands in mid-twentieth-century culture. Reed had a thorough grounding in literature and, through the influence of Delmore Schwartz (his tutor at Syracuse) and Bob Dylan, an interest in the interface between literature and music: 'a record could be like a novel, you could write about this. It was so obvious, it's amazing everyone wasn't doing it. Let's take *Crime and Punishment* and turn it into a rock-and-roll song!' (Reed qtd. in Bockris 2014: 66). John Cale had early formal musical training and studied music at Goldsmith's College in London, where he organized Fluxus events, conducted and performed contemporary music, and later worked with the avant-garde composer La Monte Young. Sterling Morrison shared Reed's knowledge of literature and was familiar with the underground cinema and performance scene in New York. Moe Tucker contributed a drumming style that was experimental in itself; she played a simplified kit with no cymbals, and she did so standing up. Finally, Nico provided a link to European culture; she had appeared in Fellini's *La Dolce Vita* (1960) and had recorded tracks with Rolling Stone Brian Jones. Warhol, in other words, chose his house band well. The Velvets' music was formed from a rich blend of cultural and musical influences and was performed by musicians willing to employ avant-garde and unconventional musical techniques (Cale's use of drones, Reed and Morrison's feedback, Tucker's drumming) alongside a love of the simplest rock and roll chord progressions.

The Velvets, then, were fortunate both in their first artistic sponsor and in the influences and approaches each band member brought with them. They were also, it could be said, uniquely fortunate in the location in which they found themselves:

> By most accounts, New York was an unpleasant, dirty, and even dangerous location to live in the 1960s and 1970s. Through a combination of population decline, governmental neglect, and bureaucratic tangles, New York City reverted to a seemingly ungovernable – and unlivable – place. In official, governmental literature as well as the popular media, New York was portrayed as a city that was broken.
>
> (Gluibizzi 2021: 2)

This general depredation not only gave Reed and the band their subject matter; as with the punk scene in the 1970s, it meant that the musicians could actually afford to live in the heart of New York and experience the rich cultural life of the city. It was a particularly good time to do so; New York, at this time, was establishing itself as one of the key centres of contemporary culture. In addition to Warhol and the Factory, the city had accommodated influential groups of visual artists (chief amongst them the New York School of abstract expressionists, and the artists following in their wake), performance groups like the Judson Dance Theatre and Richard Schechner's Performance Group, and musicians (John Cage, Morton Feldman and Christian Wolff among them). There was a proliferation of New York Schools running across all of the creative and plastic arts. Warhol's Factory was only one of the city's important cultural sites, and it was open to the influence of the various artistic currents that ran through the city. In particular, the performance events mounted at the Factory (first called Up-Tight, and then given the name the Exploding Plastic Inevitable) owed much to the emerging Fluxus movement, which grew out of the practices of composers like John Cage. Fluxus – an art movement notoriously difficult to define – tended to favour spontaneity and was interested both in the idea of art as process and in the blending together of different media. The membership of the movement was fluid and covered a great deal of artistic ground; it could be thought of both as a loose organizational term, pulling together work by a wide range of artists, and as a particularly porous network of sites and practices, easily accessible by younger, emerging artists.

In 1963, John Cale moved to the United States to take up a scholarship at the Eastman Conservatory at Tanglewood in Massachusetts, where he studied under composer Iannis Xenakis. On finishing the course (where memorably, during a performance, he pulled an axe out of a piano and slammed it into a tabletop) he moved to New York and contacted John Cage and La Monte Young, both affiliated with the Fluxus movement. In doing so he was following a path already taken by another musician who played a pivotal role in the nascent Velvet Underground. Angus MacLise was an actor, poet and film-maker but it was as the Velvets' first drummer that he had the greatest cultural impact, not just because his approach to percussion was as experimental as Tucker's but also because he was embedded in the New York cultural scene. MacLise's cultural preoccupations marked him out as someone who would be sympathetic to Fluxus and the kind of multimedia experiments Warhol would undertake at the Factory, and for the kind of blend of pop and rock chord progressions and experimental music the Velvets made. As Sterling Morrison stated, 'Angus was the most rabidly artistic of us all, with interests in literature, dance, music, film, lights, slides, incense, diaphanes, and religion – all at once. He mused day and night on a stage spectacle that might combine them all, and on what the dizzying effects of such a cataclysm might be' (qtd. in Unterberger 2009: 12).

Crucially MacLise was also already an integral part of the New York scene: he was in contact with La Monte Young in the very early 1960s – the composer had read, and admired, his second collection of poetry. MacLise went on to play in the La Monte Young trio (alongside Young and his wife Marian Zazeela). Through this connection he was also part of a larger group of musicians including Billy Linich, who would later rechristen himself 'Billy Name' and become a key member of Warhol's Factory. There are no guarantees as to which band or artist becomes culturally significant, but with connections like these, the Velvet Underground were almost bound to figure somewhere in the history of American culture. When one considers the music the band produced, and its relation to the surrounding culture, one could almost say that there was a Velvet Underground-shaped hole in the cultural story of New York – one which the band were uniquely able to fill.

The above might explain why the Velvets were so closely woven into the culture of the city in the 1960s; it also helps explain why the band became key cultural touchstones in the years to come. As the tide of the counterculture retreated, a succeeding generation of musicians found in the Velvets the antithesis of everything the hippie movement seemed to support. As Simon Reynolds (2014) points out, Reed in particular appealed to David Bowie, not only because the music Reed produced was melodically, harmonically and rhythmically direct but also because Reed could be co-opted as a fellow herald of the apocalypse. During a 1972 press conference, in which he introduced Reed and Iggy Pop as both his key influences and – given their relative career positions, his protégés – Bowie told the crowd of largely American journalists '[p]eople like Lou and I are probably predicting the end of an era … I mean that catastrophically … We're both pretty mixed up, paranoid people, absolute walking messes. If we're the spearhead of anything, we're not necessarily the spearhead of anything good' (Reynolds 2014: 230–1). An endorsement like this might have given Reed something to live up to (and it could be argued that, in terms of his performances in the early 1970s, Reed tried and failed to be the kind of proto-Glam figure Bowie thought he was) but it did mean that, very soon after the Velvets' dissolution, the significance of their music was hardwired into the popular cultural narrative of subsequent decades. And from the beginning, the band's links to the artistic culture of New York were a key part of their appeal. Speaking in 2016, Brian Eno recalled listening to the first album, not long after it came out:

> Within the first few moments, I thought, 'Okay, this is important.' I could hear the La Monte Young influence, the sort of drone thing that John Cale was doing on the viola. I think I heard *Heroin* first. So I bought that album [*The Velvet Underground & Nico*, (1967)], which not many other people did at the time. It might be hard for some people to understand, but they were a big influence on Roxy Music. Bryan [Ferry] liked them as well and we both knew about their connection with Andy Warhol, which gave them a sort of cultural position.
>
> (qtd. in Hughes 2016)

Eno therefore identifies a key part of their appeal. From the beginning, in the eyes of those influenced by them, the Velvet Underground were a cultural and intellectual force. To ally yourself to them was to link yourself to the complex cultural milieu in which they themselves were formed.

* * * *

The overall aim of this collection is to consider the trajectory of the Velvet Underground from its beginnings into the present, and to understand how the band's legacy and band member's activities developed over the ensuing decades. Rather than thinking of the band as a 1960s' phenomenon, the book aims to understand how the Velvets became and remain a formidable and far-ranging influence in popular music culture. In 2021, Todd Haynes' *The Velvet Underground* documentary was a sonically and visually intense spectacle that aimed to tell – and show – 'the story of this band through the experimental cinema of the '60s from which they emerged' using Warhol's films and those of other New York film-makers (Haynes qtd. in Taubin 2021). The emphasis of the film, on the period from 1965 to 1968, indicated that the creative relationship between Cale and Reed was vital to the radical innovations and later influence of the band, though the third eponymous *The Velvet Underground* (1969) album and *Loaded* (1970) clearly contain some of Reed's most memorable Velvets songs.

In the story as presented by Haynes, the crucial contributions of Sterling Morrison, Moe Tucker and Doug Yule became somewhat lost. It is important to point out that – as is usual with academic collections – the editors shape the book from responses received after putting out a call for papers. For this collection, alongside studies of the Velvet Underground as a whole, John Cale, Lou Reed and Nico became the dominant figures in the proposed chapters. It is not possible in a single volume to represent or encapsulate the entirety of the work of all of the Velvets, but we recognize it is important to make some attempt to address this imbalance by briefly considering Sterling Morrison, Moe Tucker and Doug Yule and their roles in the Velvet Underground – and after.

Sterling Morrison

Sterling Morrison's musical contribution to the Velvet Underground has often been overshadowed. John Cale (1995), in commenting on the fluidity of instrumental roles in the early days of the Velvet Underground, indicates '[t]here were great days and nights of rambunctious shenanigans, some of which were part of an ongoing tussle over who would play bass. I loved his bass playing as much as his guitar playing, but Sterling, not wishing to be known as the bass player, would always opt for his favorite, the guitar'. In discussing Morrison's guitar contributions to the Velvets, Buxton (2015) identified the 'sinewy slide-line up and down a blues scale in an endless loop' on 'I'm Waiting for the Man' and suggests that 'clean single-note runs, almost robotically in time, and always generous with the slides, are the Morrison signature' (e.g. on the 1969 recordings of 'Pale Blue Eyes' and 'Foggy Notion'). In contrast to Reed's meandering, syncopated rhythm guitar, and chaotic, explosive lead lines, Buxton makes a case for the steadying influence of 'the metronymic precision of Morrison's up and down chord-strokes [that] ape his hyperactive but beat-regular solos'. Doug Yule, who cited Mickey Baker as a key influence on Morrison, indicated, 'Sterling always wound up with the more organized breaks while Lou favored the longer, louder, raunchier ones' acquiring the skill of 'filling in the final pieces of a puzzle without overdoing it' (qtd. in Mercuri 1996).

Morrison was also a forthright, humorous and erudite interviewee, both during and after his time with the Velvet Underground. In a 1970 Greg Barrios *Fusion* interview he discussed Nico's time with the band with some clarity and the New York avant-garde film milieu from which the band emerged. He was happy to praise those he respected (including Quicksilver Messenger Service and The Byrds), but eagerly attacked those he didn't. He asserted that Frank Zappa was 'incapable of writing lyrics. He is shielding his musical deficiencies by proselytizing all these sundry groups that he appeals to. He just throws enough dribble into those songs'. On the MC5, when he is told others had drawn comparisons with the Velvets, he responded, '[T]hat's a comparison that would drive me to an early retirement'.

Morrison's actual musical retirement took place eighteen months later. During the recording of 1970's *Loaded*, he finished his literature degree by completing a course on the Victorian novel and began to 'cut himself off from his old way of life. He stopped smoking, stopped taking drugs and applied to graduate schools around the country' (Harron 1981). Bentley (1975) outlines how in August 1971 the Velvet Underground travelled to Houston to perform, and while there Morrison accepted a graduate place at the University of Texas, immediately leaving the band on the eve of a European tour. Morrison told Bentley that he also left the Velvet Underground for reasons other than academic ambition:

> All the big old ballrooms were closing. Either you did small clubs, where you couldn't get any decent sound out of your amplifiers ... Or else you had to do stand up/sit down concerts ... That was when rock 'n' roll was propelled into theater ...

We had the choice of going back into something that we felt we had already gone beyond, the theatrics [of The Exploding Plastic Inevitable]. It was nice to be there at the very beginning; we did do it when it was new and creative and exciting but to go back and do it because you have to, that was different.

In summarizing the Velvets' performance innovations and music, Morrison's pithy assessment given to Bentley was that '[i]n the long run, we were right'.

While studying and teaching in Austin, Morrison returned to live performance when he joined the Austin blues-based rock band The Bizarros from 1975 to 1978 (O'Connell 2015). However, Morrison's lack of any real musical ambition at this time is clear, and when asked in 1980 if he'd ever considered a solo music career, Morrison responded '[a]nd what – be Jackson Browne? I can write about lost love and "desuetude" … Who wants to listen to that stuff?' (Modern 1980). Nevertheless in 1979 Morrison began to attend local punk bars, and when John Cale performed in Austin in the same year, Morrison joined him onstage (Moser 2000). By the early 1980s Morrison had left Austin and his academic career behind, moving to Houston to work as a tugboat captain on the ship channel, though he eventually completed his PhD in 1986.[1]

With the upsurge of interest in the Velvet Underground in the 1980s, aided by the release of the archive albums *VU* (1985) and *Another View* (1986), a gradually strengthening gravitational pull drew the Velvets together. After Warhol's death in February 1987, Reed and Cale began working on the musical memorial, *Songs for Drella* (1990). Tucker worked with Reed on his album *New York* (1989) and in show's supporting its release, with Reed reciprocating on Tucker's *Life in Exile after Abdication* (1989). On 15 June 1990, Morrison joined Cale, Reed and Tucker onstage at the opening of an Andy Warhol exhibition at Fondation Cartier in Paris, and soon after, Morrison, Cale and Reed all contributed to Tucker's album, *I Spent a Week There the Other Night* (1991). February 1992 saw Morrison touring in Tucker's band, and in Paris they were joined onstage by Reed. Morrison appeared on the live album documenting the tour, *Oh No, They're Recording This Show* (1992), and a BBC John Peel session in March. In December, at John Cale's concert at New York University, Morrison played guitar, with Reed joining for two songs. In January 1993 Morrison and Cale appeared together on *The Tonight Show*.

This gradual rapprochement resulted in all the original Velvets rehearsing in New York in February 1993, and eventually touring Europe in June and July, with the final Velvet Underground show on 9 July in Napoli. Although there had been tentative plans for a US tour and a new studio album, these did not transpire. Tensions within the band had grown, and Martha Morrison stated that '[o]f course there were sparks on that tour … I know [Sterling] didn't want to do it again by the time they were through' (qtd. in Unterberger 2009: 346). However, as Unterberger writes, 'although Tucker and Morrison … [saw] … only a relatively small share of the million-dollar tour revenues' it made 'a substantial difference to their financial fortunes' (2009: 346).

In February 1994, Tucker's album *Dogs under Stress* was released with Morrison's contributions. The same year he played on albums by Shotgun Rationale, Luna and on the Cale soundtrack for the film *Antártida*, released in 1995. In November, at the opening of the Andy Warhol museum in Pittsburgh, Cale, Tucker and Morrison performed an accompaniment to Andy Warhol's films *Eat* and *Kiss* with the music described as 'incredibly sensual. Cale's keyboard playing was lushly colored; Morrison's soft guitar strumming added delicate fills. And Tucker's light, repetitive tapping provided just the right minimalist touch' (Lynne Margolis qtd. in Unterberger 2009: 348). However, it was apparent to Cale and Tucker that Morrison was very ill. Soon after the performance he was diagnosed as suffering from non-Hodgkin's lymphoma and died on 30 August 1995.

At Morrison's memorial service, Cale (1995) described him as 'a scholar and a gentleman of great resource' and Toler (1995) noted that Morrison had an 'intellect and discourse [that] soared above average', though 'conceit never overcame Holmes Sterling Morrison Jr.'. It is a tragedy that Morrison's book on the Velvet Underground, commissioned by Black Spring Press in London, was never completed. Perhaps the most well-known eulogy to Morrison came from the one band member not to attend his memorial service. Lou Reed (1995) in a *New York Times* article wrote: 'Sterl, the great guitar-playing, tug-boat captaining, Ph.D.-ing professor, raconteur supreme, argumentative, funny, brilliant; Sterl as the architect of this monumental effort, possessor of astonishing bravery and dignity. The warrior heart of the Velvet Underground'.

Maureen 'Moe' Tucker

Maureen 'Moe' Tucker joined the Velvet Underground in December 1965 following the departure of Angus MacLise. Though Tucker's gender has been viewed over the years as significant for its perceived novelty among rock drummers, Tucker herself has often stated that it was of no significance, joking, 'one of my theories is that everybody was so drugged back then that they didn't notice I was a woman' (Smith 1997). Her drumming is widely viewed as a crucial contribution to the Velvet Underground's sound and appeal. Her attitude to percussion complemented the improvisational approach she first encountered in rehearsals, and Tucker outlined how 'Lou would take off in one direction, John would take off in some other direction, all at different tempos, I would be keeping the beat so there was something for them to come back to … to keep them organised' (qtd. in Burke [1993] 2014). Elsewhere she indicated that her interplay with Sterling Morrison was also key: 'Sterling and I were holding down the fort, but I literally had to count to myself, 'cause when you hear a different rhythm, it's difficult to ignore it.' (Reiff 2018). According to Smith (1997), Tucker and Morrison were central to the impact and influence of the Velvet Underground, with many bands emulating 'the grinding, metronomic support-guitar-on-minimalist-drum axis … [of] … Tucker and Morrison'.

Tucker initially used a minimal drum set up with a vertically placed bass drum on a stand, a snare, tom toms and a cymbal that she played standing up, allowing her to easily reach each part of her kit (though later other drum setups and a drum stool were used). She used a mallet in her right hand on the bass drum, and a stick in her left, or two mallets on songs such as 'Heroin'. Tucker mostly eschewed the use of cymbals as she 'always hated cymbals and wanted to stay away from using a cymbal for every accent'. She also loved 'African drumming and was trying to get a sort of African sound (deeper sounds)' (Harrison 2009).

Tucker was particularly influenced by US-based Nigerian drummer Babatunde Olatunji, whose highly successful album *Drums of Passion* (1960) was arguably 'the first album to bring genuine African music to Western ears' (Planet 2003). Tucker first heard Olatunji's music on the New York DJ Murray the K's radio show and soon after met him in 1962: 'in our silly little Levittown school, we got Olatunji and his full troop with ten or twelve musicians and ten or twelve dancers. It was just stunning ... I got an autographed picture which I still have on my bulletin board here' (Gross 1998). She has also identified Bo Diddley's rhythms and the minimalist drumming styles of Charlie Watts and Ringo Starr as influences.

Tucker contributed to the Velvet Underground's first three albums and recording sessions eventually released on *VU* (1985) and *Another View* (1986). She was unable to take part in recordings for *Loaded* (1970) as she was pregnant with her first child, though in 2015 she remarked that she was happy to know 'Doug, Lou, and Sterl all said on separate occasions ... that they should've waited for me. That made me happy' (qtd. in Amorosi 2015). After Reed and Morrison left the Velvet Underground, and after a European tour with Yule leading the band, Tucker left the music industry: 'When the Velvets were done, it never really occurred to me that I should find some other musicians to play with ... I had a family and it wasn't even a thought that I could do music while the kids were all little' (Smith 1997).

After the Velvet Underground, Tucker worked as a computer data input operator, moved to California and eventually settled in Phoenix, Arizona, raising her family. However, by 1980 she began to experiment with a 4-track tape recorder, eventually releasing the album *Playin' Possum* (1981). Tucker's DIY approach included playing all the instruments on a number of cover versions and one original track. She began to work on projects with a number of collaborators including with Jad Fair of Half Japanese in the band Between Meals. Fair became crucial in the 1980s in aiding Tucker's return to music making. After a divorce, she relocated to Douglas, Georgia, and while working for Walmart collaborated with Fair on the 1987 *MoeJadKateBarry* e.p.

Tucker began writing songs on guitar and gained confidence in her singing voice (having previously sung on the Velvet Underground tracks 'The Murder Mystery' and 'After Hours' (*The Velvet Underground*, 1969) and 'I'm Sticking with You' – released on *VU* (1985)). Lou Reed encouraged her efforts, and Tucker released the album *Life in Exile after Abdication* in 1989 with contributions from Reed, Sonic Youth, Jad Fair and Daniel Johnston. She toured Europe supporting Half Japanese, and it became clear that she could earn enough money touring to replace her Walmart salary. In 1992 she warily left her job and supported her family with Velvet Underground royalties and touring revenue, stating, '[i]t's a tenuous existence – the cheques could stop tomorrow' (North 1992).

Alongside her interpretation of the Velvet Underground's 'Pale Blue Eyes', her own songs expressed anger at the difficulties she had faced in her family life in a kind of *domestic punk*. When asked about this subject matter, she said, '[w]hen I started writing songs, I was so embroiled in Wal Mart and trying to pay the bills on this ridiculous salary and being stuck here ... it all came out in my songs' (qtd. in Gross 1998). *I Spent a Week There the Other Night* (1991) was in a similar mould, with Cale, Reed and Morrison contributing. After the 1993 Velvet Underground reunion ultimately ended in disappointment, Tucker continued to pursue her revived career. *Dogs under Stress* (1994) featured Morrison, who toured with Tucker in October 1994 though it was clear even then that Morrison was suffering from ill health (Smith 1997).

After Morrison's death in 1995 Tucker fell into a temporary lull, but encouraged by Reed, she returned to music and drumming, joining the band Magnet for an album and tour in 1997 and began producing a number of artists in the 1990s, including Half Japanese and Shotgun Rationale. Tucker also contributed drums and vocals to The Kropotkin's *Five Points Crawl* (2000) and to the Raveonette's *Pretty in Black* (2005). However, after 2005 her musical activities seemingly came to an end. She explained why in 2015: 'I used to book our tours myself. What a chore that was – a chore I dreaded – and as time went on, I would just keep putting it off: tomorrow, tomorrow, tomorrow. That and my taking care of my grandson, which made it impossible for me to go away' (qtd. in Amorosi 2015). On Lou Reed's death, Tucker (2013) reflected on her time in the Velvet Underground:

> We had a lot of fun, and a lot of fun upsetting people ... We split when we should have, and we left behind just a handful of great albums ... Now Andy's gone, Sterling's gone, Nico's gone and Lou's gone. It feels strange. I miss them all, but I really miss Lou. He was a great songwriter who pushed the boundaries in terms of what he was writing about, but more importantly, he was a good and loyal friend.

Doug Yule

From August 1970 after Reed walked away from the Velvets through to May 1973, depending on how the period is framed, the Velvet Underground continued as a b(r)and under the leadership of Doug Yule. Morrison left the Velvets a year after Reed in August 1971, with Tucker following in late 1972. This period saw the release of the Velvet Underground's fourth album *Loaded* in the United States (late 1970–March 1971 in Europe). In May 1972 the album *Live at Max's Kansas City* was released, sourced from a bootleg quality cassette recording, documenting Reed's last days with the Velvets. Alongside many gigs in the United States, two European tours took place from October to November 1971 and November to December 1972. In 1973, the album *Squeeze*, recorded at Trident Studios in London, was released in the UK featuring only Doug Yule and drummer Iain Paice of Deep Purple. In May 1973, after a number of small-scale gigs were misadvertised as featuring the Velvet Underground by promoters, Yule brought things to an end.

From October 1968 until the band's final demise, Yule performed on the studio albums *The Velvet Underground* (1969) and *Loaded* (1970), on recordings that later appeared on the archive albums *VU* (1985) and *Another View* (1986) and *The Velvet Underground: Peel Slowly and See* (1995) box set, and the live albums *Live at Max's Kansas City* (1972), *1969 Velvet Underground Live* (1974) and *The Velvet Underground: The Complete Matrix Tapes* (2015). Hamelman (2016: 192) describes how Yule was central to defining the later sound of the Velvet Underground. Drawing from a 'training on piano, baritone horn, and tuba', his contributions on bass, keyboards, guitar and drums, as well as in singing lead and harmony vocals, were important in defining an increasingly accessible melodic pop sound.

In describing his creative relationship with Reed, Yule suggested, 'I think my own value at that point to Lou was that I was … much more of a facilitator than I am a leader. I like to take what's going on and make it work' (qtd. in Unterberger [2008] 2018). Over time Yule increasingly took on more vocal duties, giving Reed a break from the pressure of being continually centre stage, providing him with musical and emotional support. On the specifics of working with Reed, Yule described how '[w]hen Lou had already written words for and had a melody in mind, he'd play them and he'd be trying to find a chord and I'd be there and he'd sing the note, and I would sing a harmony note to that … so I acted more to help him … finish out stuff' (qtd. in Hamelman 2016: 198).

When carrying on after Reed's departure, the motivation from all sides seems to have been to capitalize on the work undertaken in completing *Loaded* that 'was in the can when Lou quit' (Yule qtd. in Thomas 1997), and that was written and produced to be a fully commercial prospect. Yule claims that Reed's exit made little difference at the time to their reception by audiences: 'Every time we went to England after Lou left, in various forms … people didn't care. Never in all those performances did anyone come up and say, "You're not really the Velvet Underground"' (qtd. in Unterberger [2008] 2018). Therefore for many discovering the Velvet Underground post-1970, the Yule-led version of the band played an important role in introducing the Velvet's music to new audiences. Personally, professionally, musically and financially, it is understandable that both band and management attempted to sustain the b(r)and that was fatally wounded by Reed's departure. However, recording and releasing *Squeeze* under the banner of the Velvet Underground was later viewed by Yule with some ambivalence: 'I was very much caught up in my own hubris at the time … That's what came out of it, I don't even have a copy of it. But it's kind of a nice memory for me and kind of an embarrassment at the same time … but it was nice to get my name and my songs out there' (qtd. in Thomas 1995).

Although Yule clearly played a crucial role in the final years of the Velvet Underground, he has largely been lost from histories of the band. He was omitted from the 1993 reunion, the 1996 induction into the Rock and Roll Hall of Fame and more recently the 2021 Todd Haynes documentary. Since the 1960s it has been the Cale, Reed, Morrison and Tucker (with Nico) band formation that has become canonized, though later songs from the Yule era such as 'Sweet Jane' and 'Rock and Roll' remain fan favourites. Yule's focus on workmanlike musicianship and his lack of the kind of notoriety and profile that Cale and Reed possessed meant that over the years he faded from view. He remained sporadically active as a musician, but his priorities eventually shifted, to a career as a luthier and to his family life.

*   *   *   *   *

Given the scope of the work of Cale, Morrison, Nico, Reed, Tucker and Yule inside and outside the Velvet Underground, it is not possible to cover everything in a single collection. However, the book does provide a variety of critical perspectives on aspects of the band members' work in collaboration and in their solo work from the 1960s until the present. Collection contributors include academics from the fields of popular music studies, musicology and music history, film studies, media and cultural industries, drama and theatre arts, and English literature. Collectively, they also have experience as musicians and music producers, journalists, promoters, DJs, creative writers and label heads. This diversity of disciplinary approaches and experiences is reflected in the diversity of perspectives in the collection.

The book is broadly organized chronologically. Roessner examines the Velvet Underground in their 1960s context. Hopkins and James' first chapter in the collection considers and outlines transatlantic connections in the early days of the band. Davis undertakes an analysis of Andy Warhol's films of the Velvet Underground and Nico, and Robinson locates Reed's literary interests in the 1960s American literary underground. Papazova undertakes a musicological analysis of the Velvet Underground and considers their ongoing influence. Griffiths analyses Reed's claims that his collected work constitutes a novel through the frame of the notion of the Great American Novel. Haddon investigates Nico's solo work and creative identity in the 1960s and 1970s. Manning focuses on the 1970s and aspects of European identity in Nico, Cale and Reed's solo work. Hopkins and James' second contribution examines David Bowie's creative appropriation of the Velvet Underground in the early 1970s. Pattie's first chapter considers performative issues in Reed's album *Berlin* (1973) in the 1970s and on its revival in the 2000s. Albiez and Kaul present a detailed and balanced analysis of a notorious 1974 concert by Nico, Cale and Brian Eno in Berlin. Goodall (re-)evaluates Reed's *Metal Machine Music* (1975), and Tenreiro Uzal examines Jonathan Richman's love of the Velvet Underground and broader issues of fandom and influence. Pattie's second contribution considers Reed's *Live: Take No Prisoners* (1978) and the role of improvisation in this recorded performance. Lindau examines the Cale and Reed collaboration *Songs for Drella* (1990) through issues around portraiture. Finally, Albiez explores the diverse creative work of Cale and Reed in the twenty-first century through an examination of their late musical voices.

Companion website

This collection uses short URLs for online references. However, a full and extended research bibliography with complete URLs, alongside other materials related to the book, is available on the companion website:

bloomsbury.pub/velvet-underground

Note

1 Morrison's PhD thesis was titled 'Historiographical Perspectives in the Signed Poems of Cynewulf' and is held at the University of Texas repository (https://bit.ly/3oioeYd).

References

Amis, M. (1973), *The Rachel Papers*, London: Jonathan Cape.
Amorosi, A. D. (2015), 'In Conversation: Moe Tucker's Velvet Mornings', *Flood*, 17 December. Available online: https://bit.ly/34maqVA (accessed 27 October 2021).
Bannister, M. (2010), '"I'm Set Free…"; The Velvet Underground, 1960s Counterculture, and Michel Foucault', *Popular Music and Society*, 33 (2): 163–78.
Barrios, G. ([1970] 2005), 'An Interview with Sterling Morrison', *Fusion*, 6 March, in C. Heylin (ed.), *All Yesterday's Parties: The Velvet Underground in Print 1966–1971*, Boston, MA: Da Capo.
Bentley, B. (1975), 'Up from the Underground: Sterling Morrison', *Austin Sun*, 19 October. Available online: https://bit.ly/3scBcIp (accessed 26 October 2021).
Bockris, V. (2014), *Transformer: The Complete Lou Reed Story*, London: Harper.
Burke, Chris ([1993] 2014), 'Drum Heroes Week: Moe Tucker' [originally published, in *Rhythm Magazine* August 1993], *Music Radar*, 20 September. Available online: https://bit.ly/3ofaopq (accessed 27 October 2021).
Buxton, R. (2015), 'The Case for The Velvet Underground's Sterling Morrison', *PopMatters*. Available online: https://bit.ly/3IUANAR (accessed 25 July 2016).
Cale, J. (1995), 'Friends for Life' [obituary], 30 August. Available online: https://bit.ly/3reVamq (accessed 26 October 2021).
Gilbert, J. (1999), 'White Light/White Heat: Jouissance beyond Gender in the Velvet Underground', in A. Blake (ed.), *Living through Pop*, 31–48, London: Routledge.
Gluibizzi, A. (2021), *Art and Design in 1960s New York*, London: Anthem.
Gross, J. (1998), 'Maureen Tucker Interview', *Perfect Sound Forever*, May. Available online: https://bit.ly/3ugW1ow (accessed 27 October 2021).
Hamelman, S. (2016), '"Music Is My First Language": An Interview with Doug Yule', *Rock Music Studies*, 3 (22): 192–214.
Harrison, B. (2009), 'Velvet Goldmine: Moe Tucker in Her Own Words', 29 May. Available online: https://bit.ly/3reVphk (accessed 27 October 2021).
Harron, M. (1981), 'The Lost History of the Velvet Underground: An interview with Sterling Morrison', *New Musical Express*, 25 April. Available online: https://bit.ly/35IlH3h (accessed 26 October 2021).
Hattenstone, S. (2003), 'Interviewing Lou Reed: Not a Perfect Day', *The Guardian*, 19 May. Available online: https://bit.ly/3H2DH6a (accessed 26 April 2022).
Hughes, R. (2016), 'Brian Eno on Roxy Music, The Velvet Underground and David Bowie', *Prog*, 24 September. Available online: https://bit.ly/347Cr3q (accessed 25 November 2021).
Mercuri, S. (1996), 'The Loaded Lowdown: Doug Yule', *The Velvet Underground Fanzine*, 5. Available online: https://bit.ly/35uwFtb (accessed 26 October 2021).

Modern, N. (1980), 'Sterling Morrison: Reflections in a Lone Star Beer', *New York Rocker*, July/August. Available online: https://bit.ly/32YoDYy (accessed 3 February 2022).

Moser, M. (2000), 'Velvet Underdog: Sterling Morrison: An Oral History with Interviews', *The Austin Chronicle*, 17 March. Available online: https://bit.ly/3HmPqfV (accessed 26 October 2021).

North, R. (1992), 'Moe Tucker: Tucker's Luck', *Siren*, February. Available online: https://bit.ly/3uj94pG (accessed 27 October 2021).

O'Connell, C. (2015), 'What Goes On: The Improbable Story of How Sterling Morrison Left VU for UT', *The Alcade*, 26 August. Available online: https://bit.ly/34qiAMu (accessed 26 October 2021).

Planet, J. (2003), 'Babatunde Olatunji: 1927–2003', *The Beat*, May. Available online: https://bit.ly/3uihM7i (accessed 27 October 2021).

Reed, L. (1995), 'The Lives They Lived: Sterling Morrison; Velvet Warrior', *New York Times*, 31 December, Section 6, 21.

Reiff, C. (2018), 'View from The Drummer's Seat: Moe Tucker Remembers Her Time in The Velvet Underground', *Uproxx*, 15 March. Available online: https://bit.ly/3GoExJ7 (accessed 27 October 2021).

Reynolds, S. (2014), *Shock and Awe: Glam Rock and Its Legacy*, London: Faber and Faber.

Smith, J. E. (1997), 'Interview with Moe Tucker', 21 December. Available online: https://bit.ly/3ofHWE5 (accessed 25 November 2021).

Snow, M. (1993), 'The Velvet Underground: Party On, Dudes!' Q, July. Available online: https://bit.ly/346NDx6 (accessed 26 October 2021).

Taubin, A. (2021), 'You'll Be My Mirror' [Todd Haynes interview], *Artforum*, October. Available online: https://bit.ly/3IVpDMh (accessed 25 November 2021).

Thomas, P. (1995), 'Doug Yule Interview', *Perfect Sound Forever*, 21 October. Available online: https://bit.ly/34s5q1E (accessed 29 November 2021).

Toler, L. J. (1995), 'Morrison: "An Inspiration" – 100 Mourn Rock City Virtuoso', *Poughkeepsie Journal*, 3 September. Available online: https://bit.ly/3ISJuvA (accessed 26 October 2021).

Tucker, M. (2013), 'Lou Reed Remembered by Moe Tucker', *The Guardian*, 15 December. Available online: https://bit.ly/341qqwB (accessed 25 November 2021).

Unterberger, R. ([2008] 2018), 'Doug Yule: The Forgotten Velvet', *Please Kill Me*, 16 October. Available online: https://bit.ly/3KZc3Jz (accessed 29 November 2021).

Unterberger, R. (2009), *White Light/ White Heat: The Velvet Underground Day-By-Day*. London: Jawbone Press.

Warner, S. (2012), 'The Banality of Degradation: Andy Warhol, the Velvet Underground and the Trash Aesthetic', *Volume! La revue des musiques Populaire*, 9 (1). Available online: https://bit.ly/3upYWv0 (accessed 25 November 2021).

1

Saved by rock and roll: The Velvet Underground in and out of history

Jeffrey Roessner

In 1965, just about the time Petula Clark headed downtown to the movie shows to forget all her worries, forget all her cares, the Velvet Underground were gathering force, getting ready for the trip uptown to meet their man and score. Surely, these travellers would never meet; it's almost impossible to believe that they share a city, let alone a rail line. Indeed, the opposing directions could be an apt metaphor of the Velvet's career in their perverse refusal of mid-1960s popular culture. In the summer of 1965, they recorded a demo of 'Venus in Furs' – a song probing the complex desires of a sadomasochistic relationship, one that ultimately moves from description to participation as the song shifts from third to first person and the singer gives instructions to his submissive partner. Who was this band? And who, exactly, did it imagine as its audience?

Subsequent rock histories have struggled mightily with such questions. The consensus seems to be that the band just doesn't fit. Depending on your perspective, the Velvet Underground arrived either ten years too late or ten years too early. Either way, the band was out of key with its time. The mélange of neo-Beat poetics, street attitude, three-chord raunch and Brill Building pop arrived from an earlier hipster era, while the thrashing metal machine music and avant-garde explorations pointed far ahead – it just took a decade or so for the world to catch up. Whether busy tending the vital force of early rock and roll or forecasting its punk resurgence, this band was untimely – hence their unpopularity and lack of commercial success in the 1960s.

But the received wisdom about the Velvet Underground easily misleads. Despite the idiosyncratic sensibility that distinguished them from their peers, they were more representative of their times than we might believe. In that same era, Frank Zappa offered a West Coast critique of hippie-dom; the Fugs incorporated performance and self-conscious poetry; and the Beatles and Pink Floyd, among many others, explored radical sonic possibilities, including the use of the drone in Western music, John Cage-inspired chance operations and tape loops. Reading specific elements of the Velvets' style next to experiments by their contemporaries, we find analogues for almost every radical gesture the band made. Their distinctiveness, then, is less about musical style than about the rejection of the florid psychedelic image and countercultural politics that have become the dominant image of the time. For the Velvet's most ardent admirers, their iconoclasm ultimately helped rescue rock from the self-absorbed excesses of psychedelia and recuperate the radical gestures of its 1950s origins. In this telling, it's not that the band doesn't fit into rock and roll history. Rather, they are central to it. Forming a crucial link between the originating moment of rock rebellion and the punk provocations to come, this band – with its Nordic chanteuse, androgynous girl drummer, electric violist and dark shades – made it possible for rock's subterranean history to be written.

Baby, you're out of time

Producing musical echoes that still reverberate, the Velvet Underground also loosed a critical torrent that shows little sign of abating. Their comparatively brief catalogue has been dissected, rehashed and mythologized in minute detail. Two full volumes have been devoted solely to the critical reception of the band (Zak 1997; Heylin 2005), while Richie Unterberger (2009) promises and indeed nearly gives us the Velvet Underground day by day.[1] This is a band that inspires rabid love, zealous devotion. Their place in rock history, though, has been complicated by a reluctance to see them as part of that history. They somehow exist outside of time, in an ethereal rock otherworld that can't be tied to mere historical circumstance. But that's a metaphor. You can't be ahead of your time – or behind it, for that matter. You're always in it, stuck right there in the present just like the rest of us. We seek metaphors when we're having trouble explaining something, and the Velvets have always refused easy assimilation. When we say they don't fit, we must mean that they don't fit our conception of the era. That's one clue that the problem is less with the band and more with our restricted, stereotypical view of the era.

Matthew Bannister (2010: 164) summarizes the Velvet's oppositional appeal, noting that in the context of the late 1960s, '[r]ock musicians were heralded as the voice of a hopeful new generation with the power to subvert the Establishment'. With their black sunglasses and aura of perverse sexuality, the band did not fit this template. As Bannister enumerates, '[t]he points of difference with the counterculture were almost endless – psychedelic drugs/heroin and amphetamines; free love/S&M; good times/bad times; West Coast optimism/Eastern cynicism; heterosexuality/homosexuality; transcendence/negation; community/alienation; popularity/obscurity'. While he goes on to complicate these too-easy binaries, Bannister argues that the band was rescued from obscurity by those who formed a deeply personal and idiosyncratic attachment to it – particularly because of these signs of negation: these fans were 'critics and musicians who recruited the band into their own personal projects for enlightenment'. Finding deeply personal meaning in the Velvets' public challenge to the counterculture, such listeners helped cement the band's iconoclasm as the defining element of its legacy.

But the band's meaning was also always more than personal. Or perhaps more precisely, we should remind ourselves that personal meaning always emerges within a specific cultural context. From this perspective, fans and critics wrote the Velvet Underground into the nascent history of rock – one whose story had become increasingly complicated by the mid-1960s. The dominant image of countercultural protest, festivals, tune-ins and turn-ons obscured latent fissures in the boomer 'youthquake'. Even as rock music increased its cultural reach, projecting images, eliciting fantasies and opening spaces for desire, its meaning was shifting: countercultural music increasingly seemed like another part of the culture industry. Sterling Morrison expresses his distaste for the Summer of Love, as he describes the West Coast scene at the time: 'every creep, every degenerate, every hustler, booster, and rip-off artist, every wasted weirdo packed up his or her clap, crabs, and cons and headed off to the promised land …. then descended upon the hapless hippies (and their dupes) in San Francisco' (qtd. in Bockris and Malanga 1983: 86). In this context, like the return of the repressed, the Velvets sprouted from the avant-garde underground to voice its throbbing dissent. The band symbolized not only the possibility of an alternative music but an alternative identity, an alternative sensibility and an alternative sexuality, just for starters. But just as neurosis gathers energy through the force of repression, the Velvet Underground could not exist outside time: the band – and its fans and critics – needed an oppressive dominant culture to achieve its vivid expression. In crucial ways, then, as the band defined itself both against and within the currents of its time, it made rock history possible.

From its inception, the Velvet Underground signalled a strong connection to mid-1960s culture. In particular, the early demos from the 1999 *Peel Slowly and See* box set vividly display the band's folk beginnings. On these tracks, Lou Reed's faltering, nasal delivery perfectly suits the strummed acoustic settings. Dylan serves as a main role model, with his literate, hipster lyrics and his own distinctive, highly mannered vocal delivery. In this vein, Reed's 'Prominent Men' is almost embarrassing: its bleating harmonica and finger-pointing moralism would not have been out of place on *The Times They Are a-Changin'* (1964) – indeed, the song even borrows the waltz-time (3/4) rhythm of Dylan's title track. And despite the band's famous injunction against blues licks (Fricke 1989), we're even treated to a lurching slide guitar on 'I'm Waiting for the Man'. Lyrically, too, many of the songs are cast as folk ballads. But here the subway addict replaces the gunslinger, and the just-ready-to-be-debauched ingénue – or the already terminally jaded recusant – stand in for the grieving widow and murderer.

Reflecting the growing complexity of 1960s folk-influenced popular music, these early demos present an ironic contrast between lyrics and music, with the bouncing rhythm and jaunty tune of 'All Tomorrow's Parties' featuring vocal harmony from Cale. Although the melodies are not all modal, they often emphasize jumps of a third, fourth or fifth in scale, which give the tunes an odd, stately elegance. Listen to the opening of 'Venus in Furs', for example, as Cage makes the thrilling melodic leap between the repeated first words. Cage's Welsh accent, too, heightens the peculiar sense of otherness in the songs: his restrained, affectless tone with those long, rounded vowels serves as the perfect placeholder for Nico, who will step seamlessly into that vocal role within a year. Taken as a lot, the demos show that the band did not emerge solely from an erudite, avant-garde context but with a clear look to past musical traditions and a serious nod to contemporary 1960s music – particularly in the debt to Bob Dylan. Despite Sterling Morrison's later insistence that the Velvet Underground 'most certainly did not want to be compared with Bob Dylan or associated with him' (qtd. in Bockris and Malanga 1983: 36), Dylan's influence remained well into their career. For example, Lou Reed's vocal performance on 1970's 'Rock & Roll' has direct echoes of Dylan's on 'Ballad of a Thin Man', with both singers wringing irony out of every stressed syllable as they spit contempt for middle-class, pseudo-intellectual culture.

Even as the Velvets gained momentum as a performing act and abandoned the obvious folk trappings, they managed to simultaneously baffle listeners and cement their connection to 1960s culture. From the very early performances, they evoked a visceral response that polarized the crowd, with a large group seeking the nearest exit, while the few acolytes drew closer to the manic storm of sound (Lugg [1967] 2005: 48). The gigs were peculiar for a rock band with this outré sensibility. Their first billed show, in December of 1965, was at a high school in New Jersey, which calls to mind later punk provocations – see Sex Pistols' notorious tour through ill-suited venues in the southern United States (Young 1978). Their first appearance with Nico occurred, infamously, at the Annual Dinner of the New York Society for Clinical Psychiatry, which seems somehow oddly fitting – prompting one psychiatrist to remark to a reporter, 'You want to do something for mental health? ... Kill the story' (Glueck [1966] 2005: 5). Such gigs can be read in the context of Andy Warhol's glaring self-promotion, but they also, counterintuitively, suggest that the Velvets didn't see themselves as that outrageous or confrontational. Referring to their New York crowd, Lou Reed suggests that the band's approach 'didn't strike them as far out. It struck other people, say outsiders, as far out .... Whereas we never considered it far out in the first place and neither did he [Warhol]' (Wilcock [1971] 2009). In the press coverage of the time, they were seen as so much a reflection of their time that they were hardly worth mentioning, even to the point of being dismissed as a stereotypical rock act: Warhol was the story, after all (Heylin 2005: xviii).

At the same time, though, we see the emergence of the out-of-time narrative. Praising the Velvet's third album as a 'suite' of related songs, Richard Williams in 1969 called it 'so subtle and sophisticated that it's on a par with *Tommy*, and so far ahead of *Sgt. Pepper* that it makes that album sound like a series of nursery rhymes' (2005: 121). For his part, Wayne McGuire in 1968 castigated his peers for 'being "probably too occupied delving into the subtleties of *Sgt. Pepper*, due to an astigmatism of the mind," to notice the one band that was "musically and mentally two years ahead of its time"' (qtd. in Heylin 2005: xxviii). McGuire's incensed comic rant beautifully draws the battle line, as he accuses wannabe rock critics of being

> too busy listening to the Beatles and the Stones and into adolescent masturbation (I can't get no satisfaction; you call that slop rebellion?), and now you've learned some musical terms and have taken some speed for insight and are busy fueling the Beatles-Airplane-Doors syndrome or are into every-so-tired black blues riffs via Cream, Butterfield, Bloomfield, Canned Heat, or Traffic.
>
> ([1968] 2005: 68)

It's a breathtaking condemnation of the counterculture that succinctly takes down the drug scene, pseudo-intellectual pretension, hackneyed psychedelic blues (played by white kids) and the utter delusion of a generation that had convinced itself that its music was going to save the world.

Flash-forward a half-century, and we find the same refrain still being sung. Reviewing the Velvet Underground's first album on its fiftieth anniversary, Sam Leith (2017) compares it to *Sgt. Pepper's Lonely Hearts Club Band*, also from 1967, and declares the Beatles' album 'a period piece'. He suggests that you '[p]lay Heroin and Lucy in the Sky With Diamonds back to back. One of them sounds like it belongs to 1967. The other one sounds like it belongs to yesterday night' (17). Leith happily confirms the band's prophetic stature, marking them as our contemporaries. But, of course, we can also see this story as reverse engineered. The Beatles' album sounds like 1967 because it was an era-defining masterpiece. The Velvet Underground album doesn't sound like that; therefore, it must have been ahead of its time. Discussing the scant mainstream media coverage of the Velvets in the 1960s, Clinton Heylin bemoans 'the disproportionate significance of those glaringly few bite-sized reviews the Velvets generated in 1967 and 1968, just when the pop world was yet to stir from its self-induced torpor in Pepperland' (2005: xxviii). Once again, the Beatles serve as whipping boys – the overwhelmingly popular but, alas, too popular and thus too commercial anti-heroes. The Velvets were awake while the rest of the youth culture dissolved into a soporific psychedelic illusion, like an LSD tab on a warm tongue.

Keeping it 'real'

One problem with this narrative is that the Velvet Underground members routinely praised other 1960s artists, including the Byrds and the Beatles. In 1968, Lou Reed recommended the Byrds as 'divine', singling out Roger McGuinn as 'a very good guitar player, really exciting' and contending that 'to this day, no one has done a better solo than "Eight Miles High"' (Martin [1968] 2005: 111). It's worth noting that in the same interview, Reed also praises the Lizard King himself, Jim Morrison – a major source of McGuire's deleterious 'Beatles-Airplane-Doors syndrome' – for 'trying to do something' (Martin [1968] 2005: 112). Given Reed's effusive praise of the Byrds, we shouldn't be surprised to hear direct musical echoes. On *Loaded*, for example, the reverential harmonies on the refrain in 'I Found a Reason' sound as if they were lifted straight from the Byrds' 1968 country turn, *Sweetheart of the Rodeo*.

And despite Lou Reed's later dismissal of them as 'garbage', the Beatles earned frequent high praise from the band (Grow 2015). In *Thirdear* magazine as the Velvets were recording *Loaded*, Reed himself calls them the 'most incredible songwriters ever', and claims, 'I don't think people realize how sad it is that the Beatles broke up ... There's nothing like sitting around listening to those songs' (The Velvet Underground 1970: 11). Sterling Morrison, too, was a fan, as he makes clear in one of his many vivisections of Frank Zappa. Having elsewhere dismissed him as 'horrible' and a 'triumph of self-promotion' (Julia [1996] 1997: 208), Morrison highlights the contrast with the Beatles and claims that 'If he [Zappa] comes out with a song that is as good as any song on *Sgt Pepper*', he would revise his opinion. Heaping praise on the Beatles' masterwork as 'a great album', he singles out the 'real perception and talent' it exhibits (Barrios [1970] 2005: 150).

Such admiration suggests how intently the band listened to others, especially the Beatles, who provide multiple musical analogues for the Velvets. Noting the simplicity and stripped-down nature of the music and packaging of *The Velvet Underground*, Richie Unterberger (2009) suggests, 'Perhaps The Beatles' recent double LP, issued in 1968 as *The Beatles*, is a subliminal influence; just as *The Beatles* will become more commonly known as *The White Album*, so *The Velvet Underground* will often be referred to by fans and critics as the third album' (225). While acknowledging that he does not want to read too much into 'what is almost certainly a coincidence', Unterberger nonetheless points to a few very specific parallels between the records by the two bands. He notes that both 'The White Album' and *The Velvet Underground* end 'by following a defiantly avant-garde exercise ["Revolution 9" and "The Murder Mystery"] with a song that could almost have come from the pre-World War II era ["Good Night" and "After Hours"]'. He also notes that both records contain an 'amelodic noise-collage wedged into a batch of very song-oriented material' (213). Without claiming direct or simple influence, Unterberger suggests compelling ways that the Velvets reflected the aesthetic currents of their time.

The band members themselves reinforce an intimate connection to song-craft and production of their era. Discussing 'I'm Waiting for the Man' – presumably one of the tracks that makes *Sgt. Pepper* sound like a 'period piece' – John Cale notes, 'It's very British-sounding, mid-'60s pop like The Honeycombs' "Have I The Right?"' (qtd. in Pinnock 2012). As for the lyrics, he places those firmly in the context of Greenwich Village folk: 'The song's about a trip up to Harlem, a conversational piece based on real experience. There was a lot of that stuff around: Dave Van Ronk, Arlo Guthrie … talking street poetry.' And most famously, of course, 'There She Goes Again': 'The riff is a soul thing, Marvin Gaye's "Hitch Hike" with a nod to The Impressions.' Here we find arguably the most radically experimental member of the band claiming inspiration from the sugar confections of mainstream pop, along with healthy dose of folk and R&B.

None of which is to deny Velvet Underground's originality or take anything away from what they so ingeniously did with those influences. As Cale contends in his description of 'European Son', 'We wanted to break the rules, so we broke every fucking rule we could' (qtd. in Pinnock 2012). That rule-breaking, however, took place in a 1960s context, one that inspired and shaped the band's lyrics and sounds. Such connections should give us pause when considering the casual (often retrospective) assessment that the band arose *sui generis*, disconnected from their era, without peers or influences. If they sound like nothing else you've heard, perhaps that's because you're listening to the wrong records.

Still, the 'out-of-their-time' narrative, like any mythos, radiates power and fascinates – and so invites interrogation. The question then isn't 'How was the band ahead of its time?' but 'Why are so many invested in separating the band from its era?' In one sense, this fable of un-timeliness reflects Velvet Underground fans' desire for identification with the group, as rock moved from teenage subculture to the purported soundtrack of a generation. In this context, the band represent perhaps the first alternative band in rock – an alternative that was, paradoxically, linked directly to the rock 'n' roll pioneers of the 1950s.[2] In this history, mid-1960s psychedelia represents the first great self-betrayal in rock. Of course, fans have always split over their allegiance to their favourite artists. But the Velvet Underground, with their 'anti' aesthetic, stood in caustic relief from the peace and love of the flower power generation. Given its subsequent mythologization, the counterculture seems to present a unified front and underscores rock's place as the soundtrack for that romanticized and so ultimately doomed rebellion. But battlelines were being drawn *within* the counterculture, and not just between the Beatles and the Stones. Hence Dylan's mid-1960s put-down songs, which are not solely directed at the suited squares of the complacent middle class. As 'Like a Rolling Stone' and 'Positively Fourth Street' suggest, the pseudo-hipsters are fair targets for vitriol. Because they aren't going far enough, they're sullying the dream. Barely finished with its first decade, rock is being co-opted.

Against the boomer's dream of empowerment and revolution, the Velvets offered dissent, and we see a clear fault line emerging in youth culture. Remarking on the band's shows in 1968, someone only identified as John (a road manager for the band – perhaps Cale putting on a journalist?) contended, 'It's not supposed to be psychedelic. The newspapermen just seized on that word and used it to death. Any clown can see that this isn't like taking LSD' (Altman [1966] 2005: 38). Those in the know get it; the rest – the pseudo-hipsters, con artists, sell-outs, corporate shills, *clowns* – do not. This defiant assertion of alternative taste signals a major rift in the counterculture. For some fans, popular rock – such as the Doors, Airplane, Stones, Beatles – didn't represent them or their identities. But listening to different music isn't enough: the rest of the culture had to be *wrong*. Lulled into complacency, the taste of the masses had been defiled by corporate consumerism, which most casual fans couldn't recognize in their drug-addled haze. In this context, the Velvet Underground were the adults in the room; they were 'real', man.

Let us pause to recognize the irony. A band that came to its initial, limited fame in the context of Andy Warhol's Exploding Plastic Inevitable is held up as the epitome of 'real'. The word 'plastic' is literally in the title of the show. We might profitably ask, what makes 'Heroin' more 'real' than, say, Scott McKenzie's top 10 hit from 1967, 'San Francisco (Be Sure to Wear Some Flowers in Your Hair)'? Couldn't we make the argument that, as saccharine and dated as some might see it, McKenzie's song represents the 'reality' of the Summer of Love more effectively than 'Heroin' – if only because it reflects the experience of a far larger number of people?

Considering the Velvet's reception, we quickly see that we are dealing with the 'reality effect', or more broadly, the 'authenticity effect'. Lou Reed wrote about darker material, so it strikes some listeners as heavier, deeper, more authentic than what those flaky hippies were up to. In his take on the construction of authenticity in popular music, Richard Middleton emphasizes the centrality of this kind of 'honesty', defined as 'truth to cultural experience' (1990: 127). Such a perspective helps clarify the band's connection to folk music, long seen as the authentic expression of the common people: folk represents the 'real' stuff that existed outside the dictates of rampant consumerism, linked to 'tradition and an older form of social organization' and, importantly, 'unpolluted by artifice' (Machin 2010: 16). Unvarnished truth and an 'unpolluted' assault on artifice: that's precisely what many fans value in Lou Reed's anti-psychedelic street poetics. But if the countercultural dream of freedom, sexuality and hallucinogens strikes some as naively romantic, we should recall that, historically, romanticism as an aesthetic practice has a very dark side – including frightening elements of the gothic. The Velvet Underground catalogue can be seen to be as romanticized in its jaundice-eyed view of the world as the paradisiacal vision of the psychedelic dropouts, yet it was received by many die-hards as less starry-eyed, more truthful to their (imagined?) experience and thus more real.

When we talk about the Velvet Underground, then, we are rarely simply talking about music, or fashion, or art. The Velvets are a remarkable band. But they have also come to play a crucial narrative function in the story of rock. And that function is directly tied to their *outré* persona. They represent the psychic underside, the repressed other of the 1960s. In this sense, for them to have the meaning that they do in rock history, they paradoxically *cannot* yet *must* exist outside time. Representing an alternative imaginative space for fan identification, the band has to be pitted against the excesses of hippie flower power: they lose vital meaning without this context. Imagine, for a moment, the Velvet Underground emerging as a band in the mid-1970s. They would seem far less radical and perhaps even oddly nostalgic. No, for the band to be itself, it must remain a product of the febrile 1960s – both immensely influential and sadly overlooked.

The Holden Caulfield effect

In the history of rock aesthetics, the Velvets might be important in another way, too. They could be the first rock band to evince what we might term 'the Holden Caulfield effect'. In J.D. Salinger's 1949 novel *The Catcher in the Rye*, the adolescent anti-hero ponders art and success, only to conclude, 'I'd swear to God, if I were a piano player or an actor or something and all those dopes thought I was terrific, I'd hate it. I wouldn't even want them to clap for me. People always clap for the wrong things. If I were a piano player, I'd play it in the goddam closet' (1951: 84). Holden encapsulates the conflicting desires that drive artistic ambition. If you have too many fans, or the wrong kind of fans, your art is not authentic. The only way to guarantee the purity of your intentions is to play 'in the goddamn closet' – for yourself or at best for a select few who can appreciate your craft. That potent drive for authenticity remains strong in contemporary culture and has been taken to extreme ends: witness the underground metal scene with bands that refuse to release records or play live, or a label 'such as California's Rhinocervs, which released albums and EPs without titles, artist names or track listings' and 'festivals that decline to inform fans who's actually playing' (Petridis 2017). Obsessed with avoiding the slightest whiff of material consumption or, god forbid, being listened to by the wrong 'fan', these bands enter Holden's closet and lock it from the inside.

The Velvet Underground members themselves presaged this dilemma regarding authenticity. They frequently expressed the desire for commercial success, and years later were still wrangling with that failure. Sterling Morrison underscores the band's aspirations when, in referring to the release of the Velvet's first album, he stated, 'I was never more excited about anything, and used to call up Cashbox to find out our chart position before the magazine hit the stands. I couldn't wait to know' (Bockris and Malanga 1983: 66). Nearly twenty years after the album's release, Morrison's excitement still rings through. Documents at the Velvet Underground archives at Cornell University reproduce detailed lists he made of the charts for 1967, noting the place of their albums and singles in relation to other major acts of the day, including The Grateful Dead, Cream and The Beatles.[3] Even committed avant-gardist John Cale wasn't simply seeking to offend middle-class taste. Upon meeting Lou Reed and hearing him play the likes of 'Heroin' and 'Waiting for the Man' – 'on acoustic guitar as if they were folk songs' – Cale admits that he 'was terrifically excited by the possibility of combining what I had been doing with La Monte [Young] with what I was doing with Lou and finding a commercial outlet' (qtd. in Heylin 2005: xiii). To suggest that the band wasn't interested in popular success is simply not true. Morrison again, from 1970: 'I'd like to see us have a hit single. It's really important that you do that' (Barrios [1970] 2005: 151).

Ironically, that very lack of success has become central to the Velvet Underground's significance in the story of rock. In a 1969 essay for *Melody Maker*, Richard Williams bemoans their lack of success, writing, '[i]t's beginning to look as if the Velvet Underground will never make it, commercially. Nevertheless, groups like them do the spadework which enables less-talented musicians to progress. It's just a shame that nobody listens' ([1969] 2005: 121). In his lament, Williams both emphasizes the band's advanced work, thanklessly forwarding the aesthetic aims of rock music, and decries their obscurity. Although the band members, and many fans and writers, seem to have wanted hits for the group, such an achievement would have meant emerging from Holden Caulfield's closet – and that would have posed an identity problem. Stay locked away, and no one hears you. Become too popular, and you lose any credible stance as an outsider. From the beginning, the Velvet Underground embodied this contradiction: they wanted to make provocative art that was popular, a delicate dance in the best of circumstances.

Some forty years after Williams' complaint that no one was listening, Bannister suggests how the band's eccentric status has, in effect, become their story. In fact, sounding a lot like Williams, he argues that '[t]he very unpopularity or marginality of the band is adduced as proof of their prophetic role as an avant-garde intervention that extends the boundaries of popular music' (2010: 165). Exactly right – but we should also note that the Velvet's project wasn't only extension, it was also recovery. Writing in 1969, Robert Somma places the Velvet Underground in their era, as he notes that '[s]everal clearly catalogued figures in art, music and urban development contribute to the material and performance technique of the Velvets'. But he also takes care to note that, existing outside the major commercial trends in music, the band 'recall in some way the sound and attitude of the first rock era' ([1969] 2005: 94). Somma perfectly captures the critical mood surrounding the Velvets: they had little to do with contemporary rock culture (sullied in its commercialized forms), but a lot to do with the original impulses of the music in the 1950s – wild unbridled, threatening and clearly 'alternative' in its gestures, moods and looks.

For Bannister, such recuperation again separates the Velvet's from the mainstream history of rock: he describes them as

> a band that seemed to affirm the vitality of rock and roll, while never having been compromised or vitiated by its mass cultural agenda (commodification) or by countercultural rhetoric about saving the world. The Velvets' insistence on specificity and their ironic awareness of their own practice, their sceptical refusal to believe in the 'grand narrative' of rock, equipped them for an age of disillusionment and reassessment.
>
> (2010: 176)

Ironically, these gestures also ensured their inscription into the grand narrative of rock – because that narrative is about resistance, rebellion, tastelessness and vulgarity, among other things. In fact, the grand narrative of rock can't exist without the Velvets precisely because, as Bannister notes, '[p]unk and '80s alternative rock are all unthinkable' without them (2010: 174). What's clear is that if they'd achieved something like commercial success, they would, in some important way, cease to be the Velvet Underground. Or put another way, if the Velvet Underground didn't exist, rock historians would have had to invent them.

Is there a band in this history?

The Velvet Underground strained against the commercial and aesthetic practices of rock in the 1960s. But how disconnected from popular music were they? Perhaps one other reason that they strike many as an uneasy fit within rock culture is that, in some ways, they didn't operate as a typical band. Of course, like all rock acts, the Velvet Underground stands as a collective noun, functioning as 'author' of its catalogue. But consider this: the Velvet's original output essentially consists of four studio albums and two posthumous live records. Other bands have forged a legacy with less, of course. But the oeuvre is fairly slim. More significant, they never made two albums with the same line-up. After the first album, Nico was gone. After the second, Cale left, to be replaced by Doug Yule. After the third, Moe Tucker stepped out to have a child, Billy Yule came on board and Reed himself contends that he exited before it was completed. Doug Yule did release a fifth album credited to the Velvet Underground, 1973's *Squeeze*, but it features no original member of the group. By that point, we have fully peeled the onion – or the banana, as the case may be.

Considering this shifting history, we might be tempted to deny the collaborative practice of the band and see its members as sidemen for Lou Reed. Such a vision seems to have been in the offing when they hired Steve Sesnick as manager, after parting ways with Andy Warhol in 1967 (Unterberger 2009: 153). As John Cale notes about his own dismissal, 'Lou wanted to keep it pure. He was right. I wanted to push the envelope and fuck the songs up. That's why we split. He wanted me to be a sideman in my own fucking group' (qtd. in Pinnock 2012). If we apply a theory from film studies, we might conclude that Lou Reed, as the band's songwriter and most consistent voice, functions as 'auteur', the central shaping vision that ties everything together. But that notion doesn't square with the serious collaboration that occurred throughout the band's career. Nico's hollow, richly aspirated voice will be forever wed to those songs on the first album. And if there hadn't been a power struggle of some sort over the direction of the band, Cale would not have been dismissed. The first voice on the third album is one we've never encountered before: the sweetly hushed, almost whispered tone of Doug Yule on 'Candy Says'. By the time of *Loaded*, Yule provides lead vocal on four of the ten tracks, again including the opener, 'Who Loves the Sun?', and supplies bass, lead guitar and drums on many others (Yule 1996).

With the cavalcade of members and voices, the Velvet Underground trouble our desire for coherence in their sound and, indeed, in their very identity. They drew from a remarkably varied musical palette, encompassing everything from light pop to thrumming rock to disjunctive sound collage. It's very difficult to identify a signature style in this mix when every record seems like a one-off. In some ways the band's journey was away from the avant-gardism of the first two records and towards the more conventional rock of *Loaded*, with its literal celebration of 'Rock and Roll'. It's impossible to imagine that track on the earlier records – mainly because they mostly weren't playing rock in any conventional sense of that genre. But despite their famous early injunction against blues licks, some tracks from *Loaded* sound as though they could be outtakes from a Rolling Stones session.

All of which suggests, again, that we may be misled if we try to make them conform to our expectations of a 1960s rock band. Viewing them as a rock group feels restrictive and they strike us as misfits, resistant to being woven into the fabric of their era. Such an ad hoc practice helps account for the tension surrounding the group's identity and direction. In *The Velvet Underground: New York Art*, his marvellous collection of the artefacts, photos and essays surrounding the band, Johan Kugelberg makes the case that they were not responsible for the hippie vibe of their promotional material. Referring to the florid posters and handbills, Kugelberg notes, 'The random nature of these aesthetic choices, rarely chosen by the band themselves, mirrors them as a distorted reflection of ... the customs and the zeitgeist of the world they inhabited – a time the Velvets were in the midst of, yet outside' (2009: 9). That liminal state, both inside and outside time, may be the best way to understand this musical project we call the Velvet Underground.

Although they never embraced the stereotypical politics, fashion, drugs or idealism of the counterculture, the Velvet Underground were made possible by their historical context. Insisting that '[t]he Velvets were definitely a sixties phenomenon' that 'enjoyed the same cultural freedoms as the Jefferson Airplane did', Richard Mortifoglio argues that 'The counter-culture allowed the Velvets to rip off the freedom they needed to do what they did but their vision was solely their own' ([1979] 1997: 66–7). From this perspective, the Velvet Underground align more deeply with the themes (and bands) of their era than we might imagine. Such freedom allowed them to turn the 1960s ethos of radical personal liberty, free love and ecstatic, drug-fuelled communion against itself, offering a subversive critique from within. And that's precisely the unapologetic, dissident note that the band sounds in the history of rock and roll as well: it represents the opportunity for insurrection and can still be heard clearly all these many years later.

Conclusion

Ultimately it may not be Velvet Underground themselves, their music or their lyrics but their reception that separate them from their times. When critics insist that the band exists outside the trajectory of rock in the 1960s, they paradoxically reinforce the band's centrality to that history. During the dark ages of psychedelia and self-indulgent hippie-dom, who kept the rock and roll fires burning? Who assured that the rebellious spirit of rock's originating moment survived? Who kicked against the corporate pricks, even as rock went mainstream and heard the siren song of money? Who never looked down at the three-minute pop confection? Who started underground and stayed there, said 'no' when everyone was saying 'yes', stubbornly declined to join anything but their own party? In their principled stance against the themes of the counterculture, the Velvet Underground kept rock alive when it faced its greatest temptations – to aspire to high art, and to make itself culturally dominant. In this way, the band made room not just for alternative music but also crucially for *alternative taste* in rock music.

It is perhaps a neat coincidence that the Velvet Underground ended with the 1960s. Despite all the insistence on their un-timeliness, the band literally could not forge on into the next decade – at least not with Lou Reed at the helm. As with the Beatles, the Velvet Underground broke up officially in 1970, and thus remain forever sutured to their era. But unlike the Beatles, fans and critics won't let them rest easily in their context. They're too peculiar in too many ways, too deviant, too unsettling for the popular image of the decade of demonstrations, peace signs and be-ins. But if we are to understand the larger arc of rock history, we cannot remove the Velvet Underground from it. They must remain there, firmly in place in the 1960s, constantly questioning our very idea of what that decade meant, and trying mightily, perhaps vainly, to save rock and roll from itself.

Notes

1. An expanded eBook edition is available – see Unterberger (2017).
2. Such connections, of course, continued to inform the story of rock: witness the Sex Pistol's version of Eddie Cochran's 1959 'Somethin' Else', among other punk resurrections.

3 These Morrison artefacts, including a 1983 private letter with material reproduced by Bockris and Malanga (1983), can be found in Box 2, Folder 4. 8105 Velvet Underground Collection, 1964-2015. Rare and Manuscript Collections, Cornell University Library, Ithaca, NY (accessed 20-21 October 2017).

References

Altman, J. ([1966] 2005), 'Warhol "Happening" Hits Like a Noisy Bomb', in C. Heylin (ed.), *All Yesterdays' Parties: The Velvet Underground in Print, 1966-1971*, 37-9, Boston, MA: Da Capo.

Bannister, M. (2010), '"I'm Set Free…": The Velvet Underground, 1960s Counterculture, and Michel Foucault', *Popular Music and Society*, 33 (2): 163-78.

Barrios, G. ([1970] 2005), 'An Interview with Sterling Morrison', in C. Heylin (ed.), *All Yesterdays' Parties: The Velvet Underground in Print, 1966-1971*, 139-54, Boston, MA: Da Capo.

The Beatles (1967), *Sgt. Pepper's Lonely Hearts Club Band*, Parlophone PMC 7027.

Bockris, V. and Malanga, G. (1983), *Up-Tight: The Velvet Underground Story*, London: Omnibus.

Fricke, D. (1989), 'Lou Reed: The Rolling Stone Interview', *Rolling Stone*, 4 May. Available online: https://bit.ly/3nYFv8G (accessed 1 December 2021).

Glueck, G. ([1966] 2005), 'Syndromes Pop at Delmonico's: Andy Warhol and His Gang Meet the Psychiatrist', in C. Heylin (ed.), *All Yesterdays' Parties: The Velvet Underground in Print, 1966-71*, 3-5, Boston, MA: Da Capo.

Grow, K. (2015), 'Lost Lou Reed Interview: "I Never Liked the Beatles"', *Rolling Stone*, 17 February. Available online: https://bit.ly/3FWNoSp (accessed 1 December 2021).

Heylin, C. (2005), *All Yesterdays' Parties: The Velvet Underground in Print, 1966-1971*, Boston, MA: Da Capo.

Julià, I. ([1996] 1997), 'Feedback: The Legend of the Velvet Underground, the Fully Revised Version (1986-1996)', in A. Zak (ed.), *The Velvet Underground Companion*, 173-233, New York: Schirmer.

Kugelberg, J. (2009), 'The Velvet Underground: New York Art', in *The Velvet Underground: New York Art*, 9-11, New York: Rizzoli.

Leith, S. (2017), 'The Velvet Underground Made the Beatles Sound Dated', *The Evening Standard*, 13 March: 17.

Lugg, A. ([1967] 2005), 'Warhol's Drugtime Phase Brings Exploding Inevitable', in C. Heylin (ed.), *All Yesterdays' Parties: The Velvet Underground in Print, 1966-71*, 47-9, Boston, MA: Da Capo.

Martin, J. ([1968] 2005), 'Interview with Lou Reed', in C. Heylin (ed.), *All Yesterdays' Parties: The Velvet Underground in Print, 1966-1971*, 109-18, Boston, MA: Da Capo.

Machin, D. (2010), *Analysing Popular Music: Image, Sound, Text*, London: Sage.

McGuire, W. ([1968] 2005), 'The Boston Sound', in C. Heylin (ed.), *All Yesterdays' Parties: The Velvet Underground in Print, 1966-1971*, 65-78, Boston, MA: Da Capo.

Middleton, R. (1990), *Studying Popular Music*, Buckingham, UK: Open University.

Mortifoglio, R. ([1979] 1997), 'The Velvet Underground and Nico', in A. Zak (ed.), *The Velvet Underground Companion*, 57-62, New York: Schirmer.

Petridis, A. (2017), 'Porno grind and Flying Intestines: My Journey into the Labyrinth of Underground Metal', *The Guardian*, 7 November. Available online: https://bit.ly/3H2N0mp (accessed 1 December 2021).

Pinnock, T. (2012), 'John Cale on the Velvet Underground and Nico [Interview]', *Uncut*, 28 September. Available online: https://bit.ly/33MSfsn (accessed 1 December 2021).

Salinger, J. D. (1951), *The Catcher in the Rye*, New York: Bantam.

Somma, R. ([1969] 2005), 'Problems in Urban Living', in C. Heylin (ed.), *All Yesterdays' Parties: The Velvet Underground in Print, 1966–1971*, 86–97, Boston, MA: Da Capo.

Unterberger, R. (2009), *White Light/White Heat: The Velvet Underground Day-By-Day*, Boston: Jawbone.

Unterberger, R. (2017), *White Light/White Heat: The Velvet Underground Day-By-Day* [revised and expanded ebook edition], Self-published [Amazon Kindle].

The Velvet Underground (1970), *Thirdear*, Box 9, Folder 3, 8105 Velvet Underground Collection, 1964–2015. Rare and Manuscript Collections, Ithaca, NY: Cornell University Library (accessed 20–21 October 2017).

Wilcock, J. ([1971] 2009), 'Interview with Lou Reed', in J. Kugelberg (ed.), *The Velvet Underground: New York Art*, 84–9, New York: Rizzoli.

Williams, R. ([1969] 2005), 'It's a Shame that Nobody Listens', in C. Heylin (ed.), *All Yesterdays' Parties: The Velvet Underground in Print, 1966–1971*, 119–21, Boston, MA: Da Capo.

Young, C. (1978), 'The Sex Pistols in Texas', *Rolling Stone*, 23 February 1978. Available online: https://bit.ly/3qXT3Dj (accessed 1 December 2021).

Yule, D. (1996), 'The Lowdown on Loaded', *The Velvet Underground*, 5. Available online: https://bit.ly/35uwFtb (accessed 1 December 2021).

Zak, A. (ed.) (1997), *The Velvet Underground Companion: Four Decades of Commentary*, London: Omnibus.

2

The Velvet Underground and the networks of sound, vision and words of the fertile transatlantic crescent 1965–7

Johnny Hopkins and Martin James

In the wealth of texts that have explored the Velvet Underground's early days, the popular history of their origin is largely constructed around the primary role of key actors such as Andy Warhol, his Factory scene and their geographical location in New York. It is an ideal that is supported by the nature of Lou Reed's lyricism that locates its studied narratives among New York's underclasses. This simplification supports a Romantic concept of New York, driving an aspect of underground pop culture in an enclosed creative cultural network associated with the multimedia impacts of Pop Art and the experimental avant-garde. However, closer investigation suggests that the emergence of the Velvet Underground is couched in the close transitive links between London and New York. These links were afforded by readily available travel and investment in the cultural and economic capitals of each city's underground by creative intermediaries, especially within the fields of art, film and literature. Contrary to the New York-centric perspective of the Velvet's origin story, there is strong evidence to support the notion that it was in (early) *countercultural* London where the band achieved a significant level of awareness through a transatlantic network, even before Warhol's insertion into the band's biography. From their earliest demo recordings, the Velvet Underground were enmeshed in a 'web of interaction' (Crossley 2015: 87) that, expanding on countercultural activist John 'Hoppy' Hopkins' concept of west London as a 'fertile crescent' (Palacios 2010: 98), can be viewed as the fertile transatlantic crescent.

Drawing on Becker (2004), Crossley, McAndrew and Widdop (2015) note that 'the networked character of music worlds is not restricted to their human participants nor SNA (Social Network Analysis) to the analysis of human networks' (2015: 4). Thus 'sites of activity' are important too; most obviously for this research such locations include Warhol's Factory in New York and public venues including the *UFO* club and *Better Books* shop in London. We extend this idea to include various private flats and houses that were crucial sites of 'musicking' (Small 1998) and countercultural activity. As Crossley, McAndrew and Widdop (2015: 1) state, '[t]hese activities tend to cluster along ... geographical lines', hence the intense concentration of activities in both Manhattan's Lower East Side and London's Notting Hill area, along with other connected countercultural sites. This clustering enabled the construction of a countercultural network and the flow of information, ideas and music within it. These locations and the actors involved serve as 'the generative force and building blocks' (Crossley 2015: 12) for the cultural location of the Velvet Underground.

This study investigates this intricate network of countercultural contacts that formed the fertile transatlantic crescent. It explores the vital place that London's key countercultural actors played in the creation of the early mythology of the Velvet Underground and the cultural intermediation of the transatlantic networks. These networks linked the band to the cultural economy of London's creative underground of the 1960s via New York's interconnected experimental art, avant-garde film and beat poetry countercultures. Through this we employ 'relational sociology', formed on the fundamental notion that 'social interactions, relations and networks are the most basic elements in social life; the generative force and building blocks from which all else emerges' (Crossley 2015: 12). The study will therefore explore the foci of New York and London's underground 'social networks'. The dynamics of the networks can be understood through the filter of key actors active in both New York and London's underground and countercultural scenes. These include music industry personnel, musicians, artists, experimental film-makers, poets, photographers, fixers, journalists, event promoters and independent newspapers, presses and distribution networks. These key actors developed a strategic attachment to each other in pursuit of shared ideologies, and in collaboration created the space that the Velvet Underground would eventually inhabit upon the release of *The Velvet Underground & Nico* (1967).

New York's experimental music, film and literary networks

Drawing on Durkheim's idea of 'collective effervescence', Crossley (2015) states that '[b]ands and stylistic innovations take place within a web of interaction whose participants encourage, stimulate and provoke one another without any sense, initially, of where it is taking them' (87–8). The main actors come together through shared interests, attitudes and lifestyles as well as the opportunities provided in cities like New York and London. He further suggests that network formation by different actors within a scene can be analysed through the triumvirate of *foci, strategic attachment* and *transivity*. Foci are the environments that offer physical spaces for cultural production that actors with a shared interest converge upon. Strategic attachment occurs where participants target each other in order to gain some form of advantage. Transivity occurs in the way that linked actors tend to cluster, interact, share contacts and then grow through clustered participants repeatedly meeting each other in key spaces.

Transivity within and between both the creative pulses of 1960s New York's avant-garde underground and London's countercultural underground initially occurred through the foci of shared living spaces, multimedia happenings, cafes, bookstores and creative events. Strategic attachment can be seen to have occurred through the clustering of musicians, film-makers, poets, alternative media operators and other creatives with a shared interest in experimental, avant-garde and countercultural approaches. While Crossley (2015) may define scenes as 'networks of sound, style and subversion', it is more accurate to consider the scene that birthed the Velvets as a network of *sound, vision and the spoken/written word*. This network initially clustered in the loci of the Lower East Side of Manhattan, New York, and the countercultural 'villages' of Notting Hill, Ladbroke Grove, Covent Garden, Cromwell Road, Bayswater and Chalk Farm in west London – John 'Hoppy' Hopkins' 'fertile crescent' (Palacios 2010: 98). These loci were networked via transatlantic flows of influence through the various strands of cultural production that were working closely together and impacted upon each other.

As viewed in the formative New York scene, the clustering of people was inextricably bound to the activities of avant-garde musicians, poets, actors and film-makers centred on the Lower East Side, specifically the locus of a decrepit block of apartments at 56 Ludlow Street. Experimental film-maker, musician and composer Tony Conrad says this address 'came to stand for a lot in terms of some kind of liberating musical influence' (Bockris and Cale 1999: 65). Importantly for this study, 56 Ludlow Street was home to key figures in the production and dissemination of the Velvet Underground's music and myth. English experimental film actress Kate Heliczer (now Archard) states that she and her then husband, poet and film-maker Piero Heliczer, lived in a fifth-floor apartment next to musician and composer John Cale and Conrad – the latter having studied at Harvard alongside Piero (Archard 2020a). An old school friend of Piero's, the actor, poet, drummer and composer Angus MacLise lived in an apartment across the hall from Cale. Other inhabitants of the block included film-maker Jack Smith and 'Warhol superstar' Mario Montez (aka René Rivera). This creative cluster collaborated on numerous interrelated projects such as La Monte Young's drone ensemble Theatre of Eternal Music (aka The Dream Syndicate), of which Cale, MacLise and Conrad were all members. The trio would also produce the soundtrack to Jack Smith's 1963 film *Flaming Creatures*, which featured Kate Heliczer and Mario Montez in acting roles. Kate Heliczer also featured in Warhol's film *Couch* (1964) alongside the poets Allen Ginsberg, Gerald Malanga, Jack Kerouac and Gregory Corso, providing links to Warhol's creative cluster at another important locus, the Factory, then at 231, East 47th Street, in Midtown Manhattan.

One night at a party in 1964, Cale and Conrad met Jerry Vance of Pickwick Records, who recruited them on account of their style to help support the promotion of a pop song called 'The Ostrich'. Cale and Conrad soon met songwriter Lou Reed, and they were joined by sculptor and drummer Walter de Maria.[1] Together, Reed, Cale, Conrad and de Maria became known as The Primitives. Reed, Cale and a rotating crew of associates were 'always recording' often for 'bread and butter' in their pop work for Pickwick Records (Archard 2020b). As Reed developed a songwriting partnership with Cale, he became drawn into the 56 Ludlow Street avant-garde cluster and soon started commuting from Long Island to share the squalid apartment with Cale and Conrad at weekends. An early incarnation of the Velvets, now with Sterling Morrison and known initially as The Warlocks, and then as The Falling Spikes, would jam in the apartment (Archard 2020a) with percussion occasionally provided by MacLise. As Unterberger (2017) has identified, there were also two female members of the band at this time.

Most notably Elektrah Lobel sang with the fledgling band at several Greenwich Village club performances and appeared in two 1965 Andy Warhol films. Later Daryl Delafield also briefly joined the band.[2] The Falling Spikes were soon renamed The Velvet Underground at the suggestion of Tony Conrad, sourced from an investigative book on subversive sexual practices he found on the sidewalk in the Bowery.

The Velvets were thus a creative product of the processes of transivity among the Lower East Side avant-garde milieu of experimental film-makers, musicians and poets. Significantly the first two 1965 Falling Spikes/Velvet Underground gigs were at groundbreaking avant-garde film-maker Jonas Mekas' *Cinematheque* events with films by Andy Warhol, Barbara Rubin and Jack Smith (Landemaine n.d.). By December's run of shows at Café Bizarre, Greenwich Village, the band had attracted the attention of Warhol and the Factory set. Gerard Malanga (2020) outlined that he 'was not aware of the Velvets until Barbara (Rubin) personally brought me to Cafe Bizarre to hear them play. That was when I stood in front of them and did my whip dance. It was pure coincidence that they had this song "Venus in Furs" that related to my whip which I wore around my belt as a fashion accoutrement'.

The importance of the network of avant-garde film-makers in the Velvets' formative stage is further illustrated by the role of Mekas and Rubin as connectors. Mekas allowed the band to rehearse in the *Cinematheque* venue's loft, filmed them at the Annual Dinner of the New York Society for Clinical Psychiatry in January 1966 (as did Rubin) and also at the Dom in April 1966. Mekas introduced beat poet Allen Ginsberg to Rubin, who further connected the Velvets to the Warhol crowd. Given the existing connections through Montez, de Maria and Mekas, it is conceivable that Warhol was aware of the band as part of the Ludlow Street cluster before the Café Bizarre show. Furthermore, Cale already had an association with Ginsberg: 'Allen Ginsberg, John Cage and La Monte Young were the first three figures of the New York avant-garde I met when I arrived in the city in 1963 ... Allen was the conscience of the underground/avant-garde to whom we all deferred' (Bockris and Cale 1999: 278).

British photographer Adam Ritchie became another part of this network. While working for Conde Nast magazines like *Esquire* and *Mademoiselle*, he took photographs for avant-garde New York record label ESP Disk and worked nights at the Bleecker Street Cinema, where he met Barbara Rubin, Jonas Mekas and the Fugs. At Rubin's insistence, Ritchie attended and photographed the Velvets playing in Piero Heliczer's (1965) *Venus in Furs* film. Rubin instigated a working relationship between Ritchie and the band that saw him shoot them on various occasions, including at Café Bizarre, the New York Society for Clinical Psychiatry's Annual Dinner, the Filmmaker's *Cinematheque* and an Exploding Plastic Inevitable show at the Dom. In April 1966 at the Velvets' first Dom show, Rubin encouraged Ginsberg to sing with them. Curiously he performed 'Hare Krishna' while the band improvised and Malanga did his whip dance (Miles 1990: 387).

Warhol had been aware of Piero Heliczer's multimedia 'ritual happenings', with films projected through veils hung in front of a screen and coloured lights and slides superimposed over them, while dancers performed onstage with musicians playing in the background (Watson 2003: 210). The spring 1965 show *The Launching of the Dream*

Weapon featured a Falling Spikes performance. In January 1966 Warhol debuted his own multimedia events *The Exploding Plastic Inevitable*, a name created from words that Paul Morrissey found in the 'amphetamine babble' of Dylan's *Bringing It All Back Home* sleeve notes (Miles 1990: 387) that featured Dylan, Rubin and Ginsberg (Miles 1990: 334). The opening night imitated Heliczer's 'ritual happenings' with the Velvet Underground, now also featuring Nico, providing music. Cale and Reed also provided experimental scores for a trilogy of black-and-white films in which Warhol submitted friends to close-up interviews. The first of these, *Hedy* (1966), starred Montez in the title role. The soundtrack comprised of twenty-six minutes of music by Cale and Reed that is reminiscent of the experimental work of La Monte Young's Theatre of Eternal Music.

Transatlantic networks of sound, vision and the written word

Through the connections made with Ginsberg, other beat poets and avant-garde film-makers, and later with the Warhol scene, the Velvets were able to interact with a professionalized transatlantic network of organized underground creatives and successful music industry actors. These included British managers like Simon Napier-Bell and Ken Pitt (Pitt 1983) along with artists such as Bob Dylan and a new breed of rock stars including the Yardbirds and the Rolling Stones. James (2019) notes that networks of sound within major cities were also reliant on both cultural commuters and activities in the provinces. He extends Crossley's (2015) model to propose a further, fluid notion of transivity that shows the relationship between localized clusters and transient 'commuter' actors. This understanding that 'social networks' are able to exist in differing spaces but with key figures simultaneously enacting change upon geographically distant but subculturally linked spaces allows for the notion of a transatlantic network. The cultural presence of the Velvet Underground within the interconnected spaces of New York and London illustrates this proposition.

Following the Beatles' Ed Sullivan Show performance on 9 February 1964, there was a teenage hunger across America for British music. '[T]he vast increase in contact during this period' (Malchow 2011: 1) was facilitated by business expansion, a greater focus on the demographics and aesthetics of popular culture, cheaper travel and the broader media, including the mid-1960s emergence of alternative newspaper distribution and syndication services such as the Underground Press Syndicate and HIPS.

This facilitated a steady stream of acts like Herman's Hermits, The Hollies, The Kinks, The Yardbirds and The Rolling Stones crossing the Atlantic to tour, and encouraged the British music press to invest in sending people to cover music in the United States. In 1964 John 'Hoppy' Hopkins went to New York in his role as *Melody Maker* photographer, initially to shoot the jazz scene. He had already met Kate Heliczer in London but soon became acquainted with British ex-pats journalist John Wilcock (a founder of *The Village Voice*), photographer Adam Ritchie and, of course, John Cale, all of whom would become associated with the Warhol network. Hoppy subsequently alerted friends in London about the New York avant-garde scene. He became a key instigator in London's countercultural movement and an important actor in the Velvet Underground's early mythological status in London's underground network.

When British artist managers and other music industry professionals visited the States, they inevitably came into contact with American creatives such as Andy Warhol, who, through his fascination with popular culture and celebrity, had been increasingly drawn towards the potential of the rock star. This is evidenced by his *Double Elvis* and *Triple Elvis* pictures (1963), the filmed screen test of Bob Dylan (1965) and his early experiment with developing the avant-noise band The Druds (Russeth 2012). Yardbirds manager Simon Napier-Bell met Warhol in New York in 1965/66 and confirms that 'Andy wanted to learn more about the music industry. Haha! So did I' (Napier-Bell 2019). Initially, Warhol was interested in managing the Fugs, a plan that did not come to fruition. By late 1965, encouraged by film-makers Rubin, Malanga and Morrissey, he recruited the Velvet Underground instead. Stephen Watson states, 'Paul Morrissey suggested a bigger plan: Warhol should emulate Brian Epstein and sponsor a band. Showing movies behind the band would give them a chance to recycle movies that had had a very limited distribution' (2003: 11). Warner (2014) argues that Warhol linking up with a pop group represented the continued collapse of the high-brow and low-brow, elite and popular cultural divide where 'Ginsberg and Dylan could establish shared agendas and Andy Warhol would feel able to invite the Velvet Underground into his own palace of mysteries' (2014: 81). In a sense the band were the perfect embodiment of this transatlantic traffic that was an early feature of the networks created through the high/low collapse featuring as they did three Americans (Lou Reed, Maureen Tucker and Sterling Morrison) and two Europeans – a Welshman (John Cale) and a German (Nico). While the Velvets were clearly their own people and very much an entity before Warhol's involvement, they came to be seen as an extension of his art practice and personal brand. Indeed, the only words on the front cover of their debut album are his name.

London's countercultural networks

It is significant that the transatlantic flow of music creatives and music business people was bidirectional, and as Miles (1990) indicates, 'London was the place to be, and Americans were flocking across the Atlantic to join in the action' (371). Young Americans headed to England in the 1960s for a variety of reasons – for jobs and career development, education, to avoid the Vietnam War draft and to party – as London was then considered the epicentre of popular culture. These included producer/A&R man Joe Boyd, documentary film-maker/promoter Steve Stollman and Shel Talmy (producer of early singles by the Kinks, the Who and David Bowie/Davy Jones). Musicians also made the journey, including The Walker Brothers, Jimi Hendrix, PJ Proby and PP Arnold. Stollman ran the Spontaneous Underground, which put on acts like the Pink Floyd Sound and AMM (featuring John Cale's London friend and mentor Cornelius Cardew – a John Cage disciple and former Stockhausen assistant). His brother Bernie ran ESP, the avant-garde New York label that was home to the Fugs, Sun Ra, Pharoah Sanders and Albert Ayler. In August 1966 ESP released *The East Village Other* album that featured early Velvets track 'Noise', as well as contributions from Malanga and Ingrid Superstar, Ginsberg, the Fugs' Tuli Kupferberg and Warhol, again situating the band within the spheres of the counterculture and its media.

Other American ex-pats played important roles within the infrastructure of the London counterculture. Malchow (2011) identifies Jack Henry Moore and Jim Haynes in particular. Moore produced the *14 Hour Technicolor Dream* event and for a period edited *International Times* (95; 131). Haynes, an ex-US Army member stationed near Edinburgh (130–1), was key in setting up *International Times* and founding the Arts Lab in Drury Lane (1967–9), where Bowie rehearsed and performed. Warhol's films, popular with the UK student/counterculture crowd (119), were screened at the Arts Lab, which may also have raised awareness of both Nico and the Velvet Underground in London.

These transatlantic networks helped lay the foundations for the UK counterculture, providing a route through which knowledge of the Velvets could be transmitted. Events in New York were a blueprint for London's countercultural activists. 'It was a very particular urban, bohemian, beat, jazz vibe which echoed quite strong in Notting Hill. [Notting Hill] certainly wasn't a laid back, cool, hippy Chelsea fashion thing. It was harder', says Mike McInnerney (2020), art editor of Hoppy's *The Grove* community newspaper and, later, *International Times*. Indeed, this radical countercultural London had distinct locations and a distinct moment (1965–7), a similar time frame to its 'Swinging London' counterpart, but a world away in social, cultural and political terms (Rycroft 2011) and ended with 'the hippy invasion' of Notting Hill sometime in 1967 (McInnerney 2020).

During this countercultural moment, Barry Miles, 'a facilitator of cultural interface' (Farren 2001: 87), talked about the 'various plans to develop Covent Garden as a London Lower East Side' (Miles 1967a:12), later reflecting that 'it was very much the Lower East Side drug scene that we were emulating' with *International Times* (Green 1988). Knowledge of New York was gleaned from the underground press and other cultural activities, film and the jazz scene as well as transatlantic visitors (McInnerney 2020).

It is worth considering the cultural geography of London in 1965–7 when the countercultural network developed out of the transivity that connected the communal loci of houses, cafes, venues and community spaces like All Saints Hall and the London Free School in the 'villages' of Hoppy's 'fertile crescent'. As with the Lower East Side, this 'crescent' was, to apply Crossley's term, 'a web of interaction whose participants encourage, stimulate and provoke one another' (2015: 87–8). Key catalysts in this were Miles and Hoppy. Archard (2020a) says that Hoppy was '[o]ne of those wonderful energetic people who had his fingers in every pie going' and Miles 'knew everyone who was anyone' (2020b). McInnerney (2020) states that 'a vibe was being engineered, pushed' by Hoppy, and that 'Miles had a strong feel for the idea of a Bohemian beat scene'. They initially centred their activity in Notting Hill as 'a petri-dish to see how something could grow', developing infrastructure, locations and forms of communication such as *International Times* crucial for a self-sufficient community. Miles called this 'a contained economic community' and told *IT* readers, 'DON'T SPEND OUTSIDE THE UNDERGROUND' (Miles 1967b:8). McInnerney (2020) states that 'walking around [Notting Hill] gave a strong feeling of kindred spirits ... You could meet interesting people in the street ... [it] put you in contact with people on the scene then you started talking', with ideas, plans and action growing out of this contact, whether creative, communal or political. Though not based in Notting Hill, the Indica Gallery and Bookshop, established by Miles, John Dunbar and Peter Asher in September 1965, acted as a one-stop shop for the countercultural community 'a ticket to the magic kingdom', 'the epicentre of osmosis' (Farren 2001: 84). Its bookshop featured a range of key texts, including William Burroughs, Timothy Leary, Malcolm X, J.G. Ballard, Hubert Selby Jr, the Marquis de Sade and a selection of American underground newspapers like the *Village Voice* and the *East Village Other*. There was also a curated rack of albums of music and spoken word such as Sun Ra, the Fugs, Lenny Bruce and Melvin Van Peebles (Farren 2001: 84–5) many on the New York label ESP. *International Times* was printed in the basement.

Houses and flats were also central within this network, for example, 108 Westbourne Terrace, home to Hoppy, Miles and Adam Ritchie (Green 1988). Wherever Hoppy lived was 'a conduit for a lot of information that was coming from abroad from Europe or America' (McInnerney 2020). In the mid-1960s Hoppy also lived at 115 Queensway, where he installed an off-set litho printer in order to produce *Long Hair* magazine. As McInnerney (2020) states, 'Hoppy's flat was an epicentre of activity and all kinds of things came out of that'. McInnerney's own flat at 212 Shaftesbury Avenue was another hot spot. Mick Farren, who lived there immediately after McInnerney, said that it became 'a three-ring circus', 'a pitstop in the night-time perambulations of friends, acquaintances, total strangers' on their way back from the Middle Earth club, the Arts Lab or elsewhere (2001:200–1).

Further, 101 Cromwell Road provided a key countercultural location, being home to, amongst others, Syd Barrett and Roger Waters of Pink Floyd, the poet John Esam and the painter Duggie Fields. Visitors included Rudolf Nureyev, Judy Garland, rock 'n' roller Vince Taylor, Phil May and Viv Prince of the Pretty Things, and Donovan, who immortalized it in his song 'Sunny South Kensington' (Palacios 2010: 138–9). Key countercultural actors were regularly orbiting each other, and these locations enabled a meeting of minds and an explosion of creativity. Indeed, as Rycroft (2011: 160) states, 'London's enclaves of countercultural living, Notting Hill Gate, Ladbroke Grove, and to a certain extent Chalk Farm and Kentish Town, dictated the pattern of the London and national underground scene.'

These flats/houses were so much more than transient homes, party places or crash pads. People within the counterculture tended to keep closely to these familiar countercultural locations as they 'were quite vital, quite important for the secure taking of drugs and being able to discuss your trips ... and that was an aspect of "the village" that would grow out of certain activities and individuals who would group together' (McInnerney 2020). These locations were also 'safe spaces' for radical political discussion, planning cultural events and political demonstrations and sharing countercultural knowledge. They were also spaces for experimental living and subversive cultural production, such as writing, designing and printing underground newspapers. Because of controversial content many printers would not print these newspapers, so they were forced to operate alternative DIY presses. Furthermore, they were spaces to listen to and analyse new music. McInnerney (2020) recalls that in these locations 'I could chill and cool out and listen to some new stuff that was coming in'. Thus, artists such as the Velvets, John Fahey, Philip Glass, Frank Zappa and Tuli Kupferberg were accessed 'hot off the press or pre-release'.

The Velvet Underground and the London counterculture

Despite Warhol's important place in the transatlantic acculturation of 1960s popular culture, the Velvet Underground's links with 1960s London actually pre-date his involvement with the band. Indeed, as previously noted, there were already important links between London's countercultural literary, film and avant-garde music worlds and those of New York, providing channels through which knowledge of the Velvets and several of their early tapes flowed, aided by key actors.

Central to and illustrative of these links were two 1965 Bob Dylan gigs at the Royal Albert Hall, London (9 and 10 May), and a reading by beat poet Allen Ginsberg at *Better Books* (11 May). The shop, managed by Barry Miles, was a key incubator of the British counterculture, situated at 4 New Compton Street near Denmark Street, the epicentre of London's music industry. *Better Books* released spoken word albums by Ginsberg and Lawrence Ferlinghetti with sleeves by the early psychedelic artist Alan Aldridge (Palacios 2010: 80). Through his contacts and interests, Miles brought together transatlantic countercultural scenes and music, film, literary and art worlds, strands later reflected in the content of *International Times* (Rycroft 2011: 88). The Dylan and Ginsberg events brought many of the protagonists in the Velvets' story into each other's orbit in London without them fully connecting. The Dylan shows were a focal point for the nascent counterculture bringing together, backstage and at Dylan's hotel, an intriguing mix of creatives: beat poet Allen Ginsberg, Barry Miles, Warhol's London art dealer Robert Fraser, the Beatles, folksingers Joan Baez and Donovan, Marianne Faithfull, Dylan's UK PR agent Ken Pitt, Dylan's producer Tom Wilson and Dylan's sometime girlfriend, Nico.

Miles engaged Ginsberg for the talk at *Better Books*, while Hoppy took photos, with emerging film-maker Peter Whitehead also in attendance (Kane 2011: 109). The event has become viewed as a key moment in the emergence of London's underground scene which author Jeff Nuttall argued 'could well turn out to have been a very significant moment in the history of England – or at least in the history of English Poetry' (Fountain: 1988: 16).

Through his connections, Miles invited Warhol, Edie Sedgwick, Gerard Malanga, Baby Jane Holzer and Barbara Rubin (Palacios 2010: 81). Ginsberg had been acquainted with Malanga from poetry circles since 1958 and, from 1964 onwards, had visited Warhol's Factory with on-off lover Barbara Rubin, who was involved with Warhol through her films (Miles 1990: 334–5). Also present was Kate Heliczer, who was carrying, as Miles noted, reel-to-reel tapes of a Velvet Underground demo (Green 1988: 65–6). She had flown over with Rubin, whom she found 'very fascinating' (Archard 2020b). This suggests that the Velvets music landed in the heart of the emerging London counterculture seven months before Warhol first saw the band at Café Bizarre in December 1965, before he recruited Nico and before the band signed a record deal.

Based on the timing of the *Better Books* event, Heliczer's tapes must derive from one of the various pre-Velvets practice sessions. Indeed, Reed, Cale, Morrison and sometimes Angus MacLise spent much of 1965 writing and rehearsing at 56 Ludlow Street. Cale recorded many of these rehearsals on a Wollensak reel-to-reel tape recorder given to him by Tony Conrad (Fricke 1995: 14). Heliczer's tapes pre-dated both the July 1965 demo tape that Cale later distributed and the November 1965 recordings filmed by Heliczer's husband Piero for his film *Venus In Furs*, documented in the December CBS News feature *The Making of an Underground Film*.[3] While it is unclear exactly which songs were on the tapes, it is certain that the band were keen to get their music to the UK music industry. Archard (2020a) reveals, 'When they heard I was going to London they, I think John Cale, asked "Do try and find someone who would like to take us on"'. Interest was instant, as Archard (2020a) notes: 'When Hoppy heard that I had the tapes he wanted to hear them. He was very excited about it. He listened to them again and again … [and he] thought it was marvellous' (2020b). As Hoppy was the DJ at *UFO* 'he chose all the records up until June '67 when he was sent to prison' (Boyd 2019). Did he or Simon Barley, who succeeded him on the turntables, play the Velvets to the gathered countercultural crowd? McInnerney (2020) feels that the Velvets and Warhol provided 'an underground template for Hoppy' for a range of activities, including the Pink Floyd shows at All Saints Hall, Notting Hill. A while later, Archard (2020a) notes, 'John Cale wrote to say: "Hold on. Don't play it to anyone" and I sent it back' – presumably once Warhol had become their manager or the Verve deal had been signed.

From our research it is clear that several other tapes from different sessions made it into the sonic bloodstream of countercultural London. A few months after Heliczer's tapes arrived, another set was in circulation thanks to Cale's promotional efforts in late summer 1965 when door-stepping Marianne Faithfull at her London home and handing over a demo tape in the hope that she would give it to Mick Jagger (Cale in Fricke 1995: 15; Bockris and Cale 1999: 80). The tape featured early versions of 'Heroin', 'Venus In Furs', 'I'm Waiting For The Man' and 'Wrap Your Troubles in Dreams'. It is not clear whether Jagger received the tape but talking to Nick Kent in the NME (1977), he acknowledged the influence of the Velvets' 'Heroin' on the Stones' 'Stray Cat Blues' (1968). The American music journalist Lester Bangs further suggested that the Stones' albums *Sticky Fingers* (1971) and *Exile on Main Street* (1972) were 'blatantly influenced by' the Velvets (cited in Julià 1996: 178).

On the same London trip Cale passed tapes to what he identified as 'the more adventurous record companies' and to one of his old tutors at Goldsmiths (qtd. in Fricke 1995: 15) that included 'Heroin', 'Venus In Furs', 'Black Angel's Death Song', 'Wrap Your Troubles in Dreams' and 'Never Get Emotionally Involved with Man,

Woman, Beast or Child' (Bockris and Cale 1999: 80). Despite some interest, no record deal was secured, but Cale acquired early Kinks and Who records that were 'played constantly' in the Ludlow Street apartment. Cale reflected that these English groups 'were sniffing around the same musical grounds as we were …. With considerable psychological depth and insight, the Kinks' Ray Davies compared with Lou as a lyricist, and their guitarists were using feedback on records' (Bockris and Cale 1999: 80). This inspired a sense of confidence and urgency in the Velvet Underground, and they even considered moving to England to build their career (Julià 1996: 182).

Mick Farren claimed that his band the Social Deviants covered the Velvets' 'I'm Waiting for the Man' and their Dylan-esque 'Prominent Men' before anybody else, after hearing early demo versions likely to be the July 1965 recordings that later resurfaced on the Velvet Underground's *Peel Slowly and See* boxset (Unterberger 1998). Farren told Unterberger, 'Joe Boyd brought over some tapes of the Velvet Underground, which we stole off him, and somebody immediately stole off us.' However, Boyd (2019) states while he 'heard about the Velvets through reading the Village Voice', he had never had tapes of the band before the debut album came out. Nevertheless, Farren, due to his countercultural connections and role in London, was certainly in a position to have heard one of the circulating Velvets tapes. He knew Miles, Pete Jenner and Hoppy, worked the door at *UFO*, wrote for *International Times* and had a long correspondence with John Peel, who gave support to the Deviants. The Deviants were, in effect, one of the house bands of the London counterculture. The Velvets' influence can be detected in the chugging rhythm of 'I'm Coming Home' on their 1968 debut album *Ptooff!*. In 1968 Farren and the Deviants toured with the Pretty Things and would finish their set with a 'mutated version' of 'Sister Ray', 'which went down so well with speedfreaks, but tended to disturb or enrage music lovers' (Farren 2001: 196).

Just as David Bowie's manager Ken Pitt brought back an acetate of the first Velvet Underground album from New York in December 1966 (see Hopkins and James, Chapter 9, in this volume), so too did Beatles manager Brian Epstein, after, as Unterberger notes, a taxi ride with Lou Reed. Epstein seems to have been keen on the record as he played it at his salons in London (Shaar-Murray 2013). With these tapes, acetates and promo copies in circulation, it cannot be beyond the realms of possibility that someone made copies for personal use or further distribution through the counterculture network beyond the core activists. Mike McInnerney (2020) recalls: 'There was quite a buzz, a lot of excitement around the band. It was doing the rounds … maybe through Hoppy's connections. They were definitely part of the conversation before *The Velvet Underground & Nico* album was released.' Intriguingly he states that when he first heard it, the album just had 'plain white bits of card covering the disc, no packaging'. Was this a bootleg? McInnerney replies, 'It makes you wonder.' Could the disc have been an acetate? This seems possible as Ken Pitt's Factory story shows that Warhol's team gave out at least one acetate of the Velvets' first album. McInnerney believes he first heard the album at his flat in 212 Shaftesbury Avenue. This makes things all the more intriguing as Mick Farren (2001: 202) has stated that Bowie was a regular visitor to the flat, thus raising questions as to whether McInnerney might have heard Bowie's infamous acetate, even though they never met in person.

1967: The Velvet Underground live in London?

Surprisingly the Velvet Underground did not perform in London until 6 October 1971, by which time Doug Yule was on vocals and only Moe Tucker remained from the original line-up. However, there were concerted efforts on both sides of the Atlantic to organize gigs in Britain even before their debut album was released in the UK. Some of these attempted efforts were by the London countercultural network. These suggest a clear awareness of the band's artistic validity and a belief that there was already an audience for them in Britain. Amongst the key cultural intermediaries also involved were Ken Pitt and Brian Epstein.

Between 10 November 1966 and 11 January 1967, Pitt met Denis Deegan twice in New York and once in London, and Warhol once in New York to thrash out details of a proposed Warhol and the Velvet Underground visit to London (Pitt 1983: 60–1; 66). In a coordinated strategy, Pitt arranged a week of gigs at playwright Arnold Wesker's Roundhouse venue in the countercultural 'village' of Chalk Farm, to start 21 May 1967, and a BBC broadcast of Warhol and Morrissey's *Chelsea Girls* film starring Nico, Malanga and others from the Factory crowd. Further, he sought to secure a Warhol exhibition at the influential Whitechapel Art Gallery (Pitt 1983: 70). However, the promoter pulled out in mid-April after the Roundhouse hire costs rose and his other commitments took him to the States (70–2). Pitt tried other options, including Jim Haynes' countercultural space the Arts Lab, but ultimately the Velvet Underground shows were shelved, with the cost of nine transatlantic flights also an issue. This was not the end of the band's UK story, and there were other attempts to bring them over.

In April 1967 *Melody Maker* ran a short news story with a quote from the Yardbirds' Chris Dreja saying that Warhol would be over for the *14 Hour Technicolor Dream* event on 29–30 April at London's Alexandra Palace. This was accompanied by a photo of Warhol taken by Dreja at one of the Yardbirds/Velvets gigs in Detroit (see Hopkins and James, Chapter 9, in this volume). As evidenced by a letter to one of the performers, the *14 Hour Technicolor Dream*'s organizers believed that it would be 'the largest gathering of "underground" people there has ever been in this country' (Howson and Hopkins 1967). It starred Pink Floyd, Tomorrow, the Pretty Things, the Social Deviants, the Creation and John's Children and others from the counterculture/mod/psychedelic scenes. Significantly one of the flyers for the event listed the Velvets and Warhol in the actual line-up.[4] Yet, again, they did not appear. Mike McInnerney (2020), who designed the more well-known official poster, says the bill was always changing so for the poster he added the artist names in Letraset. Indeed, an *International Times* news story (21st April) does not mention them at all; the line-up in the news story is essentially that of the McInnerney poster. Intriguingly the 2 June 1967 issue of *International Times* announced that the Velvets would play *UFO* five weeks later, in early July (Velvet Underground at U.F.O. 1967). Elsewhere in the issue Warhol also discusses this imminent VU visit (Vosper 1967: 10).

According to Ignacio Juliá (1997), the Beatles manager Brian Epstein had, before his death in August 1967, been hoping to organize a European tour and wanted to manage the Velvets and buy into their publishing company (1997: 205). This may seem an unlikely move for Epstein, but given the prompting of Rubin, Epstein's genuine love of the record and his own drift towards the counterculture, it was perhaps inevitable. He had ties with the London Free School, established by Hoppy as a community adult education project based on the model of American free universities. Joe Boyd's Osiris Visions produced psychedelic posters for Epstein's Saville theatre. When *UFO* was evicted from the Blarney club on Tottenham Court Road, Epstein offered them a room at the Saville. There were further links as Paul McCartney helped to fund the Indica Gallery and Bookshop run by Miles and John Dunbar and even designed their wrapping paper. Yoko Ono staged an exhibition there at which she met John Lennon in November 1966.

During a discussion about the Velvets' debut album with John Peel on Pete Drummond's Radio London *Coffee Break* show in July 1967, another gig is mentioned that was due to happen 'later this year', perhaps around the November UK release of their debut album.[5] Here, Peel spins 'European Son', and as the album was not out for another four months (November) in the UK, it seems unlikely that Peel had a promo copy. However, as the album was released on 12 March in the United States, it is possible he had bought an import copy from One Stop Records or Musicland, record shops that catered to discerning music fans (Barnett 2018; Sheehan 2019) and musicians such as Marc Bolan and Jimi Hendrix. An advert for One Stop in *Record Mirror* (11 November) proclaimed, 'CAPT. BEEFHEART ... VELVET UNDERGROUND ... TOUSSAINT McCALL ... Does your Record Shop know these artistes and have discs by them? No? EVERYONE AT ONE STOP RECORDS KNOW! American Imports arriving weekly'.

The underground press, pirate radio and John Peel

Kate Heliczer (Archard) and Barbara Rubin's roles as key early cultural intermediaries are central to the Velvet Underground's place within the UK countercultural movement. Some of the key appearances of the Velvets in the countercultural press came about through Heliczer's association with John 'Hoppy' Hopkins, linking them to Pink Floyd and the *UFO* club. Rubin 'believed they (The Velvet Underground) could be cultural heroes of a new age. In her mind that select group included Allen Ginsberg, Bob Dylan, the Beatles, and Jack Smith. She directed her energy in exposing all of them to one another' (Watson 1995: 252). Indeed, at some point, as Archard reveals, Rubin made contact with Beatles manager Brian Epstein to discuss the Velvets (2020b).

At the *Better Books* reading and in subsequent discussions with Ginsberg at the London flat she shared with Heliczer, Rubin conceived the International Poetry Incarnation/The Poetry International event – organized by John Esam (Donnelly 2011: 130) – that took place at Royal Albert Hall on 11 June 1965. It drew an audience of 7,000 people, Indira Gandhi among them. The poets featured included Allen Ginsberg, Gregory Corso, Lawrence Ferlinghetti, Michael Horovitz, Adrian Mitchell and Alexander Trocchi. Rubin succeeded in making it happen on a grand scale by quickly plugging into the London network. As Archard (2020) notes, 'Barbara knew everyone on the scene in London within two weeks'. Rubin and Kate Heliczer, amongst others, handed out flowers at the event that was filmed by Peter Whitehead and released as *Wholly Communion* (1965). Helicxer (Archard 2020) also recalls, 'It was not a great poetry reading – everyone drunk or stoned – everyone behaved badly, but it was an amazing scene. The venue said they would never have a poetry reading again.' Despite the response, as Rycroft (2011: 83) notes, it acted as 'a prelude to the kinds of cultural politics that were about to emerge in London'.

Inspired by the International Poetry Incarnation and the way it had brought out many like-minds, journalist Miles started a counterculture magazine with Hoppy in order to cater to this new audience. *Long Hair* (subtitled NATO [North Atlantic Turn-On], a name that was suggested by Ginsberg) was an eighty-page magazine with contributions from Miles' contacts. In the first issue these included pieces by Ginsberg, Ferlinghetti, Malanga and the Fugs' Tuli Kupferberg, as well as their British counterparts Michael Horovitz, Brian Patten, Pete Brown and Jeff Nuttall. A poem about heroin by the American free jazz saxophonist Archie Shepp also featured (Miles 2017: 116; Malchow 2011). At this time Miles was also the London correspondent of the *East Village Other*, which had been co-founded by John Wilcock.

Some photography for *Long Hair* was provided by Adam Ritchie after he returned to London in 1966 and met up with Hoppy and Boyd at their *UFO* Club. Here he took photos of Pink Floyd's earliest performances and forged a friendship with Hoppy. Later in 1966 Hoppy would team up with Pink Floyd manager Pete Jenner and offer to manage the Velvet Underground. Pete Frame (1972: 54) suggests that they called John Cale, although it's not clear if they already knew him or if either Cardew, Kate Helicxer or Ritchie provided his number. Nevertheless, the Velvets were by then tied up with Warhol. However, it is interesting to imagine how the band would have benefited from the management expertise of Brian Epstein, or Pete Jenner and Hoppy and the strong countercultural networks in the UK, rather than being 'managed' by Warhol.

The importance of the underground press and the strength of links between publications on both sides of the Atlantic cannot be underestimated. However, it is significant that some of the Velvets' earliest press actually appeared in the UK – not only *Long Hair*, through the links in the New York–London countercultural network but also Nottingham-based *The Flower Scene and the Love Generation* (November 1967). The *Flower Scene* article alerted the future music journalist Kris Needs to the Velvet Underground, although Nottingham local Richard Williams, who would pen the first Velvets album review in the UK, claims his interest came from 'East Village Other (John Wilcock's famous piece) and the Village Voice (Richard Goldstein)' (see Hopkins and James, Chapter 9, in this volume).

In April 1966 *Long Hair* evolved into THE Global moon-edition Long Hair TIMES (the immediate forerunner of *International Times*). Alongside articles on LSD and the London Free School, it featured a letter to Miles from John Wilcock, discussing his trip with Warhol and the Velvet Underground for two EPI events at the Ann Arbor Film Festival, Detroit and Rutgers University, New Jersey. Wilcock (1966: 5) noted enthusiastically: 'they use lights, films, rock & roll, & all kinds of turn-on stuff. Very exciting.' He asked Miles to find a London house rental for Warhol and his entourage of fifteen people, potentially including the Velvets. By this point Miles and Hoppy had also been alerted to the band by Ritchie's photos and Kate Heliczer's tapes.

Heliczer helped sell *Long Hair* at the CND march in Trafalgar Square on 11 April (Miles 2017: 138-9) at which they shifted all 500 copies. While this may not have been a massive exposure in terms of numbers, the majority of those 500 readers were likely to be actively involved in the counterculture and highly engaged with music. Each was an influential node on the tastemaker network in their own way. Indeed, despite claims that the Velvets received little or no coverage in the press, our research shows that they had a small but semi-regular presence in *International Times*, the most important UK underground newspaper. Indeed, they appeared in the first issue (14 October 1966), where their New York correspondent Bobo (1966: 6) gets it slightly wrong when stating, 'Andy Warhol's Exploding Plastic Inevitables are back at the Velvet Underground with Supergirl Nico and The Man With a Snake', presumably Malanga. To underline the links between the New York and London scenes, the same issue mentions Barbara Rubin at a Rolling Stones after-party (Millionaire 1966: 11) and features Piero Heliczer's 'American in London' column (1966: 3). The Velvets, Nico and Warhol also appear in a paragraph about an EPI event at the Dom in John Wilcock's Other Scenes column (27 February 1967: 4). Overall, the Velvet Underground were featured six times in IT's first year of production in the run-up to their debut album.

While these were not big features, they must be seen in context. First, *International Times* reached a significant audience of engaged individuals. Miles told Green (1988) that they printed 15,000 copies of their first issue in 1966 and by May 1968 were selling 44,000. Second, music was only part of the mix for countercultural publications. As Richard Neville, the founder-editor of *OZ*, noted, the main preoccupations of the underground press were 'Vietnam, pot, police, Black Power, pop' (1971: 122). Surveying the UK underground press from 1966 to 1967 shows that feminism (Germaine Greer wrote for *OZ*), sex, radical politics, gay rights, accommodation, CND, LSD, art, film, poetry and theatre were also important. *International Times* carried a few big interviews with British music artists – Paul McCartney, Pete Townshend – or visiting Americans who were in town – Albert Ayler, Paul Butterfield Blues Band – or material syndicated from US counterculture magazines such as Frank Zappa from the *East Village Other* (13 March 1967). Furthermore, Pink Floyd did not secure that much more coverage despite them being arguably the most important act for the UK counterculture, and closely tied to the key players at the paper. So the coverage of the Velvets shows they were already accepted into the publication's pantheon of significant artists contributing to an awareness of them in the wider UK counterculture.

In the UK the alternative press was not the only source of support for the early Velvets. As already noted Richard Williams was evangelical about them from 1967, writing the first printed review of *The Velvet Underground & Nico* (1967) in the *Nottingham Guardian Journal* (Williams, 2020) as well as providing early coverage in *Melody Maker* and later *The Guardian*. Pioneering British music journalist Geoffrey Cannon also wrote about them in *New Society* and *The Guardian* in 1968. An indication that the mainstream British music press understood the Velvets came through *Record Mirror*'s exposure in 1967–8 (including an 8 June 1968 review of *White Light/White Heat*). *Disc and Music Echo*'s review of their debut album (18 November 1967: 14) both nail the band's appeal and their differences to 'hippy' West Coast artists:

> The Velvet Underground is an East Coast – New York – group whose material is largely taken from the opposite side of life – evil and ugliness. Their music is hard rock'n'roll brought up to date with electricity. An electric viola adds a distinctive cruel, harsh note – it's particularly evil on 'Venus In Furs' and 'Heroin', two of the best tracks on the album which are never likely to get played by the BBC. The drummer is a girl, the lead singer often sounds like Dylan and the beautiful Nico sings sweetly on the strange 'Femme Fatale' and the lovely 'Mirror'.

While 'Venus in Furs' and 'Heroin' may have been too extreme for the BBC, Peel had already played 'Sunday Morning' on Radio 1. Nico is the only member named, and the piece included a photo of her from her time on Immediate Records in 1965, so the publication must have implicitly made this connection even if they didn't explicitly mention it in the review. Peel became another influential cultural intermediary for the Velvets, whom he first became aware of during his time on radio in America (1960–7). In early 1967 he returned to the UK, where he presented the *Perfumed Garden* show on the pirate station Radio London. For Mick Farren and others, the show 'came as close to magic as a radio show can', and it was where Farren 'first heard the innovative, the influential and the just plain weird' (Farren 2001: 90). Similarly, McInnerney (2020) states that the programme was 'a very important conduit into something interesting'.

Brian Eno (2015) acknowledges that it was Peel who switched him onto the Velvets in 1967 through his radio show. Duggie Fields (2019) confirms that he was another of those who had heard the Velvets through Peel's *Perfumed Garden* while living at 101 Cromwell Road. Throughout the summer of 1967, before the release of *The Velvet Underground & Nico*, Peel regularly played and discussed tracks from the album. On 14 August 1967, the last day of Radio London, he played two Velvet Underground tracks, dedicating 'Venus in Furs' to Mick Farren and the Social Deviants saying, 'He [Farren] explained it to me, you see. Filthy.' In the process Peel confirmed Farren's place within the counterculture. As the song finished Peel said, 'Those are the Velvet Underground with their strange, haunting and sometimes frightening things.' Peel's support of the band did not waver even when he moved over to the more rigid environment of the BBC's new station Radio 1, playing 'Sunday Morning' on his very first day on the *Top Gear* radio show[6] on 1 October 1967. Inevitably Peel's shows were a staple for London's countercultural network, connecting the Velvets with a primed audience. He also performed other roles which made him a significant actor within the London counterculture. He was involved with the *14 Hour Technicolor Dream*, compered at *UFO*, Middle Earth and the Roundhouse, and wrote for *International Times*. In two of his 'Perfumed Garden' columns, Peel briefly discussed the debut Velvets album ahead of release and mentioned Nico's imminent solo album (Peel 1967a; 1967b).

Nico's London life

Nico, of course, had her own fascinating pre-history that places her, briefly, at the centre of Swinging London's vibrant music scene. This was facilitated in the early 1960s by her continual travel through the transatlantic cultural networks linking Europe and America, making connections and pursuing careers in fashion and film and becoming a catalyst for other's creative activity. Exploring Nico's brief but productive time in London in 1965, prior to joining the Velvets, opens up a new perspective on early Velvet Underground networks. It was then and there that she connected with an array of established and emerging musicians and executives including the Rolling Stones, their manager Andrew Loog Oldham and future Yardbird Jimmy Page and his future Led Zeppelin band mate John Paul Jones.

Following a period in Italy and France acting and modelling, in 1965 she headed to London at the request of photographer David Bailey. She was quickly adopted by the Rolling Stones and their entourage, and manager Andrew Loog Oldham (2019) states that he was introduced to her by her then boyfriend Brian Jones, who had said that she could sing. Oldham felt she had commercial potential, and after a successful audition, he booked her into Pye studio in Marble Arch to cut her debut single with Jimmy Page as producer (Oldham 2019). Nico had wanted to record 'I'll Keep It with Mine', the song she believed Dylan had written for her, but they recorded Gordon Lightfoot's 'I'm Not Sayin' and a Page/Oldham song 'The Last Mile' with Page and Brian Jones on guitars. These recordings became one of the first singles on Oldham's Immediate label. Indeed, Nico played a key role in raising awareness of Immediate. As Oldham (2019) states, 'Nico was a great assist to the launch of Immediate. She did all the PR asked of her, everybody wanted to meet her. To the UK she was folk rock's Hildegard Neff or Dietrich. Great fun, a real trouper.' She even 'joined us on the launch of Immediate as we promoted thru [sic] the factories all over the north of England and Europe' (Oldham 1998).

In the *Record Mirror* story on Immediate (28 August 1965), which was illustrated by a large photo of Nico with Mick Jagger, editor Peter Jones (1965: 6) captured the appeal of Nico's vocals: 'Nico tackles a good song with a good, big voice; an antidote to the current rash of girls who whisper fearfully through folksey (sic.) lyrics.' For her part Nico lamented, 'I have a habit of leaving places at the wrong time ... just when something big might have happened to me' (1965: 6). This was an issue that blighted her career, though her return to New York later that year proved a little more successful.

Although Nico had met some of the peripheral figures in the Warhol crowd at Danny Fields' JFK Assassination party in New York in 1963, which she attended with Denis Deegan (Fields in Shore 2016), her first meaningful interactions with them came in 1965. On a trip to Paris she ran into Deegan, Warhol, Malanga, Edie Sedgwick and Chuck Wein at the Castel nightclub (Witts 1993: 109). Back in London she met Malanga again with Deegan (Malanga 2020) while out with Brian Jones at one of Allen Ginsberg's parties. Malanga (2020) says that he gave 'Nico the Factory phone number and suggested that if ever she found herself in New York to give me a call'. She duly arrived in New York with her Immediate single as a calling card and phoned the Factory. Malanga remembers the call came 'around the time the Velvets were performing at the Bizarre [December 1965], and I asked Andy to join me and we met her at a favorite Spanish restaurant of hers' (2020). Witts (1993: 123) writes that Brian Jones took her to the Factory, where she sat a screen test and a few days later acted in Warhol's film *The Closet* (1966). Soon she found herself drafted into the Velvet Underground. Her time in London had given her confidence and platform for her singing, while creating a network of contacts who had a part to play in the Velvets story. And, of course, *The Velvet Underground & Nico* producer Tom Wilson had only wanted to sign the band because of Nico (Witts 1993: 149), whom he had met on Dylan's 1965 UK tour (Savage 2015: 192).

The Velvet Underground and the 'fertile transatlantic village'

Popular histories have located the Velvet Underground's emergence and mythology as inextricably linked to the Warhol biography. This chapter notes that the band's pre-Warhol story is located simultaneously within a web of interaction between the countercultural undergrounds of New York and London. Each scene found key actors clustered around a range of loci with specific focus on residences. In New York this was viewed through the effects of transivity among a group of avant-garde and experimental creatives operating in the Lower East Side. In the UK the loci were situated within the 'villages' of London's 'fertile crescent'.

As a result of strategic attachment, individual clusters connected with other professionalized, or high-profile, creative clusters. For New York this included Andy Warhol's Factory, while in London it was spaces such as *UFO* club and *Better Books*. The poets, musicians, managers, film-makers and other underground cultural producers associated with these spaces connected New York and London through transient, or 'commuter transivity' (James 2019). Further connections were made through the underground presses and distribution networks that promoted notions of deterritorialization in which the web of interaction that connected loci transcended geographical location. The countercultural underground thus acted as a 'fertile transatlantic village' of shared participants who creatively sparked off each other. The Velvet Underground was initially disseminated through the transatlantic creative networks that connected through countercultural activities and experimental creativity. The professional music industries and media would subsequently play a role in legitimating the Velvet Underground through the authenticating knowledge of, and association with, the 'fertile transatlantic village'. The final clusters in the social network that enabled the spaces for the emergence of the Velvet Underground were located in the rock, fashion and art film aristocracies that not only associated themselves with the 'commercial' energy of the transatlantic underground but also linked the professional scene orbiting the Rolling Stones to the Velvets' Lower East Side cool via the introduction of Nico.

Notes

1. In 1963 de Maria was a member of the short-lived avant-garde noise band the Druds founded by Andy Warhol. Warhol wrote some of the Druds' songs, with artist Jasper Johns contributing lyrics. The band initially included La Monte Young on saxophone, as well as painter Larry Poons on guitar and artist/poet Patty Oldenburg (later Mucha) on vocals (Russeth 2012).
2. Bockris and Cale (1999: 76–7) also discuss The Falling Spikes members Lobel and Delafield. They claim Lobel played guitar with manic intensity resulting in bleeding fingers – Lobel states this is untrue (Unterberger 2017) – but give no details of Delafield's musical contribution. Instead they discuss Cale and Reed's personal relationship with her and note she inspired elements of Reed's *Berlin* album.
3. Available online at https://bit.ly/3KKU89s (accessed 27 January 2022).
4. The flyer can be viewed online at https://bit.ly/3IFuYXS (accessed 21 October 2021).
5. An excerpt of the show can be heard at https://bit.ly/3o00Ezp (accessed 21 October 2021).
6. The show can be heard at https://bit.ly/3H5D0Jl (accessed 21 October 2021).

References

Archard (Heliczer), K. (2020a), *personal phone interview*, 2 April.
Archard (Heliczer), K. (2020b), *personal phone interview*, 16 June.
Barnett, I. (2018), *personal interview*, 7 January.
Bobo (1966), 'New York… Leary's Spiritual League, Warhol, YMCA, Mark Lane, The Bible', *International Times*, Issue 1, 14 October, 6. Available online: https://bit.ly/3rRXRcH (accessed 30 November 2021).
Bockris, V. and Cale, J. (1999), *What's Welsh for Zen: The Autobiography of John Cale*, London: Bloomsbury.
Boyd, J. (2019), *personal email interview*, 28 January.
Cale, J. (1999), 'Memories of Allen', in H. George-Warren (ed.), *The Rolling Stone Book of the Beats: The Beat Generation and the Counterculture*, London: Bloomsbury.
Crossley, N. (2015), *Networks of Sound, Style and Subversion: The Punk and Post-Punk Worlds of Manchester, London, Liverpool and Sheffield, 1975–80*, Manchester: Manchester University.
Crossley, N., McAndrew, S. and Widdop, P. (2015), *Social Networks and Music Worlds*, Abingdon: Routledge.
Donnelly, M. (2011), 'Wholly Communion: Truths, Histories, and the Albert Hall Poetry Reading', *Framework: The Journal of Cinema and Media*, 52 (1): 128–44.
Farren, M. (2001), *Give the Anarchist a Cigarette*, London: Pimlico.
Fields, D. (2019), *personal interview*, 15 July.
Frame, P. ([1972] 1974), 'The Year of Love Including the Birth of the Pink Floyd', *Zig Zag*, 25, August, in P. Frame (ed.), *The Road to Rock: A Zig Zag Book of Interviews*, London: Charisma.
Fricke, D. (1995), 'Essay', in The Velvet Underground. *Peel Slowly and See* [boxset], Polygram 527 887-2.

Green, J. (1988), *Days in the Life: Voices from the English Underground 1961–1971*, London: William Heinemann.

Heliczer, P. (1966), 'American in London: Time Exposure', *International Times*, Issue 1, 14 October, 3. Available online: https://bit.ly/3KKsRnp (accessed 30 November 2021).

Howson, D. and Hopkins, J. (1967), *Letter to Pete Brown*. Available online: https://bit.ly/3IFuYXS (accessed 30 November 2021).

James, M. (2018), '"No I don't like where you come from, it's just a satellite of London": High Wycombe, the Sex Pistols and the Punk Transformation', *Punk & Post-Punk*, 7 (3): 341–62.

Jones, P. (1965), 'Nico Leads Andrew's Off Beat Company…', *Record Mirror*, 28, 6 August.

Julià, I. ([1996] 1997), 'Feedback: The Legend of the Velvet Underground (1986–1996)', in A. Zak (ed.), *The Velvet Underground Companion: Four Decades of Commentary*, London: Omnibus.

Kane, D. (2011), 'Wholly Communion, Literary Nationalism, and the Sorrows of the Counterculture', *Framework: The Journal of Cinema and Media*, 52 (1): 102–27.

Kent, N. (1977), 'Mick Jagger Hits Out at Everything in Sight!', *New Musical Express*, 15 October. Available online: https://bit.ly/3u5mDJ0 (accessed 30 November 2021).

Landemaine, Olivier (n.d.), 'The Velvet Underground: Live Performances and Rehearsals 1965–66'. Available online: https://bit.ly/34eVjxi (accessed 20 July 2011).

Loog Oldham, A. (1998), 'Sleeve Notes', *Nico. The Classic Years [album]*, Polygram 314 565: 185-2.

Loog Oldham, A. (2019), *personal email interview*, 10 January.

Malanga, G. (2020), *personal email interview*, 19 March.

Malchow, H. L. (2011), *Special Relations: The Americanization of Britain?*, Stanford, CA: Stanford University Press.

McInnerney, M. (2020a), *personal phone interview*, 24 March.

McInnerney, M. (2020b), *personal interview by email*, 14 May.

Miles, B. (1967a), *International Times*, Issue 14, 2 June, 12.

Miles, B. (1967b), 'Miles'. *International Times*, Issue 18, 31 August, 8.

Miles, B. (1990), *Ginsberg: A Biography*, London: Viking.

Miles, B. (2017), *In the Sixties*, London: Rocket, 88.

Millionaire (1966), 'Pop. Pop. Ouch!'. *International Times*, Issue 1, 14 October, 11. Available online: https://bit.ly/3KOisHI (accessed 30 November 2021).

Napier-Bell, S. (2019), *personal email interview*, 14 January.

Neville, R. (1971), *Playpower*, Boulder, CO: Paladin.

Palacios, J. (2010), *Syd Barrett and Pink Floyd: Dark Globe*, London: Plexus.

Peel, J. (1967a), 'Perfumed Garden', *International Times*, Issue 18, 31 August, 9. Available online: https://bit.ly/34gaGoQ (accessed 30 November 2021).

Peel, J. (1967b), 'Perfumed Garden'. *International Times*, Issue 20, 27 October, 11. Available online: https://bit.ly/3G0q9qB (accessed 30 November 2021).

Pitt, K. (1983), *David Bowie: The Pitt Report*, London: Design Music.

Platt, J., Dreja, C. and McCarty, J. (1983), *Yardbirds*, London: Sidgwick and Jackson.

Russeth, Andrew (2012), 'Six Feet of the 1960s and '70s: Patty Mucha – Once Mrs. Oldenburg – on Her Archives and New Memoir', *Observer*, 16 January. Available online: https://bit.ly/3AwvgNS (accessed 30 November 2021).

Rycroft, S. (2011), *Swinging City: A Cultural Geography of London 1950–1974*, Farnham: Ashgate.

Savage, J. (2015), *1966: The Year the Decade Exploded*, London: Faber and Faber.
Shaar-Murray, C. (2013), 'Lou Reed: A Frontline Member of the Awkward Squad', *Independent*, 27 October. Available online: https://bit.ly/3o2cPLY (accessed 30 November 2021).
Sheehan, T. (2018), *personal email interview*, 12 January.
Shore, S. (2016), *Factory: Andy Warhol*, London: Phaidon.
Unterberger, R. (1998), 'Mick Farren Interview'. March. Available online: https://bit.ly/3H5ohy7 (accessed 30 November 2021).
Unterberger, R. (2009), *White Light/White Heat: The Velvet Underground Day-By-Day*, London: Jawbone Press.
Unterberger, R. (2017), '1965 The Birth of The Velvet Underground: Concerts: The Falling Spikes, Café Wha?, New York, NY', in *White Light/White Heat: The Velvet Underground Day-By-Day* [revised and expanded eBook edition], San Francisco: Self Published [Amazon Kindle].
The Velvet Underground (1966), 'Noise', *The East Village Other*, ESP Disk 1034.
Velvet Underground at U.F.O. (1967), *International Times*, Issue 14, 2 June, 4. Available online: https://bit.ly/3r0QwYY (accessed 30 November 2021).
Vosper, P. (1967), 'Warhol!', *International Times*, Issue 14, 2 June, 10. Available online: https://bit.ly/3u0PGNL (accessed 30 November 2021).
W, E. (2017), 'Lou Reed and Jim Morrison: Magic and Loss', *Weirdland*, 25 April. Available online: https://bit.ly/3o0GeGl (accessed 30 November 2021).
Warner, S. (2014), *Text and Drugs and Rock 'n' Roll*, 2nd edn, London: Bloomsbury.
Watson, S. (1995), *The Birth of the Beat Generation: Visionaries, Rebels and Hipsters 1944 1960*, New York: Pantheon.
Witts, R. (1993), *Nico: The Life and Lies of an Icon*, London: Virgin.

3

Andy Warhol films the Velvet Underground and Nico

Glyn Davis

There is a founding tale about an early meeting between the Velvet Underground and the artist Andy Warhol which, repeated with slight variations across various sources, has become semi-mythical. As this chapter is centrally concerned with the band's formation of its identity, the conscious and careful fabrication of its image around the time of debut album *The Velvet Underground & Nico* (1967), I want to open by reiterating the story. In December 1965, Warhol was taken to see the Velvet Underground at Café Bizarre on West 3rd Street in Manhattan by Paul Morrissey, a Factory denizen and collaborator, Warhol's studio assistant Gerard Malanga and the film-maker Barbara Rubin, who had initially alerted the Factory crowd to the Velvet Underground. Morrissey's reason for inviting Warhol to the gig was that he had 'been looking for a band to work with for some time as part of the Factory's general expansion into multimedia activities' (Unterberger 2009, 64). 'It was a Thursday night', wrote Victor Bockris and Malanga (2002), and 'Nobody paid any attention to their arrival. The art and rock worlds were still quite separate and the ten or fifteen people scattered among the tables didn't recognize the new arrivals' (7–8). Despite the alleged segregation of artistic and musical spheres, Morrissey identified a conceptual link (call it a foggy notion, perhaps) between Warhol and the band: 'They were a unique group and they were called The Underground ... And this was the term always connected with Andy, too' (qtd. in Bockris and Malanga 2002: 7). Warhol recounted the concert in his memoir, *POPism: The Warhol Sixties*, stating, '[t]he Bizarre management wasn't too thrilled with [the band]. Their music was beyond the pale – way too loud and insane for any tourist coffeehouse clientele ... We talked to them ... and invited them to come by the Factory' [Warhol's studio, located at 231 East 47th Street] (Warhol and Hackett [1980] 1996: 144). Pivotal to the group's appeal for Warhol was their aesthetic. On the night of the Bizarre gig, they were 'dressed from head to foot in black' (Bockris and Malanga 2002: 8). But their sartorial choices usually combined several modes – beatnik stylings, American casual T-shirts and jeans, Cale's more esoteric dandyism, Tucker's androgyny – and the admixture ignited the artist's interest.

At this point in his career, Warhol was at a peak of cultural visibility: he was regularly seen out and about town at night with his raucous entourage, and stories about members of the gang featured weekly in newspapers and magazines. He had temporarily stopped painting and was investing considerable time and energy into making films. The films were not making money, however, and so Warhol was on the lookout for new ventures. In considering options, Morrissey 'thought of the idea of finding a rock group that Andy could appear to manage, or present' (qtd. in Unterberger 2009: 64) though Warhol was initially wary of this suggestion until encountering the Velvet Underground. Morrissey collaborated with Warhol in managing the band, primarily dealing with day-to-day legal and organizational duties, and suggested that the German model and singer Nico, who had just arrived in New York from London, could front the band (Warhol and Hackett 1996: 146). In Warhol's view 'Nico was a new type of female superstar. [Factory regulars] Baby Jane [Holzer] and Edie [Sedgwick] were both outgoing, American, social, bright, excited, chatty – whereas Nico was weird and untalkative. You'd ask her something and she'd maybe answer you five minutes later' (Warhol and Hackett 1996: 183). Despite reservations on both sides, the Velvet Underground and Nico eventually agreed to work together.

Warhol and the Factory's short but intense collaboration with the Velvet Underground and Nico lasted around eighteen months, spanning all of 1966 and the first half of 1967. In addition to enabling the production of their debut album, Warhol repeatedly turned his film camera on the band or involved them in his prolific film-making endeavours. He made over thirty Screen Test portraits – each only a few minutes long – of individual members of the group. He recorded the band jamming in the Factory (*The Velvet Underground & Nico*, also known as *A Symphony of Sound*, 1966, which ends with a police intervention) and performing live (*The Velvet Underground in Boston*, 1967). Members of the band provided live, offscreen music for the films *Hedy* and *The Chelsea Girls* (both 1966). Nico appeared in a number of Warhol films, including *The Chelsea Girls*, *Nico/Antoine* (1966), *Ari and Mario* (1966), *I, A Man* (1967) and *Imitation of Christ* (1967). According to the late curator and art historian Callie Angell, she also appeared in 'at least eighteen reels shot for, or included in, **** *(Four Stars)* (1967)', Warhol's 25-hour film experiment that has only ever been staged once (Angell 2006: 145). In addition, Warhol's films were a crucial component of the Velvet Underground's live multimedia performances – a touring show primarily known as the Exploding Plastic Inevitable (EPI) though it also operated under other names. In this chapter, I want to scrutinize the film element of the Velvet Underground's relationship with Warhol, and specifically to explore the ways in which Warhol's films of the band contributed to the shaping and solidification of their identity; I will concentrate on the Screen Tests and the EPI as the most substantial and significant components of their cinematic collaborations.

Testing, testing

White leader tape, briefly marked by a barely legible scrawl of numbers, zips past. The white screen gives way, via some residual flares, to an image of Lou Reed. He is shot in close-up, drinking from a glass bottle of Coca-Cola. Reed is framed centrally: his image is cut off at the forehead and ends at the neckline of his T-shirt. He wears sunglasses, a black choker around his neck, a dark jacket with an upturned collar; his hair is shaggy, wavy. The reel is silent, black and white, and features no camera movement or editing cuts. Shot against a dark background, Reed is lit from the right by a strong white light which casts the left side of his face in shadow. He inserts the neck of the bottle into his mouth and gulps. He turns his head to the left and swigs. He inspects the bottle. Reed's attention is caught by someone off camera – he seems to say 'yeah' – and he quickly returns his gaze to the lens, positioning the bottle between himself and it. Having finished the drink, he adopts an advertising-like pose and maintains it, slumped into the lower-left corner of the frame. The impending end of the reel casts grey washes over the image; in the final seconds, it swiftly flares to full white.

This short film, just over four minutes in length, is one of eleven Screen Tests that Warhol made of Reed. Equal parts amusing fake commercial and probing investigation of rock star iconicity, it also serves as a paradigmatic document of the relationship between the Pop artist and the band: an everyday consumer item that Warhol had previously made the focus of a number of silkscreened artworks vies with Reed, within the film frame, to be the camera's focus of attention. The film of Reed is just one of the 472 Screen Tests that the artist produced between 1964 and 1966. A considerable number of the components of this vast, sprawling serial work feature Nico or members of the Velvet Underground. To be precise, there are thirty-four: eleven each of Nico and Reed, seven of John Cale, three of Sterling Morrison and two of Moe Tucker. Most of this batch seem to have been intended as material to project behind the band during their live Exploding Plastic Inevitable performances.

The Screen Tests were all shot on a silent 16 mm Bolex camera; each was recorded on a 100-foot roll of film, giving them all roughly the same running time. Shot at sound speed (24 fps, or frames per second), they were projected at silent speed (16 fps) which slowed them down by a third, giving the films a somewhat oneiric quality. Warhol deployed this decelerated projection with many of his other silent cinematic experiments with stasis and duration, including *Sleep* (1963), *Empire* (1964) and *Henry Geldzahler* (1964). Almost all of the Screen Tests were shot in black and white, with only nine in colour. Influenced by the formats of official portrait photographs, the rules for the shooting of the Screen Tests swiftly took shape: the camera must remain fixed in position, the background should be plain, the test subject should be centrally framed, facing the camera lens, and they should keep as still as possible, not talking or smiling. Some of these guidelines were broken later in the cycle of production as, for example, the Screen Tests of John Cale reveal. Two begin with close-ups on Cale's left eye, a third a close-up of his mouth; near the end of these films, the camera pulls back to reveal his full face. (There are similar 'eye' and 'mouth' reels – one each – of Sterling Morrison; Lou Reed also gets one of each, though his 'eye' Screen Test does not zoom out.) A further two John Cale Screen Tests feature frantic camera movement: as Callie Angell puts it, they 'are filled with wild zoomings, single-framing, in-camera edits, and other experimental techniques, with the camera sometimes tilted left and right or even turned horizontally on its side' (Angell 2006: 49). Two of Nico's Screen Tests also feature agitated camera activity that zooms in on, or cuts to, close-ups of her mouth and eyes. The larger body of the Screen Tests, however, adheres to the rigid portraiture rules established at the start of the series.

According to Angell in her catalogue raisonné of the Screen Tests, Warhol's film series had its roots in two earlier projects: his experiments with photo-booth photographs, some of which he used as the basis for paintings; and a police brochure featuring mugshots of criminals entitled *The Thirteen Most Wanted*. This pamphlet served as the inspiration for a controversial mural that Warhol installed in 1964 for the World's Fair in Flushing Meadow, New York, but it also affected the instigation of the Screen Tests: some of the first reels he shot in the series were intended to serve as elements of a composite work entitled *The Thirteen Most Beautiful Boys*. This idea was not jettisoned – indeed, it was joined by a partner project, *The Thirteen Most Beautiful Women* – but the accumulated number of Screen Test reels swiftly exceeded the minimum required for these small collections of portraits, and kept amassing. These roots of the Screen Tests inflect the entire series: as Hal Foster notes, the films are, 'in effect, photo-booth pictures, mug shots, and publicity images rolled into one' (Foster 2010: 39). And certainly, the Screen Tests had the power to bestow their subjects with the allure of commercial imagery: as Mandy Merck notes, 'the close-up framing, the sculptural effect of the lighting and the contrasts of the black-and-white film tend to render even Warhol's less glamorous sitters photogenic' (Merck 2013: 94).

Warhol's Screen Tests were not intended to serve, like Hollywood screen tests, as auditions for roles in feature films. In fact, Warhol and his Factory collaborators did not initially refer to the films as 'Screen Tests', instead preferring the terms 'film portraits' or 'stillies' (Angell 2006: 15). The latter – a witty alternative to 'movies' – alluded to the virtually static content of many of the Screen Tests. Warhol's sitters were required to be patient and unmoving: this serves, as Brigitte Weingart notes, as 'a nod to the media history of the static pose, most notably to the long times of exposure in early photography that required the sitter's extended immobility; but of course one may also think of the sitting for a painted portrait' (Weingart 2010: 50). If a contemporary viewer may find it a challenge to sit through a four-minute-long still and unchanging film of a human face, then this echoes the experience of the sitter depicted. The use of the term 'stillies' also draws attention to the way in which the Screen Tests reveal the porous border between photography and cinema. At times, the images seem to have frozen: are we looking at a film, still or a still from a film? In one of the two Screen Tests of Ann Buchanan, who had connections to the Beat scene on the east and west coasts of the United States, she attempts not to blink. This eventually causes involuntary tears to well up and start running down her face. As Mandy Merck writes, 'The tears that flow from Buchanan reveal this test not as the still image it initially seems to be, but as a filmed study of incremental motion, fluidity, life' (Merck 2013: 95). Although most of Warhol's Screen Tests of the Velvet Underground feature a significant amount of activity – movement of the actors themselves, as well as of the camera – there are also more standard, 'stillie' portraits of all five of the group. Moe Tucker's two Tests, for instance, lack pyrotechnics: in one she appears sober and earnest, in the other more relaxed and warm, but in both the camera does not move and there are no edits.

Warhol's Screen Tests of the Velvet Underground and Nico need to be seen as part of the larger body of his short film portraits. The subjects of the Screen Tests vary widely, the reels capturing for posterity the variety of individuals passing through Warhol's Factory. There are Tests of musicians, actors, curators, artists, dancers, models, drag queens and a host of other hip and edgy figures. Among the better-known personalities making appearances are John Ashbery, Salvador Dali, Donovan, Marcel Duchamp, Bob Dylan, Cass Elliot, Allen Ginsburg, Dennis Hopper and Susan Sontag. Taken as a whole, as Angell notes, 'the network of individuals whose pictures Warhol collected in the *Screen Tests* offers a unique map of the New York downtown arts scene during a watershed period' (Angell 2006: 13). Like the Tests, Warhol's memoir of the time also offers compelling insights into the extent to which different social worlds overlapped within the space of his studio. His account of 1966, for instance, contains the following typical anecdote:

> We did screen tests of Brian [Jones] and [Bob] Dylan while Gerard fought with [Factory fixture] Ingrid Superstar over whose turn it was to pay for the malteds: the poor delivery kid from Bickford's stood around, frustrated, until [arts patron] Huntingdon Hartford arrived and finally settled the tab. [...] Nico sang some of the new songs for Brian and Dylan that Lou and John had just written for her – 'I'll Be Your Mirror' and 'All Tomorrow's Parties'.
> (Warhol and Hackett 1996: 151)

With some of the Screen Tests of the Velvet Underground – such as the one of Moe Tucker in which she seems chatty and relaxed – there is a sense of a social scene happening just beyond the view of the camera.

The Screen Tests could be seen as endurance tests, or tests of character. They are tests that could be failed, as Jonathan Flatley highlights: 'the Screen Tests are dramas of self-presentation, and what they dramatize above all is the singularity of each sitter's failure to hold onto an identity, the singular way that each person comes together and falls apart' (Flatley 2010: 92). The glare of the camera lens may put the sitter on the spot, but the individual depicted is responsible for projecting a coherent and sustained image. Thus, as Callie Angell notes, 'the *Screen Tests* should be recognized as true collaborations, films in which the subjects have at least as much control as the artist in determining the outcome of the finished work' (Angell 2006: 14). In this sense, it is useful to approach the Velvet Underground and Nico Screen Tests as records of the individual members of the band attempting to mould and present concrete identities, testing out roles, the camera capturing rock stars in the making. As Hal Foster writes, the Screen Tests 'were pure tests of the capacity of the filmed subject to confront a camera, hold a pose, present an image, and sustain the performance for the duration of the shooting' (Foster 2010: 39). Warhol was working with the band to craft their personae. Unlike many of the other earlier Screen Tests, Warhol was also thinking about projecting the films of the band members, was anticipating the enhanced visual scale of showing these Screen Tests as an element of the band's live shows. Filming the band members individually required them to distinguish themselves from one another (in the way that, say, the Beatles, the Rolling Stones or even the Monkees were able to do); segregating the band members, presenting them as visually and temperamentally distinct, could potentially enhance their appeal. Prior to his career as a Pop artist, Warhol had worked for a decade in advertising and illustration, including designing a number of album sleeves, and he maintained throughout his career a sophisticated understanding of the power and impact of bold commercial aesthetics.

Members of the band also had prior knowledge of the ways in which the commercial music industry operated. From September 1964 to February 1965, Lou Reed worked as a songwriter for Pickwick International, a company that 'specialised in producing bargain-basement rip-off albums for a naïve mass audience'; nevertheless, his five months there 'provided the best on-the-job training he could possibly have had for a career in rock and roll' (Bockris 1995: 77, 79). At Pickwick, Reed penned a would-be dance-craze song entitled 'The Ostrich', which was attributed to the fictitious group the Primitives. When TV companies began to express interest in the record, Pickwick threw together a fake band for a short tour, composed of Reed, John Cale and the artists Tony Conrad and Walter de Maria. The record bombed, but it facilitated Reed meeting Cale, and enabled both a glimpse at the machinations of commerce-driven pop. Nico also had previous experience of working in commercial mass culture. When she first met the members of the Velvet Underground, she was in the process of recalibrating her identity as a performer: in 1965, prior to arriving in the United States, she had released a folk-pop single, a cover of the Gordon Lightfoot song 'I'm Not Sayin''. The image on the sleeve of that record, a black-and-white photograph of Nico looking up out of frame, eyes wide open and crowned by thick black lashes, blonde hair bobbed, makes for an intriguing contrast with the version of Nico that appears in Warhol's Screen Tests. As a former model and actress, Nico was fully aware of how to harness photographic and moving images to create enduring and seductive personae.

Warhol's Screen Tests of the Velvet Underground and Nico were part of a larger series, the continuation of an ongoing long-term portrait project, but they had an alternative function as a tool in the promotional arsenal of the band. Toying with this potential, a number of the Tests of the band members took the form of 'pseudocommercials' or 'parodistic celebrity endorsements' (Angell 2006: 265). Only three earlier Screen Tests – all of 'Baby' Jane Holzer – mocked or disassembled the components of advertising: two depicted her unwrapping and chewing on gum; a third featured her brushing her teeth. All distended the running time of advertisements and notably lacked their direct messages and mimed gestures of satisfaction. There are a further eight riffs on adverts in the Velvets' Tests: four of Lou Reed and four of Nico. Reed eats an apple in one reel, drinks a Coke in another (as previously described); in two further Tests, he is depicted with a Hershey bar. Nico swigs from a can of Ballantine beer in one reel, a bottle of Coca-Cola in a second. There are also two *Screen Tests* of her with a Hershey bar. Reed and Nico both have one Hershey Test each in which they hold the chocolate bar close to their face but do not move, as though they are being photographed rather than filmed; in the other Hershey Tests, they both consume small amounts of the bar.

Tom Day has referred to these 'pseudocommercials' as 'Pop portraits', film portraits in which 'time is distended and the aesthetics of advertising are broken down' (Day 2020). Perhaps the most obviously 'Pop' of the Reed and Nico fake advert Screen Tests are those featuring a Coke bottle – a household object whose design aesthetics Warhol had appropriated and arguably celebrated in a series of paintings, including the black-and-white *Coca-Cola* (1962), which features just one bottle and part of the brand logo, and *Green Coca-Cola Bottles* (also 1962), which depicts a grid of 112 identical bottles. Warhol is, of course, often identified – along with Roy Lichtenstein, Claes Oldenburg, James Rosenquist, Ed Ruscha, Tom Wesselmann and others – as one of the central figures in the history of American Pop art. Pop's dominant aesthetic device, as Bradford Collins notes, was to draw on existing commercial or mainstream cultural products and imagery as a source, often with very little transformation: comic book panels and advertising images were blown up in scale to fit large canvases; sculptural reproductions of household items (boxes of Brillo soap pads, for instance) were virtually indistinguishable from the originals; photographs snipped from newspapers were multiplied across a painting, coated with washes of bright colour (Collins 2012: 5–6). In his collaborations with the Velvet Underground and Nico, Warhol's Pop sensibility sometimes dominated – perhaps most notably in the bold yellow and pink 'peel slowly and see' banana that featured on their album cover. If Warhol's Screen Tests were a collaboration, or even a tussle, between film-maker and sitter, then in Reed and Nico's Coke-featuring Tests, the bottle served as his proxy, a Pop branding that they failed to enthusiastically endorse. Their disaffection or studied coolness, of course, was a key constituent of the Velvet Underground's projected image.

Erupting, exploding

Early in 1966, soon after Warhol and the Velvet Underground and Nico had agreed to work together, Warhol was invited to give a talk at the annual dinner of the New York Society for Clinical Psychiatry. The event was due to be held 13 January at the Delmonico Hotel. Warhol said that he would speak if he 'could do it through movies', and with the Velvet Underground, both of which were accepted (Warhol and Hackett 1996: 146). The ensuing performance was the first manifestation of what was called 'Andy Warhol's Up-Tight', the precursor to the EPI. 'Uptight', write Bockris and Malanga, 'meant interesting. Uptight meant something, as opposed to the perennial nothing, would happen' (Bockris and Malanga 2002: 38). Warhol provides an account of the Psychiatry Society event:

> There were about three hundred psychiatrists and their mates and dates – and all they'd been told was that they were going to see movies after dinner. The second the main course was served, the Velvets started to blast and Nico started to wail. Gerard and Edie jumped up on the stage and started dancing, and the doors flew open and [writer, filmmaker and curator] Jonas Mekas and Barbara Rubin with her

crew of people with cameras and bright lights came storming into the room and rushing over to all the psychiatrists asking them things like: 'What does her vagina feel like?' [and] 'Is his penis big enough?'

(Warhol and Hackett 1996: 146–7)

Rubin's interventions were central to the dynamic of the event. As Branden Joseph writes of her actions, 'The shock they effected was intended not only to destroy the audience's traditionally contemplative attitude toward the spectacle taking place on stage, but also to make them – as exemplars of bourgeois culture, norms, and comportment – reveal themselves and the society of which they were a part as "up-tight"' (Joseph 2002: 77). Further 'Up-Tight' events followed: at the Film-Makers' Cinematheque in New York in February, at Rutgers and Ann Arbor in March. Variations on the format of the show were experimented with. Sterling Morrison remembers, 'At Rutgers we were all dressed entirely in white. The effect, with all the films and lights projected on us, was invisibility' (qtd. in Bockris and Malanga 2002: 38). Not so much underground, perhaps, as buried.

In April 1966, Warhol rented a performance space, a Polish dance hall upstairs at the Dom on St Mark's Place in New York, for the entire month. The Up-Tight show moved into the space and expanded. A press advert for the launch of the residency announced: 'Come blow your mind: the silver dream factory presents the first erupting plastic inevitable with Andy Warhol, The Velvet Underground and Nico.' In small print, the announcement continued: 'Starting Friday April 1 come at 9 o'clock – stay till 2 – Music, movies, food, dancing, Gerard Malanga, refreshments, lightworks, Ingrid Superstar, ultra sounds, and multiple films including: Sleep, Eat, Kiss … etc.' The show, soon thereafter rebranded as the Exploding Plastic Inevitable, was a huge success. Seven hundred and fifty people showed up for the opening night, and the income for the first week reached $18,000. In *POPism*, Warhol provides an extraordinary account of the show at the peak of its popularity, the breathless tumble of his words heightening the impression of sensory overload:

[T]he Velvets played so loud and crazy I couldn't even begin to guess the decibels, and there were images projected everywhere, one on top of the other. I'd usually watch from the balcony or take my turn at the projectors, slipping different-coloured gelatin slides over the lenses and running [Warhol] movies … Stephen Shore and Little Joey and a Harvard kid named Danny Williams would take turns operating the spotlights while Gerard and Ronnie and Ingrid and Mary Might (Woronov) danced sadomasochistic style with the whips and flashlights and the Velvets played and the different-coloured hypnotic dot patterns swirled and bounced off the walls and the strobes flashed and you could close your eyes and hear cymbals and boots stomping and whips cracking and tambourines sounding like chains rattling.

(Warhol and Hackett 1996: 162–3)

The EPI events projected some of Warhol's longer films complemented by assemblages of Screen Tests which were also bolstered with additional reels of material. Photographs included inside the gatefold sleeve of *The Velvet Underground & Nico* reveal members of the band performing in front of projected Screen Tests of John Cale, including one of his eyes in close-up. John Wilcock, in his account of the Up-Tight event at Rutgers, notes that as the band were performing, 'the movies were playing, movies of Nico, the bland, blonde singer. Nico's face, Nico's mouth, Nico sideways, backwards, superimposed on the walls and the ceiling, on Nico herself as she stands onstage impassively singing' (Wilcock 2010: 164).

The archive of Warhol's films contains seven compilations of Screen Test reels designed to be shown behind the Velvet Underground as they performed. Two four-minute-long reels of Gerard Malanga and Mary Woronov dancing with whips in the Factory – a routine that they would often replicate onstage at the EPI as the band performed 'Venus in Furs' – were grafted into some of these. One of the compilations, 42 minutes in length and known as 'Gerard Begins', has ten reels spliced together: a joint Screen Test of Malanga and Woronov; a Test of John Cale; a whip dance reel; another Cale Test; the second whip dance; and then five Screen Test reels of Morrison, Reed, Malanga, Tucker and Cale. A second compilation, lacking a title, has eleven reels and lasts for 49 minutes: it consists of two Screen Tests of Nico, one of Cale, two of Reed, a second of Cale, two copies of the second whip dance reel, a reel of someone clipping their fingernails in close-up (possibly a member of the band?), another Test of Reed and a further Cale Test (see Angell 2006: 269–73).

The projection of Warhol's films was an integral part of the EPI. But what did the screening of the Test compilations achieve for the Velvet Underground? As Morrison's comment about the band disappearing in white clothes at the Rutgers performance suggests, there was a possibility that the band could get somewhat lost in the audio-visual cacophony of Up-Tight and the EPI. Warhol associate Danny Fields (who would go on to author the liner notes for the Velvet Underground's *Live at Max's Kansas City*) saw this as a problem: 'I was a big critic of not showing the band. I thought that was retarding their popularity. You had to watch a fucking psychedelic light show! All these fucking plaids and water-colours and drippings. I thought The Velvets were fabulous-looking people and there they were drowned out by this god-damned psychedelic mediocrity' (qtd. in Bockris and Malanga 2002: 51). Warhol, however, would have also thought that The Velvet Underground were 'fabulous-looking': 'I've never met a person I couldn't call a beauty', he once wrote (Warhol 1975: 61). Projecting, in gigantic form behind the band, images of their faces enabled them to be seen clearly, markedly more so than if the band had adopted a standard stage performance mode. At the EPI, the images of the band were given equal weighting to the music. At times, they paired together neatly. As Callie Angell notes, the 'frenetic camerawork, with rapid zooms and pans, single-framing, and deliberate jigglings and blurrings' seen in some of the Screen Tests of the Velvet Underground not only 'added still more layers of visual disorientation to the choreographed chaos of loud music, flashing lights, and wildly dancing bodies that constituted the EPI', but arguably 'approximated the avant-garde "noise" of the Velvets' music' (Angell 2006: 265). Aural and visual agitation combined, complementing each other.

Following the residency at the Dom, the EPI toured to other venues, including Los Angeles, San Francisco, Chicago and Provincetown. Responses to the show varied widely. Cher Bono infamously stated, 'It will replace nothing, except maybe suicide' (qtd. in Bockris and Malanga 2002: 67). Journalist Larry McCombs wrote that there was 'too much happening' in the EPI; 'it doesn't go together. But sometimes it does – suddenly the beat of the music, the movements of the various films, the pose of the dancers, blend into something meaningful, but before your mind can grab it, it's become random and confusing again. Your head tries to sort something out, make sense of something' (qtd. in Joseph 2002: 86). Stephen Koch, in his account of Warhol's cinema, was critical of the overwhelming nature of the EPI:

> as the music alternated between cacophony and the hideous 'acid' maundering of the Velvet Underground's insufferable navel-gazing guitars, the effort to create an exploding (more accurately, imploding) environment capable of shattering any conceivable focus on the senses was all too successful. It became virtually impossible even to dance, or for that matter do anything else but sit and be bombarded – 'stoned', as it were – until that bludgeoning made weariness set in and one left, cursing the six-dollar admission fee.
>
> (Koch 1991: 71)

Jonas Mekas, writing in his regular 'Movie Journal' column for the *Village Voice*, read the EPI as an expression of psychological excess. In a piece published on 26 May 1966, Mekas compared the Exploding Plastic Inevitable with a number of other intermedia shows. He claimed that Warhol and the Velvet Underground's events 'are dominated by the ego. Warhol has attracted toward himself the most egocentric personalities and artists. The auditorium, every aspect of it – singers, light throwers, strobe operators, dancers – at all times are screaming with screeching, piercing personality pain. I say pain; it could also be desperation' (Mekas 2016: 249). This made the EPI, though, 'the most dramatic expression of the contemporary generation'; 'at the Plastic Inevitables', he wrote, 'it is all Here and Now and the Future' (250).

Mekas' pronouncements may seem exorbitant, but tally with other accounts of the EPI that have attempted to account for its wider cultural significance. The show appears in some accounts of 'expanded cinema', a form of cultural activity that Sheldon Renan attempted to define: 'Expanded cinema is not the name of a particular style of filmmaking. It is the name for a spirit of enquiry that is leading in many different directions … Its work is more spectacular, more technological, and more diverse in form than that of the avant-garde/experimental film so far' (Renan 1967: 227). Gene Youngblood included the EPI in his survey of expanded cinema, which he believed 'isn't a movie at all: like life it's a process of becoming, man's ongoing historical drive to manifest his consciousness outside his mind, in front of his eyes' (Youngblood 1970: 41). An alternative perspective is offered by Bockris and Malanga. They drew attention to the fact that a photograph of the Velvet Underground performing the EPI show at The Trip in Los Angeles appeared in Marshall McLuhan's book *The Medium Is the Massage* (1967). They quoted McLuhan, who tried to capture the character of contemporary experience:

Information pours upon us, instantaneously and continuously. As soon as information is acquired, it is very rapidly replaced by still newer information. Our electrically configured world has forced us to move from the bait of data classification to the mode of pattern recognition. We can no longer build serially, block by block, step by step, because instant communication ensures that all factors of the environment and of experience coexist in a state of active interplay.

(qtd. in Bockris and Malanga 2002: 66)

For Bockris and Malanga, the EPI serves as a paradigmatic example of McLuhan's thesis. Writing more recently, Jon Savage seems to combine these various perspectives in his account of the Exploding Plastic Inevitable, which he argues 'was the most fully worked-out staging, up to this time, of the inexorable high-sixties pop drive towards the dissolution of hierarchies, linear perception and overt meaning. By 1966, many strands of art, music and entertainment were all coming to the same point by different means: the total focus on the instant' (Savage 2016: 213). At a more basic level, from a contemporary perspective it could be suggested that key elements of the EPI – large-scale projections of the band members that allow the audience in the venue, no matter how distant from the stage, to see the performers; dazzling light shows and pyrotechnics – have now become standardized, even expected, components of the large-scale touring pop concert.

Coda

In 2008, the musicians Dean Wareham and Britta Phillips (formerly of Galaxie 500 and Luna) began touring a show entitled '13 Most Beautiful: Songs for Andy Warhol's Screen Tests'. They had been commissioned to score a selection from the artist's series of short portrait films by the Warhol Museum in Pittsburgh; in light of Warhol's own groupings of thirteen, this was an appropriate number to opt for. Wareham and Phillips were a suitable choice for the project. Not only were there evident Velvet Underground influences on the music of Galaxie 500 and Luna but the latter group toured Europe supporting the reformed Velvets in 1993 and covered the band's 'Ride into the Sun' the same year. Sterling Morrison had played guitar on two tracks on Luna's second album, *Bewitched* (1994). The songs that Wareham and Phillips put together for the '13 Most Beautiful' project included original compositions (songs and instrumentals) and some covers: a Screen Test of Nico was accompanied by a cover of the singer's 'I'll Keep It with Mine', originally written by Bob Dylan; the band performed the Velvet Underground track 'Not a Young Man Anymore' to accompany the Coke-consuming Lou Reed Screen Test.

The live tour of the '13 Most Beautiful' films and songs obviously lacked the drama and discord of the Up-Tight and EPI shows, but it retained the combination of projected film portraits and live music central to the 1966 and 1967 gigs. '13 Most Beautiful' subsequently became available as a soundtrack CD, as well as a DVD of the selected Screen Tests, on which the score was included as an optional audio track. Aside from a single Screen Test of Susan Sontag released on disc by MOMA in New York in 2011, this DVD remained the only official release of any of Warhol's films to date (though they do appear extensively, intercut with other material, in Todd Haynes' 2021 documentary film *The Velvet Underground*). Some of the Screen Tests parodied commercial forms, as we have seen, but with the production of this DVD a selection from the larger corpus – including some of those parodies – became a commercial object available for purchase. Watching the DVD with the soundtrack playing, each original silent reel is transformed into something akin to a pop promo, which has long been a commercial form with occasional artistic aspirations: indeed, it is notable that the standardized length of Warhol's Tests fits neatly with the regulated music industry expectations of pop singles and their accompanying videos. Wareham and Phillips' song rhythms and structures propel the viewing experience, alleviating some of the challenges of watching four minutes of silent, static cinema; lyrics and tonal shifts provide meaning that was previously absent. The cacophony of the EPI is far distant, but the magnetic allure of the Screen Test reels – only enhanced through the subsequent loss of many of those whose performances and personalities were captured by Warhol's camera – persists.

References

Angell, C. (2006), *Andy Warhol Screen Tests: The Films of Andy Warhol Catalogue Raisonné Volume 1*, New York: Abrams / Whitney Museum of Modern Art.

Bockris, V. (1995), *Lou Reed: The Biography*, London: Vintage.

Bockris, V. and Malanga, G. (2002), *Up-Tight: The Velvet Underground Story*, London: Omnibus.

Collins, B. R. (2012), *Pop Art*, London: Phaidon.

Day, T. (2020), '*Andy Warhol Eating a Hamburger* and the Pop Cinema Portrait', *Short Film Studies*, 1 (2): 153–6.

Flatley, J. (2010), 'Like: Collecting and Collectivity', *October*, 132: 71–98.

Foster, H. (2010), 'Test Subjects', *October*, 132: 30–42.

Joseph, B. W. (2002), '"My Mind Split Open": Andy Warhol's Exploding Plastic Inevitable', *Grey Room* (8): 80–107.

Koch, S. (1991), *Stargazer: The Life, World and Films of Andy Warhol*, 3rd edn, New York: Marion Boyar.

McLuhan, M. and Fiore, Q. (1967), *The Medium Is the Massage. An Inventory of Effects*, Random House: New York.

Mekas, J. (2016), *Movie Journal: The Rise of the New American Cinema, 1959–1971*, New York: Columbia University.

Merck, M. (2013), 'Susan Sontag's *Screen Tests*', in G. Davis and G. Needham (eds), *Warhol in Ten Takes*, 92–107, London: BFI.

Renan, S. (1967), *An Introduction to the American Underground Film*, New York: E.P. Dutton and Co.

Savage, J. (2016), *1966: The Year the Decade Exploded*, London: Faber and Faber.

Unterberger, G. (2009), *White Light/White Heat: The Velvet Underground Day by Day*, London: Jawbone.
Warhol, A. (1975), *The Philosophy of Andy Warhol (From A to B and Back Again)*, New York: Harcourt Brace.
Warhol, A. and Hackett, P. (1980/1996), *POPism: The Warhol Sixties*, London: Pimlico.
Weingart, B. (2010), '"That Screen Magnetism": Warhol's Glamour', *October*, 132: 43–70.
Wilcock, J. ([1971] 2010), *The Autobiography and Sex Life of Andy Warhol*, New York: Trela Media.
Youngblood, G. (1970), *Expanded Cinema*, New York: P. Dutton & Co.

4

'The riskiest kind of writing available': Lou Reed, Grove Press and the literary underground

Thom Robinson

Lou Reed had a stock response when asked about the controversy the Velvet Underground had provoked during their lifetime. Expressing incredulity that a song like 'Heroin' could have been shocking to a 1960s audience, Reed would invoke a familiar litany of literary examples: 'Why would people write these incredibly vitriolic attacks against us? *Naked Lunch* was out there. Allen Ginsberg was out there with "Howl". Hubert Selby was out there with *Last Exit to Brooklyn*. What could The Velvet Underground possibly add to that?' (DeCurtis 2017: 92).

Reed had understandable reason to feel aggrieved. The decade before the release of *The Velvet Underground & Nico* (1967) had seen a radical transformation of print censorship in America, courtesy of a series of high-profile obscenity trials beginning with Ginsberg's *Howl and Other Poems* (1957) and ending in William S. Burroughs' *Naked Lunch* (1965–6). At the forefront of this fight for the 'freedom to read' was Grove Press, helmed by dogged free speech advocate Barney Rosset. After landmark courtroom battles over Grove's unexpurgated editions of D.H. Lawrence's *Lady Chatterley's Lover* (1959) and Henry Miller's *Tropic of Cancer* (1961), the company published a series of novels in the early 1960s that offered unprecedentedly frank treatments of homosexuality, urban violence, transgenderism and drugs: *Naked Lunch* (1962), John Rechy's *City of Night* (1963) and Hubert Selby Jr.'s *Last Exit to Brooklyn* (1964). All three brought decidedly underground subcultures to the attentions of a mainstream readership, and all three had a deep and lasting impact on Lou Reed.

The publication of these titles coincided with Reed's time at Syracuse University, where he majored in English from 1960 to 1964. Reed would remember that he first read *Naked Lunch* when he was at college, a book he would later praise for its 'savaging of right-wing, straight-laced, average America' (Goddard and Lester 2005: 72). Friend and fellow student Erin Clermont recalls that in September 1963, at the start of Reed's final year, he pinned a poster of the cover of *City of Night* to his bedroom wall (Sounes 2015: 37). Reed's taste for transgressive literature then proved an important point of connection during the formation of the Velvet Underground. In John Cale's memories of his first introduction to Reed in late 1964, he stated, 'We hit it off straight away. We started talking about literature and what was the riskiest kind of writing available, what prose most gave off the stink of threat. And Lou said, "You've got to read *Last Exit to Brooklyn*." And we went roaring off into the sunset' (Jones 2009: 51).

The legacy of these particular books can be identified in Reed's lyrics from the Velvet Underground onwards (see Griffiths in this collection). His unflinching accounts of drug use bear an obvious debt to Burroughs, while the cast of damaged and self-destructive characters that populate his songs can be traced to the examples of maligned, outsider protagonists in Rechy and Selby's work. In particular, the drag queens Miss Destiny in *City of Night* and Georgette the 'hip queer' (Selby 2000: 15) of *Last Exit to Brooklyn* show a clear influence on songs as varied as 'Sister Ray' and 'Candy Says', with the latter's chorus chiming with Miss Destiny's cri de coeur: 'And at night in bed drowning in the dark ... I want to fly out of my skin! jump out! be someone else! so I can leave Miss Destiny far, far behind ...' (Rechy 1984: 116).

Beyond these points of influence, the publications of Grove Press have a wider significance in relation to the Velvet Underground. Through both their wide-ranging book titles and the contents of their house journal, the *Evergreen Review*, Grove helped to foster a cultural climate in which a band like the Velvet Underground could come to exist. In particular, *Evergreen Review*'s changing contents over the course of the 1960s show the gradual shift of the 'underground' from being the preserve of a hip cognoscenti to an increasingly commercialized and marketable commodity.

Beginning in 1957 as a quarterly publication, *Evergreen* initially mirrored the ethos of the contemporary 'little magazines' of the period, albeit with the luxury of greater circulation figures. *Evergreen*'s unique role was to 'deliver the "underground" to a large audience' (Clay and Phillips 1998: 103), as seen in the magazine's epochal second issue, a special on the 'San Francisco Scene' of Beat poets, in which Grove printed Ginsberg's 'Howl' while City Lights' edition of the poem was still on trial (with *Evergreen* substituting the poem's offending words for ellipses). By the time the Velvet Underground came into being, *Evergreen Review* had switched from a quarterly to a glossy bimonthly (and finally monthly) format that featured an increased focus on the more sensational and sexualized elements of the emergent counterculture (with nude photoshoots a recurring theme and rocketing circulation as a result).[1]

Grove's courting of a wide readership has led Loren Glass to argue that the company's 'most significant achievement was to establish and expand the circuits through which experimental and radical literature was distributed, particularly to the burgeoning college and university populations that were the seed-bed of the counterculture' (2013: 12). It is clear from surveying Reed's years as a student at Syracuse that his own identity as a writer was made in the image of the examples provided by Grove Press and *Evergreen Review*. It was during his time at college that Reed and friends published three issues of the literary magazine *Lonely Woman Quarterly* (copies of which are held in the Syracuse University archives). Named after the Ornette Coleman track of which Reed was a lifelong devotee, the magazine's contents demonstrate concerns that are markedly similar to those being steadily introduced into the mainstream by the efforts of Grove Press. By examining Reed's writing for *Lonely Woman Quarterly* alongside the wider campus culture of Syracuse at the time (as revealed through the pages of the university newspaper, the *Daily Orange*), we can see the beginnings of Grove's influence on youth culture throughout the 1960s, initially achieved through the targeting of experimental drama to a student audience.

Syracuse University

Lou Reed's first experience of higher education came in September 1959, with an abortive year at New York University. Here, Reed suffered what his family referred to as a 'nervous breakdown', an episode that resulted in the series of electroshock treatments that became a defining part of his mythology (Reed Weiner 2015). The following year, Reed began studies at Syracuse in upstate New York, with the colourful events of the next four years providing much material for his future biographers. It was here that Reed hosted a campus radio show, named after Cecil Taylor's 'Excursions on a Wobbly Rail'; met future Velvet Underground bandmate Sterling Morrison; played in rock and roll bands, including LA and the Eldorados; entered into a relationship with fellow student, Shelley Albin, whose influence has been identified on Velvets songs, including 'I'll Be Your Mirror', 'The Gift' and 'Pale Blue Eyes' (De Curtis 2017: 49); and came under the sway of Delmore Schwartz, who joined the Syracuse English staff in September 1962 and who Reed remembered as 'the greatest man I ever met' (2012: i).

The fact that the literary example of Schwartz made so strong an impression on Reed highlights the extent to which, at this time, his interests were divided between literary and musical ambitions. Sterling Morrison remembered that, during their initial meetings at Syracuse, 'Lou was pretty guarded about himself, but he did let it be known that he was an English major and he liked to write poetry. He didn't say anything about playing music' (Julià 1997: 184). Though Reed's rebellious stance at college can be seen as a harbinger of his later 'rock and roll animal' persona, it is important to recognize that at this time his rebelliousness was at least partly defined in terms of literary tastes. As Daniel Kane notes, at Syracuse, Reed 'grew to understand late-modernist and New American writing as capable of transmitting discordant ideas in the face of consensus culture' (2017: 44). In this, Reed was clearly not alone. High school friend and Syracuse contemporary Allan Hyman remembers that at college, 'Lou was hanging out with a group that was on the beatnik side, different than the average fraternity guy' (Levy 2016: 54); this group evidently had enough members to constitute a sizeable minority. Though Morrison recalled that 'out of the whole university there might have been only one per cent that we considered the lunatic fringe … it still was a hundred people maybe, and we had a great time' (Julià 1997: 184).

The archives of the university newspaper, the *Daily Orange*, indicate that the members of this 'lunatic fringe' found a natural home in the world of campus drama. During Reed's time at Syracuse, students staged a range of experimental theatre productions indebted to the publications of Grove Press. Reed's own involvement came when he served as director of a two-act play by the Spanish dramatist Fernando Arrabal, entitled *The Automobile Graveyard* (1958).[2] Arrabal's absurdist drama takes place in a junkyard where, amidst a backdrop of rusting cars, a 33-year-old jazz trumpeter is hounded by a mob that ultimately savage him after he has been betrayed by one friend and denied by another.[3] Though Arrabal's play may seem an outré choice of directorial debut, it is in keeping with an enthusiasm for the theatre of the absurd that flourished on campuses at the time and which can be directly attributed to the publishing efforts of Grove. Having made his company's name in 1953 with the first English translation of Samuel Beckett's *Waiting for Godot*, Barney Rosset continued to build Grove's reputation for publishing experimental theatre, developing a roster of 'relatively obscure European writers who had come to artistic maturity in the decade following the end of World War II, people like Beckett, Robbe-Grillet, Genet, Ionesco, and Duras' (Rosenthal 2017: 72). Arrabal was among these names, with Grove publishing *The Automobile Graveyard and The Two Executioners* in 1960, packaged in the trademark abstract cover art of the company's resident designer Roy Kuhlman.

Glass has demonstrated that Grove's publication of contemporary drama was directly linked to the company's nurturing of a student readership. With Beckett established as their star attraction, Grove next focused on the work of Eugene Ionesco, whose plays enabled the company to repeat the strategy that had proved so effective with Beckett of 'marketing the printed text in conjunction with student performances' (Glass 2013: 75). The archives of the *Daily Orange* show the success of Grove's approach, with Reed's time at college coinciding with productions of a wave of absurdist plays all recently published by Grove Press: Ionesco's *The Lesson* (February 1961), *The Chairs* (directed by Reed's friend and fellow *Lonely Woman* contributor Peter Maloney), *The Leaders*, *A Maid to Marry* (all December 1962) and *The Bald Soprano* (April 1964); Beckett's *Endgame* (November 1962) and *Waiting for Godot* (July 1964); and Jean Genet's *The Maids* (April 1964).[4] Highlighting a gulf between these productions and the Syracuse mainstream, a January 1963 *Daily Orange* review has a withering take on the popularity of experimental theatre on campus: 'SU's drama department is really going wild over French playwrite [sic] Eugene Ionesco. No wonder. To student directors and actors this "theater of the absurd" author offers innumerable opportunities for mugging, dancing, yelling, screaming, kidding and all around mayhem.'[5] If the campus mainstream took a dim view of avant-garde drama, then one can only assume this would have served to heighten its appeal for Reed and his circle, as indicated by the oppositional and contrarian stance adopted by the *Lonely Woman Quarterly*.

Alongside Grove's use of drama publications to cultivate a student audience, a further notice in the *Daily Orange* demonstrates additional means by which the company addressed their marketing to a campus demographic. Beneath a front-page notice headlined 'Grove Offers $100 in "Kitten Contest"', the *Daily Orange* of 6 February 1963 reports: 'Grove Press will award $100 to the college student who can best write an application to a mythical southern university in the style of Kitten, a beautiful Negro prostitute. Kitten and a white college sophomore, J.C., are the characters in Rovert Grover's [sic] best-seller *One Hundred Dollar Misunderstanding*, published by Grove.'[6] In addition to the winner's prize money, the contest's '100 runners-up' are promised 'a full year's subscription to the *Evergreen Review*, Grove's bi-monthly literary magazine'.[7] Presumably aware of how far they could push their luck, Grove's announcement of their competition fails to note that the 'beautiful Negro prostitute' in Robert Gover's comic novel is fourteen years old. However, the fact that Grove were keen to market one of their more controversial titles to a student audience shows a keen awareness of the developing liberal counterculture taking root on college campuses. This sensibility is amply illustrated by *Lonely Woman Quarterly*, a magazine whose contents reflect the stylistic and thematic preoccupations of the contemporary publications of Grove Press and *Evergreen Review*, while showing a marked antipathy towards mainstream campus culture.

Lonely Woman Quarterly[8]

The publication in May 1962 of the first issue of *Lonely Woman Quarterly* was heralded by a front-page interview in the *Daily Orange* with Reed's co-editor and roommate Lincoln Swados. In his role as magazine spokesman, Swados adopted a confrontational stance, explaining *Lonely Woman* as having been born of dissatisfaction with the university's established literary journal, the *Syracuse 10*: 'The people who turned out the *Quarterly* felt that this year's *Syracuse 10* was not only less literary but also that the vision of the material in the first issue was about two feet in front of its nose' (Millstein 1962: 1).[9] In attacking Syracuse's established campus journal, Swados was besmirching a literary magazine of some repute. As reported in the *Daily Orange*, the *Syracuse 10* 'received an All American Honor rating in the 1960 Associated Collegiate Press magazine critical judging',[10] and the magazine's popularity ensured that the December 1961 issue was published in a print run of 2,200 copies.[11] The first issue of *Lonely Woman Quarterly* was a more modest success, with the *Daily Orange* reporting that 'the initial 75 copies printed were sold out by noon Tuesday and a second printing of 25 copies was gone by Wednesday afternoon' (Millstein 1962: 1). Given this disparity, one can understand Swados' dismissive attitude towards a mainstream literary rival, particularly when considering that he observes of the *Lonely Woman* contributors: 'While all of us have a collection of rejection slips, only [Joseph] McDonald has had material accepted for publication in the *Syracuse 10*' (Millstein 1962: 9). Another of Swados' swipes at other literary magazines provides perhaps the most revealing insight into the ethos of their publishing endeavour: 'The magazine doesn't contain great literature, but it has material in it that couldn't be printed elsewhere on campus' (Millstein 1962: 1). Evidently a point of honour for the editors of *Lonely Woman Quarterly*, this stance suggests a rejection of conventional hierarchies, with transgressive or experimental writing afforded greater artistic validity than mere 'great literature'.

As Kane has noted, in publicizing the magazine in the *Daily Orange*, Swados' attitude was in keeping with that of the contemporary literary underground: 'Typically for the underground press at the time, the editors of *Lonely Woman Quarterly* promoted their new adventure using oppositional, arrogant, and funny language that clearly demarcated an edgy in-the-know "us" versus a mainstream, milquetoast "them"' (2017: 47). That this antagonistic stance is indebted to the contemporary publications of Grove Press is demonstrated by a message from 'The Editors' that greets the reader opening the first issue of *Lonely Woman Quarterly*:

> As the sun sinks slowly in the west, the air clears, the pungent odor of the syracuse arts festival plops solemnly on its rump, and the militant vociferous underground raises its shaggy head, gnashes its rabid molars in rhythm, and squats – in one of its infrequent appearances in front of its collective mirror and bellows, a trifle off key perhaps as Miller says, but raise its voice it does, cause boy its SPRING, and the world IS mudluscious.
>
> (*LWQ* 1: 2)

This opening makes the magazine's sensibilities readily apparent, revealing the literary cultures with which its editors sought to align themselves. *Lonely Woman* is shown to belong to the contemporary 'underground', through a playful and irreverent tone suggestive of Beat poetry; as existing within a modernist tradition, via the E.E. Cummings reference, 'mudluscious'; and as occupying a realm of anti-authoritarian defiance, through an assertion of kinship with Grove Press' most notorious publication to date, Miller's *Tropic of Cancer*. In bellowing 'a trifle off key', the editors invoke Miller's novel's opening credo, in which the author expresses sentiments that were clearly endorsed by the editors of *Lonely Woman Quarterly*:

> This is not a book, in the ordinary sense of the word. No, this is a prolonged insult, a gob of spit in the face of Art, a kick in the pants to God, Man, Destiny, Time, Love, Beauty … what you will. I am going to sing for you, a little off key perhaps, but I will sing. I will sing while you croak, I will dance over your dirty corpse …
>
> (Miller 1993: 10)

In Miller's description of his novel as 'a gob of spit in the fact of Art', we can see a harbinger of Swados favouring material that challenges and provokes in lieu of 'great literature'. Following the message from the editors, the first story in *Lonely Woman Quarterly* is an untitled one-page piece credited to 'Luis Reed' that precisely fulfils this purpose: 'He'd always found the idea of copulation distasteful, especially when applied to his own origins. His mother would never do that. No. No, she wouldn't' (1962a). Boldly introducing the Oedipal dread that Reed would later invoke in numerous songs,[12] the story rapidly progresses to a discomfiting climax between mother and child: '"Daddy hurt Mommy last night," she said and looked toward the ceiling, "Daddy hurt Mommy but," she pulled him tighter, lowering her hands to his haunches, "Mommy's little man would never do that would he?"' (1962a). Reed's opening story shows a characteristic desire to shock that succinctly proves Swados' promise that *Lonely Woman Quarterly* 'has material in it that couldn't be printed elsewhere on campus'.

Alongside a playful, absurdist poem, Reed's other contribution to the first issue is a story that, without overtly seeking to shock, nonetheless bears redolent traces of the stable of writers that were published by Grove Press. 'Prologue' has been described by Kane as offering 'a charmingly direct depiction of present-day Greenwich Village', which invites comparison to the poetry of Frank O'Hara: 'there is not much distance here between Reed's urbane sociability and so many of O'Hara's most beloved prosaic "I do this, I do that"-style poems – poems published throughout the late 1950s and early 1960s in fugitive mimeos and magazines like *Evergreen Review*' (2017: 48).[13] In another move redolent of O'Hara, Reed's story encompasses a range of cultural references, in this case indicating a youthful tendency towards intellectual precocity. A quotation from 'The Rime of the Ancient Mariner' appears alongside namechecks for Freud and Jung, Dostoyevsky and De Sade, while the use of 'tintinabulary' (*sic*) evokes the verbosity of Edgar Allan Poe's poem 'The Bells' (pointing towards both Reed's 1979 album of the same name and his 2003 Poe tribute, *The Raven*).

The second issue of *Lonely Woman Quarterly* (which, belying its title, was published within a month of the first) further showcases Reed's desire to court controversy, with the profile piece, 'Michael Kogan – Syracuse's Miss Blanding'.[14] The subject of Reed's profile (a fellow student and active member of the right-wing Young Americans for Freedom) is contemptuously described as a 'seventeen year old elder statesman, nouveau riche attache case in hand … American flag placed neatly up his rectum' (1962b). Reed also finds room to ridicule Kogan's political opponent on campus, Robin Craven, imagining, 'Maybe these two opposite yet kindred souls should meet, and perhaps marry, sperm to ovum, so to speak' (1962b). This portrait of Kogan (and the pressure placed on the university by the student's father) resulted in *Lonely Woman*'s very own censorship controversy. According to fellow contributor Karl Stoecker: 'That got it banned. They told us we couldn't sell it on school property' (Levy 2016: 66). By the time the third and final issue of *Lonely Woman Quarterly* appeared in April 1963, the magazine was sold off-campus, and Lincoln Swados was no longer involved (after leaving college due to increasingly severe mental health problems, he was diagnosed with schizophrenia and committed to a private institution) (Swados 1991: 24). As such, Reed is the only contributor whose work appears in all three issues of the magazine.

The *Daily Orange* announced the third instalment of *Lonely Woman Quarterly* with less fanfare than they awarded to the first, noting the return of

> that off-campus, independent, uninhibited collection of stories, poems and illustrations … on sale Friday at Marshall Street's newest bookstore, the Syracuse Book Center. Priced at 35 cents the *Quarterly* is the combined efforts of local talent that do not want to be printed in the official university literary publication, *Syracuse 10*. Last spring two issues of the *Quarterly* were published, each one a sellout.[15]

The print run of the third issue is announced as '200 copies'.[16] It is this final issue of the magazine that includes the most impressive of Reed's contributions, the short story 'And What, Little Boy, Will You Trade for Your Horse?' (the only contribution credited to 'Lou Reed', rather than 'Luis' or 'Lewis'). In this story, Reed embraces the content of writers published in the *Evergreen Review*, while looking towards to the urban terrains that he would later make his own as a songwriter. In particular, 'And What, Little Boy, Will You Trade for Your Horse?' shows a direct debt to John Rechy, the member of Reed's pantheon of Grove Press authors whose influence on his work has been commented on the least.

'And What, Little Boy, Will You Trade for Your Horse?'

Of Reed's key influences, Rechy is the figure whose literary development was tied the most closely to *Evergreen Review*. While Burroughs and Selby appeared in numerous little magazines prior to their first appearances in *Evergreen* (Burroughs in 1960 and Selby in 1964),[17] Rechy was fostered by Grove as a home-grown talent. His first publication came with the appearance of 'Mardi Gras' (later part of *City of Night*) in the *Evergreen Review* of Summer 1958. Before Grove's publication of his debut novel, Rechy's work had appeared in a further five issues of the magazine, including three further excerpts from *City of Night*: 'A Quarter Ahead' (July/August 1961), 'It Begins in the Wind' (May/June 1962) and 'Three Kinds of Angels' (September/October 1962). A reader's letter printed in the issue of September/October 1962 demonstrates the popular interest generated by these appearances: 'I was so glad to see John Rechy is finally having his novel published, and by the only firm fit to bring it out, Grove .... When is someone going to publish *Naked Lunch*?'.[18] Typical of Grove's publishing acumen, at the time this letter appeared the company had already printed 10,000 copies of *Naked Lunch*, ready to be distributed to booksellers pending legal advice (Rosenthal 2017: 125).

Rechy's subject matter in *City of Night* demonstrates that, as Glass has discussed, after the publication of *Lady Chatterley's Lover* and *Tropic of Cancer*, Grove were keenly staking out new frontiers in the fight for the freedom to read: 'As the trajectory from Lawrence to Miller to Burroughs economically illustrates, Grove's battle against censorship began with a quintessentially high modernist preoccupation with adulterous women – inaugurated by *Madame Bovary* and *Ulysses* – and ended up with the highly homosocial and increasingly homosexual preoccupations of late modernist figures such as Burroughs and Jean Genet' (2013: 123). Rechy takes his place in the latter camp, with *City of Night* comprising the author's fictionalized account of his experiences as a hustler in the gay underworlds of New York, Los Angeles, Hollywood, Chicago and New Orleans. Inevitably, the taboo subject matter of this writing would have helped to cement its appeal for Reed. The testimony of friends demonstrates that, from adolescence onwards, his taste in literature showed a preference for writing that challenged the boundaries of his peers. School friend Richard Sigal remembers: 'He was always ahead of us .... If we were looking at *Playboy*, Lou was reading *The Story of O*; if we were drinking quarts of beer, Lou was smoking joints' (Levy 2016: 30).[19] When it came to his own writing, it seems Reed embraced gay subject matter at least partly through an ongoing desire to shock. Allan Hyman remembered of their time at

Syracuse: 'Lou's view started becoming increasingly bizarre. It became more bizarre in his poetry, and his writing generally took on what would be described today as a gay tone, if you will. He started talking about having relationships with men, which I found amazingly rebellious at the time. That's the only way I could describe it' (De Curtis 2017: 27). Reed was typically unforthcoming as to the precise nature of his attraction to this material: 'I would say to him, "What is this about, why are you writing about this?" He would say, "It's interesting. I find it interesting"' (Bockris 1995: 23).

A wide variety of things that Reed found 'interesting' are on display in 'And What, Little Boy, Will You Trade for Your Horse?'. In addition to marking territory that Reed would later cover in his songs, the concerns of the story bear such strong similarities to *City of Night* to suggest that Reed had been following Rechy's work in the *Evergreen Review*. In particular, there are clear resonances between the story and Rechy's 'A Quarter Ahead', printed in *Evergreen* two years before and, like Reed's story, taking place in the night-time underworld of New York.[20] Rechy's story documents the author's unnamed narrator as he temporarily pairs up with a fellow hustler called Pete. Their partnership breaks off after the two of them spend a night sleeping in the same bed, an act which threatens their fragile self-identification as heterosexuals. In tackling similar subject matter, Reed's story documents a young man named David (implicitly identified as middle-class and a college student) as he navigates the seedy underworld of Times Square.

In 'A Quarter Ahead', Rechy sets the scene for his characters' sexual exchanges by establishing a New York landscape recognizable as that later inhabited by the denizens of Reed's songs. The story begins:

> From the thundering underground – the maze of the New York subways – the world pours into Times Square. Like lost souls emerging from the purgatory of the trains (dark rattling tunnels, smelly pornographic toilets, newsstands futilely splashing the subterranean gray depths with unreal magazine colors), the new-york faces push into the air: spilling into 42nd Street and Broadway – a scattered defeated army.
>
> (Rechy 1961: 14)

Reed's story begins in similar style, with his protagonist David exiting the subway into the sexualized carnival of Times Square. Rechy's descriptions of 'the different types that haunted those places' are mirrored by Reed, with both focusing on 'the scores ... the men who paid each other sexmoney' (Rechy 1961: 15). For example, in 'A Quarter Ahead':

> One night I saw [Pete] by the subway entrance on 42nd Street talking to an older man dressed in black …. Theyre glancing at me, Pete and the older man. They talk some more, the older man nods yes, and Pete swaggered up to me. He said: 'That scores digs you … he'll lay ten bucks on you-and itll be like cuhrazy', rolling his eyes.
>
> (Rechy 1961: 15)

While in Reed's story:

> An old man, well dressed, has stopped a dungareed boy .... The old man looks at his watch. Then he asks the boy what time it is. The boy says ten a throw. The old man mumbles something, stops, with his face to the ground, then nods hurriedly and hails a cab .... When the cab comes he opens the door quickly and slides in, gives a perfunctory glance, and is slowly followed by dungarees, who struts and saunters towards the car, hunching his shoulders and adjusting his collar. The door closes and they speed away.
>
> (1963: 24)

Reed's protagonist, David, thinks of following the boy's example, but is put off by the thought of 'his friend Jeffrey, who, desperate and lonely, one night donned a three piece suit, of all things, and went to join the meat racks in the flicks and as a result was left stabbed and bleeding in the balconies for his trouble' (1963: 24). Again, we see evocations of the sexual marketplaces of 'A Quarter Ahead', which include 'the moviehouses with the cavernous balconies' (Rechy 1961: 14). Foreshadowing the urban topography of 'I'm Waiting for the Man', Reed's character then briefly considers scoring for drugs uptown ('He wasn't afraid of 125th alone') (1963: 26), before winding up in an afterhours bar. Here, he sits with Jane, an older woman who announces: 'I'm queer for men and I think you're gorgeous doll' (1963: 28). The flirtation between the two returns us to the uncomfortably sexualized mother-and-son pairing in Reed's first story for *Lonely Woman Quarterly*, this time with the added gender ambiguity of the woman describing herself to David as 'a regular queen' (1963: 30). The story ends as the two of them leave together, after Jane has first asked David 'do you know what I'll make you do' and whispered an instruction into his ear: 'David's heart was beating loudly and he found it hard to talk. Yes. Yes, sir' (Reed 1963: 30).

It is hard to imagine how a mainstream campus readership would have responded to a story so openly in thrall to transgressive and hard-edged subject matter, written not by an author for the urbane *Evergreen Review* but instead by one of their peers. Perhaps a clue is offered by an editorial in a *Daily Orange* edition of November 1963; the author may well have had 'And What, Little Boy, Will You Trade for Your Horse?' in mind when praising the latest issue of the *Syracuse 10*: 'The fall issue [of *Syracuse 10*] is not only a testimony to the editors' taste and good sense, but it finally affirms the ability of Syracuse's undergraduates to produce work that is entertaining, intelligent and provocative, without being ultra-controversial.'[21]

If Reed's college writings were received by his contemporaries as 'ultra-controversial' exercises in attention-seeking shock, then this placed him in good company. Similar criticisms are manifest in the contemporary reception of the Grove Press books that Reed valued so highly. Reviewing *Naked Lunch* in the *New York Times*, Charles Poore noted that 'the glaringly gaudy way Mr. Burroughs has chosen to present his case – using shocking words by the shovelful and concentrating on perverted degeneracy to a flagrant degree' (1962). Following this example, reviewers explicitly greeted *City of Night* and *Last Exit to Brooklyn* as Grove Press titles (i.e. as further scandalous releases from the publishers of *Naked Lunch*). Writing in the *New*

York Review of Books, Alfred Chester described Rechy's novel as 'the worst confection yet devised by the masterminds behind ... Grove' (1963), supporting Rechy's later belief that 'many of the attacks on *City of Night* were also attacks on what Grove had come to represent' (1990: 138). The following year, *Time* received *Last Exit to Brooklyn* as 'Grove Press' extra special dirty book for fall ... even more extreme than *Naked Lunch*, *City of Night*, or any of Grove's earlier peddlings in the same line' (Books: Borderline 1964).

Reed evidently cared little for such dismissals. Reading at the St. Mark's Poetry Project in 1971, he introduced his story 'Do Angels Need Haircuts?' with the explanation that it was intended as an alternative ending to Rechy's novel: 'One of my favorite books of all time is called *City of Night* and it's by somebody named John Rechy. I've read all the criticisms of it and I think they're full of shit. I like the book and I think he's brilliant' (2018: 22). The criticisms of reviewers did not prevent Rechy's book from becoming 'Grove's fastest-selling novel ever, enjoying six months on the *New York Times*'s bestseller list in 1963 and at one point selling more than one thousand copies per day' (Glass 2013: 126). In publishing a novel that dealt with hustlers, drag queens, unusual sex acts and casual drug use, and which became a bestseller as a result, Grove readied the path for Lou Reed to form a band with the songs, aesthetic and, indeed, the very name of the Velvet Underground.

'Join the Underground'

In the memory of Sterling Morrison, it was the wider cultural connotations of the term 'underground' that in 1965 attracted the band to the title of Michael Leigh's exploitation paperback: 'Angus [MacLise] saw the book, *The Velvet Underground*, and brought it down to Ludlow Street. We thought it was a good name because it had underground in it and we were playing for underground films, we considered ourselves part of the underground film community. We had no connection with rock and roll as far as we were concerned' (Julià 1997: 190).

In choosing a name that would emphasize their underground credentials, the band's decision was timely. At the same time as the Velvet Underground were naming themselves in tribute to 'the underground film community', Grove Press were exploiting the commercial potentials of the term as part of a concerted marketing campaign. As Glass has explained:

> Grove almost single-handedly transformed the term "underground" into a legitimate market niche for adults in the second half of the 1960s, starting with a campaign inviting readers to 'Join the Underground' by subscribing to the *Evergreen Review* ... In the opening months of 1966, 'Join the Underground' appeared in full-page ads in *Esquire*, *Ramparts*, *New Republic*, *Playboy*, the *New York Times*, the *New York Review of Books*, and the *Village Voice* and on posters throughout the New York City subway system.
>
> (Glass 2013: 129–30)

As testament to readers' eagerness to follow Grove's invitation, the campaign proved so successful that 'circulation for the *Evergreen Review* ... nearly doubled from fifty-four thousand to ninety-thousand in the first half of 1966' (Glass 2013: 130). With this success came the attendant irony that, at the same time as Grove Press were most explicitly aligning themselves with the 'underground', the core readership of *Evergreen Review* was anything but. Following a survey undertaken by Marketing Data Inc., Grove were able to identify 'the average subscriber in 1966 as "a 39-year-old male, married, two children, a college graduate who holds a managerial position in business or industry, and has a median family income of $12,875"' (Carroll 2018: 1–2).

These ironies have ensured that *Evergreen*'s role in marketing the underground has not passed without criticism. For Jed Birmingham, the magazine's 'mass marketing of the underground' resulted in a product that 'seemed on the surface to be cutting edge, but was instead merely just another version of the mass media's sensationalized interpretation of the underground and avant-garde, which played up sex, drugs, and rock and roll rather than exploring any new creative ground' (2009). Demonstrating this fact, by the mid-1960s the magazine had come to share many of the more lurid themes that would soon appear in the Velvet Underground's lyrics. To pick an example, the issue of March 1965 features Hector Rodriguez's confessional account of drug addiction, 'The Addict in the Street', alongside Lenore Kandel's 'Poem for Perverts', an ode to S/M that utilizes a strikingly similar lexicon to 'Venus in Furs', with 'leather boots', 'whips' and 'thongs' all present and correct (1965: 20–1).

Consulting an issue from two years later (June 1967) helps to further establish the distance that *Evergreen Review* had travelled in its ten-year history to date. On the one hand, the magazine links back to its origins as a dedicated literary journal, seen in the inclusion of Samuel Beckett's story 'The Calmative' (the author's 'Dante and the Lobster' had appeared in the first issue of *Evergreen*, back when he was Grove Press' flagship writer). Elsewhere though, the issue is largely unrecognizable from the earlier *Evergreen*, as signalled by its front cover, which bears a scene from 'The Adventures of Phoebe Zeit-Geist' (the long-running comic strip of *Evergreen*'s later years) and shows the titular heroine in characteristic pose, naked and in handcuffs. Further shifts are demonstrated by Eric Salzman's article 'The Prevalence of Rock or Rock Lives!', which, in focusing on new developments in rock culture, eschews *Evergreen*'s earlier focus on modern jazz. In surveying the rock scene for *Evergreen Review*, Salzman provides a striking description of 'Andy Warhol's "Exploding Plastic Inevitable" featuring the Velvet Underground – East Village Others hacking away at grotesque guitars, straddling, stroking, and screaming into phallic microphones, amplifiers turned up to ear-splitting distortion levels; chicks in black leather slowly twirling whips and gyrating expressionless buttocks' (1967: 44).

It is difficult to relate Salzman's description of 'straddling, stroking, and screaming' to the onstage demeanour of the Velvet Underground (nor is it clear how 'expressionless buttocks' are distinguished from the ordinary kind). The important detail, though, is that Salzman describes the Exploding Plastic Inevitable precisely in terms of the extreme and sexualized 'underground' being enthusiastically devoured by *Evergreen*'s readers (perhaps from the comfort of their managerial positions). It is fitting, therefore, that among the other contents of the June 1967 issue, alongside advertisements for erotic photo books and the Riviera shaver, we find a rare advert for *The Velvet Underground & Nico*. Represented by an image of Warhol, eyes masked in black shades and face partially concealed by the open gatefold of the album, the tagline promises, 'So Far Underground, You Get The Bends! What happens when the daddy of Pop Art goes Pop Music? The most underground album of all! It's Andy Warhol's hip new trip to the current subterranean scene.'[22]

Again, there is no small irony in the fact that the same magazine that had published the transgressive authors who helped to define Reed as a writer should herald the very underground cachet of *The Velvet Underground & Nico* at the same time as *Evergreen* itself had become decidedly overground. Just as Grove Press writers had inspired Reed, the underground rock press showed a clear debt to the cultural shifts engendered by Grove in their critical responses to the Velvets' music. Contemporary critiques make repeated comparisons between the band and the work of Burroughs (who by this point had four books published by Grove Press). Hence, Wayne McGuire describes the Velvets in *Crawdaddy* in 1968 as 'sons of metallic Burroughs and leather Genet' (McGuire 2005: 65); Sandy Pearlman reviews *White Light/White Heat* (1968) in the same magazine and compares the album to the closing section of *Naked Lunch* ('That's how pretentiously humorous it is') (Pearlman 2005: 62); Adrian Ribola assesses the band's third album in *Oz* and describes their music as 'always unsettling and disturbing: their heads adrift in Burroughsland' (Ribola 2005: 107); and Lester Bangs reviews the same record in *Rolling Stone* and borrows a character from Burroughs' *Nova Express* (1964) to describe Lou Reed as 'the malevolent Burroughsian Death Dwarf' (Bangs 2005: 100).[23] These displays of the terms in which the band's music was originally received testify to the changes in the cultural landscape established by Grove Press and the *Evergreen Review*; just as *City of Night* and *Last Exit to Brooklyn* were initially reviewed in response to *Naked Lunch*, so the Velvets were posited in the lineage of an imagined 'Burroughsian' (or 'Grove Press') aesthetic.

Despite Reed's other avowed literary inspirations (including Edgar Allan Poe, Raymond Chandler and Delmore Schwartz), he continued to bracket Burroughs, Rechy and Selby's work together throughout his life. That the connection between these influences remained strong for Reed is evidenced by his first meeting with Burroughs in 1979 (as arranged by Victor Bockris). Alongside questions on the precise method of how to inject heroin using a safety pin, Reed inquired of Burroughs: 'So I wanted to ask you what you thought about two books like *City of Night* by John Rechy and *Last Exit to Brooklyn* by Hubert Selby. Now, like, these two books, for example, couldn't have been written without what you'd done' (Bockris 1995: 423).[24] Reed's question is revealing as, more pertinently, he could not have mapped out the lyrical concerns of the Velvets or of uncompromising solo albums such as *Berlin* (1973) and *Street Hassle* (1978) without the examples of Burroughs, Rechy and Selby before him. While it may not be true that, as Reed argues, *City of Night* and *Last Exit to Brooklyn* could not have been written without Burroughs' example (material from both novels having already appeared in print before Burroughs came to prominence), it is inarguable that the publication of these novels was the direct result of Grove Press' determined commitment to the erosion of print censorship in America. From introducing European avant-garde theatre onto American college campuses to liberalizing print censorship through the groundbreaking trials of works by Lawrence, Miller and Burroughs, to the eventual marketing and commercialization of the 'underground', the shifts produced by Grove Press had an indelible influence on Lou Reed and helped to establish the cultural context in which the music of the Velvet Underground was varyingly celebrated, denigrated and misunderstood.

Notes

1. See Rosenthal (2017: 79): 'The public welcomed the magazine's new format; it eventually achieved a subscription level of forty thousand and newsstand sales of approximately one hundred thousand.'
2. Unterberger (2009: 17) dates this production to Reed's sophomore year of 1961/62.
3. The Christ parallel has led one of Reed's less charitable biographers to view the production as evidence of a budding Messiah complex on the part of its director (Bockris 1995: 48–9).
4. All references to the *Daily Orange* are from the paper's online archive (with the exception of Alan Millstein's article of 11 May 1962, which is available in Syracuse's archival collection of the *Lonely Woman Quarterly*).
5. *Daily Orange*, 10 January 1963.
6. *Daily Orange*, 6 February 1963. Though little known today, Gover's novel received praise from Bob Dylan in a May 1963 radio interview with Studs Terkel: 'That's one of the more hip things nowadays, I guess … I mean it actually comes out and states something that's actually true.' The interview can be heard online: https://bit.ly/347pQNi (accessed 24 October 2021). In November 1963, Reed attended when Dylan played Syracuse University's Regent Theatre.
7. *Daily Orange*, 6 February 1963.
8. My readings of *Lonely Woman Quarterly* follow Kane's (2017) excellent chapter on Reed.
9. In considering Swados' oppositional stance, it is interesting to bear in mind Shelley Albin's memories of Reed at this time: 'He was trying to pick up on Lincoln's traits and abilities. Much of Lou is Lincoln' (Bockris 1995: 66).
10. *Daily Orange*, 21 March 1961.
11. *Daily Orange*, 14 December 1961.
12. See 'How Do You Speak to an Angel?' (1980), 'The Blue Mask' (1982), 'Sex with Your Parents' (1996), 'The Rock Minuet' (2000), etc.
13. For more on Reed and Frank O'Hara and friends, see Epstein (2013).
14. The title is a reference to Sarah Gibson Blanding, president of Vassar College, 1946–64.
15. *Lonely Woman Quarterly*, 18 April 1963.
16. *Lonely Woman Quarterly*, 18 April 1963.
17. Amongst Burroughs and Selby's magazine appearances, the seventh and final edition of *Black Mountain Review* (1957) is notable; alongside Jack Kerouac and Allen Ginsberg, the issue features the first publication of material from both *Naked Lunch* ('Naked Lunch, Book III: In Search of Yage') and *Last Exit to Brooklyn* ('Love/s Labour/s Lost'), which later formed 'The Queen Is Dead', the opening section of the novel.

18 *Evergreen Review*, 6 (26), September/October 1962: 127.
19 Sigal's memory is perhaps inaccurate; Pauline Réage's *Story of O* did not appear in English until 1965, on Grove Press.
20 With minor amendments, the text of 'A Quarter Ahead' can be found in *City of Night* (Rechy 1984: 30–2, 36–52).
21 *Daily Orange*, 12 November 1963.
22 *Evergreen Review*, 11 (47), June 1967: 100. The advert is reproduced in Unterberger (2009: 137), who tied this advert to the album's lack of commercial success: 'It doesn't help that only a few magazines run print ads for the album, and that one of these is the *Evergreen Review*, which might be a respected literary publication, but is hardly the most effective outlet for the overwhelmingly young audience by which most rock records are bought' (2009: 136).
23 Bangs reused the phrase for his 1975 interview with Reed for *Creem*, 'Let Us Now Praise Famous Death Dwarves'.
24 Burroughs' response: 'Well, I admire Last Exit to Brooklyn very much …. And I like Rechy's work very much too' (Bockris 1995: 423–4).

References

Bangs, L. ([1969] 2005), 'Review of *The Velvet Underground*', in C. Heylin (ed.), *All Yesterday's Parties: The Velvet Underground in Print 1966–1971*, 99–100, Cambridge, MA: Da Capo.

Birmingham, J. (2009), '*Evergreen Review* Archive', *RealityStudio*. Available online: https://bit.ly/3IBBoHF (accessed 24 October 2021).

Bockris, V. (1995), *Lou Reed: The Biography*, London: Vintage.

Books: Borderline Psychotic (1964), *Time*, 30 October. Available online: https://bit.ly/3nZBBN3 (accessed 24 October 2021).

Burroughs, W. (1962), *The Naked Lunch*, New York: Grove.

Carroll, J. S. (2018), 'White-Collar Masochism: Grove Press and the Death of the Managerial Subject', *Twentieth-Century Literature*, 64 (1): 1–24.

Chester, A. (1963), 'Fruit Salad', *New York Review of Books*, 1 June. Available online: https://bit.ly/3u9hm30 (accessed 24 October 2021).

Clay, S. and R. Phillips (1998), *A Secret Location on the Lower East Side: Adventures in Writing, 1960–1980*, New York: New York Public Library.

The Daily Orange. Available online: https://bit.ly/3IDe7oD (accessed 24 October 2021).

DeCurtis, A. (2017), *Lou Reed: A Life*, London: John Murray.

Epstein, A. (2013), '"I'll Be Your Mirror": Lou Reed and the New York School of Poetry'. Available online: https://bit.ly/3g0TJ4K (accessed 24 October 2021).

Ginsberg, A. (1956), *Howl and Other Poems*, New York: Pocket Poets Series.

Glass, L. (2013), *Counterculture Colophon: Grove Press, the Evergreen Review, and the Incorporation of the Avant-Garde*, Stanford, CA: Stanford University.

Goddard, S. and Lester, P. (eds) (2005), 'The Uncut 100', *Uncut*, 100, September: 30–93.

Heylin, C. (ed.) (2005), *All Yesterdays's Parties: The Velvet Underground in Print 1966–1971*, Cambridge, MA: Da Capo.

Jones, A. (2009), 'The Velvet Underground', *Uncut*, 151, December: 48–60.

Julià, I. (1997), 'Feedback: The Legend of The Velvet Underground', in A. Zak (ed.), *The Velvet Underground Companion*, 173-233, London: Omnibus.

Kandel, L. (1965), 'Poem for Perverts', *Evergreen Review*, 9 (35), March: 20-1.

Kane, D. (2017), *'Do You Have a Band?' Poetry and Punk Rock in New York City*, New York: Columbia University.

Lawrence, D. H. (1959), *Lady Chatterley's Lover*, New York: Grove.

Levy, A. (2016), *Dirty Blvd. The Life and Music of Lou Reed*, Chicago, IL: Chicago Review.

McGuire, W. ([1968] 2005), 'The Boston Sound', in C. Heylin (ed.), *All Yesterday's Parties: The Velvet Underground in Print 1966-1971*, 65-78, Cambridge, MA: Da Capo.

Miller, H. ([1961] 1993), *Tropic of Cancer*, London: Flamingo.

Millstein, A. (1962), 'New Literary Magazine Started by Five Sophs', *Daily Orange*, 11 May: 1, 9.

Pearlman, S. ([1968] 2005), 'Round Velvet Underground', in C. Heylin (ed.), *All Yesterday's Parties: The Velvet Underground in Print 1966-1971*, 61-3, Cambridge, MA: Da Capo.

Poore, C. (1962), 'Books of the Times: *Naked Lunch*', *New York Times*, 20 November 1962. Available online: https://nyti.ms/3fXAVDd (accessed 24 October 2021).

Rechy, J. (1961), 'A Quarter Ahead', *Evergreen Review*, 5 (19), July-August: 14-30.

Rechy, J. (1984), *City of Night*, New York: Grove Press.

Rechy, J. (1990), 'On Being a "Grove Press Author"', *Review of Contemporary Fiction: Grove Press Number*, 10 (3): 137-42.

Reed, L. (1962a), Untitled Story ('He'd Always Found the Idea of Copulation Distasteful'), *Lonely Woman Quarterly*, 1: 3.

Reed, L. (1962b), 'Michael Kogan - Syracuse's Miss Blanding', *Lonely Woman Quarterly*, 2: 12-13.

Reed, L. (1963), 'And What, Little Boy, Will You Trade for Your Horse?', *Lonely Woman Quarterly*, 3: 23-30.

Reed, L. (2012), 'Preface', in James Atlas (ed.), D. Schwartz, *In Dreams Begin Responsibilities and Other Stories*, i–iii, New York: New Directions. Available online: https://bit.ly/3AwGXEu (accessed 24 October 2021).

Reed, L. (2018), *Do Angels Need Haircuts? Early Poems*, New York: Anthology Editions.

Reed Weiner, M. (2015), 'A Family in Peril: Lou Reed's Sister Sets the Record Straight about His Childhood'. Available online: https://bit.ly/3u2UEK2 (accessed 24 October 2021).

Ribola, A. ([1969] 2005), 'Review of *The Velvet Underground*', in C. Heylin (ed.), *All Yesterday's Parties: The Velvet Underground in Print 1966-1971*, 107-8, Cambridge, MA: Da Capo.

Rosenthal, M. (2017), *Barney: Grove Press and Barney Rosset*, New York: Arcade.

Salzman, E. (1967), 'The Prevalence of Rock or Rock Lives!', *Evergreen Review*, 11 (47): 42-5, 82-4.

Selby Jr., H. (2000), *Last Exit to Brooklyn*, London: Bloomsbury.

Sounes, H. (2015), *Notes from the Velvet Underground: The Life of Lou Reed*, London: Doubleday.

Swados, E. (1991), *The Four of Us: A Family Memoir*, New York: Farrar, Straus and Giroux.

Unterberger, R. (2009), *White Light/White Heat: The Velvet Underground Day-by-Day*, London: Jawbone.

5

The Velvet Underground and musical archetypes

Julijana Papazova

The impetus for writing this study derives from published rock and pop encyclopaedias or monographs that often comment on the wide impact and influence of the Velvet Underground on numerous glam, punk, post-punk and alternative bands or musicians. In order to define this influence, this study deals with an analysis of the first two studio albums recorded by what is widely regarded as the band's classic and most influential formation – John Cale, Sterling Morrison, Lou Reed and Moe Tucker, with Nico contributing to the first release. This analysis will be undertaken through an examination of the main melodic, rhythmic, harmonic, instrumental and formal features of the albums, and through comparative analysis and research data on the presence of archetypes in the Velvet Underground's music. An archetype is defined as an original pattern or model from which all things of the same type are representations or copies. Thus the examination of the Velvet's music and the identification of archetypes aim to provide a better understanding of the Velvet Underground's influence on popular music since the 1960s.

Methodology

Over the past five decades, popular music criticism has been developed mostly through the criteria of originality, complexity and whether there is sustained interest over time in a band or artist. Often music analysis in this critical work is limited to a discussion of the sonic characteristics of recordings, and the feelings or emotions suggested by the songs and their production. An entire album or part of it may be analysed in detail with an emphasis on its sonic qualities. For example, the description of the album *The Velvet Underground & Nico* in the *VH1's 100 Greatest Albums* outlines how '[t]he squealing feedback that ends Heroin which sounds like subway brakes and is in its way the record's defining moment retain both a thrilling rockin' primitivism as well as a forward-looking form-shattering originality' (Specktor 2003: 53). This example demonstrates, as Carys Jones (2008: 33) suggests, that originality is one of the central criteria for the formation of the popular music canon or in the evaluation of a particular album, mostly through emphasizing qualities of sound or production. Furthermore, originality is viewed as synonymous with strange, weird and subversive elements that challenge conventional values, and this has become central to the formation of the canon in popular music (17).

In identifying popular music criticism as an important source in studies of popular music, it is also important to evaluate the relationship between the musical knowledge and sources of popular musicians, and how this informs their practice. Popular musicians acquire information, experience and knowledge about music both from listening to themselves and others perform, and from publications with musical notation. Standard musical notation and the aural tradition are complemented with a third category: phonographic aural analysis. For example, 'Sweet Jane' by the Velvet Underground was covered by the Cowboy Junkies, and this was achieved entirely by listening to studio recordings and live versions of the song (Gracyk 2001: 28, 29).

In general, in popular music publications, historical or biographical analysis has been dominant, with topics of music analysis of particular songs or albums present only in modest numbers. But in recent years, and with the rise of popular music studies over the last four decades, the number of studies that contain music analysis of rock music has increased. For example, Nobile (2014) undertook a comparative approach examining methodologies of music analysis in classical and rock music through the use of Schenkerian analysis.[1] Schenkerian analysis, developed in the late nineteenth and early twentieth centuries by Heinrich Schenker as an aid to understanding tonal Western classical music, has been used previously in studies of popular music (see below). However, Nobile's aim was to investigate the ways in which Schenkerian analytical techniques can be updated to better reflect the structure of rock music, focusing on harmonic function and contrapuntal relationships between melody and harmony (1–3).

A common approach in the field of music analysis is to feature elements of narrative theory in an attempt to describe how a piece of music develops and changes over time, and how certain structures and elements afford effects and understanding in the listener. Music presents to the listener certain sonic expectations which allow the identification of, and relationship between, musical features. For example, chords are said to lead to one another, and melodic lines are perceived as having directions. Schenker often categorizes music as a form of modern-day narrative theory. Another interesting aspect of Schenkerian theory is the archetypal nature of *Stufen*, which reflects Jungian views on humanity and storytelling. Jung viewed archetypes as structural phenomena that readers are able to identify within stories, such as the wise old man, or the young and noble hero. A similar narrative approach could derive from Schenkerian theory, treating music analysis as similar to the discovery and development of a story, in that an analysis develops based on new information as a piece progresses (Gresham 2016: 1, 2).

In the last couple of decades there have increasingly been examples of Schenkerian analysis deployed in music genres other than classical music such as non-Western music or Western popular music. Examples of Schenkerian analysis in popular music studies include work on the songs of George Gershwin (Gilbert 1995), the Beatles (Everett 1999, 2001) and Paul Simon (García Gallardo 2000). These analyses do not use the entirety of Schenkerian theory, but only elements of it depending on the chosen musical material and the necessity for adaptations. For example, Allen Forte (1995), in his analysis of American popular ballads, modifies Schenker's view that every structural harmony must be a consonant chord; he extends Schenker's concept of consonance, stating that a consonant chord is enhanced by one of the stable dissonances, such as a ninth (García Gallardo 2000).

In this study of the Velvet Underground's first two albums, I use a comparative approach of music analysis using the rules and theories of academic music analysis drawn from Schenkerian theory. These are centred on Schenker's concepts *Urlinie* and *Ursatz*, and by undertaking a phonographic aural method (as, of course, there are no original scores to work from). The *Urlinie* is the melodic aspect of *Ursatz*. The term is usually translated as 'fundamental descent', reflecting Schenker's belief that this archetypal descending motion underpins all tonal pieces. The *Ursatz* (or fundamental structure) is the archetypal progression of which all tonal pieces are hypothetically an elaboration. It consists of a descending line in the upper part (*Urlinie*) over a bass progression (*Bassbrechung*). The *Bassbrechung* (bass arpeggiation) is the I-V-I that underpins the *Urlinie* as part of the *Ursatz*, including any elaborations of this pattern. The basic harmonic progression is elaborated contrapuntally, typically creating harmonic patterns such as I-III-V-I or I-II-V-I.[2] Besides music analysis, a secondary aspect of analysis is the lyrics of the songs, by analysing their content, thematic features, manner of expression and potential metaphorical meanings.

The general terminology for the music analysis in this study is partly based on my previous analysis of alternative rock in Yugoslavia in the 1980s: *musical phrase* – a short musical entity consisting of two, four or eight bars; *music sections* are marked with lowercase letters a, b, c, and denote a complete formal unit that may be repeated but not necessarily exactly; in certain songs I use the terms *verse* and *refrain*; an *instrumental part* or section may appear at the beginning of the song as an introduction; it may also occur during the song between the verse and the refrain, or at the end of the song as a final part or *coda*; for shorter instrumental motives I use the term *passage*; *lyrics* – a particular song's verbal message (e.g. the analysis of the lyrics in the song 'The Gift'), or comparative messages across songs; *vocal* – melodic motion and the performative aspects of vocal delivery; *meter* (e.g. 4/4), accents; *harmonic analysis* – tonality, main harmonic functions; *use of instruments* – acoustic, electric, strings, percussion, brass, etc. (Papazova 2017: 57, 58).

The Velvet Underground & Nico (1967, Verve)

'Sunday Morning' is in 4/4 meter, the musical phrases are symmetrical, the main chords are on I, IV and V in F major, but they are also combined with borrowed chord from E flat major (VII). At the end, there is repetition of the main subject – 'Sunday Morning'. In the verse, a piano section is developed with chords on each beat. The harmonic scheme has a chord progression based on the chords I and IV, followed with a chord progression that is common in rock music: I-VII flat-VI flat but expanded with the II. The scheme of the first phrase is: F/B/F/B/F/Am/E flat major/Dm/G/C.

The harmonic scheme during the refrain does not have the chord on VI. The refrain scheme is: F/B/F/B/Gm/E flat major/C. The instruments used in this song are celeste, viola, drums, bass guitar, lead guitar and Lou Reed takes the lead vocal. The accents are on the second and the fourth beat. The ending of this song is based on the main vocal melody descending (*Urline*), over the bass/harmony progression (I, IV).

'I'm Waiting for the Man' is based on the rhythmical repetition of eighth notes during the entire song created with symmetrical phrases in 4/4 meter in two sections a and b. The a section is vocal-instrumental where the lead vocal on a narrative level is telling a personal story about an experience with his drug dealer. The b section is based on the same melody as a section but without the vocal. The harmonic scheme is: D/G/D/G/D/G. The basic major chords have added seconds which are creating dissonant sound. The guitar solo is simple, based on a minimalistic repetitive concept that creates tension or a nervous ambience.

The next song calms the mood of the album. 'Femme Fatale' is in a slow tempo, based on symmetrical phrases. The verse has two phrases of eight bars, and the refrain has one phrase of eight bars. The vocal part is taken by Nico. The meter is in 4/4, with accents on the second and fourth time in constant quarter note movements. The refrain is developed with a crescendo, in both vocal and instrumental sections.

'Venus in Furs' is in medium tempo, 4/4, based on two sections. It starts with an instrumental introduction based on a creative, impressive motive with the improvised performance of electric viola, ostrich guitar[3] and the accentuation of beats on the basic beat without a metric division in the drum section. A similar instrumental introduction is repeated in other songs, including 'I'm Waiting for the Man'. Through the song we hear a change of a couple of rhythmic motives divided between different instruments. These complementary rhythms are created through the following scheme: the drums have an eighth rest, eighth note and quarter note; the guitar has two eighths, eighth rest and an eighth note. Near the end, we hear the viola using tremolo, or Cale playing drones. At the same time Reed plays a sharp, naked, cruel solo on guitar. The song is in d minor and the main harmonic positions are on: I, V and II. The main chords are expanded with seconds that produce dissonant sounds. In the refrain, we hear modulation in the major parallel scale F flat major. An instrumental passage comes between the sections.

'Run Run Run' is in allegro, 4/4, based on three sections a, b and c. A is filled with recitative or narrative treatment of the vocal, and b is recognizable with the repetition of the title words (it could be treated as refrain). The entire song is filled with repetitive rhythmical patterns – dotted eighth note with sixteenth. The c section is instrumental, with a noise treatment of the guitar, and an intensive use of plectrum on the strings. There is free rhythmical movement in the guitar solo. The accent in the rhythm pattern in a and b is on the fourth beat which is a relatively novel new element in rock music for that time. Also, the guitar solo comprises of short chromatic and scale movements.

'All Tomorrow's Parties' is based on slow melodic movement with a solo vocal performance by Nico. The harmony scheme in the first section is similar to the opening song of the album based on I-VII-IV-I-IV-II-V. This song is created in two sections: a and b. The accents in drums are variable: in the first part they are on the first and the third beat, but in the second part of the song the rhythm accents are the same as in 'Venus In Furs', that is, on the second and the fourth beat. The b section in this part of the song becomes freer with the development of distorted elements and staccato playing on guitar.

'Heroin', the first song on the b-side of the original vinyl release, is notable for the constant change of tempo from slow to fast and back again, accomplished with accelerando. Although at the beginning there is a rhythmical repetition of eighth notes, during the next phrases there are opposing rhythmical movements between the instruments: the electric viola plays long notes and the drums eight notes. The harmonic scheme is based on I and IV expanded with II. At the beginning, the major chords are supplemented with the accent of the drums on the fourth beat (timpani sound). Afterwards, the drums display eighth note movements, followed by the gradual speeding up of the tempo of the song or accelerando. This is then followed with a deceleration of the tempo, or decelerando. At the end, there are poly rhythmical movements, forte dynamics and mutual improvisation of all instruments.

After 'Heroin', we hear two more melodic or consonant, and not very long, songs. 'There She Goes Again' is reminiscent of a rock and roll ballad. The song is calm and filled with a light soft repetitive melody in medium tempo, 4/4. The rhythm is based mostly on quarter and eighth notes, enriched with couple of quarter and eighth rests. The accents are mostly on the second and the fourth beat, and the form is based on verse with refrain. The song finishes with a coda based on accelerando.

'I'll Be Your Mirror' features Nico as soloist. It is calm, in medium tempo, 4/4, with accents on the second and the fourth beat performed with tambourine. The song has two sections with an intro and coda. The coda introduces a new short melody and new lyrics for the first time – the words from the title of the song.

'The Black Angel's Death Song' is characterized with experimental sound, and although it lasts three minutes, this is a very affecting song, with noise dominating. The viola section is based on repeated short dissonant intervals, with shrieks in the strings. In addition, this song has non-symmetrical phrases. The vocal has a feel of *Sprechgesang*, or speech singing, reciting the lyrics in a small span of melody movement up to thirds. Cale's vocal contribution consists of hissing that is reminiscent of white noise.

The noise-based, experimental and free approach returns in the last song of the album 'European Son'. The noise elements produced by the electric instruments are enriched with other sound elements, for example, the sound of glass breaking and a chair being dragged across the studio floor. It's not easy to count or to follow the phrases of the song, because they are non-symmetrical. During the first phrase, we can hear a syncopated rhythm that enriches the rhythmical patterns. Like 'Heroin', this song is longer than the usual length of popular music songs, at around seven minutes long. The song has two sections: a is vocal-instrumental, is intensive and nervous, with Reed storytelling, and the b section is created with noise and improvisation.

White Light/White Heat (1968)

'White Light/White Heat' is a hybrid between r'n'b and noise. It has an ostinato rhythm with the repetition of eighth notes, and the harmonic scheme is based on I and V (G and D). The song ends with intense guitar distortion. The musical phrases are symmetrical, and the vocal melody is moving in diapason. The lyrics, rather than simply reflecting the methamphetamine experience as is commonly understood, also reflect Lou Reed's interest in the role of white light in metaphysical studies (Unterberger 2009: 261).

The narrative treatment of the vocal continues also in the second song 'The Gift', with minimal rhythmical-melodical accompaniment on drums, bass and guitar in 4/4 meter with accents on the second and the fourth beat, repeated during the recitation of the lyrics. From the middle of the song, the instrumental part becomes more varied with a distorted guitar solo. John Cale recites the tale of Waldo Jeffers, which was written by Lou Reed during his college days, with the story lasting eight minutes. The theme concerns a young man, Waldo, who is in love with Marsha. During the summer vacation they are separated, and Waldo is worried that Marsha may not be faithful. He plans a surprise by having himself delivered as package to her. Marsha could not open the package, so she takes a sheet metal cutter and gives it to her friend, who stabs through the box and through Waldo's head. The approach to this song is based on the narrative treatment of the vocal, distortions and dark lyrics which can be heard in the songs of the following generations of gothic-rock or dark-rock bands.

'Lady Godiva's Operation' is in 4/4 meter. It has a symmetrical repetition of one phrase (a), then an instrumental part (b) and again repetition of the first part (a1). The drum section is based on a repetitive rhythm of eighths: two eighths/eighth rest, eighth note/two eighths/eighth rest and an eighth note. John Cale is again the lead vocalist in this song, and the story has some continuity with the previous song, based on black humour during the description of Lady Godiva's surgery. Lou Reed wrote the lyrics, and the inspiration for the title comes from the British legend of Lady Godiva. During the second repetition of the first section or a1, Reed is sporadically on backing vocals with dissonant, off-key pronunciation of the words. The electric viola played by John Cale enriched the end of the song, where we could also hear extra-musical sounds such as sound of an engine.

The vocal melodic development of the song 'Here She Comes Now' reminds us of the songs performed by Nico on the first Velvet Underground album. It is in 4/4 meter, with accents on the second and the fourth beat and it is the shortest song on the album at two minutes. The song has three sections. It starts with instrumental section with guitar solo (passage), based on a soft melodic development, with a very clear rhythm with quarter notes on the drums. The second part b is based on a repetitive melody and lyrics in which the song's protagonist asks if she will ever come, with a new rhythm in the drums with a repetition of eighths. The c section is developed with the use of tonic and dominant (I and V), and the upper melody movement is supported with little crescendo. Then the development of the song is based on a combination of all three sections. 'Here She Comes Now' could be viewed as an intermezzo for the next two intensive, dissonant, experimental songs. The lyrics of this song are treated as a double entendre. The 'she' of the title could be a reference to a girl or could be metaphor for drugs (Bockris and Malanga 2002: 93). Also, according to Brown (2014: 18) it could refer to Reed's guitar.

During the song 'I Heard Her Call My Name', the vocal expression is nervous and intense (which potentially anticipates punk singing). It is based on two sections: one vocal-instrumental and one instrumental. Both sections are based on the same repetitive rhythmical movement in eighth notes in drums and rhythm guitar. The tempo is in allegro or much faster than the medium tempos in previous songs. The instrumental section has a dissonant guitar solo. As in the previous song, in the lyrics we once again have a development of a relationship between the lead (vocal) character and a female character.

'Sister Ray' is an experimental song that lasts almost seventeen minutes. This is the longest song on both albums selected for this analysis. 'Sister Ray' arguably represents one of the foundations for the later development of alternative rock music. The main elements that suggest this thesis are the combination of melodic and noise elements, the combination of symmetrical and non-symmetrical phrases and the free treatment of tempo and noises. Other elements that are part of this song are rhythmic ostinato (six groups of two eighths/eighth rest-eighth note/eighth rest-eighth note); alternating vocal-instrumental with instrumental sections; accelerando of tempo; and the alternation of solo performances between the different instruments and in unison. An example of non-symmetrical phrases can be found in the last instrumental part of the song (16:47–17:05), with the phrase being twenty-one bars.

In summary, the most recognizable elements identified in this analysis of the Velvet Underground's first two albums are the concept of *contrast* – narrative and noise, calm songs versus fast dissonant, noise songs; *figurative speech* in lyrics with narrative operating at the level of connotation (metaphor, metonymy, allegory) and storytelling vocal interpretation (topics about drugs, nihilism, experiences from the street, inspiration from literature or art). Arguably, this represents the *foreshadowing* of later genres of alternative rock music.

Archetypes

The idea of incorporating the concept of archetypes into the analysis of the Velvet Underground's music is based on the frequent references to their influence on many bands and solo musicians since the 1960s. The central idea of this research was to demystify the influence of the Velvet Underground or to interpret the key essential elements in their music that influenced the music of the next generations of musicians and bands such as David Bowie, Joy Division, The Jesus and Mary Chain and many, many others.

For Carl Jung, archetypes could be inherent, cross-cultural patterns of relational dynamics that are universally recognized when incorporated in symbols or people who are carriers of archetypal projection. Just as a script exists continuously or in total on paper, an archetype exists in a ubiquitous state in the unconscious but can only emerge as an archetype through interaction with a symbol, person or event that the conscious mind detected, just as a play is only actually seen when actors are present (Davis 2010: 6, 7). Another parallel analysis of Schenker and Jung could be addressed in their theories of transmission in musical structure and the treatment of the Self. In Schenker's analysis, music's structure projects itself via energetic transmission from compositional background structures through middle-ground structures to the foreground structure, which parallels the way in which Jung's archetypical energy works through the Self to different outer elements of a person's life (Davis 2010: 34). As Burrows (2004: 13) argues, there is also a parallel between music archetypes and collective consciousness where Jungian archetypes can help us understand 'social and mythic origins of feelings and unconscious states', with musical archetypes pointing 'to the way in which emotional and spiritual elements interact … musical archetypes don't just have structural and narrative significance in musical terms, they stand for emotional states or conditions of the psyche'.

In some music theories, the archetypal element points in the direction of musical expectations during the analysis of a melody. Our musical expectations are determined by specific melodic archetypes, such as the triad or phrase symmetry (Meyer 1973). In analysing rock music, Yvetta Kajanová (2014: 151) focuses on the relationship between sound, improvisation and rhythm. In her work, more detailed attention is given to rhythm, where the beat-offbeat principle, poly-rhythms and poly-metrics are fundamental for rhythm patterns, and these are identified as the archetypes that characterize rock music and its subgenres. Considering the subject of rhythm in this analysis, one of the most common elements for all songs is the rhythm pattern created with repetitive movements in a 4/4 meter, with accents on the second and the fourth beat, created mostly with eighths or quarter notes.

Generally speaking musical archetypes therefore can be analysed through the selection of specific elements of the music, like rhythm, melody, improvisation and harmony as mentioned in the works of Meyer or Kajanová. They can also be based on an interdisciplinary approach as in recent publications by Kozel (2018) and Burrows (2004). In this study, the analysis of musical archetypes in the Velvet Underground's music has identified musical elements that perhaps foreshadowed or influenced later rock music genres and subgenres. These archetypal musical features arguably acted as an inspiration – via the conduits of early adopters such as David Bowie and Roxy Music – for the next generations of punk, post-punk and alternative rock bands. The results of the music analysis of this study are divided into seven archetypal points:

1. **Contrasts**: contrasting track lengths – short songs around two minutes, and long songs between seven and seventeen minutes; consonant versus dissonant melody development; symmetrical and non-symmetrical phrases; narrative calm songs versus noise songs.
2. **Intensive distortion elements**: particularly the electric guitar, and also the organ.

3. **Noise and extra-musical sounds.**
4. **Instruments:** electric guitar (with alternate tunings such as the 'Ostrich'), rhythm guitar, drums; celeste and non-conventional rock instruments like electric viola.
5. **Tempo:** conventional; slow, medium or fast; unconventional tempo: accelerando or changing of tempo during some songs on both albums, for example doubling the original tempo.
6. **Accents:** dominant accents are on the second and the fourth beat (followed by accents on the first and the third; there are rarely accents on each fourth count).
7. **Vocal:** narrative treatment based on two categories: personal expression of everyday life in the underground community in New York City; literary storytelling.

Influence and legacy

This study has identified seven musical archetypes that arguably form the key influential musical tropes to be found in the work of later artists and genres that look to the Velvet Underground as a creative touchstone. It is not possible in a study of this size to map the complex lines of this influence over five decades in detail. However, in publications about the Velvet Underground, the question of influence and legacy is a continual theme. The legacy of the band is mostly evidenced by bands' or musicians' own claims about such an influence, at other times in comparisons made by critics, and through cover versions of the Velvet Underground songs that are viewed as tributes or acknowledgements of creative influence. For some, including author Peter Hogan (2007),

> It's almost impossible to overestimate the influence of Velvet Underground upon ... rock music ... [w]ithin a couple of years of the Velvets' demise, both David Bowie and Brian Eno – two of pop music's most innovative pioneers – had publicly acknowledged their debt to the band. And both those gentlemen would in turn, of course, influence almost everything that followed them.
>
> (261)

According to Hogan we can hear the inspiration of the Velvet Underground's music resonating in 'Joy Division and New Order ... Television, Echo and the Bunnymen, Lloyd Cole, Talking Heads, The Smiths, Cowboy Junkies, Jane's Addiction, Simple Minds, The Cure, The Birthday Party, The Jesus and Mary Chain, The Wedding Present, Nick Cave, Massive Attack, Radiohead, The Violent Femmes, The Strokes, [and] The Vines' (261). This inspiration was not only musical as the Velvet Underground are said to have impacted visually with 'their all-black ensemble being adopted almost universally as de rigeur uniform for any band with boho pretensions' (Hogan 2007: 261–2). After Lou Reed's death in 2013, articles were repeatedly published defining the impact and influence of the Velvet Underground or Lou Reed over the next generation of important rock musicians or bands. For example, Greg Kot (2014) wrote that, alongside the music and visual aesthetic already mentioned, it was the bands values as much as their music that were part of the legacy:

> The roots of underground and experimental music, indie and alternative, punk, post-punk and art-punk all snake back to the four Velvet Underground studio albums ... The values that made The Velvet Underground such pariahs in the 1960s – the do-it yourself, under-produced record-making; the utter disregard for fashion; the sceptical, sometimes cynical attitude – were right in line with 1970s punk, 1980s indie rock and 1990s alternative music.
>
> (Kot 2014)

The Velvet Underground's songs can also be used as examples in the foreshadowing of more recent subgenres in rock. For example, 'I'll Be Your Mirror' as well as 'There She Goes Again' are perhaps precursors of what later became known as shoegaze, neo-psychedelic and later dream pop music. These types of music are identified as part of the meta-genre of alternative music, a term that became increasingly popular during the 1980s. The breathy vocal with guitar effects, moderately fast tempo and imaginative, abstract and introspective lyrics are one of the main elements of dream pop or neo psychedelic music. Dream pop tends to focus on textures and moods rather than propulsive rock riffs. Vocals are generally breathy and sung in a near whisper, and lyrics are often introspective or existential in nature (Bogdanov et al. 2001: ix). A louder more aggressive strain of dream pop has been defined as shoegaze (e.g. the band My Bloody Valentine and early Cocteau Twins releases) who channelled the noise experiments of the Velvet Underground.

Discussing the large number of bands that acknowledge a strong influence and debt to the Velvet Underground, in the early 1990s Lou Reed said,

> I just keeping thinking that when The Velvet Underground first came out with songs like 'Heroin', we were so savaged for it. Here it is a few decades later, and I have those lyrics published in a book, and I'm giving readings at art museums. We wanted to make records that would stick around like great novels or movies, and we believed in what we were doing, even if nobody else did.
>
> (qtd. in Kot 2014)

The inspiration of the Velvet Underground is also present in newer generations of bands such as Arctic Monkeys, whose album title *AM* (2013) was inspired by the Velvet Underground's 1985 compilation album *VU* (Chew 2016). Other bands have chosen their name from Velvet Underground songs, such as the neo-psychedelic band Black Angels, who derived their name from the Velvets' 'The Black Angel's Death Song'.

Cover songs are an act of historical valorisation from the past to the present (Schiffer 2010: 91). For musicians cover songs present a way to show their respect for a particular song, band or musician of the past, and sometimes to introduce a song to an audience in a creative and innovative way. A list of high-profile Velvet Underground cover versions includes 'Sister Ray' by Joy Division and 'Femme Fatale' by R.E.M. (Chew 2016). In 2021 the cover album *I'll Be Your Mirror: A Tribute to The Velvet Underground and*

Nico, released to coincide with Todd Haynes' *The Velvet Underground* documentary film, featured a variety of musicians, both old and new, acknowledging their debt to the band. Among the artists involved in reproducing *The Velvet Underground & Nico* album were Iggy Pop, Michael Stipe, Thurston Moore, Sharon Van Etten, St. Vincent, King Princess and Fontaines D.C. According to Plasketes (2010: 2) cover songs in popular music reflect a postmodern manifestation of intensive recontextualization. These and other cover songs are reinterpretations or remediations of music styles and periods and do not only have historical significance. They are also important sources and signposts in the ongoing creation of the rock canon, and the Velvet Underground's positioning with this canon.

Conclusion

This chapter consists of a study of the first two Velvet Underground albums, based on a comparative analysis of their early album releases, music theory and an interdisciplinary approach. In a study of this length it is not possible to go into great depth on lyric and vocal analysis, so the emphasis has been on instrumental musical details. The starting point for the music analysis was the listening or phonographic aural method. For this analysis I used terminology from my earlier research dedicated to alternative rock in Yugoslavia and Schenker's analytic technique that is essentially devoted to the relationship between melody and harmony. This combination was productive because Schenker himself links musical analysis to archetypes and Jung's view of humanity and storytelling. The selection of the musical elements for analysis such as melody, rhythm, harmony, lyrics and improvisation was complemented by the exploration of the relationship between these elements and the narrative approach or storytelling in vocal performances. In total, I analysed seventeen songs, and the results are summarized in seven archetypal points providing a critical perspective on the Velvet Underground's music. In addition to identifying these musical archetypes, I expanded the analysis with a discussion of the Velvet Underground's musical influence with the purpose of creating a complementary approach examining the Velvet Underground's musical legacy in the history of popular music.

Notes

1. Heinrich Schenker (1868–1935) was an Austrian music theorist best known for his system for the analysis of tonal music, examining deep structures shared by tonal compositions and foreground details that mark out a composition's uniqueness. It traditionally focuses on the analysis of musical scores rather than recorded performances.
2. Further details on key Schenkerian analytical terms can be found in Pankhurst (2008).
3. The term Ostrich guitar was used by Reed. It assigns one note to all strings (Daley 2016).

References

Bockris, V. and Malanga, G. (2002), *Up-Tight. The Velvet Underground Story*, London: Omnibus.

Bogdanov, V., Woodstra, C., Erlewine, S. T. and Bush, J. (eds) (2001), *All Music Guide to Electronica*, San Francisco: Backbeat.

Brown, B. (2014), *Words and Guitar: A History of Lou Reed's Music*, Brooklyn, NY: Collosal.

Burrows, B. J. (2004), 'Musical Archetypes and Collective Consciousness: Cognitive Distribution and Free Improvisation', *Critical Studies in Improvisation*, 1 (1). Available online: https://bit.ly/35rydUD (accessed 24 October 2021).

Chew, C. (2016), 'Lou Reed W ould Have Turned 74 Today', *Gigwise*, 2 March. Available online: https://bit.ly/3r1c6wq (accessed 24 October 2021).

Daley, M. (2016), 'Lou Reed's "Ostrich" Tuning as an Aesthetic Point of Articulation', *Rock Music Studies*, 3 (2): 148–56.

Davis, K. (2010), 'Manifesting Archetypal Energy through Music', MA diss., Pacifica Graduate Institute, Santa Barbara, CA. Available online: https://bit.ly/3G0EQK7 (accessed 24 October 2021).

Everett, W. (1999), *The Beatles as Musicians: Revolver through the Anthology*, Oxford: Oxford University.

Everett, W. (2001), *The Beatles as Musicians: The Quarry Men through Rubber Soul*, Oxford: Oxford University.

Forte, A. (1995), *The American Popular Ballad of the Golden Era, 1924–1950*, Princeton, NJ: Princeton University.

García Gallardo, C. L. (2000), 'Schenkerian Analysis and Popular Music', *Trans: Revista Transcultural de Música*, 5. Available online: https://bit.ly/3r0vv0v (accessed 24 October 2021).

Gerzić, B. (2003), *Superstars. Manijački vodič kroz Fektori Endija Vorhola i Velvet Andergraund*, trans. J. Vujanović, Belgrade, Serbia: Istar.

Gilbert, S. E. (1995), *The Music of Gershwin*, New Haven and London: Yale University.

Gracyk, T. (2001), *I Wanna Be Me: Rock Music and the Politics of Identity*, Philadelphia: Temple University.

Gresham, R. K. (2016), *An Exploration of Graphic Archetypal Theories in Musical and Literary Analysis*. MMus diss., Stephen F. Austin State University, Nacogcdoches, TX.

Hogan, P. (2007), *The Rough Guide to The Velvet Underground*, London: Rough Guides.

Jones, W. C. (2008), *The Rock Canon. Canonical Values in the Reception of Rock Albums*, Aldershot: Ashgate.

Kajanová, Y. (2014), *On the History of Rock Music*, Frankfurt am Main: Peter Lang.

Kot, G. (2014), 'The Velvet Underground: As Influential as The Beatles?' *BBC*, 21 October. Available online: https://bbc.in/3g0Klhe (accessed 24 October 2021).

Kozel, D. (2018), 'The Myth of Globalization and Contemporary Musical Culture', in D. Hebert and M. Rykowski (eds), *Music Glocalization: Heritage and Innovation in a Digital Age*, 32–51, Cambridge: Cambridge Scholars Publishing.

Meyer, L. B. (1973), *Explaining Music: Essays and Explorations*, Oakland, CA: University of California.

Nobile, F. D. (2014), *A Structural Approach to the Analysis of Rock Music*. PhD diss., Graduate Center, City University of New York: New York.

Pankhurst, T. (2008), 'Glossary', *SchenkerGUIDE*. Available online: https://bit.ly/3g0KuRO (accessed 24 October 2021).

Papazova, J. (2017), *Alternative Rock in Yugoslavia in the Period 1980–1991*, Chisinau, Moldova: Lambert Academic Publishing.

Plasketes, G. (2010), 'Introduction: Like a Version', in G. Plasketes (ed.), *Play It Again: Cover Songs in Popular Music*, 1–10, Farnham: Ashgate.

Schiffer, S. (2010), 'The Cover Song as Historiography, Marker of Ideological Transformation', in G. Plasketes (ed.), *Play It Again: Cover Songs in Popular Music*, 77–98, Farnham: Ashgate.

Specktor, M. (2003), '19. The Velvet Underground and Nico', in J. Hoye (ed.), *VH1's 100 Greatest Albums*, 52–3, London: Simon & Schuster International.

Unterberger, R. (2009), *White Light/White Heart: The Velvet Underground Day-By-Day*, London and New York: Jawbone Press.

6

Lou Reed's Great American Novel

Peter Griffiths

Lou Reed once claimed that across his songwriting and recorded output, 'if you thought of it all as a book then you have the Great American Novel, every record as a chapter. They're all in chronological order. You take the whole thing, stack it and listen to it in order, there's my Great American Novel' (qtd. in Reed 2014: 221). It perhaps seems more obvious to treat Reed's oeuvre as poetry, narrative or otherwise, rather than as a novel. In the introduction to *Between Thought and Expression* (1993) Reed emphasizes the performative aspect of the poetic form: 'Over the past few years I have done occasional "poetry" readings, always using my lyrics as the basis. I was continually struck by the different voices that emerged when the words were heard without the music, and those experiences encouraged me to consider the possibility of publishing them naked' (ix). Such performativity is closer to that of the pop song than the usually solitary and silent consumption of narrative fiction. However, when Reed spoke of influence, there was a strong showing of artists who were primarily authors of fiction, and indeed it is to their fiction to which Reed most often pointed (examples of these are William S. Burroughs, Hubert Selby Jr. and John Rechy).

My approach here is primarily formal/historical/contextual; I have preferred to approach Reed's work and its literary context as a Bloomian 'conversation' between texts and generally avoided literary theoretical approaches. I will later make use of Lawrence Buell's *The Dream of the Great American Novel* (2014), and I think that it is worth noting here that he also prefers this descriptor (10).

I will later argue that both Reed's 'novel' and the Great American Novel are intimately bound up with the form known as the 'picaresque'. Burroughs stated in a 1984 interview with Philippe Mikriammos in *The Review of Contemporary Fiction* that the picaresque 'has no plot. It is simply a series of incidents', and that as a form it can be dated as far back as *The Satyricon* ([c. first century AD] 1974) and as such pre-dates the novel as is traditionally understood. I disagree with Burroughs' claim that the picaresque has 'no plot' and would instead aver that this difference is relative. *Don Quixote* (1615) is often taken as a fairly arbitrary starting point for the novel, even though *Quixote* is itself episodic in nature. By 'episodic' in this case I mean relatively opposed to a 'diachronic' structure, which moves in a linear fashion by a series of causal events. The model of the traditional novel is often taken to be *Madame Bovary*, which in the most basic terms has a certain teleology which draws events forward: Emma has to be dissatisfied with her marriage in order to seek other men. This seems obvious, but it is markedly different from the episodic nature of *Quixote*, in which the events generally follow one another without as much weight on their causal relationships.

While *Quixote* might share the episodic nature of the picaresque, it lacks the other aspect inherent to the later form:

> The *picaro* is usually a cynical youth, brought up the hard way and determined to treat others as cruelly as he has been treated himself. His aim is to *bular* others: to deceive and play cruel tricks on them, and indeed cruelty is one of the dominant motifs of these novels, which reflect a world where the rule is 'every man for himself'. The *picaro*'s goal is respectability, which means money, and he is keen to make the best showing he can in the world.
>
> (Alpert 1969: 7)

It should be noted that only a few of these requirements are met by Burroughs' characters: they do not seek respectability, for example, though they do act in a manner that is cruel, and they exist in a cruel world (by 'cruel', here, I mean 'indifferent or taking pleasure in the suffering of others'). It is the quality of cruelty that Reed's 'protagonist' comes to share.

The resemblance between this form and those of a number of so-called Great American Novels is telling, if not entirely obvious. For example, *The Adventures of Huckleberry Finn* (1884) is a novel with an episodic structure, and a protagonist who acts as a trickster, though he lacks the cruelty described above. Twain writes in the 'Notice' at the beginning of the novel, 'Persons attempting to find a motive in this narrative will be prosecuted; persons attempting to find a moral in it will be banished; persons attempting to find a plot will be shot' (48). This is, then, by Burroughs' definition, a rejection of the nineteenth-century Realist novel and its central tenets.

While Buell (2014) seems to almost grudgingly accept *Quixote*'s influence on *Huckleberry Finn* (10), he stops short of relating Twain's novel to the picaresque. The episodicity of those novels is also related to what might be called a 'tableau' structure. The tableau is almost a mirror of the picaresque: static, with movement coming largely from the narrator, as is the case with 'Sister Ray', rather than a protagonist.

This structure also has much in common with novels of decadence, such as Huysmans's *Against Nature* (1884), in which the protagonist barely manages to leave his home, or Sade's *120 Days of Sodom* (1904) and the 'libertine tableaux' contained within (411). According to Reed, 'Sister Ray' is 'a compressed movie' and 'a parade of New York denizens' (qtd. in Reed 2014: 51). Jeremy Reed (2014) writes that the song 'best exemplifies the cool indifferent tone Reed had picked by from (*sic*) Burroughs's cold dissociation from experience on junk. Lou's flatly narrated account of deviated sex, murder and drugs is delivered glacially, nonchalantly'. The nervous young man of 'Waiting for the Man' has been replaced by an individual so cool that they are frozen. Jeremy Reed's chosen descriptor for the song is 'novella' (51).

There is also the issue of considering each album as a 'chapter' in this novel, largely because certain aspects inherent to the album (the cover art, for example) are not inherent to the novel. Therefore, a decision must be made as to whether in new critical style one chooses to isolate the lyrics, whether one chooses to read everything from interviews and personal histories and image as a single *gesamtkunstwerk* or whether one takes a position somewhere in between. I would argue that all of the available material is relevant, and that, for my purposes, to isolate the words from the context and paratext would be to deliver only a partial reading. However, I would contend that each approach has its own merits, and that there is no 'true' way to consider the work. If one is interested in the persona as a character in the narrative of the career, then some of Reed's interviews are integral to the total work of art. The fictionality of the inhabitants of the Factory is also an issue since there is a complex relationship between Reed's use of them as subject matter and their 'real' selves. Exactly what constitutes a relevant album is also contentious: Reed's *Pass Thru Fire* (2008) only collects lyrics from studio albums, telling only part of the story. The live album *Live: Take No Prisoners* (1978 – see Pattie, Chapter 14, in this collection) has a special place in the narrative of both Reed's persona and his artistic development.

Jeremy Reed writes of Reed's 'singular concern to turn rock into an intelligently literate medium of expression' (2014: 10), and I think that the complications of this idea should be addressed. The Velvet Underground began releasing albums just as the pop album as an art form was gaining currency and rock and roll, in general, was undergoing shift into becoming 'rock'. Arguably the band contributed to this shift, which is to say, made rock and roll into a more literate art form. Such a shift also partly comprises the introduction of a Romantic notion of art being a mode of self-expression for the artist, an idea inherent to rock music but not rock and roll, and it seems obvious that Lou Reed's lyrical work conforms to this notion. If Lou Reed's literary tendencies tend towards the novelistic, then in tandem with the Romantic shift, it might be said that he contributed to an embourgeoisement of a pre-existing art form.

Reed stated, 'People were offended that we did a song called "Heroin" but there's plenty of stuff about that in literature and no-one gives a shit but this is rock'n'roll so we must be pushing drugs or something' (qtd. in Hibbert 1989: 34). This may be broadly true, but such subject matter had been present in some forms of popular music for a long time, albeit in a ghettoized form and largely light-hearted tone: Cab Calloway's Minnie the Moocher is taken down to Chinatown by her 'cokey' boyfriend to 'kick the gong around', for example.

In this respect, the offence taken by audiences is more of an *epater la bourgeoisie* than an unprecedented lyrical breakthrough. Arguably, the introduction of subjects such as adultery (as in 'Pale Blue Eyes') is more radical in terms of pop music, yet these too are subjects traditionally associated with the novel, adultery being the subject of the bourgeois Realist novel *ne plus ultra*, *Madame Bovary* (1856).

There are a number of questions, each a subset of the preceding one, to be asked of Reed's oeuvre if it is to be considered a Great American Novel. First, what does it mean to consider it to be a work of single work of narrative fiction? Second, what does it mean to consider it a novel? And third, what does it mean to consider it to be a Great American Novel?

Narrative fiction

One way to approach the first of these questions would be in Aristotelean terms, which is to say to look for unities. In the case of Reed's oeuvre, perhaps the most obvious unity is that of place, given his status as 'unofficial Poet Laureate of New York' (10). Furthermore, as I will argue later, it is also possible to find unity of character, if one considers the Reed persona to be the protagonist in this narrative.

There is also the possibility of unity of theme, and this is where Reed's connection to the decadents of the nineteenth and early twentieth centuries is most visible; decadence here being defined in part by Arthur Symons as a 'beautiful and interesting disease', and defined by Matthew Creasy as 'a determination to turn a negative trait into a positive one' (Symons (Creasy ed.) 2014: xvii). Such definitions also apply to the literature of transgression in American literature to which Reed's 'novel' also belongs, and this is most apparent in the authors most often mentioned where Reed's literary heritage is concerned. Burroughs, Rechy and Selby Jr. are all representative, and are mentioned in Reed's abortive interview with Burroughs himself (Bockris 2014: 512–20). When discussing the material included in *Between Thought and Expression* (1993), Reed stated that his decision was partly based on 'whether it contributed to a narrative form. There's a narrative link that takes you through three decades, so they follow each other and make sense – certain themes became really apparent that you might otherwise not be so aware of' (Gaiman [1992] 2015: 57).

This revealing observation supports in part the technique of projecting a narrative form upon the material and producing a reading that need not have been intended at the time of composition or recording. The implication is that such a narrative is a construct rather than adhering to Realism's dubious claim to describing a definitive version of reality. I will here offer a constructed narrative concerning the anxiety of cool/hipness and the possibility of its solution. For simplicity I have placed the tracks in order as they appear in *Between Thought and Expression*, with the exception of 'Sister Ray', which, surprisingly, does not feature in that selection, and 'Foggy Notion', the exclusion of which is more understandable. While I have applied a roughly chronological order to the tracks, it should be noted that I do not think that the conversation need necessarily follow the order of the songs as they appear on the albums. While a diachronic approach is favoured by Reed (as above), to treat the work synchronically would be equally valid, if less intuitive, given the traditional flow of the Realist novel and the way in which we experience time in general.

If decadence is the embrace of the corrupt, then cool may be said to apply to the apparent nonchalance with which one has achieved such a state, especially given the glamour that been attached to decadence since at least the Romantic period. The notion of cool may be traced back to Baldesar Castiglione's *The Book of the Courtier* ([1528] 1976) and the idea of *sprezzatura*: a 'certain nonchalance which conceals all artistry' (67). Cool is similar, though distinct, from 'hipness', which is in essence a form of cultural capital. Both cool and hipness seem to have been preoccupations of Reed.

1. 'I'm Waiting for the Man': A young white man attempts to score drugs in Harlem. Confrontation arises when, while waiting for the man of the title, he is asked by a person distinguished by his non-whiteness about his reason for being there. He loses his cool (possibly due to withdrawal, given the allusion in the penultimate line to the necessity of going through the same ordeal the next day), stutters (in the delivery found on *The Velvet Underground & Nico* [1967]) and addresses his interlocutor politely in overcompensation. He is hip enough to know where to go, but not cool enough to maintain his composure under pressure. The man arrives, and he and the white boy go into a brownstone to fix. Those in the house pin him, meaning that he is identified as to his purpose, which is to say that the observers are hip (the term also conjures the image of a needle) but they appear not to care (i.e. they are cool). In the final stanza the speaker is freer and easier in his demeanour. The anxiety here, whether exacerbated by withdrawal or by unfamiliarity, is quite specifically based around whiteness, and the solution is seen to be through drugs.
2. 'Heroin': High on heroin, the narrator drifts through fantasies, realizing that he doesn't care anymore (is cool). The drug is both 'wife' and 'life' now, and one can assume that this means that concerns outside that of the drug have fallen away.
3. 'The Gift': Waldo Jeffers, left behind by his girlfriend, who has moved to college, naively assumes that their relationship will continue, even if she will occasionally socialize with other men. If Waldo understood the narrative that usually accompanies this, then he would not be absurdly sending himself through the post to her, completely unannounced. His plans for this surprise visit seem to be extremely tame considering that Marcia and Sheila spent the previous night carousing and heavy petting with college men. The parcel arrives, prompting Sheila to reveal that she considers Waldo to be a 'schmuck'. The two young women, with little care for what the contents of the parcel might be, drive a sheet metal cutter through the box, killing Waldo. Waldo's death comes primarily through a combination of naivety and an inability to temper this naivety with cool. Bockris explicitly links this track to Reed's anxiety about his college girlfriend, Shelley Albin (49).
4. 'Sister Ray': The speaker indifferently observes a party of drag queens and sailors, only concerned with finding a vein. One attendee produces a gun and kills one of the sailors. The main complaint about the dead sailor is the blood on the carpet. Someone stutters the word 'amphetamine', in what may be seen as a corollary to the nervousness often associated with the drug.
5. 'Foggy Notion': A girl is beaten almost to death; it is treated with the same enthusiasm as the parallel narrative about love at first sight, with Reed's delivery a demonstration of the jouissance brought about by rock and roll.
6. 'I Wanna Be Black': Anxiety is neutered by the admission of its underlying absurdity. The speaker paints an exaggerated portrait of the myth of Black sexual potency feared by white college-educated bourgeois males and makes reference to the notion of Black men 'fuck[ing] up the Jews'. The white college kid, as the speaker, is notably differentiated from the Jewish individual. The partial

self-knowledge, if one takes the Reed persona to be the 'I' of the title (a reflexive pseudo-hipness), allows for the indifference that is suggested by the looseness of delivery, in which the lyrics marry to the ironic levity of the blues-styled music.

In the construction of this narrative it becomes obvious that in approaching a selection of tracks from one angle adumbrates other possible narratives (e.g. that of race and ethnicity, and that of escalating drug use). Elsewhere in the oeuvre other narratives may be traced; for example, salvation in various tracks on *The Velvet Underground* (1969), the possibility of obtaining this through music in 'Rock n' Roll', and the narrative that these trace through his career. Thus, a relatively synchronous narrative may be drawn that cuts through both albums and events. While this may not conform to the narrative that Reed implies, neither is it wholly arbitrary, given the relative fixity of the units themselves.

It is also possible to see narrative connections between songs in the order that they appear on the album. This is clearest in the more formally cohesive and deliberate of the albums, most obviously *Berlin* (1973), but also *The Velvet Underground*, with its 'conversational' structure, described in some detail by Reed and Bockris and Malanga in *Up Tight* (2002: 171–3). Yet it is in the less cohesive albums that one is most tempted to read the songs as distinct entities. In either approach, the quality of episodicity is present, though this is, if not necessarily a direct result of the structures of the pop song and album, surely influenced by them.

For Borges, the distinction between short story and novel is one between a focus on plot and a focus on character (1974: 46). It is easy to see that this is in some way due to the restrictions placed on the length, however arbitrary, of the short story. I will later discuss the evolution of character in 'the novel', but in terms of 'plot', a short story's narrative often tends to 'pivot' around a revelation; sometimes this is personal, such as the revelation of mortality, of 'becoming shades' at the end of Joyce's 'The Dead' (1914: 219). Obviously, there is a character element to this particular pivot, but its consequences are never seen. This structure may also be found in genre material: for example, the detective story in its common form usually ends with the perpetrator revealed. If this is the structure of 'The Gift', then its revelation to both reader and characters is cast against the slightly absurd progression of Waldo's narrative and the banality of the college-girl talk. It is a domestic comedy that suddenly turns into a horror story, the shock of which can only be diachronically experienced once; synchronically, its domesticity is tainted, in an ironic manner, by the rest of the album.

Bockris and Malanga suggest that 'The Gift' was possibly inspired by Shirley Jackson's 'The Lottery' (150). Both stories take a banal situation – hungover college girls talking about the previous night's revelry and something resembling a town meeting in Jackson's story – and at the very end inject an unexpected act of violence. However, I think that this reading is incomplete: at the end of 'The Gift', Waldo dies, completing the narrative, yet part of the horror of 'The Lottery' is that the reader only sees one instance of a repeating cycle: the lottery will continue indefinitely.

A novel

One of the novel's defining characteristics is its flexibility: it can absorb practically any form, and while it is stretching the medium to include recorded music, I think that this inclusion is possible partially due to the need to textualize non-textual material in order to talk about it in any meaningful way. This may be described as an act of *ekphrasis*, which in this case may be described as a verbal account of a non-verbal work of art. For example, in order to discuss the cover of *The Velvet Underground & Nico*, one must describe it verbally, for example, as a reflection of the clash of low and high art within.

William Burroughs, in an interview with Philippe Mikriammos (1984), described the hegemony of a highly limited form of novel:

> What we call the 'novel' is a highly artificial form, which came in the nineteenth century. It's quite as arbitrary as the sonnet. And that form had a beginning, a middle, and an end; it has a plot, and it has this chapter structure where you have one chapter, and then you try to leave the person in a state of suspense, and on to the next chapter, and people are wondering what happened to this person, and so forth. That nineteenth century construction has become stylised as the novel, and anyone who writes anything different from that is accused of being unintelligible. That form has imposed itself to the present time.

This notion of plot suggests that one is to see a relationship, relatively causal, between each separate chapter. This highlights one of the issues with examining the albums as discrete entities in that, as with the songs, a diachronic narrative progression is suggested though this is not absolutely necessary. One of the more interesting aspects of the progression of the Velvet Underground's albums is that there is a peculiar inversion of the narrative one familiarly finds in discussion of the transition from the 1960s to the 1970s. This transition is usually framed as one of a mythic loss of innocence: the idealism of the Summer of Love (1967) falling away in the aftermath of Altamont, the Manson murders (both 1969), etc.

Yet, broadly speaking, *The Velvet Underground & Nico* and *White Light/White Heat* (1968) are sonically abrasive and lyrically dark, and *The Velvet Underground* and *Loaded* (1970) are more obviously 'pop' and feature lyrics mainly about love and even redemption, as though innocence had been relearnt in the interim. There are a number of events that contributed to this shift, but the most obvious is the departure of John Cale, whose avant-garde tendencies certainly left their mark on the sound of the first two albums. Such material shifts affect the transition between albums rather more than equivalent events would affect the transition between chapters in a novel, but at bottom artistic agency both absorbs and reacts to such contingencies.

It may be argued that 'Sister Ray' marks both the end of the Cale cycle, its sonic apotheosis, and its strongest link to a specific novel, in its striking relationship to Selby Jr's *Last Exit to Brooklyn*. In Anthony Burgess' introduction, he describes the novel as though it were diagnosing a social problem, though it is difficult to see this in the novel itself, which at 'best' is indifferent to morality and at 'worst' decadently revels in the scenes it describes.¹ Burgess is cautious about describing *Last Exit* as a novel, since it is essentially a group of linked short stories, but concludes that

> there is a unity of intention as well as scene which makes the term 'novel' – implying a larger and more complex organisation than a mere story – altogether applicable. Selby ... presents his small fictional entities; as we continue reading these appear as segments of a larger whole; the final impression is of a planned symphony (orcacophony) which is as validly a novel as, say, *The Big Money*, or *Manhattan Transfer*.
>
> (xiv–xv)

Of course, much of this could be applied to Reed's work. The literary content of 'Sister Ray' is fairly obviously a melange of a number of elements found in *Last Exit to Brooklyn*: a group of military personnel (soldiers in *Last Exit*, sailors in 'Sister Ray') and drag queens assemble for a party involving sex, drugs and alcohol, and random acts of violence erupt in a matter-of-fact way. As Reed said of 'Sister Ray', 'It has eight characters in it and this guy gets killed and nobody does anything. The situation is a bunch of drag queens taking some sailors home with them, shooting up on smack and having this orgy when the police appear' (qtd. in Bockris and Malanga 2002: 151). This condenses the first two segments of *Last Exit*: 'Another Day Another Dollar''s fight with the soldiers, and the party scene of 'The Queen is Dead'. Of course, the theme of random violence runs through the entire novel, and it is dealt with in much the same way that Reed treats violence in 'Sister Ray': when Georgette is stabbed in the calf, the onlookers are said to have 'roared with laughter' (19). Another detail that connects the novel to the Reed oeuvre is Georgette's status as a 'hip queer', whose attitude stems from 'feeling intellectually and aesthetically superior to those (especially women) who weren't gay' (13). The tableau structure is especially visible in the final section of *Last Exit*, 'Landsend'; here the narrator moves camera-like from micro narrative to micro narrative, in a similar manner to that found in 'Sister Ray', as well as certain sections of John Dos Passos's *U.S.A.* (1938).² It is also this structure that bears most resemblance to Delmore Schwartz's best known story, 'In Dreams Begin Responsibilities' (1935), which features the narrator as if he were 'in a motion picture theatre' (3), unable, rather than unwilling, to affect the narrative.

In Reed's other stated novelistic influences, such as Raymond Chandler, Dostoevsky and Sacher-Masoch, the connections are slightly more oblique. Reed seems to have been influenced by Chandler's turn of phrase, 'like his line "That blonde was as attractive as a split lip." It's the visualization and the simplicity of the words' (Cott [1989] 2014), and he seems generally to have used *The Brothers Karamazov* as shorthand for 'serious literature' (though 'The Grand Inquisitor' section is a precursor to the short fictions that the Reed 'novel' contains). *Venus in Furs* (1870) obviously has titular and thematic resonance, but its relationship to the song seems quite tangential: the character of Severin is common to both, as is the image of 'ermine furs', but the most striking element is in the shift from first to second person, a tactic which fits the submissive nature of the protagonist, but which would be out of place in the novel, which is about that protagonist's experience.

While Burroughs' influence is mainly structural (his novels being 'one book', as he told Mikriammos) and spiritual, 'Lady Godiva's Operation' is an obvious descendant of his work, which is the result of a similar leap from 'Waiting for the Man' as the phantasmagoria found in *Naked Lunch* (1959) is from the dirty realism of *Junkie* (1953). The images of surgery and dissection in 'Lady Godiva' are close to the 'Benway' section of *Lunch* (19–31). However, this is not limited to subject matter: Jeremy Reed writes, it is 'a sort of cut-up narrative in which Reed and Cale scrambled alternate lines, fed by drone, sound[ing] like the first genuine attempt to apply Burroughs' literary collage method to rock music as raw, disjointed verbal energies' (50). Notably, Burroughs also had an interest in what he called 'wising up the marks', which could easily be equated to making them 'hip'.

There are also a number of texts in both the Reed 'canon' and the Great American Novel canon that bear a resemblance to one another. Dos Passos' *U.S.A.* has an episodic narrative, which is essentially a Finn-like picaresque in its 'Mac' sections. Saul Bellow's *The Adventures of Augie March* (1953), the title of which obviously alludes to the full titles of both *Huckleberry Finn* and *Tom Sawyer* (1876), is also a version of the benign *picaro*, its protagonist being a trickster without cruelty. It is in John Rechy's *City of Night* (1963), as well as in Burroughs, that one may see the return of the malignant *picaro*. In many ways Rechy's novel is a bildungsroman (a novel of formation) about the narrator's embrace of the sadistic aspect of his personality: at first he shrinks from inflicting pain upon masochists, before eventually coming to the realization that 'I could prove irrevocably to the hatefully initiating world that I could join its rot, its cruelty' (252). Similarly, the growth of the Reed persona as it appears in the narrative (detours such as the third and fourth Velvets records aside) I described may be seen to mirror this development.

A Great American Novel

The notion of the Great American Novel has been problematic from the moment that John William DeForest coined the term in 1868. DeForest's own definition ('The picture of the ordinary emotions and manners of American existence' and 'a tableau of American society') illustrates the issue since it is a description that could be applied to any number of American novels, 'Great' or otherwise. The waters are further muddied by the feedback loop of description and prescription: as soon as description arises, it affects those works that seek to inhabit the same space as that described. The second issue that problematizes attempts to define the Great American Novel stems from the fact that there is a group of novels that unimpeachably fall under that umbrella but are so different from each other that they confound all but the broadest of definitions.

Buell's (2014) solution to the problem of heterogeneity is quite ingenious: he constructs four 'scripts', which he then applies to exemplary sets of novels. The first of these scripts follows similar concerns to one I voiced earlier about novels (the example taken by Buell is *The Scarlet Letter*) which are unimpeachably Great American Novels, but which may not resemble those novels which later might so be called. While there is a resemblance between some of these novels (notably *Huckleberry Finn*) and Reed's Great American Novel, Reed's 'novel' itself does not fit this script.

The second script 'centres on the life story of a socially representative figure (conventionally male, but not necessarily so), who strives whether successfully or not to transform himself or herself from obscurity to prominence' (7). Since this script is concerned primarily with character, it is more or less relevant depending on one's willingness to view the whole of Reed's work as a larger bildungsroman of a figure nominally representing Lou Reed. The journey from being a middle-class Jewish kid to the often self-reflexively mythic figure of the 1970s through to sobriety before finally achieving the status of elder statesman is a familiar narrative arc, and one to whose familiarity Reed himself obviously contributed. Often, portrayals of such myths use a micro-level event (such as Reed's E.C.T. experience) as a 'pivot' in their narrative. Indeed, Bockris opens his biography with this event, and ties it explicitly to Reed's 'homosexual feelings and mood swings' (1). However, Reed's sister has recently disputed whether homosexuality had anything to do with the treatment he received (Reynolds 2016: 271). This need not diminish the potency of what Jeremy Reed has called Reed's 'perpetual-self mythology' (80), which is also tied to the narrative Reed attached to his parents and his treatment, as described in 'Kill Your Sons'. This narrative has always been somewhat fictionalized; as Cale noted in 1974, 'Every time Lou told me about [it] he'd change it slightly' (qtd. in Kent 1993: 169). Yet to acknowledge such myths as constructs is not to deny their relevance but rather to merely assert their contingency, that is, their status as one story among many. It may even be said that such qualities are an integral part of Reed's fictionalization of his own experience. Perhaps he, in what is now almost a cliché, told himself stories in order to live.

There is a useful philosophical angle from which to approach this issue. Ian Hacking's adaptation of G.E.M. Anscombe's notion of 'action under a description' is illustrated by the image of a man moving a lever up and down.

> He was manually pumping water into the cistern of the house. He was pumping poisoned water into the country house where evil men met for planning sessions. He was poisoning the men who met in the house. Certainly there were not distinct physical sequences of activities, moving the lever, pumping the water, poisoning the men. Should we, however, say that there was a number of distinct actions, pumping water, on the one hand, and poisoning the men, on the other?

Anscombe argued that there was just one action, under various descriptions. Each successive description of the action involves a larger range of circumstances, but only one intentional action is being described ([1957] 2000: 234).

So, one might say that committing Reed to an institution is one intentional action, but the parents' intent is just one description of that action in a narrow context. In the larger range of circumstances, it is unlikely that disquiet over his homosexual tendencies could be divorced from the reasons given by Merrill Reed. A clearer example is the act of recording *Metal Machine Music* (1975): Reed was baiting his fans; Reed was bringing about a serious contribution to avant-garde music, Reed was baiting his fans by making a serious contribution to avant-garde music, etc.

Hacking's other use of the notion of 'action under a description' is also applicable here: criminals, for Hacking, are 'interactive kinds'; 'that is, new knowledge about "the criminal" or "the homosexual" becomes known to the people classified, changes the way these people behave and loops back to force changes in the classifications and knowledge about them' (1999: 105). In this respect, Reed was both creating and following a script of what the behaviour of 'the rock star' might be. This 'looping' effect is best seen in the 'character' that Reed became in the 1970s. As Bockris (2014) writes, 'R.C.A. began to market Reed as "The Phantom of Rock". Ironically, this epithet underlined Lou's greatest weakness: he had fashioned himself in the image of what his English fans imagined he was – a sexy wolverine, homosexual junkie hustler, and advocate of S&M' (223).

The novels of the second script often concern 'Aspiration in America' (103), and may be classified as being in the tradition of the bildungsroman, which Buell (2014) defines as 'a novel of "development" or "formation" that charts the protagonist's growth from childhood to social maturity' (105). Buell also notes, 'Literature scholars rightly continue to stress the importance of its "soul-nation allegory", as Jed Etsy puts it' (107). The term 'allegory' here is important since both the Velvet Underground and Reed throughout the 1970s generally displayed a distinct lack of interest in current events. It is possible to see the narrative of the fall into drug addiction as following a similar trajectory in the biographies of any number of rock stars of the 1960s, and, of course, any one of these could be read in the same allegorical manner. However, if one takes one of the narratives enacted by Reed in the first half of his career to be the development of a form of *picaro* as an allegory for this transition, then the situation is rather more singular.

Buell's third script, 'Romancing the Divides', revolves mainly around the relationships between the marginalization of race and the division between North and South. The most relevant chapter of this section begins with this quotation:

> Well into the twentieth century, 'American Literature' and culture continued to be painted white despite growing evidence to the contrary. 'What the powerful and the privileged mean by Americanisation,' declared W.E.B. Dubois in 1922, is 'but a renewal of the Anglo-Saxon cult, the worship of the Nordic totem, the disenfranchisement of Negro, Jew, Irishman, Italian, Hungarian, Asiatic, and South Sea Islander.
>
> (286)

I discussed above the problematic narrative that arises if one explores the issue of Jewishness surrounding Reed. Raised in the Jewish tradition, as well as being ethnically Jewish, Reed, according to Bockris (2014), on several occasions straightened his hair while at Syracuse in an attempt to disguise his Jewishness (28). There is also issue of the antisemitism in which he occasionally indulged. Reed's journalist friend Ed McCormack recalled, 'He hated Dylan. I once said to Lou, "Dylan's the only genius in your field," ... He said, "You mean you actually like that pretentious kike?"' (qtd. in Sounes 2015: 220). To take this disavowal in terms of inter-song narrative, the identification as white in 'Waiting for the Man' carries over to 'I Wanna Be Black', in which 'the Jews' get 'fuck[ed] up' and the speaker instead aligns himself with the white college kid. Buell's concentration is on race and ethnicity, but there is also the issue of the marginalized homosexual at play in Reed's work; Bockris also writes of Reed's vacillation between acceptance and disavowal of this element of himself. This narrative differs, however, from discussions of race and ethnicity in that its 'normalization' of the marginalized is quite radical. As Reed told *Rolling Stone*, 'My gay people don't lisp. They're not any more affected than the straight world. They just *are*' (qtd. in Sounes 2015: 220, italics in the original).

The final script posited by Buell, 'Improbable Communities', and its concern with 'meganovels' (2014: 349), is perhaps the most obviously applicable to Reed's work, given the compendious nature of the oeuvre. Buell takes as his examples *Moby-Dick* (1851), Dos Passos's *U.S.A.* trilogy and Thomas Pynchon's *Gravity's Rainbow* (1973). All three of these novels are large in volume, panoramic in scope and episodic in nature: *Moby-Dick* in the Pequod's pursuit of the whale and incidental chapters about whaling, *U.S.A.* in its tracking of various characters and incidental 'Camera Eye' and 'Newsreel' sections and *Gravity's Rainbow* with its fractured narrative separated (arguably) by film perforations, their lack of causal connection underlined by the novel's refusal to distinguish fantasy from 'reality'.

There is perhaps another way of talking about the Great American Novel, and that is Wittgenstein's conception of 'family resemblance' (1968, Section 66). Wittgenstein here posits that rather than one trait uniting a group, there may be a series of overlapping qualities that bring them together. Since both *Huckleberry Finn* and Reed's own 'novel' share picaresque characteristics, and *Huckleberry Finn* shares a similar time frame and the racial concerns that go with it with *Beloved* (1987), one could subsume the quite different texts of Reed and Morrison under the same umbrella. In this way, one could bring both the picaresque novels, such as Rechy's, that I have argued share traits with some Great American Novels, and Reed's oeuvre itself into the Great American Novel family. This may also be seen, in some ways, to be related to the issues of Buell's first script.

If Reed's unity of place is New York, then one could posit that the oeuvre is the tracking of the same city through the late twentieth century. However, it is also about the evolution of an artist and persona from naif to *picaro* and frozen observer to elder statesman, though, as I have argued, this is simply one of number of narratives that may be traced.

Reed's comments about having written the Great American Novel come largely from a period in the late 1980s and early 1990s, a period in which he seems to have been thinking seriously about his place in the world, and perhaps his legacy. He was even capitalizing on his image: his appearance in an advertisement for Honda scooters would have been unthinkable in the 1970s. A number of my quotations come from the promotion of *New York* (1989), an album that is as outward-looking and concerned with the world as those of the Velvet Underground are insular and removed: many of the band's songs take place in an apolitical underworld of sex and drugs and, in the case of Reed's preferred version of *The Velvet Underground* (1969), were produced as if recorded in a literal closet. Composed in one of the most tumultuous periods in American history, the Velvet Underground's songs find little room for social or political commentary. *New York*, on the other hand, refers to the AIDS crisis ('Halloween Parade'), the housing problem ('Dirty Boulevard') and the even state of the environment ('The Last Great American Whale'). As if to underline this panoramic view, it also includes its own reference to *Moby-Dick* ('The Last Great American Whale', again).

If at this confluence of circumstance Reed speaks of his oeuvre as a Great American Novel, then it comes with a reading of what that label really means. If the material of the Velvet Underground and the decade afterwards owes much to the episodic nature and cruelty of the picaresque, then this later reading appears to view the Great American Novel as a form that should speak to matters of macro-historical relevance, which is to say the moving from the micro-tableau I described earlier to the macro 'tableau of American society' upon which DeForest partly based his definition. The Great American Novel on occasion actually features historically significant people, as in E.L. Doctorow's *Ragtime* (1976), and the opening of Don Delillo's *Underworld* (1997). It is therefore notable that the protagonist of the picaresque *Augie March* actually sees Trotsky in Mexico, but the novel denies him this potentially significant brush with history (431-2). Thus when Reed begins to take in historical figures ('The Day John Kennedy Died') it is part of a narrative moving towards this kind of 'significance'.

It is, then, possible to construct a 'script' that emphasizes both the picaresque and episodic nature of many American novels, and to both recontextualize and add these novels, and therefore Reed's, to the canon. Unlike many other modern *picaros*, the Reed persona actually reaches the point of respectability, and in many ways the evolution of the Reed persona comprises a script which traces the Great American Novel from picaresque to the historical tableau it later becomes, in an echo of DeForest's original definition.

Notes

1   The book had been banned in the UK, and this defence is understandable given these circumstances.
2   It should also be noted that at one point a character reads Edgar Allen Poe's 'The Raven', given that Reed later recorded an album based on this work.

References

Algren, N. ([1956] 1999), *A Walk on the Wild Side*, Edinburgh: Rebel Inc.
Alpert, M. (1969), *Two Spanish Picaresque Novels: Lazarillo De Tormes; the Swindler (El Buscon)*, London: Viking.

Anscombe, G. E. M. ([1957] 2000), *Intention*, Cambridge, MA and London: Harvard.
Bangs, L., Gaiman, N. et al (2015), *Lou Reed: The Last Interview and other Conversations*, London: Melville House.
Bataille, G. ([1928] 2001), *Story of the Eye*, trans. J. Neugroschel, London: Penguin.
Bellow, S. ([1953] 1995), *The Adventures of Augie March*, London: Everyman.
Bockris, V. (2014), *Transformer: The Complete Lou Reed Story*, London: Harper.
Bockris, V. and Malanga, G. (2002), *Up-Tight: The Velvet Underground Story*, London: Omnibus.
Borges, J. L. (1974), *Borges on Writing*, ed. N. T. Di Giovanni, D. Halpern and F. MacShane, London: Allen Lane.
Buell, L. (2014), *The Dream of the Great American Novel*, Cambridge, MA: Harvard.
Burroughs, W. S. ([1957] 1966), *Junkie*, London: New English Library.
Burroughs W. S. ([1959] 2005), *Naked Lunch: The Restored Text*, London: Harper.
Burroughs, W. S. ([1961] 2001), *The Soft Machine*, London: Flamingo.
Burroughs, W. S. ([1962] 2001), *The Ticket that Exploded*, London: Flamingo.
Burroughs, W. S. ([1964] 1992), *Nova Express*, New York: Grove.
Castiglione, B. ([1528] 1976), *The Book of the Courtier*, trans. George Bull, Harmondsworth, Middx.: Penguin.
Cott, J. ([1989] 2014), 'Lou Reed: New York State of Mind', *Rolling Stone*. Available online: https://bit.ly/3KKX0mU (accessed 1 December 2021).
Cunliffe, M. (1964), *The Literature of the United States*, Harmondsworth, Middx.: Penguin.
Day, G. (1987), *From Fiction to the Novel*, London and New York: Routledge.
De Cervantes, M. ([1615] 2004), *Don Quixote*, trans. E. Grossman, London: Random House.
DeForest, J. W. (1868), 'The Great American Novel', *The Nation*, 9 January. Available online: https://bit.ly/3G35Rwr (accessed 1 December 2021).
De Tormes, L. ([1554] 1969), *Two Spanish Picaresque Novels*, trans. M. Alpert, Harmondsworth, Middx.: Penguin.
Delillo, D. (1997), *Underworld*, London: Picador.
Dinerstein, J. (2017), *The Origins of Cool in Post-War America*, Chicago and London: Chicago University.
Doctorow, E. L. ([1976] 1985), *Ragtime*, London: Picador.
Dos Passos, J. ([1938] 1966), *U.S.A.*, Harmondsworth, Middx.: Penguin.
Flaubert, G. ([1856] 1992), *Madame Bovary*, London: Penguin.
Gaiman, N. (1992), 'Waiting for the Man - Lou Reed' [interview], *Reflex*, 26, July. Available online: https://bit.ly/3Mt7aZg (accessed 26 April 2022).
Hacking, I. (1995), *Rewriting the Soul: Multiple Personalities and the Sciences of Memory*, Princeton, NJ: Princeton University.
Hacking, I. (1999), *The Social Construction of What?*, Cambridge, MA: Harvard University.
Hawthorne, N. ([1850] 1950), *The Scarlet Letter*, New York: Modern Library.
Herman, D. (ed.) (2007), *The Cambridge Companion to Narrative*, Cambridge: Cambridge University.
Hibbert, T. (1989), 'Growing up in Public', *Q*, 29, February: 32-6.
Huysmans, J. K. ([1884] 2009), *Against Nature*, trans. M. Mauldon, ed. N. White, Oxford: Oxford University.

Jackson, S. (1948), 'The Lottery', in R. Ford (ed.) (1993), *The Granta Book of the American Short Story*, London: Granta.
Joyce, J. ([1914] 1956), *Dubliners*, Hardmonsworth, Mddx.: Penguin.
Kent, N. (1993), *The Dark Stuff: The Best of Nick Kent*, Harmonsworth, Mddx.: Penguin.
Melville, H. ([1851] 1991), *Moby-Dick*, New York: Library of America.
Mikriammos, P. (1984), 'A Conversation with William Burroughs by Phillipe Mikriammos', *The Review of Conaatemporary Fiction*, 4 (1). Available online: https://bit.ly/33R1jfG (accessed 3 May 2018).
Morrison, T. ([1987] 2004), *Beloved*, London: Vintage.
Petronius ([c. 1st Century A.D.] 1974), *The Satyricon*, trans. J. P. Sullivan, Harmondsworth, Middx.: Penguin.
Pynchon, T. (1973), *Gravity's Rainbow*, London: Picador.
Rechy, J. ([1963] 2009), *City of Night*, London: Souvenir.
Reed, J. (2014), *Waiting for the Man: The Life and Music of Lou Reed*, London: Omnibus.
Reed, L. (1966), 'The View from the Bandstand', *Aspen*, No. 3. Available online: https://bit.ly/3IFwt8I (accessed 26 January 2022).
Reed, L. (1993), *Between Thought and Expression: Selected Lyrics*, Harmondsworth, Middx.: Penguin.
Reed, L. (2008), *Pass Thru Fire: The Collected Lyrics*, Cambridge, MA: Da Capo.
Reynolds, S. (2016), *Shock and Awe: Glam Rock and Its Legacy from the Seventies to the Twenty-First Century*, London: Faber and Faber.
Sacher-Masoch, L. ([1870] 2000), *Venus in Furs*, trans. Joachim Neugroschel, Harmondsworth, Middx.: Penguin.
Sade, Marquis de ([1904] 1990), *The One Hundred and Twenty Days of Sodom*, No credited translator, London: Arrow.
Selby Jr., H. ([1964] 1987), *Last Exit to Brooklyn*, London: Paladin.
Schwartz, D. ([1935] 2012), 'In Dreams Begin Responsibilities', in *In Dreams Begin Responsibilities and other Stories*, 1–9, New York: New Directions.
Sounes, H. (2015), *Lou Reed: Notes from the Velvet Underground*, London: Transworld.
Symons, A. ([1899] 2014), *The Symbolist Movement in Literature*, ed. Matthew Creasy, London: Carcanet.
Twain, M. ([1876] 2018), *The Adventures of Tom Sawyer*, London: Collins.
Twain, M. ([1885] 1966), *The Adventures of Huckleberry Finn*, ed. Peter Coveney, Harmondsworth, Middx.: Penguin.
Updike, J. (1995), *Rabbit Angstrom: A Tetralogy*, New York: Everyman.
Watt, I. (1966), *The Rise of the Novel*, Harmondsworth, Middx.: Penguin.
Wittgenstein, L. (1968), *Philosophical Investigations*, Oxford: Basil Blackwell.
Zak, A. (ed.) (1997), *The Velvet Underground Companion: Four Decades of Commentary*, London: Omnibus.

7

Nico, captain of her own ship: Cultural accreditation and mid-1960s experimental rock

Mimi Haddon

In her 1995 documentary titled *Nico Icon*, the film-maker Susanne Ofteringer uses the idea of transformation as her opening narrative hook. Following some voiceover excerpts of Nico's friends and associates that allude to her enigmatic persona, Ofteringer jumps forward in both soundtrack and footage using shots of Nico doing her hair as the fulcrum: we see a Velvets-era Nico cutting her fringe accompanied by the song 'Femme Fatale' (1967) and then a much older-looking Nico at first fixing her hair and then singing – live, deliriously and with a deathly stare – the song 'Sixty/Forty' from her fifth solo album *Drama of Exile* (1981). Paul Morrissey's voice accompanies this shift, 'An icon?', he says, 'You could say a freak, too. From being so beautiful she became a kind of freak act' (*Nico Icon* 1995). And thus, the story of Nico: from blonde *femme fatale* with the aura of an untouchable ice queen to unkempt brunette with an unseemly drug habit and thoroughly niche musical appeal with only vanity as the thread between the two.

This introductory portrait of Nico is significant for the fact that appears not only in Ofteringer's documentary but in several critical accounts of Nico and her music. As I'll discuss, the music press juxtaposed an image of Nico as an alluring, European enigma with depictions of her as abject – the faded beauty, the alcoholic, the junkie, the bad mother. Yet this narrative of Nico the 'fallen woman' fails to capture the continuities between one Nico and the next. Nor does it account for the complexity of Nico's musical output, especially her solo music, within the broader context of post-mid-1960s rock. Nico, reflecting on her artistic and personal desires as she embarked on her solo career in an August 1965 *Record Mirror* feature, just months before joining the Velvet Underground, enigmatically stated that 'if I wasn't modelling or singing, I think I'd like to be a farmer, or possibly captain of a ship' (qtd. in Jones 1965). This chapter therefore offers a detailed history of the reception of Nico's music from 1965 to

---

Special thanks to Vanessa Blais-Tremblay, David Brackett, Michael Lawrence, Barbara Lebrun and the editors of this collection for their helpful comments on earlier drafts of this chapter.

1985, paying particular attention to the emergence of Nico's artistic persona, with her increasingly acting as captain of her own ship. It will also consider this emergence in parallel with the eclecticism and avant-gardism of mid-1960s rock as well as the way, up until her death, Nico continued to frustrate critics' insistence that she conform to an early 1960s aesthetic of desirable femininity.

Frame: Beautiful, unmusical, other[1]

In several accounts of Nico's role in the Velvet Underground, she is framed as someone who was foisted on the band. For example, in an article in *Mojo* magazine from the late 1990s, the music journalist Johnny Black depicts Nico as an unwanted accessory, someone who was beautiful but lacking in musical skill, the 'price to pay' for Warhol's patronage. Black writes, 'The Velvet Underground without Nico had become New York's hottest new rock ticket' but Andy Warhol only agreed to fund the band's album on the condition that they made Nico their vocalist (Black 1997).[2] According to Black, the Velvet Underground's reasons for resisting Nico's admission included the 'perforated eardrum' that 'made her deaf in one ear' and meant 'she would often lose control of her vocals', and her idiosyncratic singing style. Sterling Morrison described her vocals as having two modalities: 'a full-register, Germanic gotterdammerung [*sic*] voice', which he disliked, and 'her wispy voice', which he preferred (Black 1997). Thus, Black's introduction of the Velvet Underground as hot *without* Nico accompanied by the band members' observations regarding her musicianship frame Nico as an interloper, an outsider, an Other: she was 'strikingly beautiful' but lacked musicality and wasn't 'rock "n" roll' (Black 1997).

The idea that Nico was at once beautiful, unmusical and Other gives rise to a significant discursive trine that underscores Nico's overall 'freakery'; it is a transgression, a disappointment, perhaps, that her voice should be so low and booming rather than pleasingly 'wispy'. While drummer Moe Tucker's tomboyish lack of glamour perhaps meant she could 'pass' as one of the boys, Nico's earlier work as a model and actor may have compounded expectations that her musicality should conform to or align with the 'beauty' of her appearance. Indeed, the media scholar Gary Needham suggests that some of Nico's film work serves as an important nodal point in her transformation from 'the cheerful fashion ingénue' of her modelling years and in her appearance in Federico Fellini's *La dolce vita* (1960) to the aloof, glamorously joy-less ice queen she was associated with in the Velvet Underground and thereafter. Needham points specifically to Nico's performance in Jacques Poitrenaud's film *Strip-tease* (released in Europe in 1963) and argues that Nico's lack of sexiness in her strip-tease in the film can be read 'reflexively' as resistance against being sexually objectified, and that her 'doll-like woodenness and refusal to be sexy, anticipates the reviews of her later career and comments made by others' (Needham 2016: 131).

Needham's argument is interesting for the way it identifies the theme of resistance in Nico's persona, but Needham doesn't sufficiently problematize Nico's agency in his analysis. While Nico's wooden strip-tease in Poitrenaud's film certainly stages resistance, her performance is not necessarily sui generis and may participate in broader cinematic convention. Her character's awkwardness might, for example, be put in dialogue with strip-teases in near-contemporary films, such as Brigitte Bardot's performance in *En Effeuillant la Marguerite* (1956), where the club audience's enjoyment hinges on what they infer as her staged and comic incompetence, and the uncertain will-she/won't-she drama of the final reveal. Nico's boredom and disconnected-ness in *Strip-tease* similarly resonate with Anna Karina's Brechtian cabaret in Jean-Luc Godard's *Une femme est une femme* (1961), which suggests that such reluctance to be 'sexy' is not specific to Nico.[3]

Nevertheless, the Poitrenaud's film-as-text might foreshadow Nico's resistance towards, estrangement from and undermining of an aesthetics of desirable femininity, and this is something that is amplified by the film's music. The track to which Nico performs her 'strip-tease' – titled 'Some Small Change' – offers little in the way of continuity between early Nico and her later incarnations. But *Strip-tease*'s title song, by Serge Gainsbourg and Alain Goraguer, not only supports Needham's observation that certain aspects of Nico's performance in this film provide a transitional stage from ingenue Nico to joy-less ice queen but also stages Nico as a figure of resistance, and therefore inadvertently pre-empts the creative agency and independent 'voice' associated with her post-Velvet's music. The song 'Strip-tease' has morbid lyrics characteristic of Gainsbourg's other work, and these are accompanied by 'exotic' signifiers in the musical arrangement. This combination produces both the 'glamour of anti-joy' comparable with Factory Nico and the Velvet Underground, and an emergent 'voice' for Nico's artistic persona, one characterized by a resistance towards being objectified and, more radically, a rebellion against her own 'beauty' as owned and projected by the male critical gaze.

Although the film's accompanying EP did not feature Nico, she did demo the track and it is notable for the way it partakes in the long-standing traditions of musical exoticism and eroticism with chromatic reed instruments (saxophones in this case) and 'exotic' hand-percussion. Furthermore, true to the 'impassive coldness' and 'elegantly formulated nihilism' of Gainsbourg's work (Hawkins 2000: 159, 163), the lyrics convey the possible tedium, disengagement and aloofness of the strip-tease act, with an inner monologue employing the metaphor of a plant or tree that repeatedly and disinterestedly sheds its leaves each night.[4] In Nico's demo, the combination of her deadpan vocal performance, the lyrical *ennui* and the kitschy instrumentation seems to presage Velvet Underground songs such as 'Femme Fatale' in a way that supports the idea that this 'text' – Poitrenaud's *Strip-tease* – connects Nico's ingénue actor persona and her Factory persona. Indeed, *chanson* analyst Peter Hawkins even suggests that Gainsbourg's particular brand of irony 'was perhaps inspired by a similar ironic minimalism' of the Velvet Underground (Hawkins 2000: 163). Furthermore, Nico's inner monologue and estrangement from being a figure of 'beauty' presage the kind of resistant 'voice' that comes to fruition in her post-Velvets solo music.

Accounts of Nico's disarming beauty inflect the music press reception of her first solo single, 'I'm Not Sayin', released on Immediate Records in May 1965. Like her recording of the title track for *Strip-tease*, this song is another transitional point in Nico's shift from actor to singer, from ingénue to abject. The Rolling Stones' manager Andrew Loog Oldham owned the label and, according to Nico's biographer Richard Witts (2006), her recording of 'I'm Not Sayin'' was a result of her brief affair with Brian Jones while in London in 1964 (40–1). In an article on the single in *Record Mirror* from 28 August 1965, Nico's striking appearance is the frame. The writer Peter Jones opens by describing Nico as looking 'a shade like Ursula Andress' with her 'long-flowing blonde hair'; he concludes the article by saying he'd be 'keeping a close eye on Nico' – presumably both her and her music (Jones 1965).

However, sandwiched between these comments on her appearance (which, as I'll discuss, recur throughout her career) we're given an impression of Nico as a musician and a sense of her artistic persona. Jones is struck first by the seemingly alternative femininity offered by Nico's voice: 'Nico tackles a good song with a good big voice; an antidote to the current rash of girls who whisper fearfully through folksey lyrics' (Jones 1965). We might infer from Jones' comments about the 'rash of girls who whisper' that he is thinking of performers such as Marianne Faithful singing 'As Tears Go By', another Oldham-associated track released in June 1964. Nico's unusually 'good big voice' at this time could be connected to her own musical interests and listening habits. In the interview, Nico says Bob Dylan was the 'biggest influence on [her] career' at the time and that Nina Simone was one of her favourite singers (Jones 1965). Thus, Jones' article and interview with Nico highlight her deviance from convention from the very start of her musical career: her voice was both exciting ('good' and 'big') and may have acted as a citation of the voices to whom she was listening. Furthermore, and perhaps more significantly, Jones' review alludes to what kinds of musical performance were permissible or legible for one's body, gender and race in 1965; that this 'big' voice emerges from Nico's white European female body is perhaps a transgression and, like *Strip-tease*, another early step on her journey to 'freakery'.

In addition to perhaps citing Dylan and Simone in her unusually 'big' voice, across her musical career Nico drew on other musical influences from a range of genres and backgrounds. In accounts of her musical influences written sometime after Jones' 1965 article, Nico cites the following important figures: Iggy Pop; Patti Smith; Jim Morrison, who Nico described as a soul brother, someone who 'gave [her] permission to be a writer' and encouraged her to compose poems and songs (Witts 1993: 186); Ornette Coleman, who advised her on writing her own music (Dadomo 1978); and Chet Baker, whose version of 'My Funny Valentine' she performed while singing at New York City's Blue Angel[5] in the mid-1960s (Witts 1993: 91) and recorded for the 1985 album *Camera Obscura*.

Recalling Jones' comments about Nico's 'good big voice', one of the most striking things about Nico's 1985 recording of 'My Funny Valentine' is the pitch at which she sings the song. Nico performs in the same key (C minor) and at the same tessitura as Baker, which means that the lowest note is the C an octave below middle C and the highest is the E flat above middle C. While not unusual for a high baritone like Baker, this range is unusually low for a woman; or, perhaps more strikingly, their two voices share a vocal range that is of ambiguous gender. The song's lyrics about an awkward lover, with a 'figure less than Greek' and a lack of smarts, are appropriately ironic for two conventionally beautiful cultural icons of the 1950s whose lives unravelled in part as a result of addiction, especially Nico, whose German pronunciation and forceful vibrato make for a 'sweet comic' melancholy. Furthermore, Nico's imitation of Baker is another illustration of the kinds of musical fields from which she was borrowing and it contributes to our hearing of her 'big voice'; is Nico citing Baker's baritone in 'My Funny Valentine'?

My suggestion that Nico may have been citing Baker, and perhaps Dylan and Simone in her early musical work, is important for the way it stages her relationship to her musical influences, particularly those who are male. In his review of Ofteringer's documentary, Archie Patterson (2012) highlights how Nico rolled naked with Morrison, was lovers with Jackson Browne and was romantically involved with both Iggy Pop and Lou Reed. Nico's relationship to male artists is ambiguous terrain. On the one hand, Nico asserts her attractiveness to men in interviews, relishes rejecting them and downplays their artistic achievements; she famously rebuffed Leonard Cohen, for example. On the other hand, cultural gatekeepers have implied that Nico's male lovers played an integral role in shaping her career and that she thrived only because of their creativity. The relationship with Jones might be taken as the context or even pretext for both 'I'm Not Sayin'' and her introduction to Warhol's Factory in November 1965 (Witts 2006: 40). Furthermore, the songs on her 1967 baroque-folk or chamber-folk album *Chelsea Girl* were written by Tim Hardin, Jackson Browne and Bob Dylan – the latter two were apparently former lovers. Cale, Reed and Morrison are credited as songwriters here too.

This tendency to refer to Nico's male lovers, and to emphasize their creativity, not only detracts from her agency but recalls the familiar rockist trope, that all truly creative artists must write their own songs. A good example of this kind of gatekeeping and journalists' tendency to credit male songwriters is Cynthia Rose's review of a Nico concert in London in the *NME* in 1983. It is striking for its cruelty, for its criticism of Nico's seeming betrayal of her 'beauty' and for the way it attributes her songwriting skills to others – Rose states inaccurately that Nico's songs were 'of course written by other people and always, of course by men' (Rose 1983). She writes as well that there was

> something unbearably pathetic about a once-beautiful woman, now around 40, conducting a public search for some vestige of her former self, in front of a bunch of pretentious kids armed with guitars, sax and drumkit ... every phrase Nico sang or mumbled took on an irony that might have been awful if it hadn't by now become so truly banal. There she stood, intoning 'All Tomorrow's Parties' in a voice an octave deeper but with no increase in its three-or-so note range – wearing her own 'hand-me-down gown' of sheepskin coat, sloppy black polyester pantsuit and cowboy boots.
>
> (Rose 1983)

Rose's review is a merciless but nevertheless useful summary of much of what I have discussed so far in terms of Nico's musical persona. In her criticism, Rose cites: (1)

Nico's reliance on men (and perhaps male lovers) to write her songs; (2) her purported lack of musical ability ('three-or-so note range'), which echoes comments about her unwelcome-ness in the Velvet Underground; (3) her unusual voice, 'an octave deeper' now; (4) her inability to stay convincingly current with either fashion or music; and (5) an insistent emphasis on her appearance and, specifically here, her inability to age well ('a once-beautiful women, now around 40'). This last observation about Rose's emphasis on Nico's appearance can be traced across the reception of Nico's career. (Male) reviewers from the 1970s onwards highlight a tension between Nico's ability to sustain her allure against process of ageing. Nick Kent (1974), in the *NME*, remarked that her 'face and form [had] lost a lot over the years – almost haunted more than haunting these days, even though the occasional profile flashed against a certain light can set the hairs on the neck a-bristling still'. Giovanni Dadomo (1978), in *Sounds*, wrote, 'Time's tugged at the corner of her eyes a little but she's still a strikingly beautiful woman' and she's as 'enchantingly unique' in person as she is on record. And, as Nico arrived at the concert venue for a performance in Cincinnati, Richard Riegel (1980), writing for *Creem*, charmingly felt his '(appendages) standing on end'.

Thus, taken one way, Nico's appearance has functioned as a frame for her artistic output across her career. Jones in *Record Mirror* in August 1965 planned to keep an 'eye on Nico' and her Ursula Andress looks, and here in the *NME* in 1983, Nico is reduced to 'a once-beautiful woman'. This emphasis on attractiveness and relationships with male artists has in some ways underwritten Nico's musical skills and approach to performance and composition. However, running contrary to some of the more pernicious reception of her music that emphasizes or indeed imagines her many love affairs, I suggest that Nico sought male allies and influences such as Morrison and Coleman in order to be like – or sound like – them, rather than to 'love' or be around them. It seems telling, for example, that towards the very end of Ofteringer's documentary, Nico tells an interviewer that her 'only regret' was that she was 'born a woman instead of a man'.

As I indicated earlier, we might understand perceptions of Nico's persona as 'freakish' or a 'freak act' as underscored by the discursive trine as beautiful, unmusical and Other. This final thread, Nico's Otherness, is rooted to some extent in her European identity and its connotations, which include a real or presumed closer linkage to Western art – and even ancient musical practices. Indeed, as much as Nico was influenced by Coleman, Dylan, Morrison and Simone, she also claimed to enjoy Western classical music. In fact, in 1978 she stated that she listened *exclusively* to classical music and had 'very conventional' taste (Nico qtd. in Dadomo 1978). And in terms of reception, Richie Unterberger (n.d.) has suggested that Nico's 1968 album *The Marble Index* owes more to 'European classical and folk music than rock'. In the liner notes for the 1991 reissue of *The Marble Index*, Richard Williams (1991) describes the music as being the first of Nico's albums to 'abandon conventional structures and instrumentation' and that it was 'really the work of two European sensibilities'.[6]

It is worth noting that such references to Western art music went further than *The Marble Index*. Witts (1993) notes how her 1971 album *Desertshore* was compared to the Gustav Mahler revival of the 1960s (252). In addition to the Western art music connotations evidenced here, critics also compared Nico's music with medieval, liturgical or ecclesiastical music. Dalton (2002) writes of Nico's 'Transylvanian voice' on *The Marble Index* and that 'words mutate into tonal shapes where meaning is overridden by archaic rhythms' and refers to Nico and Cale's modern approach to 'medieval modes'. These references to Western art music practices and so-called medieval music raise two issues. On the one hand, they rely on assumptions and mistakes about Nico's biography and identity, often prompted by the ambiguities and false claims Nico propagated. On the other hand, they are reasonable responses to the sound of her music.

Regarding the first issue, Nico's European-ness alone perhaps connoted the old-world, primarily Austro-Germanic tradition of so-called 'serious' music or Eastern European folk musics. In addition to stressing how conventionally attractive she was, journalists often commented on Nico's German-ness. In this regard, Nico's embodiment of post-war German femininity finds a significant predecessor in the German actor and singer Hildegard Knef, whom Witts (1993) says was an early model for Nico, and who modelled her voice on Zarah Leander, described by Witts as the 'Nazi version' of Marlene Dietrich (38–41). Significantly, many of the framing devices journalists employed for Nico resonate with performances by and representations of Knef in post-war German cinema. In her work on post-war European cinema, Ulrike Sieglohr suggests that representations of women in films of that era often responded to, or were in dialogue with, the status of the particular country at that time. In post-war Germany, then, so-called *Trümmerfrauen* (rubble women) were important figures. These were the women 'who cleared the debris from the ruins of bombed-out towns and cities' and might be depicted living amongst Berlin's ruins as in films such as *Zwischen Gestern und Morgen*, which starred Knef (Sieglohr 2000: 113–17). Such images of Nico's alleged predecessor stalking a collapsed Berlin are (unconsciously) resurrected in criticism that describes Nico's compositional landscapes thus: 'not unlike Berlin ... desolate and wind-blown, scarred yet futuristic' (Micklo qtd. in Witts 1993: 230). And Nico's own words about Berlin seem to convey the same sense of desolation: 'dead bodies lying in the rubble as I walked through the wilderness at the end of the street where we live' (Nico qtd. in Witts 1993: 19).

Such images of post-war Germany as the destroyed 'old world' (*vis* US rock 'n' roll) or the *femme fatale* enemy perhaps inflected critics' tendency to hear Western art music influences in her music and to 'make sense' of her eccentricity within the Anglo-American pop soundscape. However, it is undeniable that the sound of her music invites such descriptions as well, and, as we've seen, Nico cited Western art music as an influence. On *The Marble Index*, for example, Nico uses harmonium backed by Cale's arrangements using a mix of acoustic and electronic instruments. Cale's background as well as training in Western art music complements Nico's untrained instinctive musicality, thus forging an arresting figure-ground relationship that is best exemplified on tracks such as 'Ari's Song'. On other tracks from *The Marble Index* we hear unaccompanied recitation-like melodies with lyrics that refer to nature and mythology. There's also a marked absence of rhythmic groove, which would seem to coincide with music by near-contemporary German progressive rock bands.[7] The reedy sound of the harmonium, with it sonic similarity to the organ, coupled with the a-rhythmic nature of her melodies might explain comments such as this, where one critic suggested she sounded like 'Hildegard of Bingen singing mystic hymns from an interior Middle Ages' (Dalton 2002).

'Ari's Song' is an effective example of Nico's recitation-like approach to composition, since all of the phrases close on the same note (B flat), giving the feeling of a modal final. 'Ari's Song' also employs characteristics of Western classical common practice, such as the 5–1 descent (from F to B flat) that concludes the song. In order to produce drama in otherwise very sparse textures, Nico sometimes mixes modes. In the unaccompanied version of 'Nibelungun', for example, in G natural minor she sharpens E from E flat for the words 'strike the alarm'. And in terms of arrangement, Cale's strings on 'No One Is There', are remarkably redolent of other 1960s Western art music such as Luciano Berio's *Folk Songs* arranged in 1964 that include 'Black Is the Colour of My True Love's Hair' and 'I Wonder as I Wander' arranged for the American singer Cathy Berberian.

Nico's inclination towards a non-rock compositional style that alludes to Western art- or folk music practices thus contributes to her outsider status in the context of both mid-1960s rock and to some extent the Velvet Underground. This outsider status or Otherness is reinforced by her non-US (or even non-Anglo-American) background, which fuses with her appearance, unusual approach to rhythm and her unconventional voice to produce a persistent discursive trine that has, to date, tended to frame Nico's musical artistry.

Excess: Resistance and accreditation

By taking into account some of her influences and thinking through the musical comparisons that critics made, rather than view Nico as an outsider, it becomes clear that her solo music, in particular, was very much in dialogue with the broader cultural trends of the mid-1960s, which tended towards eclecticism and experimentation. In fact, 'medieval-ness' was more widespread than the critics' reception of Nico's music would appear to suggest. Nico's label-mate Judy Collins included, for example, a performance of a fourteenth-century piece, 'A Ballatta of Francesco Landini – Lasso! Di Donna' alongside tracks by Leonard Cohen such as 'Sisters of Mercy' and 'Hey, That's No Way to Say Goodbye' on her 1967 album *Wildflowers*, which might be effectively compared to Nico's *Chelsea Girl*. What is curious, then, is Witts' (1993) assertion that most critics agreed that Nico's solo music of the late 1960s was 'weird' (226). Indeed, 1968's *The Marble Index* didn't sell well when it was first released. Danny Fields jokingly suggested that it sold 'three and a half copies' and asserted in 2002 that it remains inaccessible for many listeners 'today' (see Fields in Dalton 2002), and in 1970 *Melody Maker* referred to Nico as 'the High Priestess of Weird' (Williams 1970).

According to Dalton, part of Nico's 'weirdness' stems from the shift in persona outlined at the beginning of this chapter. Dalton wrote that Nico's first solo album *Chelsea Girl* fitted critics' image of her as 'haute couture model warbling ballads in a chilling voice' (Dalton 2002) but *The Marble Index* was too much of a departure from that image. Importantly, Nico's friend Danny Fields suggested that *Chelsea Girl* wasn't the 'real Nico'; it was rather a 'Judy Collins-ish approach' to music by Browne, Dylan and Hardin (Dalton 2002), and *The Marble Index* thus represents the emergence of Nico's independent artistic voice.

Dalton rightly situates the experimental sound of *The Marble Index* amidst 'all sorts of modes' such as 'jazz, ragas, Stockhausen, and Yoko' (Dalton 2002) and, I would add, the 'classical' experiments of the Beatles and Procol Harum as well as the folk experimentation of the Incredible String Band, Syd Barrett, Kevin Ayres, Nick Drake, the Fairport Convention, Collins and German progressive rock. Furthermore, John Cale's experience with the Fluxus movement and groups such as La Monte Young's Theater of Eternal Music provides albums such as *The Marble Index* with a 'real' connection to the worlds of high/experimental music. Nico herself suggested that her way of playing the harmonium, which we hear on the record, was inspired by minimalist composer Terry Riley. She told Dadomo in 1978, 'I didn't know how to play at all. I mean, I used to improvise with the Velvet Underground but without knowing music.' She took Riley as her model: 'The repetitive way of playing, I think that's quite a good way. Especially if you sing. You know, you don't have to worry about it and you can concentrate on your singing' (Nico qtd. in Dadomo 1978). The Riley-esque approach to playing the harmonium and the minimalist style is most audible on 'Julius Caesar (Memento Hodie)' again from *The Marble Index* and the repetitive harmonium accompaniment in 'Roses in the Snow' (*The Marble Index*).

According to musicologist Susan McClary, such repetitive approaches in 1960s rock and minimalist music represent a broader trend towards cultural appropriation to the extent that such musical structures borrowed from Asian, African and African American influences. McClary writes, 'The blues and its descendants had predisposed both rockers and minimalist composers to experience time in this way, even if their attraction to Buddhism and Hindu mysticism led them to propose a somewhat different lineage' (McClary 2004: 295). There is no evidence to suggest that Nico arrived at her minimalist playing style via the blues, Buddhism or Hindu mysticism, and while Nico's models (e.g. Riley) may have appropriated such structures from Asian, African and African American practices, she seems to have arrived at them as a way to address her need to keep accompaniments minimal. Nevertheless, Nico's music shares a similar structural or harmonic foundation to other drone- or mode-inspired music of the mid-1960s (although with a marked absence of blues influences). Thus, Nico's 'medieval music' can be heard as part of a broader mid-1960s tendency to borrow sounds that pre-date functional harmony – as heard in South Asian music and 'the one-chord blues-based songs with unchanging harmony that served as a basis of rave-ups, and modal jazz' (Brackett 2020: 201).

Therefore, by closely examining Nico's solo music in relation to the soundscape of the mid-1960s, another story opens up that differs from Morrissey's dramatic sound bite – 'From being so beautiful she became a kind of freak act.' Instead, we could say that Nico's act or career demonstrates an aesthetics of resistance, from the aloof, silent voice of Gainsbourg's 'Strip-tease' through to the mid-1960s, where she partook in the 'grand dialogue' of musical experimentation, and as such perhaps even protended the punk ethos in which she later would participate in the late 1970s. What is crucial, furthermore, is that this aesthetics of resistance hinged on her physical appearance; her uniqueness and her avant-garde-ness were born in part from turning audience and critics' assumptions about desirable femininity in on themselves.

The idea that Nico's early performances prefigure her post-*Chelsea Girl* solo work (as argued by both Needham and earlier in this chapter) was proffered by rock critic Lester Bangs in the early 1970s. According to Bangs (1971), 'All Tomorrow's Parties', a song written by Lou Reed, 'presaged her own work in its sense of almost unrelieved loneliness and desolation'. Bangs' comments appeared in a lengthy article he wrote for *Fusion* magazine, which could be seen as a crucial moment and/or turning point in the reception and near accreditation of Nico as a solo artist. In his work on the intersection between pop and the avant-garde, Bernard Gendron insists Bangs was an important force in the critical and cultural accreditation of the Velvet Underground.[8] In Bangs' 1971 review of the band that appeared in *Creem*, for example, he stresses themes of avant-garde experimentalism and bohemianism and thus, according to Gendron, the Velvets contributed to the discursive convergence of these two fields (Gendron 2002: 138–42). It is interesting and significant, therefore, that Bangs wrote such a lengthy review on Nico's solo career around the same time as his Velvet Underground article that drew on similar themes, and yet Nico's legacy as an important avant-garde artist has not held in the way that of the Velvet Underground has. The early to mid-1970s could have been Nico's moment, with substantial and serious praise emerging from Lester Bangs and others in *Fusion* magazine in particular.

For example, in June 1970, perhaps anticipating the December release of her third solo album *Desertshore*, Ben Edmonds (1970), writing for *Fusion*, returned to 1968's *The Marble Index*. His review concludes with exceptional praise, writing, '[a]lthough one gets the impression that this album was created for a small group of friends, it will be meaningful for anyone willing to open himself up to it … I can only say that for me this has been one of the most rewarding musical experiences I have ever had. Edmonds' review is also in line with Fields' comments about Nico's earlier output. He suggests that her 'work with the Velvet Underground, although uniformly pleasing, was not intimately Nico', whereas *The Marble Index* 'gives us Nico working out her own framework, she is the essence as well as the effect'. He considered the album a 'stunning accomplishment' for both Nico and Cale as arranger, producer and accompanying musician.

The following year saw the publication of Bangs' substantial article on Nico for *Fusion*. Like Edmonds and Fields, Bangs (1971) suggested that *Chelsea Girl* was a 'confused project', which reflected the fact that the record label Verve 'was apparently undecided whether to try to mould Nico into an act more acceptable (and accessible) to the general public, or simply to acquiesce to the strange music that was taking shape from her and The Velvets'. As I discussed above, *Chelsea Girl* is similar to work by Collins' *Wildflowers* but also other solo female singers of the era such as Sandy Denny. Indeed, Nico's performance of 'These Days' partakes in the same sense of 'lateness' as described by Richard Elliott (2015) in relation to the song 'Who Knows Where the Time Goes', written by Denny in 1967, with her recording with Fairport

Convention released in 1968. Elliott describes 'lateness' as 'an anticipation of experience normally associated with older people but surprisingly common among young songwriters' (142). The collection of songs on *Chelsea Girl* reflects the broader trend to include song dealing with time, the seasons and references to experiences on the timeless locale of 'the highway' in songs such as 'The Fairest of the Seasons' and 'Winter Song'.⁹

But, according to Bangs, it was with Elektra Records and *The Marble Index* that the 'real' Nico could emerge. Bangs (1971) describes Elektra as a company that 'could perhaps begin to understand what Nico was up to', and, because she was writing originals on *The Marble Index*, 'never again [would she] have to endure the all but hopeless search for other composers attuned to her ethos'. Bangs was particularly impressed with the lyrics on *The Marble Index* and quoted them extensively, especially the song 'Julius Caesar (Memento Hodie)'. It is worth noting at this point that Nico drew inspiration from the works of Nietzsche, Shakespeare and the English Romantic poets Byron, Shelley, Wordsworth and Tennyson. These last two are particularly notable: the term *The Marble Index* derives from Wordsworth's description of the statue of Isaac Newton that stands in the Ante-Chapel in Trinity College, Cambridge, and Nico said of Tennyson that he was 'best of all. He's an incredible Romantic, it's just so beautiful. You find everything there' (qtd. in Dadomo 1978).

In addition to praising the uniqueness of her lyrics, it was also through comparisons with other high-brow and/or avant-garde artists and musicians that Bangs made a case for Nico's artistry. Bangs (1971) compares Nico's work overall to the films of Ingmar Bergman, particularly *The Seventh Seal* (1957). He compared some of Nico's songs to the 'miasma of Tangierian hash' in Burroughs' *Naked Lunch* (1959), and the melody of 'Janitor of Lunacy' from *Desertshore* (1970) to Don Cherry's *Symphony for Improvisers* (1966). Bangs concludes his article on Nico in a similar way to Edmonds, naming *The Marble Index* 'a truly original [project] of our time' and calls Nico 'one of the most interesting of musical phenomenon [*sic*], and probably the most original female singer (except maybe Savage Rose's Anisette)'.

The kinds of parallels drawn by Bangs work to accredit Nico as part of the rock-as-art canon, and his article marks a crucial point in her career; this is a moment in the early 1970s when she could have been and/or was considered an original artist by the rock intelligentsia. That this view was specific to a niche of listeners or critical milieu, however, is reinforced by the editor's comments on Bangs' article, where he interjects with the fact that *The Marble Index* was cut out of Elektra's catalogue in spring 1971 and could from thereon be found in discount bins (Bangs 1971). This tension between Bangs and his editor regarding critical versus public opinions of Nico points to a key issue in rock discourse. Borrowing from Pierre Bourdieu, we might understand Nico's solo work in the context of the relationship between symbolic and economic capital. Neither Nico nor the Velvet Underground were overtly commercial successes but both garnered the critical approval bestowed by key figures such as Bangs. An important difference is that the Velvet Underground's symbolic capital and their commercial capital have gathered strength over time, whereas Nico has strengthened only her esoteric appeal.

Another way of understanding symbolic capital in the context of rock is to consider this description of Island Records, which, according to music writer Richard Cromelin (1974), in *Creem* became the '[e]soterica wing of rock'. For her third album titled *The End*, Nico was signed to Island Records, connecting her to the European psychedelic scene of early 1970s rock. The guitarist Lutz Graf-Ulrich indicates that Nico was already part of this scene, playing alongside Agitation Free, Crimium Delirium, Mahjun and Kevin Coyne at several concerts and festivals (Graf-Ulrich 2015: 10). She also appeared at the Metamusikfestival in October 1974 in Berlin (one month before the release of *The End*) with John Cale and Brian Eno (see Albiez and Kaul, Chapter 11, in this collection). Graf-Ulrich recalls the event as an 'amazing, avant-garde' festival: 'The fans were thinking they would get a synthesis of Velvet Underground and Roxy Music. Instead it was a completely different thing' (Graf-Ulrich 2015: 12). Nico, Cale and Eno's participation at the event was inspired by their three performances with Kevin Ayers at the London Rainbow, Birmingham and Manchester earlier in the year, with the former preserved on the record *June 1, 1974*. In *Crawdaddy!* Island's mid-1970s moment with Nico, Cale, Eno and Ayers was described as 'a somewhat regenerated London underground' (Brown 1975). Other psychedelic or esoteric events to feature Nico included the December 1974 performance at Reims Cathedral with Tangerine Dream and parts of Nico's performance feature in Philippe Garrel's movie *Un Ange Passe* (Graf-Ulrich 2015: 14).

During this period of the mid-1970s, the reception of Nico's music was mixed in such a way that illuminates Nico's sustained appeal to a niche, critical audience. As with earlier in the decade, the rock consecrators thought of her as an interesting and challenging musician, but others found her music insufferable. Ira Robbins (1974), writing for *Zoo World*, described her performance of the Doors' 'The End', which appeared on both *June 1, 1974* and *The End* by writing, 'nothing can salvage the nine minutes wasted by Nico on an arrhythmic, monotonic recitation' of the song. However, Colman Andrews (1975) in *Creem* viewed her performance of the same song as 'particularly impressive', adding, 'She somehow manages to add new believability, new dignity (of all ridiculous things) to what is basically just another clutter of UCLA acid-head mythico Corso pseudo-poetry. Nico shows true dramatic ability, dramatic intuition here.' *The End* was marketed by Island with the slogan 'Why waste time committing suicide when you could be buying this album?', clearly anticipating (and making fun of) the record's restricted appeal.

Thus, Nico appears to have been a constant figure on the rock music scene throughout the 1970s, dividing opinions in the serious rock establishment. What is interesting, too, is the way she navigated through the different genres during this decade: from the European avant-garde rock (or even Krautrock) of 1973/74 amidst Can, Kevin Ayers, Ash Ra Tempel, Procul Harum, Caravan, Amon Düül, Wallenstein and then becoming part of – or being reabsorbed back into – the proto-/punk/post-punk continuum. According to the Dadomo (1978), Nico's 're-emergence' during the post-punk period was a result of the efforts of Larry Debay, who was 'previously a pioneer of '70s "alternative" record distribution as half of Bizarre and a long-term affiliate of Paris-based Skydog Records'. An article in *NME* from 1981 refers to the fact that bands such as the Scars and Orange Juice expressed an interest in working with her, and Geoff Travis (of Rough Trade) tried to pair her up with Orange Juice (Bohn 1981).

It is at this juncture, towards the end of Nico's performing career and before her death in July 1988, that we can perhaps return to Nico's inability to 'age well'. Earlier in the chapter I referred to Rose's 1983 review in which she criticizes Nico as, in short, middle-aged, talentless and unfashionable. In daring to perform such experimental music later in life, Nico presented a kind of dramatic ugliness that flouted the norms of conventional femininity and perhaps presaged the punk ethos.[10] In addition to her big, deep voice and her daring to perform while middle-aged, Nico's alcohol and drug dependencies bolster this image of Nico as a threat to notions of conventional and desirable femininity, certainly before the second-wave feminist movement. Another important way in which Nico challenged normative conventions is via her relationship with her son, Ari, for example. Ofteringer's film (1995) deals specifically with how Nico left him in the care of his grandmother, how she encouraged him to use heroin and how, as an adult, he defended her decisions, stressing the importance of her commitment to her soul and her creativity. Thus, not only did Nico fail to 'age well' but she also fulfilled another abject female role, that of the 'bad mother'.[11] Perhaps the most detailed account of her drug-related 'bad behaviour' is in pianist James Young's (1999) book on touring with Nico towards the end of her career when she was living in Manchester and playing with the Faction. Lurid details such as not bathing for long stretches of time and extreme attempts to score or rescue heroin are recounted. Such details are also mentioned in Graf-Ulrich's claims about his time with Nico in the early 1970s, which include Nico getting drunk before performances, asking Lou Reed for money for heroin and missing out on a Carnegie Hall appearance because of a hangover (Graf-Ulrich 2015: 48–53).

But an interest in Nico's habits also appeared in the music press from the late 1970s onwards. In *Trouser Press*, Jim Sullivan (1979) noted such insalubrious behaviour such as taking her 'afternoon breakfast of Bloody Mary's [sic] and beer'. Importantly, rather than frame such activities within the macho context of sex, drugs and rock and roll, and as part of the rebellious life of a touring musician, Sullivan presents Nico as a tragic figure with an abject life, music and poetry, but a beautiful face. Such remarks remind us of Needham's comments about her resistant and wooden performance in *Strip-tease*, her aloofness in 'Strip-tease' the song and the idea of 'lateness' or being old before her time on *Chelsea Girl*. So unmoved was she by her own experience of ageing that when asked by Dadomo (1978), whether 'time passing' and ageing made her 'sad', she replied: 'No. It's, uh, very boring.'

This persona of Nico as gloomy and gothic seemed to fix and solidify in later reviews of her records and performances. In 1983, Mat Snow (1983) in *NME* compared her to 'poetess Sylvia Plath' and described her as 'the romantic incarnation of the bedsitterland suicidal impulse'. This reading of her seems to be a culmination of ideas about Nico that hadn't yet settled, but then settled in the mid-1980s as if she'd always been part of this 'suicidal' genealogy and she seemed to find her generic niche as a proto-goth poet. More cruelly, and again drawing on heavily gendered stereotypes about women's incapacity to 'age well', Don Watson (1985), writing for *NME*, suggested her nihilistic music and persona 'fit' with or even protended punk, but after punk she seemed like an afterthought: 'in 1982, as the blind energy of punk began to fall away, Nico's weirdo shit seemed to make more sense. But now that a lot of the death culture has largely itself died the death of a cliché, Nico is still here, plodding around in her unzipped motorcycle boots, looking like microwaved death'.

Captain of her own ship

In her work on Warhol's films, Jennifer Doyle proffers the 'feminist potential' of women such as Valeria Solanas, Brigid Berlin and Ingrid Superstar. Doyle argues that the performances given by these women in Warhol's films are an 'intervention in the representational codes that shape mainstream representations of women and female sexuality', especially to the extent that these women appear as something other than sex objects (Doyle 2006: 72). The dramatic juxtaposition between Nico's appearance, and her unusually deep voice and her experimental music and her purported abjection similarly position Nico outside of the mainstream representational codes of women and desirable femininity. What is significant, furthermore, is to observe how Nico's challenge to mainstream femininity was simultaneously facilitated and contained by narratives in the mid-1960s rock press. In some ways Nico's persona and her music were a foil to, or test of, the aesthetic and cultural 'freedoms' of rock post-1960s; while she pushed its generic and gendered conventions, she was almost always hemmed in by the language of the rock patriarchy.

In this reception history of Nico, I have thus tried to demonstrate how contemporary representations of her and her music in the music press drew heavily on aspects of her physical appearance, her perceived lack of musicality and her status as an outsider. The representational modes allotted to her were a blend of the fetishization of European beauty worth ogling and fantasies of German coldness, and, in later life, a tragic figure clinging to her faded looks, an alcoholic, a junkie and in some cases a 'bad mother'. But I have also demonstrated how she ranged artistically, including a crucial moment in the early 1970s, when she was heralded a genius by some rock connoisseurs, before petrifying to become a 'suicidal' goth-poet in the 1980s.

Of course, all of these interpretations are mediated representations of who Nico was and who she strove to be. So, turning to her own words, there is a curious phrase that bookends the twenty-year span covered in this chapter, a phrase that subtly reveals something about what Nico was trying to do. Returning to Jones (1965) interview for *Record Mirror*, Nico remarked that if she wasn't modelling or singing, she'd 'like to be a farmer, or possibly captain of a ship'. It seems significant that twenty years later she says almost exactly the same thing, telling *Melody Maker*:

> I would have liked to be a captain on a ship. But I am not a man so I can't do that, it would be so picturesque. It would be very lonely which is why I would like it. I feel more comfortable when lonely. It's like when you find it hard to smile or laugh – happiness is a strain, and I am too lazy.

(Nico: Shrink Rap 1985)

This statement encapsulates what is perhaps Nico's most strongly feminist claim (though she would almost certainly have rejected the 'feminist' label). Not only did she feel thwarted by her gender ('I'm not a man so I can't') but the requisite demands of her as a woman – smiling, laughing – didn't resonate with her as a person or an artist. To depict Nico as 'suicidal' and 'gloomy' is to fundamentally misunderstand her project. Even if Nico used her conventional beauty strategically, as some have argued, her lyrics and music reveal a musician reaching beyond the policing of her identity towards a kind of freedom, forming aesthetic allegiances with eclectic influences including male singers, Black female singers, Western art music and Romantic poets. It seems not coincidental, furthermore, that her image of the lonely sea captain, sailing over strange oceans, also appears in Wordsworth's *The Prelude*,[12] from where she gained inspiration for the title of her first authentic artistic statement, *The Marble Index*.

Notes

1. I have borrowed the terms 'frame' and 'excess' from McClary (1991) in order to explore the tension between the way the music press represented Nico and her resistance against such depiction.
2. Witts (2006: 41) claims Nico was Morrissey's decision rather than Warhol's.
3. See also Roland Barthes' essay 'Striptease' in *Mythologies* (1957).
4. An English translation of the lyrics of 'Strip-Tease' can be found at https://bit.ly/3AvKsLn.
5. It is worth noting here the connection between the venue and the 1930 film of the same name starring Marlene Dietrich, especially given the comparisons between Nico and Dietrich.
6. There is an interesting parallel here with German progressive rock of the 1970s as described by Anderton (2010), particularly the abandonment of rock structures and, in the case of Nico, the use of organ-like instruments.
7. Anderton (2010).
8. For more on accreditation in rock, see Keightley (2011).
9. The inclusion of Nico's 'These Days' in Wes Anderson's 2001 *The Royal Tenenbaums* cements her status as an indie-weirdo icon. The relative obscureness of the record, its unusual sound in terms of vocal performance and knowledge about Nico's persona complement the 'quirkiness' characteristic of his films.
10. Cf. Yoko Ono as discussed in Shank (2006) and Lindau (2016).
11. For more on ageing and motherhood in rock, see Coates (2012) and Lindau (2016).
12. The relevant section from Wordsworth's *The Prelude* Book 3 is available at https://bit.ly/3r4qSCW.

References

Anderton, C. (2010), 'A Many-Headed Beast: Progressive Rock as European Meta-genre', *Popular Music*, 29 (3): 417–35.

Andrews, C. (1975), 'Nico: *The End* (Island)' [review], *Creem*, May. Available online: https://bit.ly/3KfwZdY (accessed 26 April 2022).

Bakhtin, M. (1986), *Speech Genres and Other Late Essays*, ed. M. Holquist and C. Emerson, Austin: University of Texas.

Bangs, L. (1971), 'Nico: A Kind of Frozen Purity', *Fusion*, 12 November. Available online: https://bit.ly/3FWNaKU (accessed 1 December 2021).

Black, J. (1997), 'Time Machine: Velvet Underground', *Mojo*, March. Available online: https://bit.ly/3rRCurX (accessed 1 December 2021).

Bohn, C. (1981), 'In the Nico Time', *New Musical Express*. Available online: https://bit.ly/3tYhyCk (accessed 1 December 2021).

Bourdieu, P. (1993), *The Field of Cultural Production: Essays on Art and Literature*, Cambridge: Polity Press.

Brackett, D. (2020), 'Improvisation and Value in Rock, 1966', *Journal of the Society for American Music*, 14 (2): 197–232.

Brown, M. (1975), 'John Cale: Fear (Island); Nico: The End (Island)' (reviews], *Crawdaddy*, May. Available online: https://bit.ly/3kdJbRM (accessed 26 April 2022).

Burroughs, W. (1959), *Naked Lunch*, New York: Grove.

Coates, N. (2012), '"It's Not Over…" Mom Rock? Media Representations of 'Mothers Who Rock', in R. Jennings and A. Gardner (eds), *'Rock On': Women, Ageing and Popular Music*, Farnham: Ashgate.

Cromelin, R. (1974), 'Kevin Ayres, John Cale, Nico & Eno: June 1, 1974', *Creem*, December. Available online: https://bit.ly/3rRVcQb (accessed 1 December 2021).

Dadomo, G. (1978), 'Nico', *Sounds*, 24 April. Available online: https://bit.ly/32BMDAy (accessed 1 December 2021).

Dalton, D. (2002), 'Nico and The Marble Index: A Conversation with Danny Fields', *Gadfly*. Available online: https://bit.ly/3G7Pdvz (accessed 1 December 2021).

Doyle, J. (2006), *Art and the Dialectics of Desire*, Minneapolis: University of Minnesota.

Edmonds, B. (1970), 'Nico: The Marble Index', *Fusion*, 12 June. Available online: https://bit.ly/3rUGA2n (accessed 1 December 2021).

Elliott, R. (2015), '"Across the Evening Sky": The Late Voices of Sandy Denny, Judy Collins and Nina Simone', in C. Haworth and L. Colton (eds), *Gender, Age and Musical Creativity*, Farnham: Ashgate.

Gendron, B. (2002), *Between Montmartre and the Mudd Club: Popular Music and the Avant-Garde*, Chicago, IL: University of Chicago.

Graf-Ulrich, L. (2015), *Nico – In the Shadow of the Moon Goddess*, Create Space Independent Publishing.

Hawkins, P. (2000), *Chanson: The French Singer-Songwriter from Aristide Bruant to the Present Day*, Aldershot: Ashgate.

Jones, P. (1965), 'Nico Leads Andrew's Off Beat Company', *Record Mirror*, 28 August, 6. Available online: https://bit.ly/3o2k0Ea (accessed 1 December 2021).

Kent, N. (1974), 'Nico: I Was a Hausfrau from Hanover – Until I Discovered Heroin', *New Musical Express*, 24 August. Available online: https://bit.ly/3nWgqLC (accessed 1 December 2021).

Keightley, K. (2011), 'Reconsidering Rock', in S. Frith, W. Straw and J. Street (eds), *The Cambridge Companion to Pop and Rock*, Cambridge: Cambridge University.

Lindau, E. (2016), '"Mother Superior": Maternity and Creativity in the Work of Yoko Ono', *Women and Music: A Journal of Gender and Culture*, 20: 57–76.

McClary, S. (1991), 'Excess and Frame: The Musical Representation of Madwomen', in *Feminine Endings: Music, Gender, and Sexuality*, 80–111, Minneapolis, MN: University of Minnesota.
McClary, S. (2004), 'Rap, Minimalism, and Structures of Time in Late Twentieth-Century Culture', in C. Cox and D. Warner (eds), *Audio Culture: Readings in Modern Music*, 289–98, New York: Continuum.
Needham, G. (2016), 'Warhol and Nico: Negotiating Europe from Strip-Tease to Screen Test', *Journal of European Popular Culture*, 7 (2): 123–42.
Nico: Shrink Rap (1985) *Melody Maker*, 27 July. Available online: https://bit.ly/3rMards (accessed 1 December 2021).
Patterson, A. (2012), 'Nico Icon: Directed by Susanne Ofteringer', Rock's Backpages, December. Available online: https://bit.ly/3AzmwXs (accessed 1 December 2021).
Pfeil, F. (1995), *White Guys: Studies in Postmodern Domination and Difference*, London: Verso.
Riegel, R. (1980), 'Nico: Bogart's, Cincinnati', *Creem*, September. Available online: https://bit.ly/3rKOdsk (accessed 1 December 2021).
Rose, C. (1983), 'Nico: When the Peroxide Fades', *New Musical Express*, 29 January. Available online: https://bit.ly/3nZNrqu (accessed 1 December 2021).
Savage, J. (1977), 'Nico: The Marble Index', *Sounds*, 24 September. Available online: https://bit.ly/3fXHK7N (accessed 1 December 2021).
Shank, B. (2006), 'Abstraction and Embodiment: Yoko Ono and the Weaving of Global Musical Networks', *Journal of Popular Music Studies*, 18 (3): 282–300.
Sieglohr, U. (2000), *Heroines without Heroes: Reconstructing Female and National Identities in European Cinema, 1945–51*, London: Cassell.
Snow, M. (1983), 'Nico/1919: Brixton, London', *New Musical Express*, 4 June. Available online: https://bit.ly/3fYQWZH (accessed 1 December 2021).
Sullivan, J. (1979), 'Strange Interlude with Nico', *Trouser Press*, July. Available online: https://bit.ly/3nYTJX8 (accessed 1 December 2021).
Unterberger, R. (n.d.), 'The Marble Index: All Music Review'. Available online: https://bit.ly/3qYpQbs (accessed 1 December 2021).
Watson, D. (1985), 'Nico: "Watch Out, the World's behind You"', *New Musical Express*, 3 August. Available online: https://bit.ly/3fVjB1Q (accessed 1 December 2021).
Whiteley, S. ([2000] 2013), *Women and Popular Music: Sexuality, Identity and Subjectivity*, [e-book], New York: Routledge; Hoboken: Taylor & Francis Group.
Williams, R. (1970), 'Nico: Desertshore', *Melody Maker*, 31 January. Available online: https://bit.ly/35uIpvL (accessed 1 December 2021).
Williams, R. (1991), 'CD Liner Notes, The Marble Index', Available online: https://bit.ly/3fZ9MQr (accessed 1 December 2021).
Witts, R. (1993), *Nico: The Life and Lies of an Icon*, London: Virgin.
Witts, R. (2006), *The Velvet Underground*, Bloomington, IN: Indiana University.
Young, J. (2013), *Nico, Songs They Never Play on the Radio*, London: Bloomsbury.

8

European Son: 'Europe' in Nico, Cale and Reed's long-1970s solo work

Toby Manning

Just as America guided British foreign policy from 1945, so, for much of the post-war period, did British music also appear to be under American hegemony. Cold War imports of blues, rock and roll and soul operated as a musical Marshall Plan, causing American landscapes, American towns and even American accents to dominate British popular music from the mid-1950s to mid-1970s. This made the term 'the British invasion' particularly ironic: for musically, as militarily, America led and Britain followed. Consequently, a European sensibility was largely absent from British (and, naturally, American) popular music until well into the 1970s,[1] as Britain remained culturally and politically aloof from continental Europe and huddled close to its powerful transatlantic protector.[2] My argument here is that the Velvet Underground produced, in embryo, and emphatically via Nico, Cale and – briefly – Reed's long 1970s' work, a body of European-orientated rock. This counter-impulse to American cultural dominance was a precursor to the 'European turn' in British music in the late 1970s, created largely by Velvets aficionados.[3] That American culture was government-sponsored to counter communism via both Marshall Aid and the CIA's Congress for Cultural Freedom (Stonor Saunders 2000) makes such Europeanism entirely political in its very conception, let alone its content.

The Velvet Underground

'The European' is defined here as distinct from 'Englishness', the mode whereby British culture intermittently asserted itself against America, primarily via folk (to which Cale was antipathetic [DeCurtis 2017: 61]), and vaudeville. While there is more folk in the Velvets' oeuvre than is conventionally admitted (Greene 2016: 151), and post-Cale the Velvets and Reed flirted with vaudeville,[4] these forms are anathema to the consensus 'Velvet-esque' as proto-punk. What is unique in the band is the combination of Reed's literate urban primitivism and Cale's classical avant-garde sensibility: the American and the European in musical and personal collaboration/collision. Cale later declared: 'I'm a classical composer, dishevelling my musical personality by dabbling in rock and roll' (Cale 1999: 218). The high/low culture language here is illuminating, but that dishevelment actually began earlier, with Cale's introduction to New York's avant-garde via La Monte Young, seeking 'the revolution under the surface' (58).

The first facet of the Velvets' European-ness was to eschew the blues root of Western pop music. Reed claimed, 'We actually had a rule in the band – if anyone played a blues lick they'd be fined' (Fricke 1989). Blues' defining 'blue notes' are flattened (3rd and 7th) trespassers from the minor scale (Crawford 2001: 559), derived from African music (Scott 2003: 56). With minor keys associated with melancholy in the European classical tradition, it is apt that American popular music should be constituted not just by blackness but 'blueness' – an enduring trace of the historical horrors of slavery. Reed's comment is somewhat overstated, however: there was still blues in VU ('Run Run Run'; 'There She Goes'). However, 'I'm Waiting for the Man' is a twelve-bar rhythm and blues number that manages to avoid blue notes, helping create a musical 'offness' to match its lyrical content. On 'White Light/White Heat' the vocal melody again avoids blue notes, riding stiffly across the stuttering chords rather than employing the characteristic loose, rhythmically flowing 'feel' of African American musics. Again, 'Sister Ray's two relentless chords (G to C) excise the dominant (D) that is blues' bridge to the tonic (Crawford 2001: 560) while again Reed's strident vocal skirts blue notes.

This excision of blues is not entirely unproblematic, as it is an excision of *blackness*: a white light indeed (Reynolds and Press 1995: 301). The European imperialism concurrent with Romanticism asserted whiteness as superior (Schwarz 2012: passim), and the Third Reich was only European nationalism's most virulent modern expression – see Mussolini's Italy; Vichy France; Portugal until 1974; Spain until 1975 (Arendt 1994: 123–304). Therefore, fascism is unavoidably a facet of the European – its European son. Consequently, a fascistic element regularly creeps into European-facing rock: usually as demon, sometimes as ghost, at others, combining both, glamour.

The second European facet of the Velvets was their deployment of classical instrumentation via Cale's viola, a 'European presence reminding American art of the heritage it attempts to take on' (Griffiths 2000: 183). Thanks to the viola, 'Black Angel's Death Song' is a Weimar jig, while the darkness of 'All Tomorrow's Parties', 'Venus in Furs' and 'Lady Godiva's Operation' is, despite American avant-garde elements, European: what would later be called 'Gothic'. European reference in titles – 'European Son', 'Femme Fatale', 'Lady Godiva' – add to this classicist un-American 'otherness'.

A third European element was Nico's German accent, which, combined with her glacial, un-girlish delivery – part Marlene Dietrich, part Hildegard Knef – pulls her three VU songs towards something both Romantically old (as in World) but also cold (as in War). For Germany was not only the *cause* of the Cold War – much of Stalinist foreign policy stemming from fear of resurgent German fascism (Reynolds 1994: 82) – it was geographically and politically central to it: wearing Europe's political divisions across its landscape (with Nico's childhood home, Lübbenau, ending up in the East). Fourthly, in terms of political economy, the Velvets eschewed the pop marketplace to create what became known as 'art rock': cultural 'statements' courting minoritarian approval rather than commercial success (DeCurtis 2017: 103–4). The Velvets' solo members – and their many European acolytes – would all follow this particular path.

Nico

While Nico's *Chelsea Girl* (1967) is more European than usually acknowledged (Witts 1993: 207–11; Frieze 2007; Hogan 2007: 199) – baroque being a European style; the lyrics moving into Gothicism – the long-1970s European turn really begins with *The Marble Index* (1968). Writing on a harmonium, an instrument developed by French instrument-makers in the nineteenth century (Remnant 1989: 155), Nico turned to former Velvets colleague (and fellow European) Cale, as producer, musician and arranger, giving him 'carte blanche to bring in … all this European stuff' (Cale 1999: 120). Or, correctly, 'bring out', given the songs' modal, European folk and lieder-derived melodies. Elektra head, Jac Holzman's reaction ('it's very European' [Cale 1999: 127]) became common (e.g. Greene 2016: 170–4). With 'European' often drifting into 'Aryan' (Reynolds and Press 1995: 300) – and Nico's voice being characterized as 'Gotterdammerung' (Hogan 2007: 138) – it can be suggested that the 'Germanic' and 'Nazi' commingled in the Western Cold War imaginary (Rau 2013: 9).

Often regarded as unprecedented, *The Marble Index*'s emergence from California in 1968 actually makes a level of cultural sense. The year 1968 marked the end of American-led 1960s optimism as the Vietnam War stepped up, and the generation gap turned violent in the streets, campuses, festivals and cults, largely centred on California. The fading of the special relationship was signalled by both Britain's refusal of troops to Vietnam and the Grosvenor Square protest at the US Embassy that year. Was America, a nation founded on European liberal ideas, itself becoming fascist (Marcuse 2014: 50)? While Americans escaped to comforting native country and folk – and Britons, conversely, dug deeper into American rock (The Who, Kinks, Led Zeppelin, even glam) – Old World exile, Nico turned instead to her native Europe.[5]

How far from comforting this European turn was can be heard by comparison of the ice-cold *The Marble Index* not just to Cale's Americana-saturated *Vintage Violence* (1970) but to any album of this rootsy, sunny post-*Big Pink* moment. 'No One Is There' features an icily stark, stop-start viola quartet that is barren rather than lush, recalling the alienation of Anton Webern's string quartets (Greene 2016: 172). The song's subject is similarly sinister: a mythic figure, a demon, dances, but amidst this sound and fury is a 'parody', a void: as the songs title suggests, there is nothing but an absence. Like most of Nico's elliptical ideas in her lyrics, this can be read in two ways. Greene persuasively argues that the figure is fascism (2016: 172), the Gothic supernatural rooted materially in the tainted Romanticism of the Third Reich. As Nico also dedicated the song to both Richard Nixon (Hogan 2007: 200) and Ronald Reagan (Greene 2016: 172), the American-dominated 'new world order' is also effectively being framed here as fascist. These two understandings combine, however. While Nico had lived through the horrors of Nazism (Young 1992: viii), culturally the figure of the fascist – largely absent immediately post-war – was becoming a stock figure of evil during the 1960s (Rau 2013: 3–4). One way of understanding this Cold War preoccupation with fascism is as endorsing the concept of 'totalitarianism', whereby communism and fascism essentially fuse (Arendt 1994: passim; in Rau 2003: 3, 7). Yet accusations of fascism were the currency of the Cold War: for the Soviet Union, the Berlin Wall's 'anti-fascist protection rampart' reflected a genuine fear of recursive Nazism – and of the West generally. For some leftists of both East and West, fascism is an outgrowth of, not aberration from, liberalism (Eagleton 1996: 57; Landa 2012: passim). In this way then, the demon in 'No One Is There' is both an American and a European son, birthed from both Nazi past and Cold War present, with the two perennially conjoining.

While seesawing harmonium and viola of 'Julius Caesar (Memento Hodie)' suggests Philip Glass, the melody is German folk, the arrangement French Romantic, recalling Poulenc. The song, whose lyrics are full of classical colonnades and political manoeuvring, continues the preoccupation with the absolute power of Cale's 'Winter Song' on *Chelsea Girls* and highlights the coexistence of high culture and tyranny. The song is haunted by very recent history: Mussolini was obsessed with Caesar (Nelis 2007: 395), while 'volk' music was a Nazi totem (Witts 1993: 220). Note the Latin addendum, however – *Memento Hodie* [remember at the present] – the past revisited as a warning against present fascism.

Medievalism was a key facet of Romanticism, and 'Frozen Warnings' shifts between medieval imagery, its modal folk melody wreathed in wheezing harmonium, and a contemporary frozen borderline, laced in icily glistening viola. The link is the timeless totalitarian imagining endless victory and power. While the Cold War did not invent borders, it made borders contemporary, iconic and combustible. And while the Cold War also did not invent the cold-weather metaphor, it was a key facet of Cold War discourse – and always assigned politically by the West to the physically frozen East. If Cold War polarities are held in tension here, they are levelled by the closing 'Evening of Light'. The song is riddled with medieval imagery – a dungeon, ringing mandolins, peasants – loosely chiming with its Bach chorale-like melody and ringing spinets (Condon 1983: 47). Yet an 'evening of light' suggests electricity – the modern – and the spinets play cyclical, minimalist motifs, while the bass-frequency string sound from 3:20 and distorted viola from 4:35 suggest Stockhausen. Cale himself cites the track's 'Carl Orff grandiosity', Orff being a Nazi favourite (Witts 1993: 220), which the medieval/modern combination fits (Pinnock 2015). This suggests the long sweep of European history, a history brought to an end here by the ultimate modern illumination of darkness: nuclear war (Greene 2016: 173). Thus the song's – and album's – musically explosive climax in the totalitarian balance of terror: mutually assured destruction.

Desertshore, released in December 1970, found Nico – now (nomadically) domiciled in Europe – extending her European vision. The lyrics may be inspired by real people (Witts 1993: 236) but Nico's choice of imagery creates a broader canvas. So 'Janitor of Lunacy' may concern Brian Jones (Witts 1993: 240), but its medieval, violent themes – paralysis, petrification, devilry and screaming – creates a two-way mirror between personal and political power. Musically, its rolling piano lines couldn't be further from the Rolling Stones' Americanisms, echoing Brecht/Eisler's leftist Weimar songs, while the vocal's modal melisma recall Schubert *lieder*. In fact, melisma originate in Arabic music and can be seen to fulfil the same function in European music as blue notes in American: an enduring trace of repressed blackness within the dominant imperial culture. With the B section again evoking Bach chorales, the song offers a historical sweep of European history from medieval to modern.

Again, 'The Falconer' may be inspired by Warhol (Condon 1983: 44; Witts 1993: 204), but the imagery is again medieval; the lord simply *sits*, enthroned – passive but controlling, while his ingratiating courtiers strive to entertain him. The analogy is, again, illuminating in both directions: not just the passive Warhol as potentate (Young 1992: xiii) but the medieval monarch exerting power via enforced play. Reflecting this past-in-present thematic, 'Falconer' begins folky, minor and modal, with Romantic harmonies (and modern Stockhausen-style electronic surges), then in the B section, a major-key piano melody summons Beethoven in its precise, classical elegance. The historical sweep of these songs operates in contrast to the compressed history of America, with its superficial emphasis on the 'modern', as satirized in – or exemplified by – the work of Andy Warhol.

In the tradition of Schubert death-lieder two songs in German are addressed to the deceased (Nico's mother had recently died [Witts 1993: 252]). The abrasive strings of 'Abschied' recall the string quartet of Schubert's lied, 'Death and the Maiden', while the melody recalls Mahler's similarly deathly 'Wenn Dein Mütterlein'. Nico's own 'Mütterlein"s arrangement again ranges across European music: the trumpets baroque; the thumping piano dis-chords Messiaen-esque, modern; the vocal melody again recalling Bach chorales, four-square on the beat like the Renaissance hymns Bach, in turn, mined. Here, directly addressing death, Nico's usually sombre language is almost joyous – 'blessedness', 'glory' and 'victorious' – half in love with easeful death, representing the Gothic morbidity at Romanticism's heart (and the Factory's [Bangs 1983: 52–3]). The *Rolling Stone* review of *Desertshore* was arguably the first application of the term 'Gothick' to popular music (George-Warren 1997: 257). That such Gothicism reappeared during the Cold War is little remarked: haunted by the fascist holocaust in the past and the fear of nuclear holocaust in the future, Nico and her Goth heirs were simply giving voice to the Cold War's cult of death.

Two songs are almost conventionally attractive for Nico, major key prettiness deployed to smuggle in darkness. 'My Only Child' hymns Nico's son, Ari, but the mysterious, threatening other, archaic language, Renaissance hymnal melody, death reveille trumpets and Gregorian backing vocals invoke a feudal oppression. The inhumanity of power is also linked to the Cold War via patented chilly imagery. The equally hymnal, piano-based 'Afraid' is a song not of faith but of nihilism. The subject here is doubtless Nico (Condon 1983: 51) but, emanating from a German exile, the song also expresses a de-anchoring from pre-war certainties about national and cultural identity, voided by the holocaust, the mythic Fatherland with its 'narrative of blood, soil, the "authentic" race"' (Eagleton 1996: 57) now literally split down the middle. Again, Cold War polarities are held in tension and again are levelled on the final number. On 'All That Is My Own' the 'early' trumpets are synthesized or processed, its dramatic tympani less dance than battle, recalling that most Cold War of composers, Shostakovich. The lyric again focuses on leaders, the exertion of power and borders: the desertshore. With beaches and deserts common images for nuclear devastation,[6] the track again unites past and present, an end-of-days song across the millennia. This is all some distance from American rock, being possessed of neither rhythm nor blues: indeed, Cale claimed Nico's work is closer to 'the European modern classical tradition' (Pinnock 2015).

Cale again produced and arranged Nico's *The End ...*, released in November 1974. The use of Roxy Music's Brian Eno and Phil Manzanera indicated how Velvets' acolytes Roxy, Bowie, Can and Faust were now channelling the solo Velvets' Europeanism.[7] 'It Has Not Taken Long' is now-patented Nico Gothic; images of being hunted, of blood and blades make the Mahler-esque Romanticism of children's chorus and sleigh bells distinctly 'off'. If the title of 'Secret Side' suggests Cold War espionage, its ships returning to port gives it a broader historical compass, echoed by its four-square Bach chorale melody and Cale's cascading violas. Another Nico hymnal, 'You Forget to Answer', complemented by Cale's Romantic piano flourishes, may concern Jim Morrison, yet the language of miscommunication, of codes misread, sounds entirely Cold War, accentuated by Eno's three-minute warning synthesizer howls. Although the backing is a rumbling, chiming Stockhausen collage, 'We've Got the Gold' again nods melodically to Mahler's 'Wenn dein Mütterlein', the invocation of dead children and the Nazi-despised composer intermeshing with the lyric's hymning of Andreas Baader (Witts 1993: 264). The Marxist Baader Meinhof gang conducted terrorist campaigns against 'fascist' European states from the death of the counterculture in 1968 to their own deaths in state custody by 1977 (Marcuse 2014: 363), and the song surely holds in tension these polar, yet similarly disfigured European sons.

Nico's German Romanticism comes into full, morbid flower with her version of 'Das Lied Der Deutschen'. The German national anthem is not *inherently* fascist: indeed the lyric was composed by noted liberal August Hoffman in 1841. However, belief in ethnic superiority was intrinsic to the imperialism that was constitutive of liberalism, and the nationalism of the Nazi-favoured first verse. Are Germans being asked to prioritize their homeland or wish to see Germany dominant over the world? Sections claiming Versailles-ceded territories as German, and the second verse (hymning German women like Nico), became, post-war, unsung – implicitly banned. Nico's rendition of all three verses was met in performance with a mix of hostility and approval by German audiences (see Albiez and Kaul, Chapter 11, in this collection). With the music deriving from a 1797 Josef Haydn hymn for Francis II, the classical, minor-key melody is typical of Nico ('Innocent and Vain' uses a similar melody, 'Secret Side', a similar cadence) and not only is it one of her most haunting – and haunted – performances, it is also deeply disturbing. As her occasional dedication of the song to Ulrike Meinhof indicated (Witts 1993: 278), Nico may have intended to reveal the palimpsest of history via the song's absolutist and fascist traces (263). But her insistence on playing the song through audience hostility perhaps suggests a more transgressive intent (Witts 1993: 270). Indeed, subjectively or otherwise, witnesses also refer to Nico as fascistic (George-Warren 1997: 258; Young in conversation 2018). Consequently fascism inhabits Nico's rendition of the 'Lied' as demon, ghost *and* glamour, the dark side of the European now inescapable in Nico's final song of the seventies, the excision of blackness meeting the virulent nationalism within the Romantic: the diseased European son.

John Cale

By rights, Cale's work should have occupied the same European space as Nico, but Cale took some time to get into his European – and artistic – stride post-Velvets. *Vintage Violence*'s (1970) thoroughgoing Americanism is close to political denial, though there are hints of Europe: the Welshness of Cale's singing; 'Charlemagne''s invocation of ancient European monarchies; the 'Femme Fatale'-ish 'Amsterdam' (albeit viewed from American distance); the way 'Ghost Story' unites Jacques Brel and Leonard Cohen (whose Gothic folk was itself Nico-influenced [George-Warren 1997: 255]). Although the track titles of Cale's Terry Riley collaboration, *Church of Anthrax* (1971), get closer to Europe, the minimalist-meets-rock music remains Stateside. So the title 'Ides of March' continues the absolutist preoccupations of 'Julius Caesar' but musically is a messy rock jam. 'The Hall of Mirrors at the Palace at Versailles' evokes the location of the signing of the Treaty of Versailles in June 1919, which sowed the seeds for the Third Reich, the disfigured European son. European history is a palimpsest, however, and Versailles was built for Louis XIV as a kind of absolutist Factory. This was a topic Cale would soon revisit with greater conviction. 'The Soul of Patrick Lee' begins the mapping of Europe of later work, while its medieval heraldic imagery recalls Nico's 'The Falconer' and is matched by a folky, semi-medieval melody.

While *The Academy in Peril* (1972) taps Cale's European classical roots (Cale 1999: 138) without the pomposity of contemporaneous progressive rock, its composition and execution are somewhat evanescent. Cale later dismissed the album as 'wishy-washy Vaughan Williams stuff' (139), and while there is plenty of such folk-orientated 'Englishness' in '3 Orchestral Pieces', 'Faust' also references Mahler and Bruckner, albeit to limited effect. 'Brahms' pays pianistic tribute to the Romantic composer regarded as 'paradigmatic of the German nation' by the Nazis (Buch et al. 2016: 75), so 'King Harry''s return to absolutist European monarchies is apposite, a reminder of that coexistence of absolutism and Enlightenment. Behind the 'comic' (homophobic) spoken vocal of 'Legs Larry at Television Centre', the droning violas are simultaneously minimalist, Romantic (Williams again) and modern (Shostakovich): West and East combined. Finally, 'The Academy in Peril' ranges across European musical history, incorporating Bach, Liszt, Debussy, Satie and Shostakovich in its impressionistic – indeed slapdash – approach.

All this changed with *Paris 1919* (1973), Cale's most overtly European album, albeit one recorded in Los Angeles with American rock musicians (Haider 2018). Significantly, Britain had joined the European Community the month before, signalling new alliances beyond the Atlanticist, at the same time as the United States finally called time on the debacle of Vietnam. Musically, *Paris 1919* again contains the past in the present: 'classical' orchestral arrangements adorning contemporary folk-pop, exemplified by the dramatic sweep of huge Hispanic Bizet-esque strings on 'The Endless Plain of Fortune'. *Paris 1919*'s lyrics are elliptical and enigmatic, but such surrealism is itself European (Gold 1973), as well as highly suggestive, and two key observations can be made. First, the lyrics are a roll-call of European place-names (Adrianopolis, Segovia, Andalucía, Dunkirk, Paris, Berlin, Barbary) – a compulsive mapping of Europe that competes with American music's self-mapping, from New York to LA via Route 66 and Highway 61– while also suggesting how the map of Europe was redrawn by the Cold War. Opener, 'Child's Christmas in Wales' deploys ship and travel imagery and mentions Columbus, Russia's European Sea port Sebastopol and Turkey's East-West straddling Adrianopolis, thus conveying the borders between both East and West and Old and New Worlds. Second, religion and the church are recurring themes: church congregations in 'Child's Christmas' echo its hymnal-via-Beethoven melody; religion encroaching on one's door ('Hanky Panky Nohow'); Crusaders in 'Andalucía' (another 'Femme Fatale'); the church/bishop who comes to make an unwelcome claim on you in 'Paris 1919'; the prejudice of the Church of England ('Graham Greene'). While this hostility to religion is hardly surprising for somebody abused in childhood by a church organist, religion surely also represents ideology here. As Cale has suggested, '[*Paris 1919*] was an oblique look at the height of the Cold War' (Haider 2018); then 'Hanky Panky Nohow's conflation of religion and sex explores not just personal trauma but the disjuncture between liberalism's signalled virtue and its often sordid practice. 'Graham Greene''s reference to racist Conservative MP, Enoch Powell and its depictions of the establishment can thus be seen to reference 1930s aristocratic fascism or indeed Britain's Cold War support of dictators like Papadopoulos in Greece. Similarly, the binary conflict between an individual and a hostile other portrayed in 'Half Past France' suggests the Manichean divisions of both old and Cold War.

'Paris 1919' itself is commonly seen to reference the Treaty of Versailles (Mitchell 2003: 85–6; Hogan 2007: 174). Thus the religious claiming feared in the song by the ominous 'iron drum' is the fascism the Treaty helped incubate (like Gunther Grass' 1959 *The Tin Drum*), its European son – religion as ideology again. This is underlined by the song's relentless staccato strings, reminiscent of Richard Wagner's *Tannhauser* overture (Adorno 2005: 4), with which – given that Wagner was Hitler's favourite composer – the correlation between tyranny and Romantic music reached a queasy peak. Given the January 1973 Paris Peace Accords ending the Vietnam War and the song's ostensible reference to William P. Rogers (the US Secretary of State), a Cold/old War link is clearly being made: perhaps that fascism arises out of imperial Western failures, or the fear that proxy East-West conflicts will lead to World War III. Thus the closing, seemingly out of place, 'Antarctica Starts Here' potentially evokes not just the faded actress of *Sunset Boulevard* but, via cold-weather metaphors, another end-of-days wasteland, a post-nuclear frozen landscape, whose once disputed borderline is now meaningless.

Despite John Cale's relocation to Europe, his *Fear* album in 1974 launched three Island albums which looked to America lyrically and musically, using less classical instrumentation, with the viola gradually disappearing from Cale's musical palette. However, *Fear* still possesses elements of Europeanism compared to most mid-1970s rock, with 'Gun' and 'Fear Is a Man's Best Friend' essaying an arty, non-bluesy angularity in the Velvets vein, which was hugely influential on the post-punk European turn (the Banshees covering 'Gun'). Musically, 'Ship of Fools' boasts a chiming, Mozart-like fanfare, 'Buffalo Ballet' a hymnal quality, while B-side, 'Sylvia Said' boasts a Beethoven-esque melody. Although *Slow Dazzle* (1975) continues the State-wards shift, Cale's Gothic version of 'Heartbreak Hotel' repeats the Velvets' trick of excising blue notes, while the lyrical surrealism of 'The Jeweller' is matched by Brian Eno's mittel-European atmospherics. *Helen of Troy* (1975), finally, was split. On the one side were pennanted baroque trumpets, the Gothic title track's invocation of Helen and Joan of Arc, the Bach-meets-50s rock of 'My Maria', alongside explicit Cold War imagery on 'Sudden Death' and 'Leaving It Up to You', which calls out a fascist while the tanks are approaching. On the other side, however, was the unabashed blues of 'Baby What You Want Me to Do', complete with blue notes. This then represented a gradual withdrawal from the overtly European in Cale's work, heralding his physical return to America in the late 1970s.

Lou Reed

The usually thoroughly American Lou Reed's *Berlin* followed mere months after Cale's *Paris 1919*, in July 1973. Reed, Cale and Nico had performed together at Paris' Bataclan in January 1972: Cale played piano on Reed's 'Berlin', while Nico arguably influenced the entire *Berlin* project: she and the song's heroine are both Berliners and both heroin addicts. *Berlin*'s Berlin-ness is, however, sometimes regarded as superficial (DeCurtis 2017: 175, 178), so the album's deliberate setting in *the* iconic Cold War location or the meaning of the avowed 'metaphor' of the Wall (175) is left unexplored by critics, who instead focus on *Berlin*'s bleakness and its biographical resonances with Reed's own relationships (Hogan 2007: 209). However, the album's Cold War iconography is not simply poetically apt for the personal drama – walls long being symbols of division – *Berlin*'s personal fiction can also be read as a political fable. The sundered alliance of two lovers who become enemies echoes Britain and America's wartime ally, the USSR, becoming their Cold War enemy, or, indeed the division of once united Germany into enemy halves, microcosmically magnified in Berlin itself. In this light, Caroline's sexual betrayals also represent political betrayals – a patented (and misogynistic) Cold War trope in Fleming, le Carré and Deighton, particularly given the cold-weather imagery used for the German Caroline (compared to Alaska, separated from Siberia only by the Bering Strait). The narrating waterboy's obsessive cataloguing of Caroline's crimes in 'The Kids' suggests both the McCarthy hearings and Soviet show trials, but similarly, such moral righteousness does not eclipse Jim's own moral culpability. Jim – apparently American – may be a victim of capitalism ('Men of Good Fortune', an Americanized rewrite of Brel's 'Fils De ...' [1967]) but he has hate-filled eyes ('Oh Jim'), and his use of violence undermines any proclamation of moral superiority ('Caroline Says II'), like the elided violence of liberalism – that distinction between signalled virtue and sordid practice again. Intentionally or otherwise, Caroline's rebuke to Jim (as she makes up her black eye in the same song) to think of others than himself berates the unfettered individualism of liberalism (implicitly invoking communism's collective 'us'). Consequently, the album's very musical and lyrical bleakness becomes not simply biographical but an elliptical expression of Cold War structures of feeling.

As ever, historical resonances go deeper in Europe, and Berlin is particularly 'weighed down by history' (DeCurtis 2017: 176). That it was the city of Mendelsohn and Strauss is suggested in *Berlin*'s Romantic orchestrations. 'Caroline Says I' features a clarinet in the verse, a dramatic surge of strings in the chorus, and oboes and flutes in the coda, adding a European classicism to its American rock base. Ancient monarchies return both here and in 'Sad Song', with Caroline compared to (Francophone) Mary Queen of Scots, and the music bedecked with ornate, courtly strings and flutes. This is all at some considerable remove from the monochrome attack of the Velvet Underground, whose lyrical street realism is otherwise continued here, high and low culture in creative tension.

Berlin was also associated with the decadence of the liberal Weimar Republic, as seen in Bob Fosse's 1972 film, *Cabaret*, another key channelling and dissemination of the European turn (Bracewell 1998: 204; Witts 2011: 171). *Berlin*'s title track's opening – a blare of distorted MC microphone a la *Cabaret*'s Joel Grey – and its jazzy arrangement both invoke this heritage. Weimar cabaret was a camp Teutonification of jazz, a suggestion of sleaze that undercuts the song's Romanticism, adding foreshadowing to the fragmentary lyric. The attention-seeking Caroline in 'Lady Day', standing atop the bar and living in a hotel, recalls Sally Bowles, whose flighty hedonism and need for affirmation are, in *Cabaret*, linked to liberalism's weakness in the face of fascism. The fascism theme is more subdued on *Berlin* than in Nico and Cale, but is found in the brutality of Jim ('Caroline Says II'), the authoritarian removal of Caroline's children ('The Kids') and in the sheer emotional *deadness* of the entire album, signalled even in the opening title track by the blank desiccation of Jim's reportage of the romance, continuing through the frozen Caroline as 'Alaska' and the final morbid nihilism of 'The Bed' and 'Sad Song' – Romanticism at its most curdled. Reed's *Berlin* was a rare instance of an American artist channelling the incipient European turn and was hugely influential on both Bowie and on post-punk.

The European turn

Both Cale and Nico would fall silent for the second half of the 1970s, and upon their return, would be chasing rather than channelling the zeitgeist. Bowie's declaration concerning the return of the European canon on January 1975's *Station to Station* was a typical channelling of cultural currents. Having joined the European Community in 1973, a June 1975 referendum gave British public approval (67.23%) to greater economic links with Europe. From 1977 a distinct 'European turn' became audible in British music, first in Bowie's France and Berlin-recorded *Low* and '*Heroes*' and then in punk (the Sex Pistols' 'Holidays in the Sun'; Wire's 'Reuters'). Europeanism largely defined post-punk from mid-1978 (Magazine's Cold War manifesto, 'Shot by Both Sides'; Siouxsie and the Banshees' 'Metal Postcard [Mittageisen]'). This increased to a flood after Margaret Thatcher's March 1979 electoral victory announced a nationalist, yet strongly Atlanticist conservatism that was overtly hostile to Europe.

Cale's aggressive *Sabotage/Live* in the final month of the 1970s seemed an 'answer' to punk's Velvet disciples. However, it sounded more like his recent American production client Patti Smith's more mainstream work than post-punk's experimental

Europeanism, with which Cale's blues cover 'Walkin' the Dog' was entirely at odds. Lyrically, however, 'Mercenaries (Ready for War)' implicitly addressed proxy Cold War conflicts in Afghanistan and Angola, while 'Dr. Mudd' confronted nuclear war. Cale's *Honi Soit* in March 1981 was a smoother version of the same approach, thus tame in comparison to producer Mike Thorne's other clients, Wire's anti-rockist guitar experiments (Reynolds 2003: 145–6) or Soft Cell's European-facing electronica. There are still hints of Europe, via the French-sung title track and the explicitly Cold War 'Russian Roulette', but these albums found Cale at his most 'rock' and his least adventurous.

Nico's only album without Cale, *Drama of Exile*, in May 1981, sounded more European than her erstwhile producer, but her lyrics lacked the European references of yore (bar 'Orly Flight'), with several songs explicitly invoking America ('60–40', 'Henry Hudson'; 'I'm Waiting for the Man'). Moreover, in a musical landscape now containing several androgynous 'ice queens' (Reynolds and Press 1995: 300–1) – Siouxsie, Poly Styrene, Pauline Murray, Patti Smith – and given post-punk's revolutionary rethinking of rock, Nico's new electric backing group sounded thin and leaden compared to recent releases by Joy Division, Bauhaus, the Cure or Public Image (*Metal Box*'s encompassing of Krautrock, Spanish folk and classicism). These artists had processed the Velvets, Velvets soloists (Witts 1993: 281), and Velvets acolytes Bowie, Roxy, Can and Faust, to create a distinctly white-sounding, blues-free European-facing art rock that evoked the very frozen borderlines Nico's work once had. Nico's cover of Bowie and Eno's '"Heroes"' highlights this problem. Bowie's original channelled both 'I'm Waiting for the Man' (O'Leary 2019: 89) and German music (Romanticism; Neu) while tapping the totalitarian and Cold War motifs of Cale and Nico's work. Nico's '"Heroes"' highlights her limitations: that she misses the song's Romantic grandeur is surprising – its passion and humour, less so.

This new Europeanism began to invade the British charts in 1980–1 (John Foxx's 'Europe after the Rain'; Depeche Mode's name), then the top 10 (Visage's French dialogued 'Fade to Grey'), peak Europeanism arguably being reached with Ultravox's no. 2 hit 'Vienna' in January 1981, complete with Romantic, Reger-influenced violin solo and Vienna-set *Third Man* video. With Ultravox admitting to the song's meaninglessness (Bracewell 1998: 217), 'European-ness' in this New Romantic moment had become style over substance – indeed, the turn's last gasp was, aptly, a hit 1982 reissue of Kraftwerk's 'The Model'. In this respect the Labour left's severe defeat in the 1983 UK election becomes a cultural, not just political, turning point, after which, under an emboldened Thatcher, an overtly transatlantic neoliberalism took hold of hearts, minds and wallets.

Invigorating as this European turn had been, the taint of fascism was never far away, whether it was Bowie hymning Hitler in 1976, Kraftwerk's ambiguous invocations of the Third Reich (Witts 2011: 167), the Pistols and Banshees' use of Nazi paraphernalia, Joy Division, Spandau Ballet and the March Violets' names (Reynolds 2003: 181–3; 435), the Skids' and Spandau's artwork, the Fall's Nietzsche fetish, Throbbing Gristle's mystic totalitarianism, the anti-humanist *hauteur* underpinning synthpop or the aristocratic Aryan posturing of New Romanticism (Bracewell 1998: 207) – all underpinned by the encroachment of the National Front upon youth culture (Reynolds 2003: 181). The gradual return of blackness to art rock via 'punk-funk' was thus a very necessary cultural development (131). Nico, Cale and Reed were hugely influential pioneers of this European turn but were themselves channelling currents which chafed against the post-war political and cultural dominance of America. Within this long-1970s work, the disfigured European son, fascism, floats, dances and demands acknowledgement, just as it did in Cold War Europe, highlighting the contrary currents of European history in liberalism and imperialism, enlightenment and absolutism, and inhabiting this European turn in music as demon, ghost and glamour.

Notes

1. Exceptions in British pop include the Beatles' Francophile 'Michelle' and Teutophile 'Girl' on 1965's *Rubber Soul* (MacDonald 1995: 140, 145 and 136).
2. France twice blocked Britain's attempts to join the European Economic Community: in 1963 (under Macmillan) and 1967 (Wilson).
3. Equally influential was the Jacques Brel-influenced work of Scott Walker from 1966 to 1970. Walker returned to American themes until 1978's Europhile, Bowie-esque, *Nite Flights*.
4. For example, the post-Cale Velvets' 'After Hours' (1969).
5. Concurrent with Cale, Nico and Reed's work, however, was progressive rock, which took inspiration from the European classical canon, though rarely featuring European themes.
6. See William Golding's *Lord of the Flies* (1954) and Neville Shute's *On the Beach* (1957).
7. For example, Roxy Music's 'Song for Europe' (*Stranded*, 1973), Bowie's Brel-like 'Rock'n'Roll Suicide' (*Ziggy Stardust*, 1972) and the Weimar nod of 'Time' from *Aladdin Sane* (1973).

References

Adorno, T. W. ([1952] 2005), *In Search of Wagner*, trans. R. Livingstone, London and New York: Verso.
Arendt, H. ([1951] 1994), *The Origins of Totalitarianism*, New York: Harcourt.
Bangs, L. (1983), in A. Zak (ed.) (1997) *The Velvet Underground: Four Decades of Commentary*, London, New York, Sydney: Omnibus.
Bockris, V. and Cale, J. (1999), *What's Welsh for Zen?*, London: Bloomsbury.
Bracewell, M. (1998), *England Is Mine: Pop Life in Albion from Wilde to Goldie*, London: Flamingo.
Buch, E., Zubillaga, I. C., and Silva, M. D. (eds) (2016), *Composing for the State: Music in Twentieth-Century Dictatorships*, Oxford and New York: Routledge.
Condon, J. (1983), 'The Perils of Nico', in A. Zak (ed.) (1997), *The Velvet Underground: Four Decades of Commentary*, 40–51, London, New York, Sydney: Omnibus.

Crawford, R. (2001), *America's Musical Life*, London and New York: W.W. Norton and Company.
DeCurtis, A. (2017), *Lou Reed: A Life*, London: John Murray.
Eagleton, T. (1996), *Literary Theory: An Introduction* [1983], Malden, MA: Blackwell.
Fricke, D. (1989), 'Lou Reed: The Rolling Stone Interview', *Rolling Stone*, 4 May. Available online: https://bit.ly/349y7jZ (accessed 1 December 2021).
Frieze (2007), '*Nico. The Frozen Borderline: 1968-70*', 6 May, 107. Available online: https://bit.ly/3GfXfTz (accessed 1 December 2021).
George-Warren, H. (1997), 'Nico', in B. O'Dair (ed.), *Trouble Girls: The Rolling Stone Book of Women in Rock*, 255–8, New York: Random House.
Gold, M. (1973), 'John Cale: Paris 1919', *Let It Rock*, October. Available online: https://bit.ly/3IHbT7A (accessed 1 December 2021).
Golding, W. (1954), *Lord of the Flies*, London: Faber and Faber.
Greene, D. (2016), *Rock, Counterculture and the Avant-Garde, 1966–1970*, Jefferson: McFarland & Co.
Griffiths, D. (2000) 'Home Is Living Like a Man on the Run: John Cale's Welsh Atlantic', *Welsh Music History*, 4: 159–85.
Haider, A. (2018), 'Programme Notes: John Cale Interview with Arwa Haider', *John Cale A Futurespective*, London: Barbican. Available online: https://sites.barbican.org.uk/johncale/ (accessed 22 November 2021).
Hogan, P. (2007), *The Rough Guide to The Velvet Underground*, London: Rough Guides/Penguin.
Landa, I. (2012), *The Apprentice's Sorcerer: Liberal Tradition and Fascism*, Chicago: Haymarket.
MacDonald, I. (1995), *Revolution in the Head: The Beatles' Records and the Sixties*, London: Pimlico.
Marcuse, H. (2014), *Marxism, Revolution and Utopia: Collected Papers of Herbert Marcuse*, vol. 6, ed. D. Kellner and C. Pierce, London and New York: Routledge.
Mitchell, T. (2003), *Sedition and Alchemy: A Biography of John Cale*, London: Peter Owen.
Nelis, J. (2007), 'Constructing Fascist Identity: Benito Mussolini and the Myth of Romanita', *Classical World*, 100 (4): 391–415.
O'Leary, C. (2019), *Ashes to Ashes: The Songs of David Bowie 1976–2016*, London: Repeater.
Pinnock, T. (2015), 'Nico and *The Marble Index*: "She Hated the Idea of Being Beautiful"', *Uncut*, 16 October. Available online: https://bit.ly/3H5Tm4u (accessed 1 July 2021).
Rau, P. (2013), *Our Nazis: Representations of Fascism in Contemporary Literature and Film*, Edinburgh: Edinburgh University.
Remnant, M. (1989), *Musical Instruments: An Illustrated History from Antiquity to the Present*, London: Batsford.
Reynolds, D. (1994), 'Great Britain', in D. Reynolds (ed.), *The Origins of the Cold War in Europe: International Perspectives*, 77–95, New Haven, CT: Yale University.
Reynolds, S. (2003), *Rip It Up and Start Again: Post-punk 1978–1984*, London: Faber and Faber.
Reynolds, S. and Press, J. (1995), *The Sex Revolts: Gender, Rebellion and Rock'n'Roll*, London: Serpent's Tail.
Schwarz, B. (2012), *Memories of Empire, Vol. 1: The White Man's World*, Oxford: Oxford University.

Scott, R. J. (2003), *Chord Progressions for Songwriters*, Bloomington, IN: iUniverse.
Shute, N. (1957), *On the Beach*, London: Heinemann.
Stonor Saunders, F. (2000), *Who Paid the Piper: The CIA and the Cultural Cold War*, London: Granta.
Thornton, A. (2005), 'Nico: The Marble Index', *NME*, 12 September. Available online: https://bit.ly/3fXCbGm (accessed 1 December 2021).
Unterberger, R. (2009), *White Light/White Heat: The Velvet Underground Day-By-Day*, London: Jawbone.
Witts, R. (1993), *Nico: The Life and Lies of an Icon*, London: Virgin.
Witts, R. (2011), '*Vorsprung durch Technik*: Kraftwerk and the British Fixation with Germany' in S. Albiez and D. Pattie (eds), *Kraftwerk: Music Non-Stop*, New York: Continnum.
Zak, A. (1997), *The Velvet Underground: Four Decades of Commentary, London*, New York, Sydney: Omnibus.

9

'I'll be your mirror': The Velvet Underground as the legacy of Ziggy Stardust

Martin James and Johnny Hopkins

The rock critic Lester Bangs stated that '[m]odern music starts with the Velvets' (Richman 2012), while Brian Eno once jokingly told an interviewer in 1982: 'I was talking to Lou Reed the other day and he said that the first Velvet Underground record sold thirty-thousand copies in the first five years ... I think everyone who bought one of those thirty-thousand copies started a band!' (McKenna 1982).[1] Popular histories initially sought to reduce the Velvet Underground's messy emergence to a one-dimensional, heroic and celebratory master narrative, through identifying a teleological progression, from great creative visionaries to great events. Eno's comment seems to hold some semblance of truth, with an MGM royalty statement showing sales of 58,476 copies[2] in the first two years of release (Gold 2013). It also echoes similar claims made for notable historical events such as the sparsely attended but culturally significant Sex Pistols gig at the Manchester Lesser Free Trade Hall in 1976, and as such denies the complexity of the creative networks that created the space for the Velvet Underground as a cultural artefact. Eno implies that the impact of the band's debut album was relatively rapid, though in truth the force of its impact wasn't felt until many years later. Indeed, it was with the emergence of punk that many artists publicly noted the importance of the Velvet Underground. But their initial discovery had been less of the band themselves than of David Bowie's performance of the Ziggy persona performing the Velvet Underground. For Bowie's own fandom Ziggy's performance of the band thus became a simulacrum – more real than the real thing (Baudrillard 1994). Indeed, the wider, post-demise popularity of the Velvets can be viewed as a legacy of Ziggy, which in itself was an expression of Bowie's own commodified fandom. Ziggy, in other words, was his own answer to Warhol's Pop Art, as a musical (per)form(ance) that embraced its own processes of commodification and was created with a limited shelf life – the popstar as a can of Campbell's soup.

This chapter explores both Bowie's pre-fame 'discovery' of the Velvet Underground and his use of the band's mythology in the creation, adornment and performance of the Ziggy Stardust character. We show his attempts at performing subcultural capital (Thornton 1996) through the early recording of 'I'm Waiting for the Man' and the inclusion of the song in his live shows from late 1966, prior to the release of *The*

Velvet Underground & Nico, through to mid-1967. We then explore Bowie's role as both 'productive consumer' (Jensen 1992) and 'cultural intermediary' (Bourdieu 1984) in the production of the Velvet Underground as 'taste culture' (Bourdieu 1984). Bowie achieved this through adopting the identity of the objects of his fandom and subsequently associating them with his own assumed identity. In fandom terms Ziggy became the religious icon (Whyton 2014) through which Bowie performs the cultural and subcultural capital (Bourdieu 1984; Thornton 1996) gained through associations with, immersion in and performance of the objects of his own active fandom (McCormick 2017). This commodifying process brought the Velvet Underground out of the shadows of rock authenticity into the artifice of pop culture that ultimately led to a generation of fans discovering the band. Bowie then performed the role of cultural intermediary through the performed identity of Ziggy Stardust long after the New York band in its original, authentic form had ceased to exist.

The Velvet Underground as Bowie's biography

In late January 1971 the still relatively unknown David Bowie attended a Velvet Underground show at the Electric Circus on St. Mark's Place in New York. Reflecting on this, Bowie (2004) stated that as the self-proclaimed 'biggest [Velvet Underground] fan in the UK', his first experience of the band live found him 'at the front by the lip of the stage', making 'sure that Lou Reed could see that I was a true fan by singing along to all the songs'. The venue itself was steeped in Velvet Underground mythology, having been the location for some of Andy Warhol's Exploding Plastic Inevitable happenings throughout 1966. For Bowie the fan, the setting couldn't have been more perfect. After the show he tells how he went backstage, knocked on the dressing room door and, '[a]fter a few gushing compliments', asked if he 'could have a few words with Lou'. He enjoyed a ten-minute conversation with the singer before he 'left the club floating on cloud nine – a teenage ambition achieved'. It was only later he realized that Reed had already left the band and the singer he sat on a bench talking to was in fact Doug Yule, who had replaced Reed as band leader.

By this point the Velvet Underground's flame appeared to be flickering to an end. Press reactions to their self-titled third album were not entirely positive and the fourth, *Loaded* (1970), was at best dismissed, at worst ignored. Any early hype around the band had dissipated, record sales had been disappointingly low and now Reed, the creative songwriting force and figurehead, had gone. The Velvets' position as an elite force of avant-gardist countercultural activity seemed over and, but for the Reed-less fifth album *Squeeze* (1973) – essentially a Doug Yule solo album – they were a spent force.

The timing of Bowie's first and only experience of the Velvet Underground live and the mistaken identity that followed is significant. On returning to England, Bowie willed that meeting with Reed into existence by penning his Velvets homage 'Queen Bitch'. *The Melody Maker*'s Michael Watts (1972) wrote that the song 'takes off to a tee the Lou Reed vocals and arrangement, as well as parodying, with a storyline about the singer's boyfriend being seduced by another queen, the whole Velvet Underground genre'. When Bowie launched his Ziggy Stardust persona live at Aylesbury Friars (15 July 1972) in front of fans and the UK and US media, the set included his New York trilogy from side two of *Hunky Dory* ('Andy Warhol', 'Song for Bob Dylan' and 'Queen Bitch') alongside covers of 'I'm Waiting for the Man' and 'White Light/White Heat'. After the Friars gig, Bowie hurried back to London to catch fellow Velvets acolyte Iggy Pop, one of his other heroes/charges, play with the Stooges at the Kings Cross Cinema (Rock 1995: 33). Bowie's self-elected role as a tastemaker meant he became a key cultural intermediary in the Velvet Underground's slowly emerging post-demise popularity. In becoming the messenger through cover versions, the Velvets-inspired 'Queen Bitch' and via his production of Reed's breakthrough 1972 solo album *Transformer*, the mainstream positioning of the Velvets was mediated in the early 1970s through Bowie's own biography, including through his fetishization of New York as a mythological space that he would eventually call home – and where he would ultimately die.

Key to Bowie's status as a cultural intermediary was his questionable claim to have been the first artist to perform and record covers of the Velvet Underground's 'I'm Waiting for the Man' before *The Velvet Underground & Nico* had even been released. At a time when the first wave of rock aristocracy had embraced the peace and love ethos of mid-1960s psychedelia, the Velvets appeared to redefine the frameworks of 'authenticity' in rock. Sonically they achieved this through a blend of disparate and seemingly oppositional styles that to the outsider appeared to capture the essence of the drug-fuelled hedonism of Warhol's Factory. Lyrically their celebration of drug abuse, sadomasochism and prostitution made the Beatles' LSD experiments appear relatively tame. Reed's explicit accounts of inner-city street life and social decay offered a voyeuristic description of life that would never be seen along 'Penny Lane'. To the British rock fan, the Velvet Underground's dystopian art rock offered access to distant urban exotica existing in a world that was inaccessible to all but Warhol's New York art elite, in a city that appeared wholly alien. It was outsider music from which its audience were excluded, themselves forever outsiders from the Warhol inner circle.

Popular history suggests that Bowie was first introduced to the work of the Velvet Underground via an acetate of the yet-to-be released debut album (Pitt 1983: 61). Bowie's manager Ken Pitt had been in New York in November 1966, when former assistant Marian Fenn offered him the chance to meet Warhol through her friend Denis Deegan, whom Gerard Malanga says 'knew just about anyone who was anyone on the planet. A true catalyst' (Malanga 2020). Pitt was keen to meet Warhol, and on 10 November, Deegan told him Warhol wanted to come to London with his new rock and roll group the Velvet Underground. Pitt was asked if he could facilitate this (Pitt 1983: 60). Pitt and Deegan visited the Factory later that day, where they met with Warhol sat beneath a huge yellow banana suspended from the ceiling. He also spotted Nico sat at typewriter, whom he remembered from being around during the Bob Dylan UK tour in 1965, for which he handled PR (Pitt 1983: 60). For Pitt 'the most significant aspect of my visit to the Factory was my meeting with Lou Reed and being given an advanced acetate copy' of the Velvets debut 'banana' album (Pitt 1983: 61). After his return to London on 16 December, he handed the record to Bowie along with a Fugs album (Pitt 1983: 70). However, there is some suggestion that Pitt may have given the acetate to Bowie at a slightly earlier date. According to Bowie his band the Buzz played 'I'm Waiting for the Man' as an encore at their last gig on 2 December 1966, stating 'not only was I to cover [a] Velvet's song before anyone else in the world, I actually did it before the album came out' (Bowie 2003). However, in a 2002 interview Bowie's memory of the chronology of his performance of the song is further confused: 'I got Riot Squad to learn it in the week I got the album before it was out. We were doing it onstage before the Velvets had an album out' (Du Noyer [2002] 2020: 68).

Despite Pitt's claims to have introduced Bowie to the Velvet Underground, it is likely he already knew of the band. In the 1960s a transatlantic network existed through which countercultural and music knowledge readily flowed (Bockris and Malanga 1983; Unterberger 2009; Hopkins and James, Chapter 2, in this collection). This network included professional services of management, promotion and record labels, and significant countercultural spaces and events inhabited by key bands, artists, poets, journalists, business figures and fashionistas from the London and New York undergrounds. The underground US rock press (e.g. *East Village Other*, *The Village Voice*) was easily available on import in specialist UK shops. The UK's underground press (e.g. *International Times*) and John Peel's radio show were also sources of transatlantic music news. Richard Williams, who wrote the first UK review of *Velvet Underground & Nico* in the *Nottingham Guardian Journal*, explains, 'I had a music column in a page called "The Younger Set" that appeared each week in the *Nottingham Guardian Journal*. This was a daily, then soon to disappear; perhaps leading a page with an ecstatic 600-word review of the VU and Nico helped it on its way to oblivion. But no one tried to stop me' (Williams 2020). In further explaining how he first became aware of the band, he outlined:

> I read about the VU in the *East Village Other* (John Wilcock's famous piece) and *The Village Voice* (Richard Goldstein). These publications came, amazingly enough, to a bookshop in Nottingham, called *Bux*, where one could also buy *City Lights* volumes and the works of LeRoi Jones and Che Guevara ... So as soon as the album came out ... I got hold of one. Disappointed that EMI had dispensed with the US gatefold and its peelable banana but only slightly so because everything else about it was so stupendous.

Bowie too was locked into the underground presses of the UK and the United States as a regular attendee of many of London's subcultural spaces, and so is likely to have already been aware of Warhol's Pop Art, the Factory scene and the Velvet Underground. Like most people in the UK, hearing the debut album would have been his first real experience of the band. Bowie was able to accentuate his subcultural capital by drawing attention to the fact that he heard the album before most other people. 'Everything I both felt and didn't know about rock music was opened up to me on one unreleased disc ... This music was savagely indifferent to my feelings. It didn't care if I liked it or not' (qtd. in Gilbert 2017: 34). Bowie's reaction made Pitt even more determined to bring Warhol and the Velvets to London, wondering, '[w]hat if they formed a mutual appreciation society, with Warhol and the Velvets singing David's praises in America?' (Pitt 1983: 70).

Interestingly the work of Reed and John Cale had already inadvertently touched Bowie some six months earlier thanks to his long-standing admiration for the UK R'n'B act Downliners Sect. In 1964 he'd been in Davie Jones and the King Bees, with Downliners Sect among the band's influences (downlinersect.com). That influence was audibly taken forward to his next two bands – The Mannish Boys and Davy Jones and the Lower Third – both of which criss-crossed Downliners Sect on the UK gig circuit throughout from 1964 to 1966. By early 1966, at the instigation of the music publishing company Campbell Connelly, Downliners Sect were including the song 'Why Don't You Smile Now' in their set. Attributed to Reed, Cale, Philips and Vance, it was the product of Reed's period as a songwriter for the Pickwick record label; it was also the first song Reed and Cale collaborated on. Reed had demoed 'Why Don't You Smile Now' on 11 May 1965 at Pickwick Studios, Long Island, with Terry Philips producing in a recording session also including the song 'Buzz, Buzz, Buzz' and two early takes of 'Heroin'. Downliners Sect released 'Why Don't You Smile Now' on their April 1966 *The Rock Sects In* album. That Campbell Connelly had pushed the song towards Downliners Sect raises the question of whether they pushed other Reed or Reed/Cale songs to British artists. Interestingly, the Reed, Philips, Vance and Sims song 'You're Driving Me Insane' performed by the Roughnecks was publicized as '[t]he sounds of England' despite actually being Reed and Pickwick session players.

After hearing the Velvet Underground via the acetate, Bowie's subsequent recordings have interest from a production perspective but as songs they were less than auspicious. On 13 December Bowie recorded 'Please Mr Gravedigger' at the Decca Studio 2 with producer Gus Dudgeon. Bowie had previously recorded a different version of the song two months earlier – then called 'The Gravedigger' – at RG Jones studio. Only the lyrics remained intact from that version. A month later, on 26 January 1967, Bowie and Dudgeon began the first of four days of recordings across two months, with 'The Laughing Gnome' and tracks destined for Bowie's debut album. While both 'Please Mr Gravedigger' and 'The Laughing Gnome' show producer and songwriter employing found sounds and pitched tape loops in performances of *musique concrète* juvenilia, the latter is often regarded as one of Bowie's song writing low points. However, 'The Laughing Gnome' can also be viewed as his first of many attempts to 'match the drone of the Velvet Underground's "I'm Waiting for the Man"' (O'Leary 2015: 67). Carlos Alomar, who appeared with Bowie live and on recordings from the 1970s to 2000s, suggests simple chord structure in the song reflected his love for the Velvets: 'the same pulsation' exists in both 'The Laughing Gnome' and 'I'm Waiting for the Man' (qtd. in *David Bowie: Finding Fame*, 2019).

A month after completing the recording of 'The Laughing Gnome', Bowie secretly joined the Waltham Forest act Riot Squad. He had been label-mates with an early incarnation of the band through his deal with Pye, but they hadn't come into contact with each other until August 1966 when David Bowie and the Buzz supported Riot

Squad at The Marquee Club in London. When Bowie joined Riot Squad, he was waiting for his Anthony Newley-esque eponymous debut album to be released and didn't have a band to perform with. As he was contracted to Deram, he was forced to perform under the assumed name Toy Soldier, which he also used when the band were featured in the 8 July issue of *Jackie* magazine.

The Riot Squad were similarly in a state of stasis; their producer, Joe Meek, had murdered his landlady and subsequently committed suicide on 3 February 1967. They felt the need to move their sound in a new, more psychedelic direction, and having unsuccessfully auditioned numerous singers, bandleader Bob Evans suggested Bowie as a temporary solution. Evans offered him the job when the pair met in March at the Denmark Street La Gioconda Café (Ceriotti n.d.). During approximately twenty-five gigs between 17 March to 2 May, Bowie encouraged the band to start wearing make-up and introduced theatricality to their shows, contributing three originals to the band's repertoire: 'Silly Boy Blue', 'Little Toy Soldier' and 'Silver Treetop School For Boys'. He instigated covers including the Fugs' 'Dirty Ol' Man', Frank Zappa's 'It Can't Happen Here' and a rendition of the as-yet-unreleased 'I'm Waiting for the Man'. O'Leary (2015) suggests that due to the locations of the Riot Squad gigs in towns like Harrow and venues such as London's Tiles Club, the Riot Squad dates with Bowie can be viewed as the birth of glam rock. Certainly their stage show drew on the performance of ambiguous sexual identity with Bowie's misunderstanding of the lyrics to 'I'm Waiting for the Man' resulting in a high camp comedy mime. At the start of the performance Bowie would set about painting the band's faces with the intention of unlocking latent homosexual tendencies. In response the band would move around the stage following each other 'in close contact' (*David Bowie: Finding Fame*, 2019). An unsophisticated performance of fluid sexual identity that was more *Carry On* than Jean Genet perhaps, but an early example of concepts that Bowie would return to with greater impact in the next few years.

The extent to which Bowie misunderstood Reed's lyrics became even more evident through the demo he produced with Riot Squad. After Bowie had convinced Gus Dudgeon to let the band use downtime at the Decca 2 studio in London, they recorded four tracks on 5 April from 10 pm to 12 midnight. These songs included Bowie originals 'Silly Boy Blue', 'Silver Treetop School for Boys', 'Little Toy Soldier' – which featured liberal lifts from 'Venus in Furs' – and a version of 'I'm Waiting for the Man'. The underwhelming results were an 'exercise in cross-Atlantic sonic dilution' (O'Leary 2009). Despite claims that this was the first recorded cover of a Velvet Underground song, the recordings remained unreleased until 2013, when Acid Jazz released the Riot Squad songs on the *Toy Soldier e.p.*. In fact the first commercially distributed covers of the Velvet Underground material emerged in April 1967, one month after the album's US release and contemporaneous with the Riot Squad's recording, when Dutch band the Riats released a single with versions of the Velvets' 'Run Run Run' and 'Sunday Morning'. Around the same time an American band called the Electrical Banana are reported to have released a version of 'There She Goes Again', recorded in a tent in Vietnam while on service in the US Army, though only a limited number of copies were pressed (Pyro 2014).

If Bowie's recent career had been notable for his convincing appropriation of Anthony Newley's exaggerated cockney twang, then on his Riot Squad experiments, he expertly showed his mimicry also extended to Reed's New York City drawl. Bowie's vocal on 'Little Toy Soldier' seems a shameless attempt at imitating Reed's deadpan enunciation. Even more shameless was Bowie's blatant steal from 'Venus in Furs' in the chorus, again delivered as a close impersonation of Reed, with the verses appropriating Newley's singing style. It was a performance of confused and duelling identities with the present Bowie already grappling with his future self. The major shift, however, can be heard in the lyrical content, which features a little girl called Sadie, a toy soldier and whipping – all of which is festooned with sound effects, including cackles, whipcracks and creaking springs which descend into whoops, explosions, shattering glass, coughing and, just as in 'Please Mr Gravedigger', a loudly blown nose.

Bowie's claims to have recorded 'I'm Waiting for the Man' before its release may have been, therefore, a classic case of self-mythologizing largely unquestioned by Bowie's numerous biographers (Sandford 1996; Trynka 2010; O'Leary 2015, etc.). *The Velvet Underground & Nico* was released in the United States on 12 March 1967, the same day as Riot Squad's Bob Evans had met Bowie at La Gioconda Café and almost a month before the band recorded their version (although the Velvets album wouldn't get a full UK release until the following November). What is clear though is that Bowie's 'discovery' of the band was before the album's release. The most significant impact on Bowie at this time may have been that the Velvets eventually saved him from a career as a mainstream entertainer. Bowie was covering popular songs from film musicals in 1965 and 1966 with his band Davy Jones and the Lower Third and also when Pitt first met and saw Bowie perform with the Buzz in April 1966 (Pitt 1983: 51).

Following disastrous sales of his debut album, Bowie was dropped by Deram. By 1968 he was thinking of giving up music to become a dancer (Reynolds 2016: 89) and joined mime artist Lindsay Kemp as part of the touring *Pierrot in Turqouise*. Bowie played the part of 'Cloud' and augmented his mime with folk renditions of songs from his debut album. His next project was the mixed-media trio Turquoise (later Feathers), who debuted in September 1968. Mick Farren, who painted backdrops for Kemp, claimed that the mime artist's scene was as outrageous as Warhol's Factory. 'If you wanted to hang out (with Kemp's scene) you had to learn heavy manners. And David came in, learning moves. He was clearly learning a lot – mutating' (Trynka 2010: 81). The songs Bowie wrote following his mixed-media experiments with Feathers presented more evidence of the influence of 'I'm Waiting for the Man'. An early 1969 home demo version of 'Conversation Piece' reveals a similar metronomic two-chord propulsion in the verse with first-person lyrics discussing urban alienation and suicidal thoughts. By the time he re-recorded it for the *Mercury Demos* with John 'Hutch' Hutchinson, it had been transformed into a Dylan-influenced folk song in keeping with the rest of his pre-'Space Oddity' set.

Despite Pitt's suggestions that he'd pushed Bowie towards the aesthetic of the Velvet Underground's New York, it would appear his protégée was also attracted to the New York of Simon & Garfunkel, as evidenced in the demos 'Life Is a Circus' and 'Lover to the Dawn' (later released in a fully reworked form as 'Cygnet Committee'). Alan

Mair, bass player in the Beatstalkers (and later the Only Ones), was managed by Pitt at the same time as Bowie and the two became friends. Mair (2019) confirms that the Velvets' sound 'was the direction that Ken Pitt had been encouraging him towards during the 60s' although Bowie didn't fully deliver on Pitt's hopes until the arrival of Ziggy Stardust in 1972.

The myth of the first live performance of a Velvet Underground cover version

Bowie's role as it developed into the 1970s can be understood by viewing him as a cultural intermediary of the Velvet Underground, with the band a 'taste culture' that is filtered according to positions of power and influence within particular 'fields' via layers of subcultural gatekeepers. Bourdieu defined tastemakers as cultural intermediaries that operate at the intersection of culture and economy and define what is good and bad in the marketplace. They perform key roles in the production and promotion of consumption through the construction of legitimization, authentication and value. The notion of the cultural intermediary is drawn from Bourdieu's (1984) work on the 'new occupations' that marked out the post-1960s socio-economic landscape. Bourdieu (1984) presents cultural intermediaries as a group of tastemakers and need merchants in an economy that requires the production of consumer tastes. For Bourdieu taste acts as a common ground that brings people and goods together and enables that taste to become situated in those goods. He argued that a new economy came into play that required not only the production of goods but also the production of needs. This entailed an 'ethical retooling' of consumer culture that 'new class fractions' (1984) in society pursue. Bowie's performance of the role of tastemaker enabled him to work at the intersection of culture and economy. He performed critical operations in the production, promotion and consumption of particular artists as a construct of good taste, in the process constructing legitimacy and adding value to the artists he promoted and his own art and consumer goods (Matthews and Smith Maguire 2014: 1).

As previously noted Bowie claimed to have first performed 'I'm Waiting for the Man' as early as 2 December 1966. Mick Farren also claimed to have performed the earliest Velvets cover with his proto-punk band the Social Deviants. Bowie seemingly learnt the Velvet's songs from an album acetate, but Farren's covers were of the versions of tracks from demo tapes that circulated in the UK in the two years prior to the album's release (Bockris and Malanga 1983; Hopkins and James, Chapter 2, in this collection). However, a band with a potentially stronger claim would be original mods the Yardbirds, who were also a huge influence on Bowie. The Yardbirds connection cannot be underestimated as they were early cultural intermediaries key to Bowie's own developing cultural capital. Bowie, whose 1965 Manish Boys single 'I Pity the Fool/ Take My Tip' included Page sessioning as lead guitarist, would cover two Yardbirds tracks – 'I Wish You Would' and 'Shape of Things' – for his 1973 covers album *Pin-Ups*. Following the huge US success of 'For Your Love', the Yardbirds embarked on a tour of the United States. According to drummer Jim McCarty they first came across Warhol when he was nearly refused entry to their record company reception in New York at the end of their first 1965 tour (Platt et al. 1983: 78). Rhythm guitarist Chris Dreja noted that on their second 1965 tour they were 'pretty soon met by the current "in-crowd", notably the Warhol clan. It was very bizarre; you'd arrive at a restaurant and discover Warhol and his entourage would be at the next table' (Platt et al. 1983: 85). However, as McCarty reflected, '[w]e always kept ourselves largely to ourselves…. [the NY scene] was a bit like meeting the Devil and being invited to join the Inferno' (Platt et al. 1983: 85).

Unlike both Pitt and Bowie, the Yardbirds experienced the original Velvet Underground live, with bassist Chris Dreja taking photographs (Platt et al. 1983: 131–3). Just a few days after Pitt's Factory visit and about a month before Bowie heard the aforementioned acetate, the Yardbirds played with the Velvets in Detroit at Dick Clark's *Caravan of Stars* festival on 18 and 19 November 1966 (Platt et al 1983; McCarty 2018). McCarty notes that during the Yardbirds' extensive tours of Britain and the United States, 'we heard new music from new bands, and sometimes it registered with us' (2018: 164). For the Yardbirds the 'highlight' of the [Detroit gigs] 'was the opportunity to learn a new song that would soon be appearing in our repertoire' (McCarty 2018: 166). That song was 'I'm Waiting for the Man', and while McCarty (2019) confesses now that 'I wasn't crazy on the Velvet Underground, though they were "interesting!"', he does concede that '"I'm Waiting for the Man" was a good song with "street cred"'. As documented on the *Last Rave-Up in L.A.* (1979) bootleg, the Yardbirds were still playing the song at the Shrine Exposition Hall in Los Angeles on 31 May 1968, one of their last gigs before Jimmy Page redefined the band as the New Yardbirds, a precursor to Led Zeppelin. McCarty (2019) concludes by saying, 'We did meet Lou when he came to our LA show, and he was very impressed we played that song.'

The Yardbirds saw the Velvets play again at *The World's First Mod Wedding Happening* also in Detroit on 20 November, an event promoted by Motown publicist Allan Abrams (Cosgrove 2016: 86). Warhol gave away the bride with the entertainment at the reception including a Velvet Underground performance (McCarty 2018: 164). As a further example of the transatlantic cultural collision between darkest New York and Swinging London, the 'Mod Wedding' was a central feature of the three-day November 1966 *Carnaby Street Fun Festival* in Detroit.

When director Michelangelo Antonioni was making *Blow Up* (1966), his film about a hip young British photographer (based on David Bailey), he had wanted to feature the auto-destructive live performance of the Who in a club scene but they turned it down. The Velvet Underground were under serious consideration to step in, both because their vicious sound matched Antonioni's brief and the film company, MGM, owned the Velvets' label Verve. However, the cost of bringing them to the UK for filming was proving an issue (Fricke 1995: 17) and Yardbirds manager Simon Napier-Bell instead negotiated the deal for his clients. It is intriguing to imagine what would have happened if the quintessential New York group the Velvet Underground had appeared as the live band in the quintessential Swinging London film.

The Velvet Underground as Ziggy's legacy

Bowie's fans expressed their fandom not only through their appreciation of the artist himself but also through knowledge of his antecedents (such as Scott Walker, Jacques Brel and the Pretty Things). As Bannister (2010) notes, 'Such awareness of the past was (at the time) subversive. Unlike today … the 1960s were virtually unheard, a kind of secret' (81). Bowie used his cultural and subcultural capital as subversive elements in his own self-creation. In so doing the artists he outwardly referenced and who informed his music and performances were subsumed into the Ziggy character as a piece of Pop Art. Bowie's attraction to the Pop Art of Warhol made perfect sense. Indeed in many ways the Ziggy Stardust creation was in itself a piece of Pop Art – one that aimed to challenge the elitist notion that 'real art' was somehow separate from daily life and commerce. This romanticism was also central to the countercultural rock industry in which musicians were able to deny the commercial nature of the products they created through the illusion of authentic artistry that permeated the rock industries. This illusion was further endorsed and mediated by so-called 'golden age' music critics such as Lester Bangs, Jim DeRogatis and Richard Meltzer, who were implicit in propagating the illusory nature of rock-art over pop-commerce. These writers emerged through non-professional, highly ideological fanzine presses and structured their work in line with the interests and language of fans. In so doing these rock critics 'valorized authenticity and originality, and developed a mythologized account of rock musicians that considered their work as art' (Atton 2009: 53).

This implied division between the authentic artist and the commercial pop star was embodied in vinyl formats. Pop was animated via the 7-inch single – the life blood of the radio DJ, fuel for the charts and the product favoured by younger teenagers and, perhaps more significantly, female music fans. The 7-inch format drove the communal nature of subcultural engagement by encouraging public sharing. Following 1967's concept album *Sgt Peppers' Lonely Hearts Club Band*, rock music increasingly prioritized private over public listening (Wald 2009). Rock music's serious nature was supported by notions of concept, cover art that might not feature the artist and performances that exaggerated the distance of authentic 'real' art. The serious art of rock aimed for a timelessness that transcended the fads and fashions of commercial taste. Pop music on the other hand celebrated style, artifice, commerce, disposable fashion and the star. Ziggy Stardust was created with a short pop life. It was the Ziggy moment in which influence and history collapsed into a performance of the Ziggy present. Ziggy as a product was defined by its own defined obsolescence, at the hands of its own consumers: a product that contributed to the wider growth of glam rock and spoke to fans through the medium of television. In 1971, 91 per cent of British homes had a television, meaning that the 'glam rock generation was the first to be socialized during a period when television, with its emphasis on the image, was pervasive and taken for granted. It was the first generation to be able to watch, as a mass, both working-class and middle-class, its rock performers on *Top of the Pops* and *The Old Grey Whistle Test*' (Stratton 1986: 16).

Bowie's 'coming out' television performances as Ziggy performing 'Starman', which many have suggested was their own awakening to Bowie (Jones 2014), personified the transition from folk artist to glam rock star, a performance discarding the authentic, real and remote of rock art to the artifice of the image-driven, disposable and commercial works associated with Pop Art. Ziggy was the product of Bowie's study of Warhol, and in many ways Bowie's vision was more aligned with the mass consumption aesthetic of Pop Art than that of the Velvet Underground. Warhol's suggestion of bringing Nico into the band and his infamous peel slowly and see banana cover were an attempt to provide the Velvets with Pop Art's celebration of commodification. In truth the band's aesthetic was initially more closely associated with the exclusivity of the avant-garde, the high culture of great poets and the elitist, countercultural ethos of the Factory.

The Ziggy Stardust product also celebrated Pop Art's connection to high camp to a greater extent than the Velvet Underground's oeuvre did. As Stevenson notes, '[c]amp exhibits a relish for exaggeration, artifice and androgyny. It depends upon a playful rather than a serious disposition as well as the "victory" of "style" over "content", "aesthetics" over "morality", of irony over tragedy' (Stevenson 2006: 51). Bowie's high camp, pop subcultural turn was an exaggeration of Pop Art's own exaggerated camp. Lou Reed may have written the songs but it took the arrival of Ziggy Stardust to turn 'I'm Waiting for the Man' and 'White Light/White Heat' into Pop Art.

Bowie's early embrace of the potential of these two songs[3] meant that they would ultimately become central to the Ziggy Stardust mythos, despite the fact that he never released his own versions of any Velvets material until 'White Light/White Heat', on the *Ziggy Stardust: The Motion Picture* live album in 1983. As Ziggy, Bowie cut another version of 'I'm Waiting for the Man' with The Spiders from Mars in January 1972 for early Velvets supporter John Peel's BBC show. 'White Light/White Heat' was recorded twice for the BBC with the Spiders. A third recorded version that had been slated for Bowie's *Pin Ups* collection was dropped, though Mick Ronson revived the recording for his solo album *Play Don't Worry* (1975).

The BBC sessions and live performances of the Velvet Underground's material again locate Bowie as a key cultural intermediary of the New York band's mythology. However, just as 'Queen Bitch' had shown Bowie writing himself into the Velvets' story, Bowie's 1970s patronage placed them in the centre of his own myth creation. Having finally met the real Reed in September 1971, Bowie hosted Reed's first UK performance. Reed's eponymous debut solo album had been released three months earlier to critical ambivalence. In this album Reed attempted to reclaim the Velvets' crown by releasing a set dominated by new recordings of unreleased Velvet Underground material. By the time of Reed's live debut as part of Bowie's show at a Friends of the Earth 'Save the Whale' charity event (8 July 1972 at the Royal Festival Hall), Bowie the student had usurped Reed the professor. Following a rendition of the Velvets-influenced 'Moonage Daydream', Bowie introduced Lou Reed to his stage, and together with the Spiders, they performed 'White Light/White Heat', 'I'm Waiting for the Man', 'Sweet Jane' as well as Bowie's 'Suffragette City'. The photographer Mick Rock, who had struck up a creative relationship with Bowie that grew from a shared love of the Velvets, took defining photos both of Bowie as Ziggy and later of Reed for the cover of *Transformer*. He gave an intriguing insight into the dynamics between Bowie and Reed at the Royal Festival Hall show, stating, 'David never did join Lou at the mike [sic]. He completely turned off his charisma and became part of the backing band for Lou. He respected Lou more than any other rocker: "Lou Reed is a master. He's messed-up, but he's a master"' (Rock 1995: 28).

Only five months later Reed released the Bowie-produced and Ronson-arranged *Transformer* album, in which Reed's New York became fetishized by Bowie's New York gaze. 'Vicious' sounded like Reed performing Bowie's idea of the Velvet Underground, while 'Satellite of Love' was Reed as Bowie within an arrangement worthy of *Hunky Dory*. Lou Reed and the Velvets were thus subsumed into Bowie's performance of Ziggy. When fans of Bowie found the Velvet Underground, it was as an aspect of his performed identity, and not the Velvets as an entity unto themselves. Yet for many Bowie's consumption would become a gateway to an authentic discovery of Reed and the band. For example, Douglas Hart, the original bass player in the Jesus and Mary Chain, discovered the Velvets through his elder brother's love of Bowie (2019). Many fans would define the late discovery as a moment of epiphany. Vic Godard of Subway Sect outlined how:

> I first heard them through being a Bowie fan. I used to buy bootlegs in Kensington Market and Bowie often did 'Waiting for the Man' and 'White Light/White Heat' in his live set in those days. Around the same time I heard Lou himself on the radio doing 'Waiting for the Man' and was immediately stunned. It was like everything you wanted to be on a record and no extraneous flab. It was comparable to hearing the Kingsmen doing 'Louie Louie' after knowing it by the Kinks, or hearing a Chuck Berry song after an English group's version.
>
> (2019)

Another example is the experience of Phil King of Felt, the Servants, Lush and later the Jesus and Mary Chain, who draws parallels between his and Bowie's experience as fans:

> The first thing of note I remember reading was an article in a short lived music magazine called *Music Scene* – titled "BOWIE Superstar Who's A Fan At Heart" – from 1972. It was just before Lou Reed's *Transformer* was released. It had some fantastic colour Mick Rock images of Bowie, Lou Reed and Iggy Pop and in the piece it said that 'Lou Reed is to Bowie what Chuck Berry was to The Rolling Stones ... Bowie has released Lou Reed's work from the greedy clutches of the esoteric underground circles which first hallowed his name.'
>
> (King 2019)

Bowie's performance of Velvet Underground songs also became a key tool in enabling him to step away from the defined obsolescence of Ziggy's disposable Pop Art into the artistic permanence celebrated in rock ideology. While Ziggy drew the disposable artifice from the Pop Art connotations of the Velvets' work, Bowie later used them to underpin his own authenticity as a serious artist. 'White Light/White Heat' was a regular source of ideological redeployment. Versions ranged from the rock standard delivered by the Spiders from Mars to the funk rendition performed during the *Station to Station* tour, and on to the anodyne middle-of-the-road recordings of his fiftieth birthday rehearsal demo that gained an official release in 2020. Bowie seemed to continually grapple with the song without satisfaction. It was as if he could never live up to it – forever the student, never the master.

Conclusion

Bowie's early adoption of the Velvet Underground was as a performance of the 'mod' identity, which places huge emphasis on knowing and inhabiting the newly discovered and celebrates modernity's forward-facing cultural production. However, Bowie's true role as the Velvet Underground's key cultural intermediary is through the creation of the Ziggy Stardust persona, an expression of Bowie's fandom, with a defined shelf life at the hands of the fandom of the performance of his creation. This was a demise hardwired into the character's narrative through the *memento mori* theme of the title song, and later eulogized as the character's death at the hands of his creator in the final Ziggy performance at the Hammersmith Odeon, London, on 3 July 1973. Witness the film of the show as Bowie performing Ziggy reaches out to the audience and urges them to give him their hands, to a fandom witnessing the end of a performance in which they are implicit. With the giving of their hands, Ziggy dies by their hands.

Ziggy Stardust thus flattens history by consuming the past and then producing it as part of a temporary, temporally defined present that is all about the highly packaged Ziggy moment. The Velvet Underground thus become subsumed into the Ziggy character and commodified through that performance of this moment. In so doing Bowie the fan re-creates and repackages all associated media as a piece of Pop Art. The fans may ultimately kill the man, but they retained his songs and seized on and then embodied Bowie's influences.

Notes

1   This often-repeated quote first appeared in the *Los Angeles Times* (23 May 1982: 291) and was repeated in *Musician* magazine in October 1982 (available at https://bit.ly/3G43dXx) in two related features on Brian Eno written by Kristine McKenna.
2   Film director Grant McPhee argues that selling almost 60,000 records by 1968 'was respectable for an era where the 7" still ruled' (2021).
3   Bowie also recorded 'I'm Waiting for the Man' with the Hype in 1970 for the BBC.

References

Atton, C. (2009), 'Writing about Listening: Alternative Discourses in Rock Journalism', *Popular Music*, 28 (1): 53–67.

Bannister, M. (2010), '"I'm Set Free…"; The Velvet Underground, 1960s Counterculture, and Michel Foucault', *Popular Music and Society*, 33 (2): 163–78.

Baudrillard, J. (1994), *Simulacra and Simulation*, trans. S. F. Glaser, Ann Arbor, MI: University of Michigan.

Bockris, V. and Malanga, G. (1983), *Up-Tight: The Velvet Underground Story*, London: Omnibus.

Bourdieu, P. (1984), *Distinction: A Social Critique of the Judgement of Taste*, trans. R. Nice, Cambridge, MA: Harvard University.

Bowie, D. (2003), 'Confessions of a Vinyl Junkie', *Vanity Fair*, 20 November. Available online: https://bit.ly/3AzxrAq (accessed 23 November 2021).

Bowie, D. (2004), 'David Bowie: What I've Learned'. *Esquire*. 1 March, 2004. Available online: https://bit.ly/3GZm5bg (accessed 23 November 2021).

Ceriotti, B. (n.d.), 'Riot Squad', *Bruno Ceriotti, Rock Historian*. Available online: https://bit.ly/3u5ZBSj (accessed 23 November 2021).

Cinque, T. and Redmond, S. (2019), *The Fandom of David Bowie: Everyone Says 'Hi'*, Cham, Switzerland: Palgrave.

Cosgrove, S. (2016), *Detroit 67 – The Year That Changed Soul*, Edinburgh: Polygon.

Downliner Sect (n.d.), 'A Quote…' [Website Home Page], *Downliner Sect*. Available online: https://bit.ly/34feEOU (accessed 23 November 2021).

Du Noyer, P. ([2002] 2020), 'I Try to Channel My Addictions', *Mojo* (322): 66–7.

Duffett, M. (ed.) (2014), *Popular Music Fandom: Identities, Roles and Practices*, Abingdon: Routledge.

Farren, M. (2001), *Give the Anarchist a Cigarette*, London: Pimlico.

Fricke, D. (1995), 'Essay', in The Velvet Underground. *Peel Slowly and See* [boxset], Polygram 527 887-2 (1995).

Gilbert, P. (2017), *Bowie: The Illustrated Story*, Stillwater, MN: Voyageur Press.

Gold, J. (2013), 'Lou Reed & Exactly How Many Albums The Velvet Underground Sold', *Record Mecca*, 10 November. Available online: https://bit.ly/3GZmGK2 (accessed 22 November 2021).

Godard, V. (2019), *personal email interview*, 22 January.

Hart, D. (2019), *personal phone interview*, 24 January.

Jones, D. (2014), *When Ziggy Played Guitar: David Bowie and Four Minutes that Shook the World*, London: Preface Publishing.

Jenson, J. (1992), 'Fandom as Pathology: The Consequence of Characterization', in L. A. Lewis (ed.), *The Adoring Audience: Fan Culture and Popular Media*, London: Nicholas Brealey.

King, P. (2019), *personal email interview*, 3 September.

Malanga, G. (2020), *personal email interview*, 19 March.

Mair, A. (2019), *personal phone interview*, 18 January.

Matthews, J. and Smith Maguire, J. (2014), *The Cultural Intermediaries Reader*, London: Sage.

McCarty, J. and Thompson, D. (2018), *Nobody Told Me: My Life with the Yardbirds, Renaissance and Other Stories*, Self-published: lulu.com.

McCarty, J. (2019), *personal email interview*, 21 January.
McCormick, C. J. (2017), 'Active Fandom: Labour and Love in the Whedonverse', in P. Booth (ed.), *Companion to Media Fandom and Fan Studies*, 369–84, New York: Wiley Blackwell.
McKenna, K. (1982), 'Lots of Aura, No Airplay', [Brian Eno interview]. *Los Angeles Times*, 23 May: 291.
McPhee, G. (2021), 'The Velvet Underground Myth?' *Into Creative*, 17 October. Available online: https://bit.ly/32ziQbz (accessed 23 November 2021).
O'Leary, C. (2009), 'I'm Waiting for the Man', *Pushing Ahead of the Dame: David Bowie, Song by Song*, 24 September. Available online: https://bit.ly/3u0xAvq (accessed 23 November 2021).
O'Leary, C. (2015), *Rebel Rebel: All the Songs of David Bowie from '64 to '76*, Winchester: Zero Books.
Pegg, N. (2016), *The Complete David Bowie*, 7th edn, London: Titan Books.
Pitt, K. (1983), *David Bowie: The Pitt Report*, London: Design Music.
Platt, J., Dreja, C. and McCarty, J. (1983), *Yardbirds*, London: Sidgwick and Jackson.
Pyro, H. (2014), 'Check Out These Rare 1967 Velvet Underground Covers from Dutch Kids and U.S. Soldiers in Vietnam'. *Dangerous Minds*. 12 June. Available online: https://bit.ly/33Lm3FO (accessed 23 November 2021).
Reynolds, S. (2016), *Shock and Awe: Glam Rock and its Legacy*, London: Faber and Faber.
Richman, S. (2012), 'The Velvet Underground: The Revolution Rocks On', *The Independent on Sunday*, 14 October. Available online: https://bit.ly/3rRsdw3 (accessed 23 November 2021).
Rock, M. (1995), *A Photographic Record 1969–1980*, Iver Heath, UK: Century, 22.
Sandford, C. (1996), *Bowie: Loving the Alien*, London: Little, Brown and Co.
Stevenson, N. (2006), *David Bowie: Fame, Sound and Vision*, Cambridge: Polity.
Stratton, J. (1986), 'Why Doesn't Anybody Write Anything about Glam Rock?' *Australian Journal of Cultural Studies*, 4 (1): 15–38.
Thornton, S. (1996), *Club Cultures: Music, Media and Subcultural Capital*, Cambridge: Polity.
Trynka, P. (2010), *David Bowie: The Definitive Biography*, London: Sphere.
Unterberger, R. (2009), *White Light/White Heat: The Velvet Underground Day by Day*, London: Jawbone Press.
Wald, E. (2009), *How the Beatles Destroyed Rock'n'Roll: An Alternative Popular Music*, New York: Oxford University.
Watts, M. ([1972] 1996), 'Oh You Pretty Thing'. *Melody Maker*, 22 January, in H. Kureishi and J. Savage (eds), *The Faber Book of Pop*, London: Faber and Faber.
Whyton, T. (2014), 'Musicians, Myths and the "Cult" of John Coltrane', in M. Duffett (ed.), *Popular Music Fandom: Identities, Roles and Practices*, Abingdon: Routledge.
Williams, R. (2020), *personal email interview*, 20 April.

10

What Caroline says: *Berlin*, 1973 and 2006

David Pattie

In Berlin

The original *Rolling Stone* review of Lou Reed's 1973 concept album *Berlin* is, to say the least, unambiguous:

> Lou Reed's *Berlin* is a disaster, taking the listener into a distorted and degenerate demimonde of paranoia, schizophrenia, degradation, pill-induced violence and suicide. There are certain records that are so patently offensive that one wishes to take some kind of physical vengeance on the artists that perpetrate them. Reed's only excuse for this kind of performance (which isn't really performed as much as spoken and shouted over Bob Ezrin's limp production) can only be that this was his last shot at a once-promising career. Goodbye, Lou.
>
> (Davis 1973)

Coming, as it did, after *Transformer* (1972), the Bowie and Visconti-produced album, more than any other release in Reed's lifetime, both saved his career and established Reed as the musical forebear of Glam, Punk and all the musical styles that followed; *Berlin* was regarded as a tasteless mistake. Stephen Davis' *Rolling Stone* review condemned the album as relentlessly negative and offensive. Robert Christgau (1974) was more damning:

> The story is lousy – if something similar was coughed up by some avant-garde asshole like, oh, Alfred Chester (arcane reference for all you rock folk who think you're cool cos you read half of *Nova Express*) everyone would be too bored to puke at it.

The generally negative reception of the album (which was accompanied by a sharp falling off of sales) was at the time enough to condemn *Berlin* to relative obscurity; at the time, the album was easily outsold by the live recordings *Rock and Roll Animal* (1974) and *Lou Reed Live* (1975). Reed's next studio album – *Sally Can't*

Dance (1974) – returned to the territory marked out in *Transformer*; a set of discrete vignettes of New York life, the album reached #10 in the Billboard charts. *Berlin* was quietly forgotten.

Thirty-three years later, the status of the album had changed. It was no longer the lamentable mistake of 1973. In 2003, *Rolling Stone* placed the album at 344, in its roll call of the 500 greatest albums of all time; and in 2006, Reed performed the album in St Ann's Warehouse in New York, with Anohni (Anthony Hegarty) on backing vocals and the album's producer, Bob Ezrin, as musical director. Jon Pareles (2006), reviewing the event for the *New York Times*, was in no doubt about the worth of the album, discerning in it a nuanced subtlety that the original reviewers missed: '[a]t first, there are sarcastically upbeat horns and swaggering guitars; later, as things spiral downhill, it is pared down to unadorned guitar or piano and a voice that, in Mr. Reed's deceptive deadpan, sounds as if it's choking back all its rage and sorrow.' What was a narrative that could inspire only disgust is now a combination of Charles Bukowski and Raymond Carver; what was an exercise in degradation is now an exercise in barely suppressed emotion. The performance (filmed by Julian Schnabel, and released as a live album and DVD [*Lou Reed's Berlin* 2007]) captures something of the music's new status: the audience's response is rapturous, and Reed himself looks, if not ecstatic, then at least quietly pleased with the way the evening is going.

Partly, the differences in reception between *Berlin* the original album and *Berlin* the filmed performance can be attributed to the circumstances surrounding their release. In 1973, Reed's position in the history of popular music was still rather precarious. The Velvet Underground's status had been boosted by acolytes like David Bowie, but Reed's solo career had got off to an uncertain start. He was only one of a number of artists (others included Iggy Pop and Mott the Hoople) whose success was significant mainly because it bore witness to the cultural influence Bowie wielded. *Berlin* posed a considerable problem for Reed and his record company; its relative failure (especially in the United States: in the UK the album reached no. 7) could have brought Reed's burgeoning solo career to an abrupt halt. By the time of the 2006 performance, Reed's place in the history of popular music and popular culture was unassailable; the Velvet Underground were venerated, and Reed himself had amassed an impressive, if uneven, body of solo work. In the pantheon of popular music, he was by now rated as highly as Bowie, and *Berlin* itself had become a key part of the Reed myth.

In some ways, *Berlin* in 2006 differs from the 1973 recording. There are musical differences; for example, the performance is framed by a short extract from 'Sad Song', the album's last track. Rather than the burst of party noise that begins the album, the evening begins with the backing vocalists, singing the track's chorus, in close harmony. By and large, though, the performance adheres to the structure and musical dynamics of the album. Guitar solos are lengthened, and some of the vocal duties are shared, but the performance attempts, as far as is possible, to replicate the album as closely as it can. And yet the performance gives a very different impression; and in understanding why that is the case, we will come closer to understanding exactly why the original album was, and remains, a profoundly unsettling musical experience.

Affect and the voice

Reed's voice is one of the most distinctive in popular music. Like other male vocalists of the 1960s and 1970s he did not have a vocal style that would automatically be designated conventionally beautiful. Bob Dylan's delivery is exaggeratedly nasal; Leonard Cohen's voice was significantly lower than the average; Tom Waits' voice is roughened by alcohol and cigarettes. In each of these three cases, the vocal traits most closely associated with each artist became more marked as the vocalist ages. Dylan's voice becomes, in many cases, an adenoidal monotone; Cohen becomes positively sepulchral; and Waits' voice becomes so distorted that it is sometimes hard to distinguish the individual notes of the melody. In each case, however, the gradual erosion of the singer's vocal capabilities is countered, and to a large extent negated, by what could be described as a change in implied or created affect. Dylan's increasingly monotone nasality comes to signal increased world-weariness; the increasing depth of Cohen's voice suggests both age and, because of the way he comes to phrase his lyrics, an amused, ironic detachment. Waits is perhaps the most adept at manipulating the profoundly unconventional grain of his voice. In his early work, his vocal default setting is that of the drunk at the piano; on the albums from *Swordfishtrombones* (1983) onwards, Waits uses his voice both to create an appropriate persona for the song and as an instrument.

Reed doesn't follow the same trajectory. On the Velvets' first album, he can hold a tune, and is capable of providing a variety of vocal styles, from the soft, almost crooning 'Sunday Morning' to the agitated, rhythmic delivery of 'I'm Waiting for the Man'. On *Ecstasy*, in 2000, we find something like the same type of delivery; rhythmic and insistent on 'Mystic Child', and the croon re-emerges on 'Tatters'. On the later album, Reed's tuning is occasionally imprecise, but it is worth remembering that this was always a feature of his singing. Cohen's range shifts; Reed's stays much the same. Dylan's voice gets more nasal as time goes on; Reed's voice (although it is perceptibly produced by an ageing man) retains the same timbre. Waits' voice roughens and thickens; Reed's voice, at the end of his life, still occupies the same space in the soundbox (Moore 2012: 29–49) his recordings create. Mark Richardson (2008), discussing Reed's performance of 'Caroline Says II', notes, '[by] any objective standard, Reed's voice sounds lousy on the track – despite his compressed range, he has some serious trouble with pitch'. However, when one listens to the original track, one could make exactly the same comment; Reed's voice is Reed's voice, whenever one encounters it. If we are to look for the differences between *Berlin* the album and *Berlin* the performance, then the most obvious route (the voice itself thickening, ageing, changing quality) is not one that is open to us.

A more promising route is not through the nature of the voice itself but through what the voice does. Allan Moore (2012: 179–214), following on from a typology first laid out by Philip Auslander, distinguishes between three positions the voice can adopt in popular music. The *person* is the real human being who delivers the song, the *persona* is the performative identity the singer adopts and the *protagonist* is the subject or central character in the song. As Moore notes, sometimes the distance between these three positions can be great, and sometimes it can be so narrow as to have apparently disappeared. In Reed's case, however, the relation between these three elements is always hard to ascertain, precisely because of the vocal tone that he adopts. Characteristically, Reed sings in a style that very closely mimics the rhythm and timbre of his normal, speaking voice; the melody of the song is always apt to devolve into speech (see Chapter 14 in this collection). Moreover, it is hard to read the emotional temperature of the track from the tone of Reed's delivery. Sometimes, the distance between the apparent content of the song and the rather affectless style of Reed's characteristic singing style can be profoundly moving. 'Perfect Day', for example, would arguably lose something of its emotional impact if the two-word phrase 'someone good' was delivered in a more emotive fashion. Reed throws the phrase away, inviting the listener to impute the nature of the emotion that the delivery fails to express. Sometimes, though, the result is rather more disturbing. *Berlin* the album charts the violent disintegration of a marriage; its lyrics deal with drug and alcohol abuse, domestic violence and suicide – and yet Reed's vocal tone stays neutral more or less throughout.

Brian Massumi, in a 1995 article credited with inaugurating a turn towards the consideration of the affective, began his argument by discussing an apparent paradox. A group of children were shown versions of a short film and were asked to rate the scenes in it for pleasantness or unpleasantness. The researchers, according to Massumi, were surprised to find that, in the most overtly emotional version of the film, the scenes that were sad or distressing were rated the most pleasurable. Massumi argues that this was because the apparent contradiction between the subject matter and the manner in which the subject matter was experienced was, in practice, easily resolvable. If instead of looking purely at the emotional content, or the quality of the material, one took into account the intensity with which the material was delivered and experienced, it was possible to gauge the piece's affect:

> it could be noted that the primacy of the affective is marked by a gap between content and effect: it would appear that the strength or duration of an image's effect is not logically connected to the content in any straightforward way. This is not to say that there is no connection and no logic. What is meant here by the content of the image is its indexing to conventional meanings in an intersubjective context, its socio-linguistic qualification. This indexing fixes the quality of the image; the strength or duration of the image's effect could be called its intensity. What comes out here is that there is no correspondence or conformity between quality and intensity.
>
> (84–5)

If, as Massumi argues, there is no automatic relation between the ostensible emotional content and the intensity generated by the effect of that content, then we have a working model that allows us to understand the impact of other tracks that Reed wrote and performed. 'Heroin', for example, generates considerable intensity; the structure of the song mirrors the rush of the drug, but the lyrics convey the protagonist's helplessness.

Any pity generated by the protagonist is countered – in fact, is overwhelmed – by the affect generated by the rising intensity of the music.

However, when it comes to the tracks on the original version of *Berlin*, it is much harder to determine the affective impact generated by the lyrics and the music. As I will argue, this is to do largely with the nature of Reed's voice. Roland Barthes (1985), in a much quoted discussion of the particularity of vocal delivery, treats the voice as the carrier of meanings that escape easy codification:

> The human voice is, as a matter of fact, the privileged (eidetic) site of difference: a site which escapes all science, for there's no science ... which exhausts the voice: no matter how much you classify and comment on music historically, sociologically, aesthetically, technically, there will always be a remainder, a supplement, a lapse, something non-spoken, which designates itself: the voice.
>
> (279)

When we take this quote, and apply it to the singing voice, it is relatively easy to determine what might count as the sign of the voice as site of difference. The expressive power of the singer is not something that lends itself easily to codification. Writing in 2020, Victoria Malawey identifies one of the elements that enables the musical voice to resist easy analysis:

> Prosodic elements in speech – such as pacing, speed, and intonation – can convey meaning, not only that which supports specific linguistic content, but also that which is independent of it (Shintel et al., Nusbaum, and Okrent 2006, 167–77) ... singing voices fuse the domains of speech and music, resulting in at least three different streams of information – semantic meanings implied by lyrics that are sung, metaphorical meanings resulting from musical content, and analog, non-semantic meanings conveyed by prosodic properties through vocal delivery. Although prosodic elements of singing differ from those of speech in several ways including speed of delivery, meanings listeners ascribe to popular song recordings are similarly contingent upon a singer's prosody.
>
> (70)

In other words, there is no clear discernible distinction between the speaking voice and the singing voice. Each vocal performance is a blend of the meanings that can be inferred from the lyrics, the meanings implied by the shape of the melody and the harmonic framework that contains it and the 'non-semantic' meanings contained within those elements of singing that use elements also employed in everyday speech.

Studies of the affective impact of differing types of emotional content have identified a number of key indicators of affective investment on the part of the singer:

> Joy and pride are generally close to anger, although less extreme, also indicating a relatively high amount of power and arousal. Pride is generally higher on the

variables loading on component 1 (voice intensity), which may be directly related to power. This suggests that power is relatively more important than arousal. The opposite seems to be true for joy … Fear is generally in between the two extremes, with a more extreme position only on low formant amplitude. Joy and pride are characterized by high loudness and low formant amplitude. Pride is distinguished from joy by high perturbation variation. Anger has a distinctive vocal profile with very strong loudness and very high dynamics. Fear has a nondescript profile with fairly level dynamics standing out.

(Scherer et al. 2017: 1812–3)

These indicators align themselves very closely with the presentation of such emotions in everyday speech; one might assume that someone who wished to express pride might do so in a tone that was more intense than it would normally be. From this, one might take the commonsensical point that emotion in song is a heightened or exaggerated version of emotion as expressed in everyday speech. In saying this, I do not intend to denigrate research into the affective impact of singing. If anything, analyses like this are very useful, because they remind us of how deeply ingrained our ability to recognize emotion is, and how much the artistic representation of emotion relies on our automatic interpretation of the emotional state of the performer. To go back to Moore's three-part division, described above, we assemble, from the lyrical, melodic, harmonic and performative aspects of the music, a composite picture of the emotional state of the persona (as this is the aspect that contains and controls the performance), which then colours our view both of the performer and of the protagonist.

This usefully direct schema breaks down, however, when we try to fit it to Reed – and especially when we try to fit it to *Berlin* the album. It might be easy to read the distanced, ironic vocal tone Reed adopts for 'Street Hassle' as a sign of world-weariness, as though the protagonist has lived through the events chronicled in the song, in one way or other, for longer than he might care to remember. When it comes to *Berlin*, such an interpretation is more difficult to sustain. The album begins with a shortened version of the track 'Berlin', first recorded for Reed's eponymous first solo album. Musically, the initial affective content of the song seems relatively straightforward; a piano starts to play under the sound of a birthday party (the chords can be heard beneath a distorted version of 'Happy Birthday to You'). The pianist (Bob Ezrin, the album's producer) plays a series of bluesy improvisations over a descending bassline – an appropriate musical setting for a song that references a late night cafe, drinking and (compared to the rest of the album) blissfully happy romance. The lyrics fit the atmosphere created by the music are playful, romantic and express the protagonist's happiness, stating, 'Oh honey it was paradise'. Sung by a vocalist employing the kind of affective investment described above, the song might be overwhelmingly, cloyingly sentimental. Reed, however, sings it in a way that holds the protagonist back from full emotional investment. He sings the first two lines quietly; one might assume that at this point the protagonist is overwhelmed by the memory. This reading is countered by the delivery of the next line ('It was very nice.'). Here, Reed drops back to the nasal, subdued, listless tone that he employs elsewhere on the album. Just for a moment, an affective distance opens up between the persona Reed adopts and the ostensible content of the song. It is here, I would argue, that we get the first and clearest clue about the particularly disturbing affect the album creates. Emotional states are indicated, but Reed's vocal delivery undercuts them at the moment at which they are expressed. The disjunction between Reed's emotional tone and the affective content of the music is, if anything, emphasized by the album's production. The musical arrangement frequently suggests an emotional impact that Reed's voice simply doesn't provide. This makes the original album an unsettling listen; deviations from the original delivery (and their physical incarnation in performance) help to make the 2006 performance easier for the audience to assimilate.

'Caroline Says II' – 1973/2006

The main models proposed above rest on the idea that the nature of the singer's performance is placeable. For Massumi, there might be a gap between the content of the material and the nature of the delivery, but the emotional content of the material is a necessary part of the way in which affect is generated. For Moore, although the lines between performer, persona and protagonist might blur, the affective content of each of the roles is key to determining their relation. A line sung with full investment by one vocalist can be reinterpreted by another. In each of these cases the interpretation of the affective impact of the track might vary, but the listener would experience an affective impact of some kind, one that could be traced along the lines suggested by Massumi, and according to the type of delivery patterns identified by Malawey and Scherer et al. Reed, however, delivers most of the songs on *Berlin* in a way that makes such identification impossible. Even when there is a sign of what could be read as conventional emotional investment, the investment is sketched in, rather than fully incarnated, as in the delivery of 'Lady Day's' key line 'No, no, no'. As the album progresses, and as Jim's and Caroline's relationship worsens, even this minimal gesture towards affect drains out of Reed's voice. The more desperate the narrative content of the track, the less invested Reed sounds; and as the discussion of the opening track above suggests, he never sounded very invested in the earlier songs.

'Caroline Says II' is the first song on the second side of the album. It inaugurates what might be one of the most harrowing song sequences in popular music; the violence it describes is followed by 'The Kids' (in which Caroline loses her children), 'The Bed' (which describes her suicide) and 'Sad Song'. Lyrically, the song is written in the omniscient third person. We watch and listen to Caroline responding to Jim's abuse, and we watch her gather herself back together after each assault. The narrator isn't Jim; the narrator is a dispassionate observer who has insight into Caroline's state of mind, and who is familiar with the people who call her Alaska. We enter into Caroline's mind, in the alarming lines that matter-of-factly describe her smashing a window with her fist. At no point, though, does the lyrical voice editorialize; it keeps a scrupulous, careful distance from judgement, recording rather than analysing. This means that the lyrics in the outro ('It's so cold in Alaska'), although they seem like a summary, are rendered ambiguous because we do not know who is speaking. If it is the narrator, then this is as close to analysis as the song gets; Caroline is frozen, numbed by violence and by the drugs she takes. If it is Caroline, then it could either reference punching the windowpane or it could be an answer to the question her friends pose about her state of mind. It could also be said by those friends; they are the ones who nickname her Alaska, after all.

It is not that, lyrically, 'Caroline Says II' is unusually ambiguous; the lyrics are only one part of the overall affect of the track. Commonsensically, one might expect that the vocal delivery would clear up the ambiguities I've described or at the least it should give the listener a clearer indication of how the song might be interpreted. As argued above, vocal intonation in singing correlates to vocal intonation in everyday speech. We would normally expect, too, that the emotional affect of the track would largely be determined by the arrangement of the music, and by other factors (the production, the pacing, and so on). 'Caroline Says II' provides us with what seems like an easily assimilable musical framework. The track begins with an acoustic guitar, playing a chord pattern over a descending bassline, which is doubled by a bass guitar; the only other musical element at the song's beginning is a lightly brushed cymbal. It sounds, momentarily, like the opening of a track by any one of the singer-songwriters of the early 1970s; when Reed starts to sing, the three-note melody (e-d-e-c) recapitulates the opening of other Reed and Velvet Underground tracks; a short, simple musical phrase that introduces either the subject of the song (as in 'Sunday Morning') or the song's protagonist (Jeanie, in 'Rock and Roll') or the song's title ('Vicious'). For those familiar with Reed's songs, there is nothing that automatically suggests the direction that the narrative will take.

The opening line is sung neutrally, and one might expect that, as the song progresses, this tone would modulate. However, Reed sings the rest of the song in the same emotional register. Even on those moments when the music suggests a changed affect (or where, at least, we might expect to hear Reed delivering the lyrics in a way that allows us to intuit an emotional response) his voice doesn't change its inflection or its intensity. There are moments where Reed approaches the kind of emotional delivery that might seem to fit the lyrics; towards the end of the second verse, he sings with a marginally increased intensity, as though for a moment the anger in the words might be matched by anger in the singing. The arrangement of the track also suggests a potential change in emotional tone. As Reed starts the second verse, a Mellotron appears; it occupies the same space in the song's harmonic framework that might, elsewhere, be filled by a string section, and it does the same work, providing a rhapsodic counterpoint to the main melody. Reed's voice is doubled on the chorus, beginning on the word 'Alaska' (subtly on the first chorus, more overtly on the second). As the song moves into its final section, the arrangement seems to prepare us for a moment of overt emotional investment. The Mellotron and piano play interweaving lines, the track's volume subtly increases, the chords move into a simple, repeated pattern (I–IV), more musical elements are added (in particular, a set of chimes); in other words, we are given every indication that the affect generated by the song is at this moment at its most intense. And yet Reed's voice stays where it was at the beginning: neutral, uninflected, uninvolved.

Reed's neutral tone is subtly unsettling; such subject matter should, one might expect, be handled in a way that allows the listener the comfort of a shared moral framework. What happens to Caroline is terrible; the music, the arrangement and the lyrics tell us as much; but Reed's voice does not. Moreover, if we go back to the schema laid out by Moore, we could say that none of the ambiguities contained within the lyrics are resolved by the delivery of the song. We don't know who the singing voice is; we don't know its relation to Caroline, or to the events it describes; we don't know what it thinks or feels about the words it sings. It is as close as any vocalist can come to a delivery that has no definable persona. Even those attributes that tend to characterize Reed's delivery of other songs and that might indicate a lack of emotional involvement (the projection of irony, the move from song to speech) are absent. Because there is no definable persona, we cannot determine the protagonist; the questions posed above about the song's point of view remain unanswerable. It is this, I would argue, that makes the second side of the album a particularly harrowing experience. This material would usually have an editorial presence, something to tell us how to interpret the information (both musical and lyrical) that we receive. In the run of tracks from 'Caroline Says II' to 'Sad Song', the music and the arrangement are designed to provoke and sustain affect. The voice – the part of the track most suited to conveying the intensity that can generate an affective response – remains emotionally and affectively blank.

The 2006 version begins in much the same way as the album; an acoustic guitar plays the opening chords with the same descending bassline, and Reed sings the opening line in the same, uninflected style as he does on the original. As he does so, we also hear (and see) the first difference in the arrangement. The bassline is played on a double bass and bowed instead of plucked; the opening arrangement sounds smoother, more like a piece of chamber music than the confessional singer-songwriter style employed on record. Reed's delivery has also changed – and the differences begin to manifest themselves during the first verse. In these circumstances, he can rely on the audience's awareness of the song's original melody; from the first line, he begins to play with both the rhythm and the tune, and the alterations he makes push the lyrics in two complementary directions. First, he allows his voice to drop from singing to speech, delivered with the anger that the studio version notably lacks. Second, the melodic changes Reed makes push parts of the song closer to the kind of affective delivery style identified by Scherer et al. On the first chorus, for example, Reed pauses between the initial 'She's' and the rest of the line; the melody he sings rises to the last word of the line ('Die') and he stretches the sound of the last syllable. The rest of the chorus has a new melody line that is higher than the original, dropping only on the last line. Affectively, this now suggests that the friends are actively concerned about her. The second chorus builds on this new reading. The line 'All of her friends call her Alaska' now has a non-verbal vocalization; an agonized, effortful 'Aaah' between 'her' and 'Alaska' – as though her friends' concern is growing. On the outro, Anhoni and the backing vocalists join Reed, transforming the final section into what sounds like a gospel song.

The vocal delivery of the song, in other words, now suggests a range of protagonists, with their own individual affective investment in the narrative. Caroline is weary, angry and sad; her friends are worried; and Reed himself now has a clear persona – the concerned onlooker, invested in Caroline's fate. Partly, this new interpretation is made possible by the way Reed sings; partly, it is based on the way that he physically inhabits the song in performance. Live, the line of demarcation between performer, persona and protagonist can blur, as it does here. At the beginning of the song, Reed looks weary; he settles the guitar strap around his neck as though it weighs more than it actually does. At one point in the performance he brushes the back of his hand over his forehead, in a gesture of tired resignation. There are moments where the physical gestures Reed enacts link directly to the lyrics. Most of the time, though, the audience watch a performer whose precise relation to the characters might not be fixed, but whose emotional investment in the material is manifest in terms of both his vocal delivery and his physical response to the track. The 2006 version of the song, in other words, gives the audience the kind of emotional clues that enable them to read, orient themselves within and have an affective response to the material. Reed does not move all the way towards direct emotional investment, but he does enough to sketch in the elements – the blend of content and intensity – on which an affective response relies.

Conclusion

John Tatlock, reviewing the recording of the 2006 *Berlin* performances for *The Quietus*, begins with a memorable account of the first time he came across the 1973 album:

> I first encountered the 1973 studio version of *Berlin* some time in the early 90s while flipping through a friend's vinyl collection. At the time, I was a big fan of Reed's previous LP, the Bowie and Mick Ronson produced *Transformer*, but I knew little else of his solo career. 'Is this any good?' I asked. 'It's brilliant, but it's fucking horrible' came the reply.
>
> (Tatlock 2008)

This, in a nutshell, is the history of the album's reception. Even though it is now accorded classic status, the subject material is still profoundly uncomfortable; and for Tatlock, this discomfort comes from the fact that Reed presents, without editorializing, the characters whose narrative we follow through the album: 'Reed is making a serious point with *Berlin*, challenging the listener to continually consider and reconsider their positions on the archetypes he is presenting us, without ever offering any conclusions of his own.' This conclusion might hold true for the 2006 live recording; as I have noted above, it is far easier to read the emotional content of the performance – and, in doing so, to be open to the affect the songs generate. However, in the 1973 recording, it is not that we are left adrift to draw our own conclusions; it is that the affective tone of Reed's voice is so consistently blank as to impede even the most basic engagement with the affective potential of the music. In place of the intensity Massumi describes, we have blankness; in place of the performer, the persona and the protagonist of Moore's typology, we have nothing – the largely uninflected transmission of narrative material, without the editorializing presence of the engaged voice. *Berlin* – the original studio recording, rather than the 2006 re-creation – remains a profoundly disturbing experience, because of the profound disjunction between the music and Reed's voice. The music (as my discussion of Caroline Says II makes clear) is all affect; it is full of the kind of musical codes and cues that we usually rely on to generate our emotional investment in the track. Reed's voice, on the other hand, gives very little away; the voice, that part of the soundscape that we usually rely on most for emotional, interpretive and affective clues, remains inscrutable. The 1973 *Berlin* is disturbing, not because it denies us a final judgement about what to feel but because it leaves us uncertain about whether we should feel anything.

References

Barthes, R. (1985), *The Responsibility of Forms: Critical Essays on Music, Art, And Representation*, trans. R. Howard, New York: Hill and Wang.

Christgau, R. (1974), 'The Christgau Consumer Guide: Lou Reed: Berlin (RCA Victor)', *Creem*, February. Available online: https://bit.ly/3ADOcun (accessed 16 December 2021).

Davis, S. (1973), 'Berlin' [album review], *Rolling Stone*, 20 December. Available online: https://bit.ly/3AEYIkY (accessed 16 December 2021).

Malawey, V. (2020), *A Blaze of Light in Every Word: Analyzing the Popular Singing Voice*, New York: Oxford University Press.

Massumi, B. (1995), 'The Autonomy of Affect', *Cultural Critique*, 31, part II: 83–109.

Moore, A. (2012), *Song Means: Analysing and Interpreting Recorded Popular Song*, Farnham: Ashgate.

Pareles, J. (2006), 'Sentimental Journey: A Return to "Berlin"', *New York Times*, 16 December. Available online: https://nyti.ms/3KRqdg0 (accessed 16 December 2021).

Richardson, M. (2008), 'That Voice Again', *Pitchfork*, 5 September. Available online: https://bit.ly/3HamV5b (accessed 16 December 2021).

Scherer, K. R., Sundberg, J., Fantini, B., Trznadel, S. and Eyben, F. (2017), 'The Expression of Emotion in the Singing Voice: Acoustic Patterns in Vocal Performance', *The Journal of the Acoustical Society of America*, 142 (1805). Available online: https://bit.ly/3o1F9OL (accessed 16 December 2021).

Shintel, H., Nusbaum, H. C. and Okrent, A. (2006), 'Analog Acoustic Expression in Speech Communication', *Journal of Memory and Language*, 55 (2) (August): 167–77.

Tatlock, J. (2008), 'Lou Reed's Berlin: Live at St, Ann's Warehouse' [review], *Quietus*, 29 October. Available online: https://bit.ly/3H9LpeX (accessed 16 December 2021).

11

Unfrozen borderlines: Nico, John Cale and Brian Eno at the Berlin Nationalgalerie

Sean Albiez and Timor Kaul

Introduction

On Saturday 5 October 1974, Nico, John Cale and Brian Eno performed together at the Metamusik Festival in Berlin. The objective of the festival was to introduce contemporary, progressive and what would later be labelled 'world music' to a young audience at the Mies van der Rohe–designed Nationalgalerie. The Metamusik festival featured American contemporary composers including Pauline Oliveros, Terry Riley, Christian Wolff, Steve Reich and Philip Glass as well as musicians from outside the Western context, including Indian sitar player Ustad Vilayat Khan, the vocalist Salamat Ali Khan from Pakistan and Tibetan Gyuoto Monks from northern India. Claus-Henning Bachmann in the festival programme characterized Bachauer's central concept as '*Daz Prinzip Offenheit* – the principle of openness' (Beal 2006: 205). Apart from Tangerine Dream there were no other representatives from the world of rock music, though the festival Bose sound system was installed and operated by Michael Hoenig of the band Agitation Free and Klaus D. Müller (road manager to Klaus Schulze), as well as John Strawn, a Fulbright scholar at the Technische Universität Berlin.

At the event Nico, John Cale and Brian Eno were billed as representing 'British Rock of the Avant-Garde'. Cale and Eno's avant-garde credentials stemmed from their 1960s student days, with Cale studying music at Goldsmith's College, London, during 1961–3 and Brian Eno art at Ipswich Civic College during 1964–6 and Winchester Art College during 1966–9. Both were inspired by John Cage; the New York School of composers including Morton Feldman, David Tudor and Christian Wolff; and British experimentalists such as Cornelius Cardew, and arranged and performed in new music events featuring works by Cage, George Brecht, La Monte Young and Cardew among others – eventually making personal connections with key figures in this milieu (Mitchell 2003: 27–33; Albiez and Dockwray 2016: 141–3). Coincidentally, Cale and Eno's avant-garde credentials are further enhanced as they arguably gave the first two British performances of La Monte Young's experimental work *X for Henry Flynt*: Cale in 1963 at Goldsmith's College, and Eno in 1968 in Winchester. Through the Velvet

Underground and Velvet acolytes Roxy Music, Cale and Eno acted as conduits bringing such experimentalism to the field of rock music, unfreezing established borderlines between and within popular, art and folk musics at a time when rock began to gain cultural weight.

By contrast, Nico was neither British nor formally acquainted with the 1960s musical avant-garde. However, she had witnessed and absorbed multimedia activities at Warhol's Factory, contributed to the Velvet Underground's live free improvisations and appeared in Philippe Garrel's experimental films. She had forged her own idiosyncratic and eccentric approach to music, creating a form of liminal 'metamusic' that sat indefinably across the borderlines of classical, folk and popular music. As such all three artists central to this study could be said to have been exploring a metamusic aesthetic in this period.

The aims of this study are first to map the road to Berlin taken by Nico and Cale after respectively drifting away from, and being cast adrift by, the Velvet Underground, and by committed Velvets fan Brian Eno before, within and soon after his time with Roxy Music. In examining the years before 1974, the musical activities, artistic *suchbewegungen* [the exploration of creative possibilities] and wider context of the three artists will be considered. The discussion will then move on to consider the two key 1974 events leading into the analysis of the Berlin Nationalgalerie concert. First, the Kevin Ayers, Cale, Nico and Eno (ACNE) concerts in June 1974 in London, Birmingham and Manchester, as well as the *June 1, 1974* album documenting the first of these, that inspired Bachauer to bring three of those involved to Berlin. Second, the recording of Nico's album *The End* in London – including her interpretation of 'Das Lied Der Deutschen' – produced by Cale with Eno's contributions. Nico performed the complete Nazi-tainted German anthem in London and on the record, and it is her repeat performance in Berlin with Cale and Eno that forms the focus of the second part of this study. As we will outline, Nico as a German and former inhabitant of West Berlin was fully aware of the potential controversy singing the unexpurgated, three-verse version of the anthem would cause. Yet, as we will suggest, there was hostility targeting Nico, Cale and Eno from elements of the West German audience throughout the concert, with the response to the anthem only part of the story. In examining the prelude to the event, and the event itself, light can be cast on Nico, Cale and Eno's work as they strove to formulate their musical identities in the early 1970s, and their struggle to overcome rock audience expectations and prejudices.

The road to Berlin, 1970–73

Nico

Nico is indelibly linked in the public imagination to the album *The Velvet Underground & Nico* (1967) and appeared on stage with the Velvets until May 1967 (shortly after recording her solo album *Chelsea Girls*) (Unterberger 2009: 144; 151). Her relationship with the Velvet Underground was temporary, sometimes fraught, and her departure (in accounts by other band members) was met with both relief and regret. Towards the end of her time with the band, Cale, Reed and Morrison (as well as Jackson Browne, Tim Buckley and others) offered support in her solo performances at The Dom in New York in early 1967. They also contributed five unrecorded songs and played on her album; the song 'It Was a Pleasure Then' featuring Reed, Cale and Nico is reminiscent of vocal and instrumental Velvets improvisations of the period and most closely foreshadows Nico's future musical identity. However, producer Tom Wilson's decision to overdub string arrangements and flute, giving the album a chamber-folk identity, resulted in her largely disowning the album. As Witts (1993) reports, after this disappointment, in July 1967 Jim Morrison of the Doors encouraged her to write her own songs (186–7).

Soon after Nico bought an Indian harmonium in San Francisco and taught herself to write songs and play keyboard over the ensuing months. This portable and practical hand- or foot-powered reed instrument connoted exotic folk musics for some in Western audiences, but it was actually introduced by Europeans to India in the late nineteenth century (Kasliwal 2001). The harmonium had been used in Europe – particularly Scandinavia – and the United States in religious and folk music settings since the late eighteenth century. By 1915 India had become the leading producer of harmoniums (Gaitonde 2016), leading to its association by the mid-twentieth century with non-Western and earlier folk musics. The instrument therefore embodied almost two centuries of cultural crossings, and its connotations in the context of guitar-driven 1960s rock music were 'other', of folk, of religious music and non-Western musical forms, contributing to Nico's distinctiveness.

Nico signed to Elektra Records in 1968 and recorded her first songs with Cale contributing instrumental overdubs and arrangements and acting as a producer in all but name. A working method was established where Nico would record her voice and harmonium before Cale created arrangements, eventually revealing the results to Nico once completed. The album *The Marble Index* was first presented publicly on 19 September at an Andy Warhol party, less than two weeks before Cale was sacked from the Velvet Underground. It defied easy categorization in terms of both Nico's songs and Cale's experimental settings, but in common with much of Nico's work, it was plaintive, dark, mournful and lacked obvious musical precedents.

From late 1968 Nico travelled back and forth across the Atlantic, playing concerts and appearing in the films of Philippe Garrel (e.g. *La Cicatrice Intérieure* [1972]; *Les Hautes Solitudes* [1974]) when living in Paris. In 1970, she again recorded with Cale, co-producing and arranging the album *Desertshore*, recorded at Vanguard Studios in New York and completed at Sound Techniques in London. Cale's diverse textures and inventive instrumental parts provided timbral differentiation between the songs, though 'My Only Child' and 'Le Petit Chevalier' remained as minimal, sparse arrangements. Album engineer and Sound Techniques owner John Wood described the working methods he witnessed while engineering sessions, observing that Vanguard 'was an old ballroom [of] about 2,000 square feet. [Nico] sat in the middle of the room with her harmonium, with her back to the control room ... Cale each day would order more and more instruments. There was a circle of ... blocks and carillons and Hammond organs and it went on and on'. Wood also described how 'Cale would run around playing them at the same time' and that Cale and Nico 'were virtually at one another's throats most of the time'. Crucially, though Joe Boyd officially produced the album, 'Cale was very, very hands on with the mixing' (Wood 2018).

Between 1971 and 1973, Nico made media appearances including BBC radio sessions for John Peel's *Top Gear* and *Sounds of the Seventies* and performed on the BBC2 television show *Disco 2*. She appeared with Cale at London's Roundhouse, and in April 1971, she rehearsed with Lou Reed for concerts at New York's Gaslight, but hastily left the city before they could happen after a violent incident involving the actress Emmaretta Marks (Otter Bickerdike 2021: Chapter 31). In Europe, Nico supported Gong a number of times, and on 29 January 1972, she appeared with Reed and Cale at a Velvet Underground reunion of sorts at the Bataclan in Paris. Following this she again supported Gong and appeared at events alongside Magma, Genesis, Ten Years After and Komintern among others. In August 1972, the British avant-garde composer Gavin Bryars remembers meeting Nico at the International Carnival of Electronic Sound (ICES) (Thompson 2017: 154) – a wide-ranging event of experimental and conceptual performances held in London (Cowley 2012). The year 1973 saw a Nico concert at the Opera Comique, Paris, and concerts supporting Magma, though a tour of the UK was cancelled in early 1974. What is notable across all these activities is that the milieu Nico was most associated with during this period was that of avant-garde and progressive rock.

John Cale

On leaving the Velvet Underground in 1968, unlike Nico, Cale possessed a surfeit of musical skills and experience ranging across classical music and avant-garde composition and practice, and a new interest – songwriting – evidenced by 'Winter Song' on Nico's *Chelsea Girls*. Elektra, happy with Cale's work on *The Marble Index*, offered him the opportunity to produce the Stooges first album. Through 1969–1970 Cale and Terry Riley, another La Monte Young collaborator, recorded sessions for a project eventually released as *The Church of Anthrax*. John McLure of CBS felt that by combining Riley – who had critical success in 1969 with *A Rainbow in Curved Air* – and Cale, he could bring Riley and other experimentalists to a wider audience. Riley was disappointed with Cale's production at the time and walked away from the project, but in 2014 he admitted, '[o]ver time, I've grown to like what they did, but I think it would have sounded good with my vision, too. I think it probably became more of a rock album because John was a rock musician and really understood what had to be done to make the record rock a little more strongly' (qtd. in Prasad 2014).

Before *The Church of Anthrax* was released, Cale completed an album of traditional pop/rock songwriting, *Vintage Violence* (released March 1970), in a process of imitation and learning. Cale admitted the album was 'very oriented to what The Band were doing, as the musicians on the album shared that same upstate New York mentality' (Bockris and Cale 2009: 123). In *Mojo* in 2004, Cale portrayed his struggles in this period: 'I was a classical musician playing catch up with everyone around me.

I was a little embarrassed and I was constantly trying to prove myself against Lou's work' (qtd. in Unterberger 2017: 25 March 1970). From May to July 1970 Cale was involved with Joe Boyd, producing and arranging Nico's *Desertshore*, released in December, and through his growing friendship with Boyd, he also contributed to two songs on Nick Drake's *Bryter Later* (1971).

As mentioned, in 1971 Cale was in London and performed with Nico at the Roundhouse, also playing songs from *Vintage Violence*. Mitchell (2003: 82) reports that Cale had established his own production company, Hit and Run Productions, and appeared now to be looking to revive his classical music activities, suggesting he wanted to record Nico backed by the English Chamber orchestra. Soon after, Joe Boyd asked Cale to collaborate with him on film music projects at Warner Brothers in Los Angeles, meaning Cale turned down an offer to become an executive producer at CBS in New York. However, his initial forays into film soundtrack work were unsuccessful, and he moved on to other projects, though details are vague (Bockris and Cale 1999: 133).

According to Mitchell (2003: 83) Cale had harboured an ambition to write a symphony after leaving the Velvet Underground. In 1972 work began on *The Academy in Peril* in the UK, but he recorded a number of non-classical tracks before the Royal Philharmonic sessions began and rejected the idea of completing a symphony. Instead Cale recorded four classical orchestral pieces, three presented side by side, and a fourth, 'John Milton', ended the album (which also included three classical piano and three rock tracks). Cale's assessment was 'it showed I could sound as much like Dvořák or Ives as Procol Harum or The Byrds' (Bockris and Cale 1999: 139). It also demonstrated that he retained the ambition and ability to write Western art music compositions.

After joining Reed and Nico at the Bataclan concert in late January, Cale returned to Los Angeles, working on projects including an ill-fated attempt to produce an album with the Modern Lovers. In late 1972, Cale returned to his own music with producer Chris Thomas on what became *Paris 1919*. Cale viewed the album as more focused after his earlier generic waywardness, but still offered variety: '*Paris 1919* put me back into the mainstream of popular music ... [it was] as musically accessible as anything I had ever done, yet its dense musical texture and lyrics made it as eclectic as *Anthrax* and *Peril* ... it struck a sort of ideal middle ground' (Bockris and Cale 1999: 141).

In early 1973, Reed and Cale met to discuss a Velvet Underground reunion as an equal partnership, though nothing came of their deliberations (Doggett 1992: 85). This was one of several examples of the former Velvets circling each other in a wary dance in the early 1970s. After *Paris 1919* was released, Bryan Ferry asked Cale to produce the second Roxy Music album, but instead eventually chose Cale's friend and *Paris 1919* producer Chris Thomas (Mitchell 2003: 88). By autumn, Cale's solo contract with Reprise Records ended, and Richard Williams, who had recently taken on an artist and repertoire (A&R) role at Island Records (home of Roxy Music), made contact. In December the *Record Mirror* announced that a three-year, six-album – more likely three album – deal had been struck, with tours planned as well as production and arrangement work with other Island artists (John Cale signs 1973: 6).

Brian Eno and Roxy Music

Towards the end of his studies at Winchester School of Art, Brian Eno began to describe himself as an 'art kleptomaniac' (Sheppard 2008: 46), and in interviews throughout the 1970s as a 'non-musician' (e.g. Goldman 1977). He instigated experimental sound art performances through 'scores for painting' and 'sound sculptures' (Poynor 1986: 42–3) and embarked on efforts to bring together the avant-garde with rock music in a number of collaborations (Sheppard 2008: 52–4). In doing so he drew from his already burgeoning knowledge of experimental and contemporary music alongside his earlier musical interests – American rock and roll, blues, rhythm and blues and doo wop – that inspired in him 'the most overpowering sense of wonder' (qtd. in Tamm: 17). However, it would be the Velvet Underground in 1967 that most significantly triggered his quest to interrogate and collapse the boundaries between art and popular music. As Sheppard (2008: 49) explained, '[h]e relished the fact that [the bands] songs were often as melodically accessible as the cream of contemporary pop, yet also proffered a dark side brimming with daring discords and experimental, atonal flights ... What's more, the VU were, with the notable exception of John Cale, all unschooled musicians.'

Just as significant was Eno's discovery of John Cage's book *Silence: Lectures and Writings*. Tamm (1995) argued Cage's influence was conceptual rather than musical, and it was those who 'rallied to John Cage's proclamation during the 1950s and 1960s that "everything we do is music"' (19; 23) that inspired Eno. Concepts around chance, indeterminacy, disrespect for Western art music conventions, the emphasis on process over outcomes and the view that all sounds can be musical were key. After Winchester, Eno further pursued his experimental music interests in Cornelius Cardew's Scratch Orchestra and Gavin Bryars' Portsmouth Sinfonia before joining Roxy Music in 1971. This came after a chance meeting with Roxy's Andy Mackay, whom Eno originally met and befriended at one of Eno's experimental performances in 1968.

Roxy Music were described by *Melody Maker*'s Richard Williams on his first encounter with them in 1971 as 'a bit of Velvet Underground, a bit of free jazz, a bit of doo-wop' (qtd. in Buckley 2004: Chapter Two). Eno joined Roxy Music after being asked to record the band by Mackay, as by this time Eno had amassed an amount of sound recording and PA equipment. He soon began tape experiments with Mackay's EMS VCS3 synthesizer (Sheppard 2008: 70–1). Roxy Music signed to Island Records after gaining support in the music press, particularly from Williams. Across the first two Roxy Music albums – *Roxy Music* (1972) and *For Your Pleasure* (1973) – and in performance, Eno played a crucial role in contributing electronic sound (using a VCS3 and tape machines) and sound design to the band's aesthetic. Through Bryan Ferry's leadership, the band aimed to draw influences from across the worlds of art and music while simultaneously embodying – and clothing themselves with – a pop art sensibility. In May 1973 Eno described the 'metamusical' intentions of the band, stating, '[w]e wanted to be able to draw on any parts of the history of music, or features of music ... [s]o we obviously wanted to keep what we were doing open and unspecific enough to do that. The other thing we wanted to do was produce the richest variety of sounds' (Robinson 1973). However, by July 1973, tensions between Eno's commitment to continual experimentation and Ferry's intent to pursue a commercial future left Eno out in the cold and Ferry, literally, centre stage.

Eno's immediate response to leaving Roxy Music, much like Cale on leaving the Velvet Underground in 1968, was an element of confusion concerning options for the road ahead. He completed work on the instrumental *No Pussyfooting* album, comprised of Eno's Revox tape machine manipulations of Robert Fripp's guitar performances. Released later in 1973, Sheppard describes its nearest musical equivalent as the work of the 'Krautrock' German bands Can, Faust, Kraftwerk, Popol Vuh and Tangerine Dream, in whom Eno had begun to develop an interest (Sheppard 2008: 141–2). Eno's debut solo album *Here Come the Warm Jets* of spikey, but sometimes mellifluous, songs provided evidence of his developing songwriting craft. Sheppard portrays the album as overburdened with ideas, including 'Anglicized Velvet Underground art pop, baroque Beatles-parody, electronic tone washes … [and] sub-1950s doo-wop pastiche' (150). *No Pussyfooting* and *Here Come the Warm Jets*, both released in November 1973, demonstrated Eno's future intentions were neither totally within nor outside rock music, and that he would pursue a career defined by metamusical play, between and beyond established musical cultures and sound worlds.

Kevin Ayers, John Cale, Eno and Nico – *June 1, 1974*

In early 1974, Velvet Underground and Roxy Music enthusiast Richard Williams in his new A&R role at Island Records had recently signed John Cale and Kevin Ayers, and by June would also sign Nico. He witnessed Eno's departure from Roxy Music and the beginnings of his solo career on Island at close hand. Nico in early 1974 contributed to a song, 'Irreversible Neural Damage', on Island artist Kevin Ayers' album *The Confessions of Dr Dream and Other Stories* (1974). Nico and Ayers had known each other for three years, and he claimed that much of his 1973 album *Bananamour* and the song 'Decadence' were about Nico (Thompson 2017: 175). In April, Williams, who had attended the Reed, Cale and Nico reunion concert in 1973 in Paris, arranged a meeting with Ayers, Eno and Cale to discuss a live album modelled on the Bataclan event. The intention was to provide a mutual boost for all concerned, capturing Ayers and Eno's new material in a live context, and providing a platform to introduce Cale and Nico as new signings to the label. Velvet Underground fan Eno was delighted to become involved and took charge of the logistics of the event (Thompson 2017: 201–3).

In April and May, Eno and Roxy Music's guitarist Phil Manzanera became involved in Cale's first Island album *Fear*, with Eno acting as a production sounding board to Cale. Eno outlined how 'I shared John's ideas and helped him develop them. It was so rewarding!' (qtd. in Demorest 1975). Cale's metamusical intention with the album was to 'keep on doing the stuff that Lou had refused to keep doing in The Velvet Underground … I saw it as what had been left undone by the Velvets' (Thompson 2017: 224). Mick Gold's (1974) assessment of the album was that Cale's songs sounded 'like dream sequences, but in place of the lush, orchestral ambience of [*Paris 1919*],

Phil Manzanera's guttural guitar work and Eno's electronics convey the mood of an uptempo nightmare, while Cale's imagery is tougher and more direct ... *Fear* is haunted by tension and black forebodings about the future.'

By mid-May mixing on the album began (Kent 1974), and rehearsals for the 1 June concert at the Rainbow Theatre in London commenced. The full band included Robert Wyatt (formerly of Soft Machine with Ayers) and Mike Oldfield (formerly of Ayers' the Whole World band), Archie Legget, Ollie Halsall, Eddie Sparrow and John Bundrick from Ayers' current touring band, as well as backing vocalists Irene and Doreen Chanter and Liza Strike. However, at the Rainbow event, Cale, Eno and Nico largely performed together, backed by the other musicians in a variety of combinations, but not with Ayers until the encore. The concert featured two Eno songs from *Here Come the Warm Jets* ('Driving Me Backwards' and 'Baby's on Fire'), Cale's 'Buffalo Ballet', 'Gun' and an eccentric reinterpretation of 'Heartbreak Hotel', and Nico's performance of 'Das Lied Der Deutschen' and 'The End', featuring only Nico with Eno on synth. On release in late June, the album *June 1, 1974* featured only Eno's tracks, Cale's 'Heartbreak Hotel' and Nico's 'The End'. Promotional and media coverage focused on the speed of the album release, only three weeks after the event, which gave it a high profile in the music press.

Soon after the first gig, stories began to appear in the British music press that the success of the collaboration at the Rainbow would lead on to an almost complete reunion of the Velvet Underground. On 8 June the *Melody Maker* (Velvets back 1974: 3) and *NME* (Tour by Eno 1974: 3) ran news stories outlining how an eight-date tour featuring Cale, Sterling Morrison and Moe Tucker, alongside Nico and Eno, would be visiting the UK, Europe and the United States in the Autumn. Nico's manager Jo Lustig was reportedly in the United States, discussing the reunion with Morrison and Tucker. However, in 1975 Eno clarified the actual intention of what proved to be an aborted project: '[w]e contacted Maureen Tucker and Sterling Morrison ... We were going to use John's songs, Nico's and my own. But it was over-exaggerated by the press ... We weren't going to call it The Velvet Underground, and I didn't want to go on stage to be judged as Lou Reed's replacement' (qtd. in Davy 1975).

Nico, *The End* and 'Das Lied Der Deutschen'

Nico signed to Island Records in June 1974, and when Cale completed his *Fear* album soon after the Rainbow concert, work began on recording her next album, *The End*. After these sessions, Ayers, Cale, Eno and Nico repeated their Rainbow Theatre performance at Birmingham Hippodrome and Manchester Palace Theatre on 27 and 28 June. According to John Wood (2018), the album was recorded over three or four days in a more disciplined manner than *Desertshore*, but still he observed antagonism between Nico and Cale. However, when Wood's daughters recorded vocal overdubs on 'It Has Not Taken Long', he remarked that 'it was the only time I've ever seen Cale not be impatient in the studio – he was great with them'.

According to Witts (1993: 262-3) Nico claimed the musical foundation – a kind of Wagnerian *leitmotiv* – for the album was the Haydn melody of 'Das Lied Der Deutschen', with five songs containing 'variants of Haydn's tune, each opening with the same three notes, while the sixth mixed the tune with that of "The End"'. However, on analysis this does not seem entirely accurate. First, the anthem is in a major key, while all the songs on the album are in diverse minor keys and modes including Phrygian ('You Forgot to Answer') and Dorian ('Valley of the Kings'). Furthermore, the first phrase of the German anthem (1.-2.-3.-2.-4.-3.-2.-7.-1. tones of the major scale) or at least its first six tones constitute(s) the specific character of the tune which allows its recognition. Witts refers to the first three notes (1.-2.-.3.). These three notes may be found in the minor scale (with the third tone a half step lower) in some of the songs of the album (e.g. at the beginning of 'It Has Not Taken Long'), but this sequence is much too common to serve as a leitmotiv in the classical sense. Finally, it has to be noted that Nico's melodies tend to avoid great intervals, usually moving up and down the given scales or modes, making the mentioned sequence of notes almost inevitable. This narrow range in melodic lines contributes to the unusual character of Nico's singing. The resulting aural impression is of Medieval litanies, supported by the frequent use of church or Gregorian modes and, of course, the harmonium as her backing instrument.

On Nico's intention in performing the anthem, Witts asserts that she wanted to make a 'provocative act' based on a dream where, as a young girl, a train of soldiers passed by and 'told her to be silent or they would kill her with a special drug'. After escaping to a cemetery where she 'saw the name of her mother' on a grave stone with a flag close by, she 'sang the anthem and the flag melted', waking before the soldiers caught her. Nico's intention was to 'sing the forbidden words to expose the old sentiment behind the new one' (qtd. in Witts 1993: 263). This rationale does not seem to have been noticed or understood by reviewers or audiences at the time. However, Batt (2012) observes that Nico's performances of 'Das Lied Der Deutschen' 'always received a mixed response in concert … [as] the song had connotations which neither tribute nor parody could quite undermine'.

As John Wood indicated, the album was more disciplined in terms of its production and arrangements than *The Marble Index* and *Desertshore*. Once Nico had completed her vocal and harmonium performances, Eno and Manzanera were brought in briefly for improvised synthesizer and guitar overdubs. Eno's synthesizer contribution added an ominous, icy sheen to 'You Forgot to Answer', while Manzanera contributed electric guitar runs reminiscent of Spanish guitar. On 'Innocent and Vain' Eno contributed some unsettling, screaming synthesizer textures, and Manzanera layered detuned guitar sounds on 'We've Got the Gold'. Throughout the album Cale again contributed piano, organ and viola, as well as textures from percussion instruments, sometimes strummed rather than hit. 'Das Lied Der Deutschen' itself began with a Velvet Underground–style viola and keyboard drone, with improvised tonal and atonal interjections on organ by Cale. As in previous albums, Nico returned to the studio towards the end of the process where Cale's work was revealed to her. Batt's (2012) assessment of the album is that 'listening to Nico is always an unforgettable experience;

turbulent, enigmatic, haunting, nihilistic and timeless ... With *The End* she is at her best, forcing you to totally rethink what a rock album should sound like'.

When the putative 'The Velvet Enoground' tour in Autumn 1974 failed to materialize, and with Kevin Ayers occupied elsewhere, Nico, Cale and Eno regrouped in Berlin at the Metamusik Festival, with Cale and Nico performing songs and Eno providing textural backing on synthesizer and a glass harp (consisting of water filled wine glasses). If 'Das Lied Der Deutschen' was met with little if any controversy at the Rainbow Theatre performance in June, this would not be true in Berlin.

Nico, Cale and Eno at Nationalgalerie, Berlin, 5 October 1974

The controversial decision to perform 'Das Lied der Deutschen' at the Berlin Nationalgalerie caused some audience consternation during a time of political upheaval in West Germany (FRG), with leftist terrorists attempting to initiate revolutionary action. To help understand the problematic nature of this decision, an overview of the historical, political, social and cultural context of this incident is necessary, and the reactions of the Berlin audience on the night will be examined in some detail.

Cold war and counterculture

In 1974 Berlin was a fractured city. The wall had been built thirteen years earlier and divided the cities' infrastructure, inhabitants and, in many cases, families. The former capital of Germany became a central symbol of the cold war and was an isolated foothold for the West, completely surrounded by Soviet soldiers and their East German allies. In the early 1960s the global political situation pitted the free Western world against communist totalitarianism, with the US President John F. Kennedy telling the West Berlin crowd: 'Ick [Ich] bin ein Berliner' in 1963. Despite this, the US engagement in the ongoing Vietnam War pursued by Kennedy and his successors contributed to anti-war protests that began in West Berlin as early as 1966.

During the 1960s, many young people of the post-war baby boom generation, from all over the FRG, had moved to Berlin for several reasons. It had three universities, it offered large and affordable flats and the cost of living in general was low. Moreover, there was no *Wehrpflicht* [conscription] into the FRG's army for male Berliners (a requirement introduced across the country in 1956) due to the specific political status of the town. The previous decade had been characterized by the *wirtschaftswunder*, a fast reconstruction and growth of the West German economy, but also a period of political and cultural conservatism and rigid sexual morality. As in other parts of the Western world, new ideas, including philosophically and politically leftist concepts, began to spread in course of the 1960s. The capitalist system at the base of the *wirtschaftswunder* and the dominance of the American way of life and its popular culture on the Western world were resisted by growing numbers in the younger generation. In the FRG, this turn towards the political left also has to be seen in the context of the country's hidden Nazi past of the country. Many members of the political and economic system at the heart of the Third Reich had been able to rapidly re-establish themselves in their former positions during the early years of the cold war. There had been some judicial attempts to make Nazi murderers and their supporters take responsibility for their crimes. Nevertheless, even several prosecutions of guards at the Auschwitz death camp, where more than 1 million Jews and other victims had been killed between 1942 and 1945, ended with relatively mild punishments or even acquittal.

These components, the rising protest movement against the Vietnam War, a climate of political and cultural stagnation in the FRG, the ongoing presence of former Nazis in many institutions, and Neo-Nazist tendencies and a supposed continuum of fascism in general, contributed to an intense radicalization of Germany's leftist scene. West Berlin became one of the hotspots of this process. The pivotal year 1967 began with the founding of Kommune 1, a community founded on leftist political ideals that propagated free love, drug use and radical political action. The visit of the Shah of Iran, a close ally of the United States, led to widespread political demonstrations in June of that year. During these events a protester, Benno Ohnesorg, was shot by a police officer. This event was a trigger for the development of leftist terrorism in the FRG (most prominently, in the activities of the Rote Armee Fraktion [RAF]).[1] This growing political radicalism coincided with new radical aesthetics, and 1967 saw the opening of the Zodiak Free Arts Lab by Conrad Schnitzler and the formation of the bands Agitation Free and Tangerine Dream, the experimental nucleus of what later became known as the 'Berlin School' in music.

Approximately 450 kilometres west of Berlin in Düsseldorf and Cologne were two progenitors of these experiments: the artist Joseph Beuys and the composer Karlheinz Stockhausen. The latter released his electronic work *Hymnen* (1969). This was a composition that combined among other snippets recordings of Germany's national anthem 'Das Lied der Deutschen' (sometimes also called 'Deutschlandlied'), the Nazi hymn 'Horst-Wessel-Lied' and protesting students singing the communist 'Internationale'. This montage was criticized by the conservative establishment as it was an obvious critical commentary on the politics of the FRG. Despite its ironic or perhaps even sarcastic character, and a totally different audience, Nico, Cale and Eno's interpretation of 'Das Lied der Deutschen' proved equally controversial at Berlin's Nationalgalerie in October 1974. For a better understanding of the disapproval of many audience members (in part representing Berlin's young generation of that time), the ideological and symbolic potential of the German *Nationalhymne* will now be outlined and interpreted.

The dark shadows of German history

The story of the German anthem began when Joseph Haydn composed its melody, as the *Kaiserhymne*, in 1797 and dedicated it to Joseph, the Habsburgian emperor during the period of Napoleonic Wars.[2] The victory over Napoleon in 1815 did not fulfil many Germans' longing for a united national state and democratic reforms, and opposition to the reinstallation of absolutism in Germany soon developed. Hoffmann von Fallersleben, a professor at Göttingen university, joined this movement as did many other intellectuals of his time, and wrote the lyrics of 'Das Lied der Deutsche' using Haydn's melody in 1841. The line 'Deutschland, Deutschland über alles' [Germany, Germany above all] in the first verse was originally intended as a strong patriotic call for a German national state uniting all German-speaking peoples, across a large section of Central Europe. But the third verse also contains liberal demands for unity, the rule of law and liberty for those in the German fatherland. However, from 1914 the first verse of the 'Deutschlandlied' began to turn into an indicator of aggressive nationalism and militarism by the emerging Langemarck myth, that young German volunteers had died singing it during a hazardous attack in Belgium.

After the First World War the song became the national anthem of the first democratic German state, the Weimarer Republik. During the following Nazi period (1933–45), only the first verse followed by the *Horst-Wessel-Lied* was used for official events. Stockhausen hinted at this in *Hymnen* with his highly ideological juxtaposition. After three years of discussion concerning the nationalistic and militaristic connotations of the song, only the third verse of the 'Deutschlandlied' was adopted for the national anthem of the new Federal Republic of Germany in 1952.

Nico as a German was not only aware of this history but had also lived through its darkest times. She was born in 1938 in Cologne, and as the Second World War began, she briefly lived in Berlin before spending the war with family in Lübbenau in the Spreewald forest, around eighty kilometres from the German capital. By 1946 she had relocated with her mother to Berlin to what Otter Bickerdike describes as 'a dystopian wasteland' with 'the once vibrant city now described as a *Geisterstadt* – a "ghost town"' (2021: Chapter 4). Nico therefore well knew the background and connotations of 'Das Lied der Deutschen' when she released it with all verses on *The End* (1974) and later presented it at the Nationalgalerie. As indicated above, she claimed she intended to 'expose the old sentiment behind the new one'[3] (Witts 1993: 263). However, at the end of her performance of the song at the Rainbow Theatre in June, after general applause, her only provocative or perhaps ironic comment was '[a] harmless little song'.

Although Nico apparently performed the song on a number of occasions (though exact details are unclear), it seems obvious that she was wise enough not to sing it at a solo set on 13 December 1974 at the Notre Dame de Reims cathedral[4] as support act for Tangerine Dream.[5] This church hosted the coronations of French kings during the Middle Ages and had been destroyed by German artillery in 1914, which was widely regarded as a barbaric act.[6]

While the symbolic character of the Reims cathedral appears to be pretty evident, it should be added that the Nationalgalerie at Berlin, where Nico's previous concert had taken place, was also symbolic, albeit less obviously. The venue was located in urban wasteland devastated by war on the edge of West Berlin. It was built directly next to the wall dividing the city and Potsdamer Platz, its former and destroyed core. The building was the final major project completed in designer Mies van der Rohe's lifetime. He was one of many members of the famous Bauhaus group and other intellectuals and artists who emigrated from Germany during the Third Reich.[7] Due to this, the building of the Nationalgalerie might be viewed as a symbol of the new, modern FRG – as part of the free Western world displaying its art next to the ruins left by the Nazi era, and the wall erected by the new totalitarian enemy in the east.

As has been outlined, the Metamusik Festival that took place from 1972–6 also has to be seen in this political and cultural context, since it presented music from across the globe, often by new or unfamiliar artists, and was regarded as 'progressive' by its young audience (Schnitze 1974). Publicity materials for the festival articulated the reasons for the choice of name: 'Meta stands for several constructive lines of the program and for its confrontations. America's new modal music is being presented in connection with its Asian models ... Meta, beyond mere aesthetics, is this aspect of a musical ritual of concentration, but *Meta is the politicisation of the avant-garde*' (Beal 2006: 205). The 'confrontations' therefore intended to probe the borders and connections between, across and beyond the music presented. Therefore, the generations of Germans born after 1945 can be understood to have become much more open to cultural influences from abroad. Of course, this musical and cultural openness[8] also implied a denial of Germany's Nazi past, as well as a more general refusal of German tradition and identity. This refusal is also shown by the fact most German pop and rock bands of that period chose English names, titles and lyrics. Rock music served as a highly distinctive generation marker and an essential part of a kind of cultural *vergangenheitsbewältigung* – a catharsis of the individual and collective past and its connections to the Nazi era (Schneider 2015:18). But Nico, who had left Germany in the mid-1950s, dared to perform songs with German lyrics during her concert at Berlin in 1974. It is enlightening to analyse the reactions of the audience to this aspect of the performance, as well as to the broader musical presentation of Nico, Cale and Eno.

Saturday Night at the Nationalgalerie

Nico, Cale and Eno's concert took place on 5 October 1974 at the Metamusik Festival curated by Walter Bachauer, a music journalist at the local radio station RIAS (Radio im amerikanischen Sektor).[9] Between 1000 and 1500 visitors, mostly students and other younger people, attended the event.[10] A light show and high-quality Bose sound system had been installed in the museum for the duration of the festival, and the audience sat on white cushions with the imprint 'Metamusik Festival'. Some people smoked marijuana, and it is fair to assume that other drugs were taken as well.

Bachauer's festival was sponsored by Berliner Festspiele GmbH and the artist section of DAAD (Deutscher Akademischer Austauschdienst) with low ticket prices for the targeted younger audience (Schnitze 1974). Nico, Cale and Eno had been booked by Bachauer after hearing of the ACNE concerts in June 1974 and the *June 1, 1974* album. As has been indicated, they were announced in the festival programme as 'British Rock of the Avantgarde'. It is to be assumed that some visitors were expecting or hoping for a hybrid performance combining the aesthetics of the Velvet Underground and Roxy Music (Graf-Ulbrich 2015). But the eclectic music presented was very different. Cale performed four songs: the Dylan Thomas–inspired 'A Child's Christmas in Wales', stylistically in the mould of a nostalgic piece of late 1960s pop; 'Guts' from his recently released album *Fear* was deceptively cut from similar cloth with unfamiliarity and language differences meaning the audience potentially missed the profanities and extreme violence in the lyrics, mistaking it for an unremarkable piano-based pop song; 'Fear Is a Man's Best Friend' began in singer-songwriter territory before descending into uncontrolled anger, fear and despair; and by contrast, 'Buffalo Ballet', a simple country-rock song of life and historical events in the Texas town of Abilene. The one crowd-pleaser was the Velvet Underground's 'I'm Waiting for the Man'. Nico's contribution was a number of songs from across *The Marble Index*, *Desertshore* and the soon-to-be-released *The End* that were hard to place in any established rock, folk or classical genre or frame. Eno meanwhile stood behind a trestle table filled with wine glasses set up as a glass harp amplified through the sound system, and contributed effects and musical parts generated from his EMS Synthi A synthesizer. While Cale's 'Guts' received the thoughtful comment '[t]hat sounds a little bit like Neil Young',[11] other visitors showed their disapproval in various and intensifying ways during the course of the gig.

The Berlin concert started with Nico. The 'Janitor of Lunacy' was met with polite applause, but some apparent confusion in the audience. For 'The Falconer', Eno accompanied Nico by rubbing the rim of the wine glasses filled with water to varying degrees, and Cale eventually joined on piano. Again the song was met with applause and approval. At the end of the third song, 'No One Is There' with a romantic, poetic interplay between Nico's lament and Cale's viola, the first booing began, with one shouting in English 'shitty music'. It was the fourth song, 'Frozen Warnings' (backed by Cale's La Monte Young/Velvet Underground style viola drone, and Eno's pulsing, high pitched synthesizer contributions), that unrest and inter-audience conflict started. A young man ironically shouted, '[b]eautiful music!' before the song began, with others answering 'get out now', 'go home' and 'stop it', followed by '[j]ust go, if you don't like it. It won't change that much here probably'. The latter person may have been correct, but the disruptive element of the audience stayed despite this observation. As the song ended, there were more boos, and a repeated cry of 'Scheiße!' ['shit!']. Cale's 'Guts' was then met with fewer, but clear shouts of 'Scheiße!' and some longer boos.

As Nico's 'Abschied' began, an attendee started counting '1,2,1,2,3' followed by laughter, an ironic statement indicating the lack of a rock beat in the performances. Notably, the negative reactions increased when Nico presented two solo songs, 'Abschied' and 'Mütterlein', in German, with shouts such as 'Scheiße!' or 'Aufhören!' [stop playing!] becoming more frequent. Moreover, parts of the audience started loud rhythmic and pointed clapping, combined with whistling, to disturb the performance of 'Mütterlein', though another audience member shouted, 'Hör auf damit!' [stop doing that!]. Others shouted at the disruptors, asking them to 'Geh nach Hause|!' [go home!] and 'Raus!' [leave]. Cale's 'A Child's Christmas in Wales' faced some minor disruption, with a call from one of the sitting attendees to others to 'Hört auf zu stehen!' [stop standing!]. Cale's interpretation of 'I'm Waiting for the Man', backed by Eno's percussive, arpeggiated glass tones and some lower pitched synth, was met more positively, with the comment 'that was fine now – [do] not [sing] in German!' However, another attendee shouted in English, '[t]hat is not music, that is noise', a puzzlingly conservative assessment at a festival presenting experimental and avant-garde musics. Cale's 'Fear' followed with Eno randomly 'playing' the wine glasses with a glass rod.

Richard Williams (2014) commented that '[f]or me, "Fear" was the real first highpoint ... Eno tapped on the glasses to make tintinnabulatory noises and then, as Cale's dramatic song neared the point of explosion, he started to smash them. Fluxus had come to the Bauhaus'. Though 'Fear' was met positively by the audience, as John Strawn (2018) reported the event organizers and museum administrators had been 'extremely nervous during the entire festival about one of their art works being damaged. One dared touch nothing or even get close ... As a result, those of us running the festival felt a shiver when the glasses started shattering'.

The performance of 'Das Lied der Deutschen' may have been suggested by Lutz Graf-Ulbrich (2016),[12] but clearly Cale and Eno played a part in the song choice. Nico on vocal and harmonium was backed by Eno producing swooping synthesizer sounds with descending pitches that have clear connotations of dive-bombing planes and falling bombs (reminiscent of Kraftwerk's 'Von Himmel Hoch' [From Heaven High] from 1970 that dramatized the horrors of air warfare). Cale contributed atonal piano improvisations, with percussive low pitches reminiscent of the sound of distant explosions, sporadic clusters of notes and some harmonic ghosting of Nico. It has to be assumed that Cale and Eno's contributions were as offensive to some in the audience as Nico's performance. Clearly linking the anthem to the sounds of warfare may have been ironic or sarcastic British humour aimed at an old enemy, or equally a condemnation of warfare as in Kraftwerk's composition. But whatever the intention, it was not incidental and contributed to the furore around the song. As Nico sang the first line there were boos, loud whistles and some laughter and shouts of 'Aufhören!' [stop playing!] and 'Bravo!'. As the song progressed there were shouts of 'Das ist ja unerhört!' [that is outrageous] and 'Mensch, super!' [great, man!]. An audience member at the song's end shouted in English at the disruptors, 'Go home, be polite, motherfucker!'. During the performance, parts of the audience had predictably reacted unfavourably and with growing hostility, shouting and booing loudly and throwing some of the Metamusik festival branded cushions towards the stage (Williams 2014).[13] At the end of the song there was clearly a mixed reaction, some applauding loudly, some jeering and booing. After the band finished their version of the *nationalhymne*, some discussion began to take place in the audience, and a man started singing the first line of the French 'Marseillaise', receiving some applause.[14]

Nico's next song, 'You Forget to Answer', was a solo performance, with further shouts aimed at the disruptive attendees – 'Hör doch auf!' [give it a rest!], 'Geh doch endlich!' [go at last!] and 'Geh doch in den Tierpark!' [go to the Zoo!] – as well as booing and jeering.

'Innocent and Vain' also features Eno contributing washes of white noise reminiscent of the sound of waves. As the song progresses, elements of the crowd began to mimic and mock these sounds, suggesting some crowd hostility towards the experimental aspects of the performance, that is, the noise and avant-garde elements. However, another possibility is that some audience members perhaps felt they should in some way participate in the event, as happened in 1969 at an abandoned Stockhausen performance of *Stimmung* in Amsterdam, where left radical Dutch composers in the audience disruptively contributed the sound of cat's meowing to the overtone singing of six vocalists (Reetze 2020: 169). During the song, an audience member accused the troublemakers of not showing any '*Kunstverstand*' [any sense of understanding art], which was answered by somebody else with the words: 'And you don't have any mind at all!'. Cale followed Nico's song incongruously with the country rock ballad 'Buffalo Ballet', with audience chatter throughout but to a generally positive response. By the last song of the concert, Nico's cover version of the Doors' 'The End' (1967), the angry part of the audience seemed pacified again. Nico sang and played her harmonium, Cale sustained a viola drone and contributed sporadic piano, with Eno contributing arpeggiated clusters on synthesizer, though an organ-like sound was also apparent at times. This ten-minute version of the song was centred again on a Velvet Underground-style drone, piano interjections and aggressive synthesizer screeches and screams towards the end; in sonic terms this was the most powerful of the performances.

Germanness as a frame of interpretation

While the bootleg concert recording and other sources allow for the reconstruction of the historical facts of the event in terms of the performance and audience reactions, this appears to be much harder in relation to questions regarding the intentions and motivations of the protagonists. It has to be assumed that the reasons why a group within the audience tried to disturb the concert are as complex as the wider contexts already mentioned. In the daily press two interpretations could be found. In his short review in *Der Abend*, music journalist Barry Graves accused many visitors of buying tickets without being aware of Nico's record releases[15] and showing impatience, ignorance and bad behaviour at the concert itself.[16] Graves proposed that the 'Protestanten-Rotte' [gang of protestors] demonstrated their inability to understand the avant-garde sense of irony underlying 'Mütterlein' and 'Das Lied der Deutschen' (Graves 1974). In his review in *Tagesspiegel*, music professor Dr Wolfgang Burde (1974) on the other hand blamed Nico and her fellow musicians for dilettantism.[17] This academically skilled critic criticized the lack of differentiation of articulation in Nico's vocal performance as much as a lack of '*swingenden Witz*' [swinging wit] and humour. Moreover, Burde contended that the depth of meaning and emotion of the lyrics, the singing and the music itself was misplaced in a rock context, and due to that the reactions of elements of the rock audience were understandable. In his own definition rock should deal with beat, gogo, wild brilliant aggression and not with sad or even depressive songs.

In his article Burde also referred to the chosen headline of the concert. While the audience expected British avant-garde rock, the Indian harmonium of Nico 'strangely sounded like a German one' (Burde 1974) (suggesting Burde was ignorant of its European origins). In this quote a double tension is evident. On the one hand, it seems to be quite obvious that the musicians should have shunned the basic genre conventions of rock. Nico's plaintive singing had never been orientated much to the African American tradition that had influenced most rock artists of that time. Furthermore, the line-up itself contained no electric guitar or any kind of rhythm section, which made the untypical harmonium become the most important instrument of that evening next to the viola, a piano, a synthesizer and the wine glasses (glass harp) used musically and as occasional sound effects by Eno. For Burde, despite the contributions of her fellow musicians, the whole setting itself and the singing and music of Nico appeared to be linked to a specific kind of musically and lyrically naïve Germanness.[18] In contrast the renowned music writer Barry Graves (real name was Hans-Jürgen Deutschmann)[19] explicitly blamed a typical characteristic of Berlins inhabitants – the '*Mutterwitz*' (Graves 1974) [the ability to judge phenomena and react quickly] as one of the causes that contributed to the incidents at the Nationalgalerie. He also mentioned aggressive *spießbürgerlichkeit* [bigoted small-mindedness] and *humorlosigkeit* [humourlessness], characteristics often regarded to be 'typically' German – even or foremost by Germans themselves – as at fault. *Spießbürgerlichkeit* is a pointed and permanent insistence on any kind of regulations, and a dramatic lack of openness towards anything new combined with a profound lack of a sense of humour. One of the rare pronouncements by Nico during the concert at the Nationalgalerie suggests she had a similar perception of the events taking place in front of the stage. After the harsh reaction to her performance of 'Abschied', she addressed the shouting and booing persons ironically: 'Das hört sich ja an wie die Nachtwächter!' [That sounds like the Night Watchman!], which provoked an immediate response inspired by *mutterwitz*: 'You too!'.[20]

As has been noted, Nico's contribution to the performance took place in the town where she had spent a large part of her post-war childhood, later working at the KaDeWe department store before heading to Paris to start a new life (Williams 2014; Otter Bickerdike 2021). The gig at the Nationalgalerie Berlin seems to be linked not only to her own biography but to German history in general and its individual and collective snares and contradictions. It is quite remarkable that the two songs that caused the greatest disapproval had German lyrics. The performance of 'Das Lied der Deutschen' and the upset it caused simply further stirred up what had been in the air before. The German language itself had been regarded as not an appropriate fit for the rock genre, no matter how avant-garde. Bands like Floh de Cologne or Ton, Steine Scherben had already made use of German as a vehicle for leftist political agitation quite successfully, but Nico's lyrics had been much more in the tradition of the obscure language and inner reflections of the Romantic era and expressionism. The troublesome audience members at the Nationalgalerie failed to discover the lyrical ambiguity and hypnotic potential of Nico's minimalistic songs, as much as the sense of humour and the irony in the group performances, and that underlying her songs including 'Mütterlein'. The way Nico made use of German lyrics probably appeared out of time, or even *reaktionär* [reactionary] in a political sense (which served as a strict oppositional stance to progressivism at that time). The performance of 'Das Lied der Deutschen', including all three verses, might have afforded interpretations of that kind if the bombastic, chromatic passages of Cale's piano and the warlike noises created by Eno were ignored. Other visitors who might have been more open minded to new aesthetic experiences perhaps had better knowledge of Nico's previous works, or might even have recalled another famous pop cultural adaptation of a national anthem: Jimi Hendrix playing 'The Star Spangled Banner' at the Woodstock Festival in 1969, where he memorably emulated the sounds of bombing and warfare as an anti-Vietnam War statement.[21] But five years after that mythical performance to the

'Woodstock generation', the live debut of Nico, Cale and Eno's deconstructive version of the German national anthem at the Nationalgalerie next to the Berlin Wall, dividing the former capital of Germany, had been misunderstood widely, which surely reminds us of other events in the history of artistic avant-gardes.

Although there is no hint of explicit politically motivated disruption to be found on the bootleg (besides the singing of the *Marseillaise*), it has to be assumed that the aesthetic preferences of the public had been influenced by their individual and collective political opinions and practices as much as by the historical circumstances of a leftist counterculture and growing terrorism.[22] But while Williams seems to take into account that the unruly members of the audience might have been leftist radicals (Williams 2014), Barry Graves refers to the scene around the pub Polkwitz (Graves 1974). Fashionable markers of the counterculture like jeans, long hair and beards had been adapted into neater forms by the crowd there, but not their politically inspired values. A newspaper report on several hip locations of that time writes that, scandalously, there were even some men wearing ties (Benzmann 1971). Another interpretation can be found in the memories of another attendee, Manfred Weiß (2021). He neither expected the melancholic character of Nico's songs nor her very idiosyncratic, monotonous performance. He felt she ignored the audience unlike other rock performers he had witnessed, thereby alienating the crowd. Weiß admits he misunderstood the performance of 'Das Lied der Deutschen' as having nationalistic intent, and it has to be supposed that he was not the only one to do so. He also portrays attendees as a typical young rock audience wearing ex-*Bundeswehr* [army] parkas. The cheap, good quality parkas were commonly worn by youngsters at the time, with West German flags removed from the sleeves to avoid nationalistic or militaristic connotations. In Weiß's view, it was this group that became angry during the concert because the music and its presentation did not fulfil their expectations.

Reflecting on Nico, Cale and Eno's concert at the Nationalgalerie and its complex background, it becomes evident that those who had started their 'revolution' around 1967, claiming to fight tradition and conservative society and its oppression and censorship, using political action and avant-garde art, soon established actualized or even re-actualized forms of distinction. In some sections, even an aggressive intolerance, culminating in the terrorism of RAF and other groups (see also: Aly 2007).[23] To what extent the tension between the common citizen, the narrow-minded *spießbürger* [bigot] and any form of radicalism – which surely includes the possibilities of the *spießbürger* becoming radical and the radical to become a *spießbürger* – is 'typically' German may become clearer by a closer examination of the Romantic era and its influential idealistic concepts that suggest continuity in romantically inspired approaches to politics and art (Safranski 2007). In 1979 Nico dedicated 'Das Lied der Deutschen' to the dead Andreas Baader during a concert in New York City (Rockwell 1979), and Witts (1993: 278) observed at other times it was dedicated to Ulrike Meinhof, whose Berlin funeral Nico attended. Following Safranskis' thesis of the Romantic era as a predominately 'German affair', all three individuals, the artist Nico and the terrorists Baader and Meinhof, might be regarded as romantic (as well as romanticized) and deeply tragic 'German' figures united by their failed attempts to get rid of a 'Germanness' contaminated by the Nazi past whose ideology had romantic implications itself (Safranki 2007: 348ff.). While Andreas Baader, Ulrike Meinhof and others chose real weapons and bombs to fight the 'system', Nico's version of the German anthem might be seen as an artistic effort to do so (Witts 1993: 262 f.).

But perhaps Witts' interpretation fits the cultural studies paradigm of 'resistance' too neatly, and Nico's motivations in performing 'Das Lied der Deutschen' remain more ambivalent, informed by awareness of the political situation of the FRG in the 1970s as much as by her own mixed feelings and experiences. To her the national anthem had also been linked to memories of her childhood in Germany during the Second World War. She decided in 1974 to sing the version she had been taught early in her life, with the 'old sentiment' (Nico qtd. in Witts 1993: 263), and this might even be regarded as an expression of the naïve 'Germanness' Burde criticized in his review (Burde 1974). Lutz-Graf Ulbrich (2017), who would be Nico's musical and personal partner over many years, assumed that she wanted to express her nostalgia concerning the country she had chosen to leave, and also might have simply liked the melody. Regarding the music itself, it becomes pretty evident that the contributions of Cale and Eno function as deconstructive counterparts to Nico's playing and singing. Just imagine her as a German performing 'Das Lied der Deutschen', singing the proscribed words, only accompanied by her harmonium at Notre Dame de Reims in December 1974. It is not too hard to guess what the perception in France and elsewhere in Europe would have been. Germany, the Germans and German culture were then, and evidently still are, inevitably tied to German history and its dark shadows culminating in the Holocaust and other Nazi crimes.

Conclusion

Nico, Cale and Eno's controversial performance at the Nationalgalerie lacked an overall sense of coherence, presenting a number of facets of their separate musical activities as boundary crossing, avant-garde musicians attempting to come to terms with their trajectory through early 1970s rock music. The trio's Berlin performance effectively marked a new beginning for Cale and Eno after a busy, fraught year of collaborations and abandoned plans. Cale after 1974, though still retaining a certain manic experimental energy, took the opportunity to attempt to emulate Lou Reed's solo success as a rock performer, and initially appeared to bury his classical and avant-garde training underground while pursuing this. He simultaneously developed a career as a record producer, notably on Patti Smith's *Horses* in 1975. Eno, after an abortive tour supporting *Here Come the Warm Jets* in February 1974, gradually disappeared from public performance into solo and collaborative projects and production work, inside and outside music, and most notably returned to Berlin to work on David Bowie's *Low* and *'Heroes'* albums in 1976–7. In 1975 he established the label Obscure Records as a vehicle for liminal, avant-garde metamusic existing in the spaces between Western art music, electronic, experimental and popular music in the work of Gavin Bryars, Michael Nyman, Harold Budd and David Toop among others. Nico hoped that after years of touring and self-management, her relationship with Island records and manager Jo Lustig would be a platform for further recording projects, though this was not to be. She ultimately drifted through the rest of the 1970s performing her distinctive music alone with her harmonium in Europe and the United States – and eventually to newer punk audiences – after being dropped by Island records due to poor sales and controversial pronouncements in interviews.

In examining the audience reception of the concert, with a specific emphasis on the historical and political context of West Berlin in the 1970s, this study has raised questions concerning the diversity and complexity of audience interpretations at the event around musical style and genre expectations. There is no doubt that Nico, Cale and Eno created a sense of dialogue across, between and beyond existing musical taste cultures and genres through their performance containing Romantic classical, avant-garde, folk, rock and pop elements. Doing so defeated audience expectations of a 'Roxy Underground' hybrid for those unfamiliar with their solo work outside of the bands they had left behind. Moreover, by examining the frames of reference through which audiences made sense of the intersection of music performance and Germany's shameful twentieth-century history in the presentation of 'Das Lied Der Deutschen', a more nuanced version of events in Berlin has been developed – in particular, concerning the contradictory responses of sections of the audience to being confronted with a past that had recently started to come into full view in West Germany. Whatever the intentions of Nico, Cale and Eno, this confrontational performance, congruent with the overall aim of openness and the politicization of the avant-garde at the heart of the Metamusik festival, created an event that provides important insights into musical and cultural currents in the FRG and beyond in the 1970s.

Notes

1. A Berlin terrorist group's name, Bewegung 2.Juni, refers to this date. The killing was used to legitimize their own violence ideologically as self-defence against a still fascist state.
2. The 'Kaiserhymne' is similar to the Croatian folk song 'V Jutro Rano Se Ja Vstanem'. Haydn perhaps referenced the melody as he did with other folk songs. The 'Non-German' origin of the musical base of 'Das Lied der Deutschen' is an ironic historical detail.
3. The first two verses of the Deutschlandlied were never censored officially in the FRG, but banned widely in social life.
4. Nico's set at Reims contained eleven songs, of which only three had not been performed at Berlin in October: 'Valley of The Kings', 'We've Got the Gold' and 'Ari's Song'.
5. This was a musical 'reconciliation project' by Tangerine Dream, with concerts at Coventry Cathedral and other places hit by German air raids during the Second World War.
6. The concert actually caused a scandal in France as attendees urinated in the church, which was reconsecrated as a result.

7   Mies van der Rohe left Nazi Germany in 1938. Others, e.g. Thomas Mann, Berthold Brecht and Arnold Schönberg, fled earlier for political reasons or due to racist Nazi ideology.
8   The festival primarily emphasized modal music (i.e. music without functional harmony), but modal jazz and contemporary jazz-rock was ignored in this conception of 'meta musik'.
9   The RIAS, founded by the American military administration of West Berlin at the end of 1945, were regarded as propaganda tools during the cold war by both sides.
10 Thanks to Bernd M. Radowicz for information on his website rockarchiv and further help; Lutz Graf-Ulbrich and Manfred Weiß, who attended the concert in 1974 for some insights and ZKM (Zentrum für Kunst und Medien); and Karlsruhe for the provision of a video containing some of the songs presented. The event was filmed by Michael Geißler, member of the leftist video art collective VAM (Video Audio Medien). Articles in Berlin's daily press in October 1974, and a bootleg recording of the set served as sources for the reconstruction of the event.
11 Audience comments are translated by Timor Kaul.
12 'Das Lied der Deutschen' was the final track of *The End*, released in November 1974.
13 While throwing cushions was of a symbolic character, rock fans from Berlin had thrown beer bottles on other occasions: e.g. Rock-Zirkus festival of 1974 (During 1974).
14 'The Marseillaise' (French national anthem) serves as an ideological counterpart to 'Das Lied Der Deutschen', as it also supports the idea of the nation and propagating the duty to fight for the fatherland. Despite this, the conception of French nationalism developed during the revolution appealed to German and other European supporters who regarded the successful French troops as liberators from absolutist rule.
15 *Der Abend* published a notice for the concert that might be read as a warning not to expect easy listening and entertainment, labelling Nico's music 'psycho rock' (Alisch 1974).
16 It is not clear how many members of the audience demonstrated their disapproval; Barry Graves estimated 60 per cent, and Lutz Graf-Ulbrich and Manfred Weiß mentioned a small group that grew over the course of the event.
17 Wolfgang Burde – lecturer at Pädagogische Hochschule Berlin – was interested in Neue Musik, jazz and music sociology and wrote for *Tagesspiegel* and other German newspapers.
18 Burde's review also contains paternalistic machismo, referring to Nico as a 'schönes Kind' [beautiful child], only able to present a poor, amateurish musical concept.
19 Barry Graves had his own RIAS radio show, wrote for several newspapers and became co-author of the first German rock dictionary (Schmidt-Joos, Siegfried, Graves, Barry, Rock Lexikon. Hamburg: Rowolth, 1973). As a regular visitor of gay clubs in Berlin and New York, he was interested in African American dance music (Der Mythos 2021).
20 While the *spießbürger* in medieval towns defended city walls, the *nachtwächter* were the night watchmen. The *spießbürger* became a synonym for the 'typical' petit bourgeois German, and *Nachtwächter* was used as an insult for forgetful and slow persons (in their actions and thinking).
21 It is conceivable that Eno and Cale intentionally referenced Hendrix's performance in Berlin. In fact as Claque (2014: 469) makes clear, Hendrix performed 'The Star

Spangled Banner', around sixty times from 1968 to 1970 aiming to express 'the transformational dreams of the countercultural 1960s, its frustrations and its hope ... Hendrix took stock of a nation in violent transition, making this process audible to his listeners as critique, as affirmation, and as call to action' (469). Nico was irritated by the fact that Hendrix was celebrated as a countercultural hero for playing the US anthem, while she was disparaged for performing 'Das Lied Der Deutschen', which she viewed as doing 'the same thing' (Witts 1993: 266).

22 On 6 October 1974 (the day after Nico, Cale and Eno's gig) a performance of Arnold Schönberg's 'Moses und Aron' at Deutsche Oper Berlin was targeted. The protestors' flyers demanded the end of the solitary confinement of terrorists at Moabit prison and support for their hunger strike (Deutsche Oper 1974).

23 Götz Aly compares students' movements in 1933 and 1968 and notes phenomenological and ideological parallels: anti-liberalism, anti-Americanism and antisemitism.

References

Albiez, S. and Dockwray, R. (2016), 'Before and after Eno: Situating "The Recording Studio as Compositional Tool"', in S. Albiez and D. Pattie (eds), *Brian Eno: Oblique Music*, New York: Bloomsbury Academic.

Alisch, J. (1974), 'Prinzessin auf der Knallerbse', *Der Abend*, 4 October, 3.

Aly, G. (2007), *Unser Kampf: 1968- ein irritierter Blick zurück*, Bonn, Germany: BpB.

Batt, A. (2012), 'Liner Notes', Nico, *The End [Expanded Two CD Edition]*, Island 518 892-2.

Beal, A. C. (2006), *New Music, New Allies: American Experimental Music in West Germany from the Zero Hour to Reunification*, Berkeley, CA: University of California Press.

Benzmann, A. (1971), 'Sause durch linke Pinten', *Der Blickpunkt*, 206, October, 32.

Bockris, V. and Cale, J. (1999), *What's Welsh for Zen: The Autobiography of John Cale*, London: Bloomsbury.

Bracewell, M. (2007), *Re-make/Re-model: Art, Pop, Fashion and the Making of Roxy Music, 1953–1972*, London: Faber and Faber.

Buckley, D. (2004), *The Thrill of It All: The Story of Bryan Ferry and Roxy Music*, London: André Deutsch [Amazon Kindle].

Burde, W. (1974), 'Ausdruckskunst für Bambusflöte', *Der Tagesspiegel*, 8 October, 4.

Cowley, J. (2012), 'Oh What a Circus', *The Wire*, February, 36–43.

Davy, S. (1975), 'Bubbly, Bubbly Eno', *Beetle*, January. Available online: https://bit.ly/347QK7I (accessed 8 November 2021).

Demorest, S. (1975), 'Eno: The Monkey Wrench of Rock Creates Happy Accidents on Tiger Mountain', *Circus*, April. Available online: https://bit.ly/3qYLe01 (accessed 8 November 2021).

Der Mythos Barry Graves (2021), *Studio 89*, 27 October. Available online: https://bit.ly/35sMqkl (accessed 8 November 2021).

Deutsche Oper von Linken gestürmt (1974), *Bild Berlin*, 7 October, 1.

Doggett, P. (1992), *Lou Reed: Growing Up in Public*, London: Omnibus Press.

During, R. W. (1974), 'Ein müder Rock-Zirkus', *Spandauer Volksblatt*, 6 October, 8.

Eno, B. (1973), *Here Come The Warm Jets*, Island Records ILPS 9268.

Fripp and Eno (1973), *No Pussyfooting*, Island Records HELP 16.
Gaitonde, V. R. (2016), 'The Harmonium Was Born in Europe – So How Did It Become Synonymous with Indian Music?' *Scroll.in*, 19 August. Available online: https://bit.ly/3H6T3qf (accessed 8 November 2021).
Gold, M. (1974), 'John Cale: *Fear*', *Let It Rock*, November. Available online: https://bit.ly/3g2kOnO (accessed 8 November 2021).
Goldman, V. (1977), 'Eno: Extra Natty Orations', *Sounds*, 5 February. Available online: https://bit.ly/3nXtGQg (accessed 8 November 2021).
Graf-Ulbrich, L. (2015), *Nico: In the Shadow of the Moon Goddess*, Self-published ebook [Amazon Kindle].
Graf-Ulbrich, L. (2017), *e-mail communication with the authors*, 16 November.
Graves, B. (1974), 'Mädels für Polkwitz', *Der Abend*, 5 October.
Grubbs, D. (2014), 'Henry Flynt'. *The Wire*, February. Available online: https://bit.ly/3H1eOrj (accessed 8 November 2021).
John Cale signs (1973), *Record Mirror*, 15 December, 6.
Kasliwal, S. (2001), 'Harmonium', *India Instruments*. Available online: https://bit.ly/3AwBEVk (accessed 8 November 2021).
Kent, N. (1974) 'The Freewheelin' Brian Eno', *New Musical Express*, 18 May. Available online: https://bit.ly/3r0GJ5j (accessed 8 November 2021).
Mitchell, T. (2003), *Sedition and Alchemy: A Biography of John Cale*, London: Peter Owen.
Otter Bickerdike, J. (2021), *You Are Beautiful and You Are Alone: The Biography of Nico*, London: Faber and Faber [Amazon Kindle].
Poynor, R. (1986a), 'The Painted Score', in B. Eno and R. Mills (eds), *More Dark than Shark*, 40–4, London: Faber and Faber.
Prasad, A. (2014), 'Terry Riley: Lighting Up Nodes', *Innerviews*. Available online: https://bit.ly/3ICW2Hj (accessed 8 November 2021).
Reetze, J. (2020), *Times and Sounds: Germany's Journey from Jazz and Pop to Krautrock and Beyond*, Bremen: Halvmall Verlag.
Robinson, L. (1973), 'Roxy Music: Terror in the Rue Morgue', *Creem*, May. Available online: https://bit.ly/3fUAfyu (accessed 8 November 2021).
Rockwell, J. (1979), 'Cabaret: Nico Is Back', *New York Times*, 21 February, 17.
Safranski, R. (2007), *Romantik: Eine deutsche Affäre*, München: Hanser.
Schneider, F. A. (2015), *Deutschpop halt's Maul: Für eine Ästhetik der Verkrampfung*, Mainz: Ventil.
Schnitze, W. (1974), 'Außenseiter-Messe', *Die Zeit*, 18 October, 7.
Sheppard, D. (2008), *On Some Faraway Beach: The Life and Times of Brian Eno*, London: Orion.
Strawn, J. (2018), *email communication with the authors*. 1 August.
Tamm, E. (1995), *Brian Eno: His Music and the Vertical Color of Sound*, New York: Da Capo Press.
Thompson, D. (2017), *The Greatest Supergroup of the Seventies*, 2nd edn, Self-Published: Amazon.
Tour by Eno and Four ex-Velvets (1974), *New Musical Express*, 8 June, 3.
Unterberger, R. (2009), *White Light/White Heat: The Velvet Underground Day-By-Day*, London: Jawbone Press.
Unterberger, R. (2017), *White Light/White Heat: The Velvet Underground Day-By-Day [Revised and Expanded Ebook Edition]*, Self-published [Amazon Kindle].

Velvets Back on the Road (1974), *Melody Maker*, 8 June, 3.

Weiß, M. (2021), 'Festival Stories: "The Room Is Unseated": Nico at the Neue Nationalgalerie', *Berliner Festspiele Blog*, 20 September. Available online: https://bit.ly/3AyNnTi (accessed 8 November 2021).

Williams, R. (2014), 'Nico, Eno and John Cale in Berlin, 1974', *thebluemoment.com*, 5 October. Available online: https://bit.ly/3AxxyfF (accessed 8 November 2021).

Witts, R. (1993), *Nico: The Life and Lies of an Icon*, London: Virgin Books.

Wood, J. (2018), *personal phone interview with the authors*, 24 July.

12

Noise annoys: Lou Reed's *Metal Machine Music*

Mark Goodall

Metal Machine Music (*MMM*) was Lou Reed's fifth solo studio LP, released by RCA in July 1975. The tales of how he duped his record label into releasing four sides of unlistenable noise, ostensibly to get out of a failing recording contract, are legion. The LP is viewed by some as an example of Reed's intransigence; when RCA, horrified by the music he delivered for release, suggested it was put out on their Red Seal classical imprint, Reed baulked at the idea as 'pretentious' (Bockris 2014: 281). Further evidence of his supposed intransigence/deceit was the list of technical specification printed on the back of the sleeve which he later claimed to be 'all bullshit' (281).

In this chapter I wish to argue that, far from *MMM* being an aberration, a provocative, self-destructive gesture made to irritate all and sundry, it was actually a continuation of a methodology developed by Reed early in his artistic career, finding particular expression in certain works of the Velvet Underground. In the sleeve notes for the CD reissue of *MMM* David Fricke asks the question: 'How do you dissect, or describe, random, mad-animal tone?' (Fricke 2002). In this chapter, I hope to answer this question by identifying the elements – conscious and unconscious – that have gone into the production of the LP. I am not so much concerned with the music that *MMM* has inspired or influenced as with its existence as a unique work of sonic art.

The roots of Reed's *MMM* lie in the connections the Velvet Underground developed with the contemporary art scene of New York before meeting Warhol, and notably during their two-year association with American pop artist Andy Warhol and the Factory. As Dominic Molon (2007) has pointed out, the Warhol period 'meaningfully established the relationship between avant-garde art and rock music'. Warhol's influence encouraged Reed and co-leader John Cale, who had previously associated with artists and film-makers in the New York scene, 'to bring sophisticated avant-garde strategies into the more widely distributed cultural context of rock music' (13). This being the case, we can view *MMM* as a logical extension of this long-term, almost permanent strategy. Ronald Nameth's film *Andy Warhol's Exploding Plastic Inevitable with The Velvet Underground and Nico* (1966) captures the 'hellish sensorium' (Youngblood 1970: 103) of the audio-visual kinaesthetic experience. *Andy Warhol's Velvet Underground and Nico*, the film of the group rehearsing an hour-long drone at the Factory in 1966 and directed by Warhol, shows how the power of improvised noise was key to the group's development.

MMM offered up the kind of polarizing experience that Reed long extoled. Many individuals purchasing the record were unable to endure a complete listen of the LP's four sides (or even one side), returning it to music shops in allegedly record numbers. *The New York Times* called the LP 'sheer self destructive indulgence'. *Rolling Stone* magazine voted it the worst album of the year. On the other hand, Japanese experimental musician Otomo Yoshihide called it 'the most interesting Lou Reed album' (*Browbeat* #2 1996: 37), while Lester Bangs acclaimed it as 'The Greatest Album Ever Made' (Bangs 2001: 195). It has also been described as an 'experimental rock masterpiece' (Molon 2007: 13). However, critics were unanimous in hating *MMM*, largely it seems, as it did not accord the decadent rock and roll image that Reed had been contriving with his solo career, particularly with his 1974 live LP *Rock n Roll Animal*, where Velvet Underground classics were treated to tedious and mostly generic rock arrangements. John Rockwell's comment that Reed 'may have gone farther than his audience will willingly follow' (Bockris 2014: 282) is particularly telling.

MMM is generally dismissed as 'four sides of guitar feedback'. Yet this description of the recording does not express the full nature of the work. From this we can infer that the recording was produced 'off the cuff', with little thought or construction (this somewhat supports the myth that Reed produced the LP simply to aggravate his record company). But he was actually extremely meticulous throughout his career about the planning of his recordings and the various methods and technologies incorporated into the production of his music. In an interview conducted in 1975 (Bloom 1996) he goes to great lengths to describe the complexity of the process behind the recording, where layers of sound were built up with drones, reverse tape effects and experiments with varied tremolo settings. Reed was obsessed with guitars and guitar technology. As his partner and fellow avant-garde musician Laurie Anderson remembers, their first 'date' together took place at an Audio Engineering Society convention, a showcase for new musical equipment. 'We spent a happy afternoon looking at amps and cables and shop-talking electronics' (qtd. in De Curtis 2017: 388).

Critics also like to perpetuate the myth of the casual rock and roll rebel who contemptuously dismisses any consideration or reflection. Yet Reed had experimented with the elements that made up *MMM* for years, using feedback, loops and open tunings (most famously the 'Ostrich' tuning[1]) in his Velvet Underground days. As he acknowledged, the core technique of *MMM* – the sound of a plugged-in electric guitar leant against an amplifier – stretched back to the mid-1960s: 'I did tons of shows with The Velvet Underground where we would leave our guitars against the amps and walk away. The guitars would feedback forever, like they were alive' (Fricke 2002). He has also claimed that the roots of the album, including some of the recorded elements, stretched back to the period around 1970 when the group was signed to Atlantic records (Bloom 1996: 33).

Phil Morris' 1970 description of Reed's guitar technique sets the scene for the technique used for *MMM*:

> Lou Reed has all sorts of pre-amps and speed and tremolo controls built into his guitar so that it would literally play itself. He could make it play sixteen notes for

every one he played, or, he could tune all the strings to one note, set the guitar up to feed back and leave the stage and go into the audience to listen to an incredible, totally mechanical music.

(Morris [1970] 2005: 167)

Morris goes on to argue that '[t]he Velvets were the first group to use controlled feedback and distortion and they used it like another instrument altogether, not as simply a variation on a guitar sound' (167). Guitar noise becomes a total sound in itself, not just a technique to be inserted intermittently and with its open tunings *MMM* develops this to the limit.

Of the music critics, only Lester Bangs seems to have properly appreciated the crazed power of *MMM*.[2] In his extraordinary account for *Concert Review* of the LP, Bangs recounts how he 'awoke with a hangover and put on *MMM* immediately' listening to the LP almost continuously across one drunken 24-hour session (Clapton 1982: 88). This chapter manages to capture the pure effect of the sound of the music on an individual psyche, albeit, in this case, a psyche mangled by paranoia and severe drug and alcohol abuse.

Reed, as a composer and musician, epitomizes what Keister has defined as a 'freak artist', suggesting 'a kind of madness, either invoked by musicians as a countercultural weapon against the sanity of mainstream culture or perceived by listeners who sometimes explain away such unlistenable records as temporary madness by their favourite musicians' (Keister 2012: 94). Indeed this is the way in which *MMM* has been received by critics and fans alike, as either a provocative 'fuck you' gesture towards the 'music industry' or an aberration within an otherwise fairly consistent musical career. Reed's decision to deliver, to a major label, four sides of feedback noise is clearly, in the minds of some, an insane gesture. While none of Keister's subsequent three criteria for 'freak art' – anarchy, absurdity and amateurism – really applies to the music of Reed or the Velvet Underground, the 'counterparty madness' within avant-garde rock Keister defines does connect with Reed's work. Keister goes on to list *MMM* as an exemplar of 'insider' freak exhibitionism, akin to a work such as John Lennon and Yoko Ono's *Unfinished Music No. 1. Two Virgins*, albeit, like the latter, one with very few listeners (Keister 2012:12).

Atton (2012) has observed how music fans listen to 'difficult albums', a category which *MMM* clearly falls into. Interestingly, Atton discusses the Beatles' infamous track 'Revolution 9' from the 1968 LP *The Beatles* [The White Album] as having avant-garde credentials and yet being also located in a 'pop sensibility rooted in everyday experience ... not a cerebral music that is inevitably separated from social and cultural meanings' (Atton 2012: 352). I think that the same can be said of *MMM*, in that while the sound experience of the recording is 'difficult' and 'extreme' (in the context of popular music), nevertheless Reed has created the recording out of a rhythm and blues 'mind-set' and the aesthetics and techniques of rock guitar music. Atton does go on to question the validity of those who express a love for *MMM* as a practice where 'specialist music fans might lay claim to in order to celebrate cultural difference' (Atton 2012: 358). There may be some truth in this. But it might also be the case that 'difficult' music takes longer to digest and appreciate (decades sometimes), especially in comparison with traditional popular music forms, where accessibility and instant gratification are the desired norm.

MMM then is not a freakish blip in the trajectory of Lou Reed but instead draws on a range of elements stretching back across his career, elements which moreover have played a strong role in alternative musical forms of all shapes and sizes. The Velvet Underground utilized a number of elements that we can now see fed into the conception and production of *MMM*: *white noise*, *free expression* and *feedback*.

White noise

Noise has always been essential to Reed's music. As early as July 1966, Velvet Underground performances were being described as 'assaults on the senses'. In an account published by the *Boston Broadside* newspaper of a Plastic Exploding Inevitable event at Poor Richard's in Chicago, the effect of the sounds and visuals on the writer was disconcerting. Larry McCombs ([1966] 2005), wrote, 'The noise builds to a climax ... the music is lost in the chaos of noise'. Most presciently, in relation to *MMM*, he observes that the musicians are 'grinding out a noise that has music in it somewhere' (27). Sections of the Plastic Exploding Inevitable shows heavily featured noise as an alienating element. As Warhol actress and dancer International Velvet testifies, such events contained a lot of 'noise and feedbacks and screeches and groans from the amplifiers' (Superstar [1967] 2005: 45). Before any recordings of the band were made, a precursor to the aesthetics of *MMM* can be discerned in the '(anti) psychedelic, amorphous, pounding blur' of the Velvet Underground live shows (Mortifolglio 1997: 62), where what became the beauty and artistry of the subsequent recorded versions of songs was subsumed under a wall of sound.

As Unterberger (2009) outlines, the Velvet Underground live sound is characterized as '12-tone rock and roll' (148), and 'the amplified throb of single disconnected guitar notes' (118). Unterberger indicates that journalist John Wilcock in 1966 claimed the band 'played about ten times louder than anybody ... had heard before' (92), signifying the overwhelming power of their experiments with volume. One legendary unreleased 28-minute jam dubbed 'Melody Laughter' was an 'avant-garde extreme, beginning with five minutes of drum-free, feedback-ridden squalling and scraping' (118) where '[t]he piercingly high amplification of the guitars and drums blast out with a sound like a jet engine running wild' (164).

Hegarty has argued that the music of the Velvet Underground (and specifically 'Sister Ray') is 'not about understanding' but that it makes music 'physical to the point of being visceral' (Hegarty 2008: 69). Much of the music on the 1968 LP *White Light/White Heat* profoundly expressed this idea. 'Sister Ray' was not an attempt at any kind of psychedelic transcendental experience through sound. The track, like most of the music of the Velvet Underground, was instead a confrontation with sound that was not always pleasant, a stripped-down 'electric pulse of the whole rock and roll feeling' (Mortifolglio 1997: 63). As guitarist Sterling Morrison put it, this LP was all 'raw electronics' (Barrios [1970] 2005: 146) – the 'ultimate statement in the new musical vocabulary of electronic abstraction' (Bangs [1971] 2005: 224).

White noise became a favoured term when new experiments with electronic instruments took off in the late 1960s, and musicians and artists began to push the boundaries of analogue sounds to their limits. The point about white noise is that it contains in combination many or all audio frequencies simultaneously, clearly a dimension of the sonic landscape of what became *MMM*. Although there are many ambiguities about what 'white noise' is and how this descriptor is used, it is clear that this description is metaphorically applicable to the intensity of the sounds on MMM (and experimental rock music more generally). That is, the way sounds are melded together, repeating and clashing to create a rich collage of noises, making difficult the identification of particular frequencies (with a few notable exceptions discussed below).

The early Velvet Underground track 'Noise' also suggests a sensory experience unlike usual musical productions. The track is a collage of heavily reverbed radio speech and snatches of an improvisation with guitars, and is 'an unpleasant listen' according to some (Unterberger 2009: 110). 'Noise' was a contribution to the *East Village Other* newspaper's compilation LP – 'the first electric newspaper' according to the sleeve notes – and was another exemplar of McLuhan's theory of media being an extension of man.

Noise has always been a critical component of rock music but it remains a nebulous and contradictory concept. Sangild (2004), however, has identified three key types of noise: *acoustic noise*, *communicative noise* and *subjective noise*. These concepts are useful when thinking about *MMM* as they all in some way help to define what Reed has produced with the recording.

In terms of *acoustic noise* Reed has deployed a range of sounds that are 'impure and irregular ... with a lot of simultaneous frequencies' (Sangild 2004: 4.1). Sangild includes 'white noise' in this category and other sounds which are hard to pinpoint and are almost unrecognizable, a strong feature of the *MMM* experience, where one's first encounter with the LP is often that of confusion as to what one is hearing and how it was made. Some of the most affective acoustic noise sounds on the LP are the rapid oscillations and the bird-like screams punctuating the recording.

Sangild's description of *communicative noise* is mostly applicable to Reed's use of distortion and overdrive (a common rock effect and one that he deployed from the early days of the Velvet Underground). Sangild notes, 'Noise is that which distorts the signal on its way from transmitter to recipient'; the artistry involved in this manipulation is what is key. It is critical for the reception of difficult noise works that when such a disturbance is integrated back into the actual musicality of a piece, that tension created 'is an important part of the musical power of noise' (4.1).

Sangild's third category, *subjective noise*, is also vital to understanding how *MMM* works on the audience. What is unpleasant to one listener (an extended recording of harsh guitar feedback) is to another listener fascinating (if not exactly 'pleasant'). The fact that the sounds on *MMM* are irritating is partly directed by the artist making their work; there is a conscious manipulation of the audiences' likely emotional response.

Sangild talks about a 'training of the senses' that needs to take place in order that noise can be experienced as something positive, 'infusing the formerly negative' (4.1) with a creative element that can be appealing. Sangild repeats the suggestion that *MMM* should be listened to with more depth, 'discovering the variations in the stream of rumbling noises and screeching feedback sounds' (4.1).

Free expression

It was Lester Bangs who argued that 'Sister Ray' 'marked the first successful attempt at applying the lessons of free jazz to rock' (Bangs [1971] 2005: 224). The model for the experimental sounds of the Velvet Underground and Lou Reed's solo career was often not the rock/blues experiments but those of the free jazz movement, Reed naming Ornette Coleman and Cecil Taylor as the reference points for this. Coleman once asked that jazz musicians 'try to play the music and not the background' (Williams 1998), meaning that the focus should be on performing music freely without constant recourse to the rules and regulations of conventional notational structure. I believe also that we can locate this influence in *MMM*. The specific 'Lou Reed noise' is not created via the 'jam' familiar to rock music, where a basic rhythm and blues structure is extended through a series of technically skilled interventions. Instead the music has more in kind with the expression of free jazz, where familiar, comfortable and recognizable patterns were rejected in favour of new modes of expression, trying out new systems of expression. Thus the lapses into pure noise and distortion (both literal and metaphorical) in *MMM* relate more to the music on Coleman's *Free Jazz* LP or the work of Don Cherry and Anthony Braxton than to any rock tradition.

In addition to the free-flow chaos of improvisational music, more persistent sounds are also in evidence. McGuire ([1968] 2005) describes the drones used by the Velvet Underground as having a very special quality that are at the heart of the Velvet Underground sound. He writes that this is 'a drone which is produced by New World Citizen nervous system plunging into the Cosmic Whirl … The drone is not always heard but rather felt as pure essence and perpetual presence' (71–2). McGuire goes on to describe Velvet Underground feedback as being projected through the 'amps which have been made perfect human extensions', with the ensuing 'wall of sound' being a 'beautifully constructed and richly textured abstract-expressionist motion picture' (72). It is not hard to see how this mythical ecstatic experience, created by use of both drones and feedback producing sound pictures and moods, feeds into Reed's realization of *MMM* where, through deep listening, sound invokes abstract pictures and colour senses.

In relation to modern jazz, specifically free jazz, we can discern in *MMM* certain other experimental tendencies. In a discussion of John Coltrane's legendary *A Love Supreme*, Lewis Porter notes the 'motivic approach' used by Coltrane in developing his extended improvised sections of music. Here, as in *MMM*, 'long passages would be devoted to a single motive' (Porter 1985: 596). While modern jazz and experimental rock music differ in instrumental form, the approach can be seen to be similar. Coltrane used this simple but effective approach throughout the more experimental phase of his career, and as a long-time fan of Coltrane's work, it is not too far-fetched to suggest that Reed adopted some of these techniques in producing *MMM*. In place of space for instrumental solos (as in jazz), he enlarged and expanded his own small recurring, motivic sound patterns to an abstract, artistic extreme. Like Coltrane, Reed was simply 'following his compositional ideas of the moment' preferring not to curtail, edit or predetermine this process' (Porter 1985: 599). He adopted the free and open spirit of the improvising jazz musician, prepared to go where sounds that are unexpectedly created lead to, without compromise or concession to the audience. In another sense, Reed's project with *MMM* can be seen as akin to the jazz musician improvising freely in the 'jam session' in order to 'get the taste of commercial music out of his mouth'. The *MMM* project then was a 'ritual of purification ... a self cleansing by the reaffirmation of his own aesthetic values' (Cameron 1954: 178).

The other aspect of free expression relevant to the conception of *MMM* is that of extended duration. Reed once noted in a 1969 interview that 'Sister Ray', the Velvet Underground's most celebrated improvised track, in its entirety 'might run three days'. At this time he was (ironically) nervous about submitting a track of such duration to a record label, stating, 'the record company would lose money and we would get it in the end' (Martin [1969] 2005: 110). As Williams notes in his 1969 *Melody Maker* article on the Velvets, 'Sister Ray' contains 'some of the most modern music ever heard. Like many of their compositions it never resolves: one gets the feeling it could go on and on' ([1969] 2005: 120). We can see tracks such as 'Sister Ray' and its many variants then as a precursor to the endurance length of *MMM*.

Reed also incorporated elements from avant-garde music of the 1960s New York scene (of which, of course, John Cale was a prominent member) – in particular La Monte Young's development of the sustained note for 'extended durations relying on the establishment of a drone and the placing of harmonically-related frequencies (overtones) around this drone' (Condon 1997a: 32). On *MMM*, Reed deployed a somewhat more violent approach than Young to the sensory overload the drone created; his sound was denser and more complex, built up of more elements than the minimalists were using. Tony Conrad also observed how Reed's early Brooklyn groups were experimenting with tuning to a single note, prefiguring *MMM*, and how that linked with what Conrad was doing contemporaneously with La Monte Young and Terry Riley. 'In fact we were tuning to two notes and they were tuning to only one' Conrad recalls (qtd. in Condon 1997b: 39). The weird combination of rock and the avant-garde that grew out of Cale's involvement with the minimalists when combined with Reed's rock sensibilities found its ultimate expression in *MMM*.

Feedback

That *MMM* incorporates a number of guitar feedback loops is well established. But another key aspect of the recording is the pleasure of repetition. Sections of 'Part II' consist of repetitive shards of noise created by guitar effects such as oscillation that are hypnotically impactful. Traces of this technique can be found in a very early

Velvet Underground track 'Loop' which is believed to have been made solely by John Cale. 'Loop' was issued as a flexi disc for a 1966 edition of the *Aspen* magazine. This was a mixed media publication inspired by Marshall McLuhan and Quentin Fiore's book *Medium Is the Massage* that featured a double-page photograph of the Plastic Exploding Inevitable, to illustrate the sensory experience of the new media landscape. The 'Loop' edition of *Aspen* – number 3 – was edited by Andy Warhol and music writer David Dalton. The track prefigures *MMM* in the way it creates a repetitive soundscape of noise but one which pulses, ebbs and flows as it progresses (in a circular manner). The original flexi disc of 'Loop', like *MMM*, contained a locked grove, an effect that Pierre Schaeffer, the inventor of *musique concrete*, observed 'produced a novel state of mind and endowed raw sound with a form of aesthetic legitimacy' (Leavaux 2016: 169). The locked groove in *MMM*, where a new multi-dimensional pattern emerges from the loop, is possibly the highlight of the recording. Cale had spoken previously of the sound that he and Reed created for the Velvet Underground (and which is located within 'Loop') as 'controlled distortion' (Goldstein [1966] 2005: 31). Mixed in with this is the use of the drone, an extended note or set of notes that can last forever. There are no 'relaxing' drones *in MMM*, yet a certain pleasure can be obtained from a single feedback note with modulations, extending across the whole side of an LP. The *MMM* assault does have some relation to the feedback noise of the Yardbirds or Jimi Hendrix's 'Star Spangled Banner', for example, but is thicker, wilder and more violent, relentless and aggressive, unfiltered by any rock guitar mannerisms or breaks into more traditional blues phrasing.

Lou Reed's use of feedback also dramatically appeared in the 1967 recording of the track 'I Heard Her Call My Name' from *White Light/White Heat*. Although the track is structured around a typical rock song of the era (as evidenced in the later, somewhat tame live version on *Live MCMXCIII*), it is augmented with extended sections of guitar noise soloing by Reed. To create this incredible burst of noise, he used a Treble Booster V806 device manufactured by Vox (equipment sponsors of the Velvet Underground), which was promoted as having a 'glass shattering sound'. McGuire ([1968] 2005) perceptively writes of this track that it 'contains one of the most pregnant and highly charged moments I've ever heard in music: a split second pause of silence after the second "my mind's split open" foreshadowing the following feedback explosion' (75). Sandy Pearlman ([1968] 2005) also argued that the rhythms on the entire *White Light/White Heat* LP sounded 'mechanistic enough to be taken for electronics' (63). This demonstrated that it is not only the sonic properties of the stringed or keyboard instruments that point towards *MMM* but also the drum patterns that hint at the repetitions created by feedback loops: the 'repetition scene' (63) inherent in many of Reed's soundscapes.

As suggested, it is also possible that a listener is required to access MMM in what one might define as a 'different dimension'. Timothy Jacobs ([1967] 2005) once remarked that while listening to *The Velvet Underground & Nico* 'it is best, perhaps, to put yourself in the frame of mind that you might assume by listening to Indian music' (51). In other words, the sounds that are 'distinctly different' from popular music must be listened to in a different way, without the expectation for satisfying rhythmic structures and poetic/romantic word-play. The feedback sounds evident in *MMM* are, as Sangild points out, tones where 'some of them have a drone like character, others swarm chaotically. There is no structure, but there is texture with the drones as temporary points of orientation between traditional opposites – the expressionist scream and the meditative mantra' (2004: 4.4.2). Thus what first seems to be a wall of noise (this is what the casual listener experiences and thus rarely gets any further) is actually replete with tiny fragments of sound, bubbling and spiralling around the listener in a confusing yet exhilarating manner (see the closing section of 'Part I' for a good example of this). It is precisely this specific and creative 'expressionist noise' that Reed has captured in the recording and by all accounts predicted, stating that 'the really fun way of listening to it is on headphones because then it will have a physical effect on you' (Bloom 1996: 33). This mode of listening reveals hidden aspects of the recording, the rise and fall and phasing in and out of sounds that are lost when playing in a typical ambient room setting.³

What Reed produced in *MMM* was also akin to what Meltzer defines as 'non-diminished intensity throughout repetition' (Meltzer 1987: 332). Meltzer argues this technique is found in 'Sister Ray'. Here, rather than the repetition of a sequence of notes or harmonies leading to boredom or a flagging energy, the successful (and scarce) tracks that manage to maintain that intensity reward the listener's perseverance (due to a trance-like spirit, the repetition becoming a powerful and hypnotic vibe). 'Intensity' is the key word here as this is what *MMM* delivers to an impressively heightened degree: a sense of 'wonder' as Meltzer puts it (332). One must approach the recording with John Rockwell's observation in mind that beneath the initial sonic assault, *MMM* contains 'a wealth of listenable detail' (Clapton 1982: 91). *MMM* offers that tension and uncertainty that improvised music offers; as Steve Lacy succinctly but eloquently put it: 'on the edge – in between the known and the unknown' (qtd. in Bailey 1992: 54).

Conclusion

In March 2002, avant-garde group Zeitkratzer produced an orchestrated version of *MMM*, arranged by Ulrich Krieger using 'classical' instruments, in collaboration with Reed. Krieger, like other listeners, must have discerned the patterns 'hidden' within the *MMM* soundscape, elements that could be notated. While impressive in terms of the technical achievement of reproducing a wall of sound made with two guitars, two amps and electronic effects, and making a more accessible 'concert' version of the noise aesthetic the LP is purported to have invented, the exercise is largely disappointing. The Zeitkratzer production makes an art house presentation of an experimental rock masterpiece that is clever, but sterile and academic. What makes the original Reed recording so affective is the relentless screaming assault it gives the listener: a purely sonic, aural experience. It is not a curiosity to be experienced in a concert hall (or on DVD) but an essential component of the Lou Reed/Velvet Underground story, one that marks a perfect synthesis between the rhythm and blues that Reed grew up with and the transgressive elements of experimental rock that he grew into and helped shape.

Reed states, 'No one I know has listened to it all the way through including myself. It is not meant to be' (Reed 1975), so why produce a concert version of the LP? In any case, scoring an experimental rock work such as *MMM* seems a rather mannered gesture.

Lou Reed has always, according to Richard Mortifolglio (1997), had 'much of the pure artist in him, despite years of cynical hackwork'. He has always been interested in 'purely formal possibilities' and has 'longstanding technological fascinations' (58). This is clearly evident throughout *MMM* – an experiment with guitar technologies in their purest and most extreme manifestation. Since *White Light/White Heat*, Reed has produced work that contributes towards an 'exceedingly strong statement of what it means to "search"' (Mortifoglio 1997: 67). It can be argued that *MMM* is the ultimate realization of that search. The deep questioning commitment he showed across his entire career (learnt from figures such as Delmore Schwartz and Andy Warhol) is exemplary, something that today's young alternative rock musicians should perhaps be cognisant of.

The Velvet Underground was once described as 'a rock group that goes beyond rock' (Unterberger 2009: 95) and Lou Reed continued this path with his solo work. He once stated (in 1969) that 'if electronic composers could play rock'n'roll then electronic music might get interesting' (Martin 2005: 117). But instead of waiting for that moment to occur he flipped the statement, becoming a rock and roll artist making electronic (tape-based) music. The wonder then is that RCA were so surprised by what he offered them with *MMM*; isn't this precisely the kind of work that an artist such as Reed would deliver? Had the label not paid attention to his career up to that point, or was it a case of simply the music industry focusing in on only the accessible aspects of his writing (the love songs and straight rock numbers) and ignoring the transgressive and experimental nature of a body of work stretching back to the early 1960s? Reed said that *MMM* 'in time would prove itself' (Bockris 2014: 283). With the veneration now heaped upon it by a new generation of musicians including, as noted, those from outside the rock sphere he mostly inhabited, the time has come for him to be proved correct.

Notes

1. See Daley (2016) for an extensive guide to this method.
2. With the exception of his remark that 'any idiot with the equipment could have made this album' (Bangs 2001: 196), which is clearly not true.
3. Reed outlined that a quadrophonic version of *MMM* was also produced (Bloom 1996: 38).

References

Atton, C. (2012), 'Listening to "Difficult Albums": Specialist Music Fans and the Popular Avant-garde', *Popular Music*, 31 (3): 347–61.

Bailey, D. (1992), *Improvisation: Its Nature and Practice in Music*, Cambridge: Da Capo.
Bangs, L. (2001), *Psychotic Reactions and Carburetor Dung*, London: Serpent's Tail.
Bangs, L. ([1971] 2005), 'Dead Lie the Velvets, Underground', *Creem*, May in C. Heylin (ed.), *All Yesterdays' Parties: The Velvet Underground in Print 1966–1971*, 220–42, Cambridge: Da Capo.
Barrios, G. ([1970] 2005), 'An Interview with Sterling Morrison'. *Fusion*, 6 March, in C. Heylin (ed.), *All Yesterdays' Parties: The Velvet Underground in Print 1966–1971*, 139–54, Cambridge: Da Capo.
Bloom, M. (1996), 'Metal Machine Music', *Browbeat #2*, 33–8, Available online: https://bit.ly/35qlAJv (accessed 2 December 2021).
Bockris, V. (2014), *Transformer: The Complete Lou Reed Story*, London: HarperCollins.
Cameron, W. B. (1954), 'Sociological Notes on the Jam Session', *Social Forces*, 33 (2): 177–82.
Clapton, D. (1982), *Lou Reed & The Velvet Underground*, London and New York: Proteus Books.
Condon, J. ([1983] 1997a), 'Angus MacLise and the Origin of The Velvet Underground', in A. Zak (ed.) (1997), *The Velvet Underground Companion: Four Decades of Commentary*, 31–6, London, New York, Sydney: Omnibus.
Condon, J. ([1983] 1997b), 'Three Interviews: Tony Conrad, Henry Flynt, Terry Riley', in A. Zak (ed.) (1997), *The Velvet Underground Companion: Four Decades of Commentary*, 36–40, London, New York, Sydney: Omnibus.
Daley, M. (2016), 'Lou Reed's "Ostrich" Tuning as an Aesthetic Point of Articulation', *Rock Music Studies*, 3 (2): 148–56.
De Curtis, A. (2017), *Lou Reed: A Life*, London: John Murray.
Fricke, D. ([1975] 2002), 'Sleeve Notes', Lou Reed, *Metal Machine Music*, Buddha Records 74465 99752 2.
Goldstein, R. ([1966] 2005), 'A Quiet Night at the Balloon Farm', in C. Heylin (ed.), *All Yesterdays' Parties: The Velvet Underground in Print 1966–1971*, 29–32, Cambridge: Da Capo.
Keister, J. (2012), 'The Long Freak Out': Unfinished Music and Countercultural Madness in 1960s and 1970s Avant-Garde Rock', *Volume!*, 9 (2). Available online: https://bit.ly/35uXJZj (accessed 2 December 2021).
Hegarty, P. (2008), *Noise/Music: A History*, New York and London: Continuum.
Jacobs, T. ([1967] 2005), 'Review of the Velvet Underground and Nico', *Vibrations*, 2., in C. Heylin (ed.), *All Yesterdays' Parties: The Velvet Underground in Print 1966–1971*, 51–2, Cambridge: Da Capo.
Levaux, C. (2016), 'Loop', *Rock Music Studies*, 3 (2): 167–79.
McCombs, L. ([1966] 2005), 'Chicago Happenings', *Boston Broadside*, July. in C. Heylin (ed.), *All Yesterdays' Parties: The Velvet Underground in Print 1966–1971*, 24–7, Cambridge: Da Capo.
McGuire, W. ([1968] 2005), 'The Boston Sound', *Crawdaddy*, 16, in C. Heylin (ed.), *All Yesterdays' Parties: The Velvet Underground in Print 1966–1971*, 65–78, Cambridge: Da Capo.
Martin, J. ([1969] 2005), 'Interview with Lou Reed', *Open City*, 78. in C. Heylin (ed.), *All Yesterdays' Parties: The Velvet Underground in Print 1966–1971*, 109–18, Cambridge: Da Capo.
Meltzer, R. (1987), *The Aesthetics of Rock*, New York: Da Capo.

Molon, D. (2007), *Sympathy for the Devil: Art and Rock and Roll since 1967*, New Haven: Yale University.

Mortifoglio, R. ([1983] 1997), 'White Light/White Heat', in A. Zak (ed.), *The Velvet Underground Companion: Four Decades of Commentary*, 62–8, London, New York, Sydney: Omnibus.

Morris, P. ([1970] 2005), 'The Velvet Underground: Musique and Mystique Unveiled', *Circus*, June., in C. Heylin (ed.), *All Yesterdays' Parties: The Velvet Underground in Print 1966-1971*, 166–70, Cambridge: Da Capo.

Pearlman, S. ([1968] 2005), 'Round Velvet Underground', *Crawdaddy*, 16., in C. Heylin (ed.), *All Yesterdays' Parties: The Velvet Underground in Print 1966-1971*, 61–3, Cambridge: Da Capo.

Porter, L. (1985), 'John Coltrane's "A Love Supreme": Jazz Improvisation as Composition', *Journal of the American Musicological Society*, 38 (3): 593–621.

Reed, L. (1975), 'Sleeve Notes', Lou Reed, *Metal Machine Music*, RCA Victor CPL2-1101.

Sangild, T. (2004), 'Noise – Three Musical Gestures: Expressionist, Introvert and Minimal Noise', *JMM: The Journal of Music and Meaning*, 2, Section 4. Available online: https://bit.ly/349OnBk (accessed 2 December 2021).

Superstar, I. ([1967] 2005), 'Index Interview with The Velvet Underground', in C. Heylin (ed.), *All Yesterdays' Parties: The Velvet Underground in Print 1966-1971*, 43–6, Cambridge: Da Capo.

Unterberger, R. (2009), *White Light/White Heat: The Velvet Underground Day-by-Day*, London: Jawbone.

Williams, M. ([1961] 1998), 'Sleeve Notes', Ornette Coleman. *Free Jazz: A Collective Improvisation by the Ornette Coleman Double Quartet*, Rhino Records R2 75208.

Williams, R. ([1969] 2005), 'It's Shame That Nobody Listens', *Melody Maker*, 25 October, in C. Heylin (ed.), *All Yesterdays' Parties: The Velvet Underground in Print 1966-1971*, 119–21, Cambridge: Da Capo.

Youngblood, G. (1970), *Expanded Cinema*, New York: Dutton.

13

The Velvet Underground is a Jonathan Richman song

Cibrán Tenreiro Uzal

In an interview with John Cale and Jonathan Richman on Australian TV in 1983,[1] the host asked Richman how he would describe the relationship between himself and Cale. Richman replied, 'kinda like Bozo the Clown opening for Jean Paul Sartre'. At that point, the camera showed them together, and one would think that Richman was completely right: Cale was dressed all in black except for his surprising white sneakers. He also wore sunglasses and looked like a parody of an existentialist, or like the nihilists in *The Big Lebowski*. On the other hand, Richman was dressed for summer, wearing his classic blue-and-white striped T-shirt and a surfing necklace. They could not look more different, but they were not there by chance.

Richman's career would not be the same if we took away his relationship with the Velvet Underground and the members of the band, and his humorous simile recalls the theory that Ernie Brooks, bass player in the original Modern Lovers, had about the relation between them and the Velvets:

> [Jonathan] also loved the Velvet Underground, but he was very conflicted about them, because of the darkness they presented. I always had this theory that our sound was almost the opposite of the Velvets, that basically we were playing into the light as opposed to the darkness. But you could argue that about anybody – any art that expresses pain is also suggesting a way out of the pain.
>
> (McNeil 2014)

If there is a moment in Richman's work that clearly shows that darkness/light dialectic, it is the fragment of 'Sister Ray' (*White Light/White Heat*, 1968) he includes within 'Velvet Underground' (*I, Jonathan*, 1992), the fan song that sums up his take on the band. 'Sister Ray' is, musically, one of the most gloriously chaotic tracks on the Velvet Underground's discography and, lyrically, an example of Reed's most provocative subject choices. However, Richman places it inside a stripped-down and completely joyful song: just handclaps, guitar, bass, a tambourine and classic rock and roll chord changes. The Velvets' minimalist approach to rhythm is still there in some way, but the chaos has disappeared. And the somewhat objective distance that Reed takes between himself and his characters and ambience is here out of context, used as a practical illustration of the description of the band that Richman has been making up to that point – a description pretty much focused on sound and attitude, not on lyrical content. The dark elements are gone and what we have is the brightness of a fan celebrating his love of the Velvet Underground: their mystery, their look on stage and their all-encompassing and powerful live sound. And we also have a summary of a particular connection between artists that transcends imitation and that can be approached by using some of Harold Bloom's thoughts on poetic influence. I will use these two theoretical frameworks (fandom and influence theory) to tackle the relation between Jonathan Richman and the Velvets, and to share some thoughts on the role of the Velvet Underground's fandom as an important creative motor for popular music in the last fifty years.

Fan songs and artists as fans

'Velvet Underground' is one of the most notable examples of a genre of pop songs where the performers present themselves as fans of another artist. By doing so, they usually place themselves within a musical tradition, but they also affirm and share their own identity like most fans do in everyday life. Cornel Sandvoss (2005: 97) explained that fans and audiences search out their own audiences for their performances of media texts: 'the individual partly constructs itself through its object of fandom and its performative display. Indeed visual signifiers of fan consumption, such as particular dress styles, stickers, buttons, posters or replica shirts, have become part of the performance structure of our everyday lives.' Often, these fan actions oriented to an audience transcend social interaction and lead to what John Fiske (1992) calls 'textual productivity'. That is, the production of cultural texts and materials like fan art, fan fiction, fanzines or even 'filk songs', a genre born to be sung collectively and informally by fans gathered at science fiction conventions (Jenkins 1992: 255–74), which differs from what I identify here as fan songs in its orientation towards organized fan communities.

A quick list of examples of fan songs that contain more or less clear expressions of fan love for an artist or a band includes Richard Thompson's (2015) 'Guitar Heroes' that mentions Django Reinhardt, Les Paul, Chuck Berry, James Burton and the Shadows; Saint Etienne's (2012) 'Over the Border' about the evolution of personal music fandom; Jeffrey and Jack Lewis' (2006) 'Williamsburg Will Oldham Horror'; Weezer's (1994) 'In the Garage' (on Kiss); and Billy Bragg's (1990) 'I Dreamed I Saw Phil Ochs Last Night'. A closer examination shows the way in which they represent different kinds of typical fan actions and feelings. Thompson's 'Guitar Heroes' describes trying to get the sound of his idols, introducing fragments of their music as Jonathan Richman does in 'Velvet Underground'. Saint Etienne's song reports a fan pilgrimage to see Peter Gabriel's house. Jeffrey and Jack Lewis' song is about the anxiety of meeting an idol, Will Oldham. Weezer's in 'In the Garage' mentions having Kiss posters on a wall, creating a feeling of intimacy and protection. Bragg presents himself talking to Phil Ochs in a dream. The fan object can therefore affect subject choice, lyrical content and also musical elements and, in general, the way the fan presents himself or herself as an artist in his or her own right. We can also sometimes see the fan addressing the original artist by presenting himself or herself as a successor as David Bowie did in 'Song for Bob Dylan' (*Hunky Dory*, 1971): 'There's even a song – "Song To Bob Dylan" – that laid out what I wanted to do in rock. It was at that period that I said, "okay (Dylan) if you don't want to do it, I will." I saw that leadership void. (…) If there wasn't someone who was going to use rock'n'roll, then I'd do it' (qtd. in Hilburn 1976).

The difference between these examples of fan productivity and those we usually understand as fan art or fan fictions is not their creativity, as any fandom can lead to imaginative interpretations of fan objects (see Vermorel and Vermorel 2011). The main difference is that these songs are not oriented to fan communities. We think of these musicians first as artists and then as fans, while a Harry Styles fan who uploads a fan fiction to Wattpad is going to be thought of first as a fan and probably never as an artist. But in essence, there is no real divide between fan-artists and artist-fans, as the relevance of their fandom when it comes to define their public identity does not show the *real* and internal relevance of that same fandom to their identity.

Fan songs have, in that sense, shaped how we understand the work of several artists by showing us the importance of fandom in their lives. Patti Smith's *M Train* (2015) shows her visiting graves, houses and other places where some of her idols lived (Sylvia Plath, Virginia Woolf, Jean Genet, Frida Kahlo, Arthur Rimbaud, Jim Morrison). These fan pilgrimages are congruent with her constant elegiac homages or celebrations of artists like Rimbaud and Morrison, as well as Kurt Cobain, Amy Winehouse, Andréi Tarkovsky, Jimi Hendrix and, on the 2016 Soundwalk Collective release *Killer Road*, Nico. On songs, poems and memoirs, she shares with an audience the kind of intimate and even mystical relation she has with all those people. We also find many fan songs in the work of Dan Treacy and Television Personalities, including his own 'Velvet Underground' (2006), where he asks the same question that Jonathan asked in his song – about the mystery of the Velvets' live sound.

Jonathan Richman has written many fan songs, a fact that also shows the importance of fandom in his life. The approach that Jonathan takes in them also shows lots of typical fan behaviour. In 'Salvador Dalí' (2004) he sings that the painter saved his life by guiding him into a world of dreams, showing a similar type of mystical and intimate relation with an artist to that of Patti Smith. In 'Vincent Van Gogh' (1985) he recalls a visit to the Amsterdam museum in which he felt that Van Gogh was with him in the hall, a feeling of proximity that is also common to many fans.[2] In 'When Harpo Played His Harp' (1988) he shares the great beauty he finds in Harpo Marx's playing and his fascination with that sound, in a similar way to how he does in 'Velvet Underground'. In some of his fan songs, this fascination turns into argumentation and discussion, a kind of action that is also part of usual fan behaviour.[3] In 'No One Was Like Vermeer' (2008) he explains how the painter used colour in a modern way, out of or beyond his time. In the recent track 'Keith' (2015) he describes why Keith Richards' playing is so unique as it combines blues techniques with a European sensibility, even pointing out Richards' use of internal melodies and minor sixth harmonies. When researching this chapter, I asked Jonathan Richman (2018) about his views on Richards' guitar playing, as well as some questions concerning the Velvet Underground. On Richards his response was as follows:

> Q. In your song 'Keith' you make a few comments about Keith Richards guitar playing style (like his use of minor sixth harmonies). You do something similar with Jan Vermeers painting style in 'No One Was Like Vermeer'. Do you usually study music & art you like to understand how it works?
> A. No. In the case of Keith Richards it finally dawned on me that he was using minor sixth in songs like 'Gimme Shelter'.

The main intention of my question was to identify the nature of Jonathan's fandom through his answers. This response, alongside his lack of a response to other questions concerning the Velvets, meant I was unable to do this. However, by looking at his work, interviews and other materials I identified in his relationship to the Velvets the same kind of fan actions we can see in the songs discussed above, showing the importance of the band in his life and in his work.

In a special tribute to Lou Reed on *Wax! Crackle! Pop!* (2014) broadcast on Radio Valencia, Jonathan shared a personal moment of revelation: 'I just heard one of the songs with Nico singing and I was intrigued, but a friend of mine brought over the album, and when I first heard the song "Heroin" I went: "These people would understand me", as a person who never thought he was understood at all.' This feeling of understanding and identification often appears when somebody describes their personal fandom. For example, in Cavicchi's study (1998: 52) John O'Brien states, '[i]t always happens that the latest single or album that comes out from him [Bruce Springsteen] in a way matches up with how I'm thinking. It's almost uncanny. It's weird!' In Giles Smith's *Lost in Music* by (1996: 74) he writes that 'not since Marc Bolan had I felt so strongly that a voice on the record had come into the room specifically to address *me*. Whatever he [Stevie Wonder] sang seemed instantly applicable. Any crush he happened to talk about was the one I happened to have'.

When I sent my questions to Richman, my intention, as a fan, was to get close to him in some way – to make real the closeness I feel to him. At the same time, I was apprehensive because some time ago I had dreamt that I met him and he was mean and rude; I was worried that his answers (or his lack of answers) would disappoint me and spoil the enjoyment of listening to him. Luckily, none of the two things happened, but it made clear for me that the reading that we fans make of our fan objects is, as Sandvoss explained, 'self-reflective' (Sandvoss 2005: 98). We create our own meanings for our favourite songs and for our idols based on our thoughts and experiences; creative reception often leads to a misreading, a take on the work of art or the person that does not match the canonical nor even the author's interpretation. Hence, there is a close relation between that main feature of fandom and the central principle of Harold Bloom's theory of influence:

> Poetic Influence – when it involves two strong, authentic poets, – always proceeds by a misreading of the prior poet, an act of creative correction that is actually and necessarily a misinterpretation. The history of fruitful poetic influence, which is

to say the main tradition of Western poetry since the Renaissance, is a history of anxiety and self-saving caricature, of distortion, of perverse, wilful revisionism without which modern poetry as such could not exist.

(Bloom [1973] 1997: 30)

Therefore, talking about fandom and talking about influence are not exactly the same, but the two things are related, and I will try to use them both to analyse how the Velvet Underground's influence on Jonathan Richman and his work evolved.

Misreading the Velvets

Sixteen years before he appeared in that Australian TV show with John Cale, Richman had that moment of revelation listening to 'Heroin' and eventually got to meet his heroes. In a DVD interview (*Take Me to the Plaza* 2003), he observed,

> it couldn't have been by chance. It was so ridiculous that it had to be fate. I just met this person who knew that person who knew that other person ... There was no way I should meet those people. I was too young to get into nightclubs, I was sixteen. But somehow the manager of one of the nightclubs let me in. He never met me before, but he just said 'oh, let him in', and he also happened to be the manager of The Velvet Underground. So I met them, I met these people and I wanted to play too.

His love of the Velvet Underground inspired his creativity, and a good part of his early work seems to revolve around the band. One of the oldest recordings of Jonathan Richman that we know of has him covering 'I'm Waiting for the Man' (on the bootleg *Songs of Remembrance*). John Cale recalls Richman visiting the band at the Boston Tea Party: 'Jonathan would show up persistently with poems, scribbled poems, that he had written about this, that and the other, mainly about the band. We had no idea initially he was going to be a musician' (qtd. in Mitchell 1999: 22). The Velvets are also the subject of an article, 'New York Art and the Velvet Underground', that Richman wrote in 1967 for the Boston fanzine *Vibrations*, a text that already offers an understanding of the band that would prevail:

> Finally, the Velvets and the New York Art Scene are about the same thing. The same old people ... have been around since early Pop. The ideas are the same. They loved honesty. The Velvets are honest. The scene has had a sense of humor and functionality. The Velvet Underground personifies this stuff. It can't really be defined, I guess. (...) The image of sexual perversion, leather stuff, and general coldness aimed at the scene and specifically at the Warhol crowd is inaccurate to the point of being a good joke.

At that time, Richman is already profoundly involved in his Velvet fandom. Apparently he saw them live more than eighty times (Burrows 2008), he moved to New York for a time to be part of the scene and he slept on Steve Sesnick's couch[4] (Greenman 2013).

Moreover, he was creating art with the band as a subject, sharing his love of their music with the world and learning everything about them. This can clearly be seen if we look at the detailed, precise description of their equipment Richman provides for Bockris and Malanga's *Up-Tight*, including the rarely discussed relation between the changes of their gear and the changes in sound (2002: 138–9). Mitchell (1999: 13) says that Richman's initial idea was to become a painter, but that the Velvet Underground changed that. Soon after he met the band, he started playing live and even got to open a show for them, during which he borrowed Lou Reed's guitar.

It is fair to say, therefore, that the Velvet Underground is the starting point for Richman's career as a songwriter. He started to get noticed after Reed had left the Velvets, and the first notable critical mention of the Modern Lovers by Lillian Roxon (1972) in the *New York Sunday News* already compares the two bands:

> Important footnote: I've just come back from Boston where I had my mind totally blown by a group called the Modern Lovers. They are not signed to a label (I can't imagine why it's taken the record companies so long) but their music is a kind of mixture of Velvet Underground, Kinks and the late Buddy Holly. Listening to 19-year- old Jonathan Richman sing 'Roadrunner' is as exciting as listening to the early Velvets. Powerful, danceable, sinister and funny all at the same time.

This comparison would become routine. Peter Laughner (1976) calls Richman 'a Lou Reed protegé' in his *The Modern Lovers* review and says it is 'the album *Transformer* could have been'. An enthusiastic *Sounds* review by Giovanni Dadomo (1976) says that 'Richman sounded like a younger, slightly more adenoidal Lou Reed, and his songs had the pump and grind of early Reed classics like "Run, Run, Run"'. One would think that initial feeling of identification from Richman ('these people will understand me') got him to imitate his idols and try to copy that fascinating sound. At first that was true, as Richman (2009: 5) says in the introduction to his songbook:

> I had no idea what to do with it [his first guitar], but I had every idea: I wanted to make a dark rumble like the Velvet Underground. From a guitar-chord book I learned E minor. Hour after hour, week after week I played E minor and then the 'open' chord over and over (…). I didn't want to make 'music'. I wanted to make sounds … noise.

In *The Anatomy of Influence* (2011) Bloom uses Longinus' treatise *On the Sublime* to explain that the experience of reading the work of a sublime poet is something akin to authorship: '[w]e come to believe we have created what we have only heard.' That feeling is close to a fans identification with an artist's song as something that speaks directly to them. Bloom believes that implicit in Longinus' celebration of the sublime is the anxiety of influence:

> What is my creation and what is merely heard? This anxiety is a matter of both personal and literary identity. What is the me and the not-me? Where do other

voices end and my own begin? The sublime conveys imaginative power and weakness at once. It transports us beyond ourselves, provoking the uncanny recognition that one is never fully the author of one's work or one's self.

(20)

Bloom uses the concept of strangeness to explain how the anxiety of influence appears for a writer, echoing Owen Barfield's idea that such influence 'must be a strangeness of *meaning*'. To Barfield (and to Bloom), strangeness is not correlative with wonder, as they define wonder as a reaction to things we are conscious 'of not quite understanding'. Strangeness in beauty has, for them, the contrary effect: '[i]t arises from contact with a different kind of *consciousness* from our own, different, yet not so remote that we cannot partly share it, as indeed, in such a connection, the mere word "contact" implies' (Bloom 2011: 20).

Richman's take on the Velvet Underground shares these elements of strangeness, as we have seen him contacting that different but shared *consciousness* in his moments of revelation; both his article 'New York Art and the Velvet Underground' and his song 'Velvet Underground' (1992) describe the work of the band as mysterious and undefinable. The constant comparison between them and The Modern Lovers is inevitable, as there are a lot of shared musical elements that distinguish both from most bands of the era: a rejection of virtuosity, a general absence of blues elements, the use of repetition, a basic approach to rhythm and a use of dynamics that could get them both from noisy aggression to delicate fragility (see Papazova, Chapter 5, in this volume). There is also the direct influence of John Cale as the producer of demos that would end up being the core of the album *The Modern Lovers* (1976). And Richman himself has explained that Sterling Morrison and Lou Reed taught him how to play guitar (*Wax! Crackle! Pop!* 2014) and acknowledged the influence of 'Sister Ray' on 'Roadrunner' (Richman 2009: 6). However, those are not the elements that make up the mystery and strangeness of the Velvet Underground, and the evolution of Richman's music would soon lead him far from the sound of his favourite band. The Modern Lovers signed a record deal with Warner Bros. and, as Mitchell puts it, were 'in a position to turn [their work] into real commercial success' (1999: 13). However, Richman was no longer interested in a sound and a repertoire he had mostly left behind. Sean Maloney (2017) describes the tension between Cale and Richman during the aborted sessions that should have led to the Lovers' debut album:

> Cale and Richman are at loggerheads. Richman and the band are at odds. The label's worried. Art and commerce are at each other's throats. Volume versus dynamics. Darkness against light. Jonathan's restless creativity … is taking him in a different direction from Cale, from the label, and from his bandmates. Jonathan, inspired by the calypso of Bermuda, and increasingly distasteful of high-volume performances, is moving in a softer direction …. Cale, still infatuated with the Modern Lovers of '72, kept pushing for more anger, more aggression. Cale wanted the brute force that the Lovers had used to forge their sound.

(92)

This clash could be used to propose that this shift in Richman's musical direction is an Oedipal moment where he kills a father figure in some way. Many visions of Bloom's theory present it as Oedipal too, regarding the way it presents poetry as a set of intertextual relations, where 'every poem is the result of a critical act, by which another, earlier poem is deliberately misread, and hence re-written' (Said 1975). Another of factor in influence theory is agon (conflict): '[t]hreatened by the prospect of imaginative death, of being entirely possessed by a precursor, they suffer a distinctively literary form of crisis. A strong poet seeks not simply to vanquish the rival but to assert the integrity of his or her own writing self' (Bloom 2011: 17–18). Jonathan Richman's self as a songwriter is undeniably unique, but it is after the breakup of the original Modern Lovers where that idiosyncrasy becomes free of obvious Velvet Underground influences. What remains is not a musical nor lyrical influence, but a general approach to art. That is, the reaction to the anxiety of influence towards his predecessors takes first the form of 'following the lead of the previous poet' and then to a stronger affirmation of his or her own self (Lydon n.d.: 6–7).

Maloney (2017) draws parallels with the Velvets when he describes the new Modern Lovers, the band that would record *Jonathan Richman and the Modern Lovers* (1976): 'the power and amplitude of the Modern Lovers had been reduced to nothing. The wailing assault of … "Sister Ray" had been all-but stripped from the Modern Lovers' sound, replaced with the playful gentle sound of tunes like "I'm Sticking With You"' (116). But even if there are similarities with the Velvets' more tender songs or with their more restrained rock and roll tunes, the general evolution of Richman's songwriting is much richer than just a shift in the nature of the influence of the band. Lyrically, Richman's writing never had much to do with Lou Reed's. Richman himself declared that he never understood Reed's lyrics (*Wax! Crackle! Pop!* 2014) and mostly presents himself and his feelings and views as the absolute centre of his songs, whereas Reed tends to inhabit different characters.[5] From this point, Richman developed an ability to address any subject in song, and to find beauty in the most unsuspected things ('Chewing Gum Wrapper' [1985] is a moving song about a chewing gum wrapper). His work always maintained the two crucial elements that, according to Richman, the Velvets also had: honesty and humour. Regarding sound, there is a conscious rejection of amplification and elaborate stage settings and a search for absolute liveness. That opened up a space for the inclusion of the different types of music Richman had been taking interest in over the years (including calypso, South American folk and country), but also especially for an independence that his signing with Warner Bros. would have prevented. Anyone who has seen Richman live with Tommy Larkins in the last twenty-five years has seen the way in which he lets his feelings shape the show: apparently there is no setlist, and the songs are constantly interrupted by impromptu dance routines, monologues or percussion solos, or modified to include new verses, both spoken and sung, and general jamming between guitar and drums. These are two more features, then, common to the work of the Velvets and Richman, even if they sound different: a music full of space and a disinclination to follow any preset rules. A music where anything could happen.[6]

My point is that both Jonathan Richman's and the Velvet Underground's approach to art is one of absolute freedom, even if their constant refusal to meet expectations induces controversy or confrontation with audiences. Pop artist Ronnie Cutrone (qtd. in Bockris and Malanga 2002: 84) identified how different the Velvets were to other bands in the late 1960s:

> The general attitude was fuck you which was very punk but nobody knew what punk was. The Velvets hated everything. The whole idea was to take a stab at everything. Before The Velvet Underground almost without exception all groups came out and said, 'Hey, we're gonna have a good time, let's get involved!, faced the audience, said, 'This is a time of love, peace, happiness and sexual liberation and we're gonna have a great wonderful time.' The Velvets on the other hand came out and turned their backs to the audience. I remember one review said this is musical masturbation. Who do they think they are? They're jerking off on stage.

The focus is, then, on honesty and not on adapting in any way to what the audience wants to see. Mitchell (1999) recalls that Richman would stop the Modern Lovers if an audience was not paying enough attention and recite the lyrics: 'The audience would be startled enough by the abrupt curtailment of the song that Jonathan would immediately have the attention that he wanted. Sometimes, too, songs would be prefaced by spoken verses – to similar effect, lyrics in rock and roll rarely being highlighted in this way' (35). When I asked Richman (2018) if he cared about how his audience reacted to his songs and if he had ever felt misinterpreted, he answered, 'I want communication: I'd rather have an audience dislike the song, but understand it than have them like it, but not understand it.'

When I said that the Velvet Underground was the starting point for Richman's songwriting work, I identified how his Velvet fandom was crucial as the main reference point in his first songs. But by looking at his work as a whole, I would suggest that between Richman and the Velvets is something of the relationship Bloom describes between Christopher Marlowe and William Shakespeare. That is, Shakespeare comes after Marlowe and the work of the latter is necessary for the existence of Shakespeare as we know him: 'without Marlowe, Shakespeare would not have learned how to acquire immense power over an audience ... to have invented a dramatic control *over the audience* in which Tamburlaine's vauntings enlist them as potential allies or victims is a surpassingly strange breakthrough. Shakespeare's infinite art far surpasses this, but required it as starting point' (Bloom 2011: 48).

It is not easy to translate anxiety theory from poetry to music, as previous attempts (Lydon n.d.; Straus 1991) demonstrate. They both point out several problems with Bloom's theory, as he focuses on the relationships between what he considers 'strong poets' (or, in particular, between poems) and hence does not provide a general model. Straus (436) uses the concept of 'anxiety of style' as a more inclusive one, which is implicit in Bloom's writing's and that has to do with the need of new composers to react to previous genres and styles more than to react to particular artists. I did not therefore want to focus here on the relation between works that would have led to a comparison of 'Roadrunner' and 'Sister Ray', for instance. Rather, I focus on an open and general way to explain the need of some pre-existing, specific voices to make new voices appear. Richman's career shows a seeming departure from the Velvet Underground's influence but, in developing the more particular features of his artistic personality, he made that influence more intense. In the early 1990s he was maybe far enough from his beginnings to create a song like 'Monologue about Bermuda' (1991) and re-evaluate his relation towards his early work. In it he compares the rigidity and snottiness of the Modern Lovers to a local calypso band, the Bermuda Strollers, of seasoned and loose musicians. He is able to convince the audience that the Bermuda Strollers were much better than the Modern Lovers, if we want to use those terms when talking about music. This re-evaluation of his youthful attitude has appeared again in recent songs like 'My Affected Accent' (2010) and 'They Showed Me the Door to Bohemia' (2015), where he mentions the Velvet Underground yet again.

'Velvet Underground' (1992), the song, does not mock the band or reject their influence. It has almost the opposite effect, as it underlines how Richman evolved from a sound that owed a great deal to the Velvets to the complete freedom he has achieved – that same freedom and determination that define the Velvet Underground. If, as Ernie Brooks suggested, the Modern Lovers and the Velvets were part of an opposition between light and darkness, Richman has continued his journey towards luminosity, but that does not mean the influence of the Velvets is gone. In fact, it is even more present: not through two-chord riffs and noise but through the development of a unique creative universe. That is the form of influence that shapes the work of the bands and artists that represent the Velvet Underground's legacy better. At this point, we should go back to Brian Eno's infamous (and often misquoted) pronouncement about the band's influence. In a 1982 interview discussing his new album release, *Ambient 4: On Land*, he was asked how he expected it to fare commercially. He responded,

> Very poorly compared with my other records – which haven't done too well either. My reputation is far bigger than my sales. I was talking to Lou Reed the other day and he said that the first Velvet Underground record sold 30,000 copies in the first five years. The sales have picked up in the past few years, but I mean, that record was such an important record for so many people. I think everyone who bought one of those 30,000 copies started a band! So I console myself thinking that some things generate their rewards in a second-hand way.
>
> (McKenna 1982)[7]

The radical quality of the Velvet Underground is what makes them so influential, even if they were relatively unsuccessful in the 1960s perhaps because of this radicalism. The Velvet Underground were important to many people because they opened a path. They created a space for voices that did not really have one in popular music at the time. That space of freedom, of constant refusal to meet expectations, has been followed by Richman, but also by artists such as Sonic Youth, Yo La Tengo, Talking Heads, Patti Smith, David Bowie and the Fall. These artists overcame the temptation to imitate and instead developed their own paths. As the Velvets have achieved mainstream appreciation, their sound has become more generally – and poorly – copied, but any Velvet Underground fan would agree that they are much more interesting as a starting point than as an endpoint; and, anyway, nobody has understood even until today how in the world they were making that sound.

Notes

1. Available online on: https://bit.ly/3o2Kjd8 (accessed 20 May 2018).
2. See, for instance, the 'odd closeness' that Bruce Springsteen fans report in Daniel Cavicchi's study *Tramps Like Us* (1998: 52–3).
3. An example of musical discussion (on 'Which band best represents the legacy of the VU's music?') by Velvets fans can be found on the Velvet Forum (https://bit.ly/3g1uNKa (accessed 25 October 2021). Jonathan Richman came second after Sonic Youth.
4. Steve Sesnick was manager of the Velvet Underground from the end of their association with Andy Warhol in 1967 until 1973 when the band line-up led by Doug Yule disbanded.
5. There is a general problem in pop when it comes to distinguish between the 'real person' (the performer as a human being), 'performance persona' and 'song character' (Auslander 2004: 6). Sterling Morrison underlines that problem when talking about 'Heroin': 'it should be pointed out that when Reed sings he's only glamorizing heroin for people who want to die. The real damage, particularly in New York, has been done through the cult of personality. Rock fans have taken heroin thinking Lou took heroin, forgetting that the character in the song wasn't necessarily Lou Reed' (qtd. in Bockris and Malanga 2002: 117). This lack of distinction has been especially intense in Spain. Many rock stars of the 1970s and 1980s did not understand the lyrics of their American and British idols and tended to mythologize Reed's drug use, as an interview with Burning's leader Johnny Cifuentes shows: 'We were ignorant because we were all fascinated by Keith Richards, Lou Reed, Bowie and some others, and we knew they used heroin and other substances to create their work and we all wanted to be like them and we believed that with two shots we would be kings, and that went out of hand because that was a lie' (Pose 2016).
6. In an article on the Stooges, Richman dismissed Iggy Pop's stage performance as 'like watching a magician from behind. Assumed spontaneity is revealed as calculation'. This rejection underpins his belief in the need for spontaneity in live music (Richman 1970).
7. In fact *The Velvet Underground & Nico* sold almost 60,000 copies in the United States alone between 1967 and 1969 (Gold 2013).

References

Auslander, P. (2004), 'Performance Analysis and Popular Music: A Manifesto', *Contemporary Theatre Review*, 14 (1): 1–13.

Bloom, H. ([1973] 1997), *The Anxiety of Influence. A Theory of Poetry*, New York and Oxford: Oxford University Press.

Bloom, H. (2011), *The Anatomy of Influence. Literature as a Way of Life*, New Haven and London: Yale University Press.

Bockris, V. and Malanga, G. (2002), *Up-Tight. The Velvet Underground Story*, 2nd edn, London: Omnibus Press.

Burrows, T. (2008), 'Strange World of… Jonathan Richman', *The Quietus*, 8 May. Available online: https://bit.ly/3rbG1T3 (accessed 2 December 2021).

Cavicchi, D. (1998), *Tramps Like Us: Music and Meaning among Springsteen Fans*, New York and Oxford: Oxford University Press.

Dadomo, G. (1976), 'Jonathan Richman and The Modern Lovers: The Modern Lovers', *Sounds*, July 3. Available online: https://bit.ly/3rbGc0F (accessed 2 December 2021).

Fiske, J. (1992), 'The Cultural Economy of Fandom', in L. A. Lewis (ed.), *The Adoring Audience: Fan Culture and Popular Media*, 30–49, London and New York: Routledge.

Gold, J. (2013), 'Lou Reed & Exactly How Many Albums The Velvet Underground Sold', *Recordmecca*, 10 November. Available online: https://bit.ly/3H4bvzX (accessed 2 December 2021).

Greenman, B. (2013), 'World on a String', *New Yorker*, 25 November. Available online: https://bit.ly/3GZu34a (accessed 2 December 2021).

Hilburn, R. (1976), 'Bowie: Now I'm a Businessman', *Melody Maker*, 28 February. Available online: https://bit.ly/3KIRIbj (accessed 2 December 2021).

Jenkins, H. (1992), *Textual Poachers: Television Fans and Participatory Culture*, New York: Routledge.

Laughner, P. (1976), 'The Modern Lovers', *Creem*, August. Available online: https://bit.ly/3KJryW2 (accessed 28 May 2018).

Longinus, C. ([1st Century C.E.] 2018), *On the Sublime*, Aylesbury Park, Ireland: HardPress.

Lydon, M. (n.d.), 'Hey, Hey Influential "Other". I Wrote You a Song: Bloom, *The Anxiety of Influence*, and the Strand of Social Protest in Popular Music'. Available online: https://bit.ly/35k4pJn (accessed 2 December 2021).

Maloney, S. L. (2017), *The Modern Lovers*, New York: Bloomsbury.

McKenna, K. (1982), 'Lots of Aura, No Airplay', [Brian Eno interview]. *Los Angeles Times*, 23 May, 291.

McNeil, L. (2014), 'Jonathan Richman: In Love with the Modern World', *Vice*, 6 June. Available online: https://bit.ly/3u9JwLg (accessed 2 December 2021).

Mitchell, T. (1999), *There's Something about Jonathan*, London: Peter Owen.

Pose, G. (2016), 'La mala fama: Johnny Cifuentes', El Estado Mental, 31 October. Available online: https://bit.ly/3G2yPg3 (accessed 2 December 2021).

Richman, J. (1967), 'New York Art and the Velvet Underground', *Vibrations*, September. Available online: https://bit.ly/3Gg8mvL (accessed 2 December 2021).

Richman, J. (1970), 'The Stooges: Side Two', *Fusion Magazine*, 16 October. Available online: https://bit.ly/3FXilG5 (accessed 2 December 2021).

Richman, J. (2009), *Jonathan Richman Songbook*, Milwakee: Hal Leonard.

Richman, J. (2018), *personal email communication* (via Debbie Gulyas of Blue Arrow Records), 9 January.

Roxon, L. (1972), 'Top of Pop: The Graceful Kinks', *New York Sunday News*, 12 March.

Said, E. W. (1975), 'The Poet as Oedipus', *New York Times*, 13 April. Available online: https://nyti.ms/3rYYMZ4 (accessed 2 December 2021).

Sandvoss, C. (2005), *Fans: the Mirror of Consumption*, Cambridge: Polity.

Smith, G. (1996), *Lost in Music*, London: Picador.

Smith, P. (2015), *M Train*, New York: Knopf.

Straus, J. N. (1991), 'The "Anxiety of Influence" in Twentieth-Century Music', *The Journal of Musicology*, 9 (4): 430–47. Available online: https://bit.ly/3sbnzcv (accessed 2 December 2021).

Vermorel, F. and Vermorel, J. (2011), *Starlust: The Secret Fantasies of Fans*, London: Faber and Faber.

14

'It's not that I don't want to play your favourites'; Lou Reed, improvisation and performance

David Pattie

Taking no prisoners

'Sweet Jane' has, it is fair to say, one of the most familiar chord sequences in rock music: I-V-IV-VI/V-I, played against a simple, solid 4-4 beat. Over this progression, and in a voice that can best be described as laconic, Lou Reed tells an apparently straightforward story – of Jackie, who works in a bank, and Jane, a clerk who are the narrator's friends – who live a life together which manages to escape the strictures of the cynical and the nihilistic. A slightly more complex bridge section did not survive into the studio version of the track (first released, in that year, on *Loaded*). The most familiar version of the song, therefore, is as close to an archetypal Reed/Velvets track as it is possible to get; harmonically simple, rhythmically precise, with lyrics that hover somewhere between poetry, conversation and reportage, delivered in a dry, New York *sprechgesang* [speech singing] that hovers around a definable, regular melody.

On the 1978 double live album *Live: Take No Prisoners* (*L:TNP*), things are not so simple. After the sound of someone fumbling in a matchbox and striking a light, Reed greets us. 'Hello', he says, 'Sorry we were late. We were just tuning'. He stresses the first syllable of tuning, giving the delivery of the word an odd, ironic twist. Then there is the unmistakeable sound of a tape spooling; we hear crowd noise for the first time, the sporadic chords and notes of musicians checking their tuning; and then, after the cheer that always accompanies the first sighting of the star, Reed addresses the audience: 'What's the matter? Did we keep you waiting?' After a moment of aggressive banter, which includes slapping down a fan ('Can't you fucking hear?'), he tells the audience that he is going to quote Yeats: 'The best lack all conviction while the best are filled … oh no, it's the other way round – the best lack all conviction (*laughs*), while the worst are filled with passionate intensity. Now, you figure out where I am.' This is as far as it is possible to get from the conventional exhortations of a 1970s rock star. Reed does not seek to gain the crowd's approval; he doesn't acknowledge the location of the performance; he doesn't attempt to invoke a shared performance history, in the way that a musician might when playing to a group of devoted fans. He challenges the crowd, but he does so in a curiously self-cancelling way. The options he lays out before his fans are that their idol is either gifted but ineffectual or a self-deluding failure. Even at a time when the performative tropes of punk had destabilized what the punks saw as an overly smooth, professional, distanced and therefore inauthentic relation between performer and audience, Reed's challenge seems rather out of place. Instead of baiting the audience (in the style of Johnny Rotten) or using the gig to create, at least in passing, a coalition of the despised, dispossessed and discarded (as the Clash did – see Double [2007]), Reed essentially dares his audience to choose what kind of artist he is, while at the same time indicating, through the off-handedness of his delivery, that the answer will not affect him either way.

Reed in the 1970s

Reed's progress through the 1970s had been uneven. The Velvet Underground's reputation had risen, in part because of the active promotion of Reed by a new wave of musicians such as David Bowie. By 1978, Reed was an established icon of the Punk movement; a cartoon of his face had adorned the front cover of the inaugural edition of *Punk*, published at the beginning of 1976. There had also been some notable commercial successes (*Transformer* [1972]; the single 'Walk on the Wild Side'; the live albums *Rock and Roll Animal* [1974] and *Lou Reed Live* [1975]; the studio albums *Sally Can't Dance* [1974] and *Coney Island Baby* [1976]). The album he was touring at that moment (*Street Hassle* [1978]) had been a critical success, even if its sales had not matched those of some of its predecessors. On the other hand, Reed had also spent much of the decade addicted to speed; his relationship with the music press had been difficult, and the recording of *Street Hassle* coincided with the end of a relationship (with a transgender woman called Rachel) that had been as stable as any in his life.

Performatively, too, Reed had difficulty engaging with the 1970s. Trends in live performance in the first part of the decade tended to favour those performers who used avowedly theatrical means (declarative gestures, themed clothing, bespoke lighting and stage design, scripted performance) to extend the world implied in their albums into live performance. Sometimes this theatricality served to foreground the star (as it did with Bowie); sometimes it enabled undemonstrative musicians to efface themselves (as with Pink Floyd); sometimes it allowed technically adept performers to showcase their skill (perhaps the most memorable example of this came in 1974, when Keith Emerson, playing with ELP at the California Jam festival, was strapped to a revolving grand piano hoisted high above the stage). Even punk was essentially a type of theatre: a self-consciously stripped-back theatricalization of the mixture of threat and ennui punks discerned in the world around them.

Reed's response to this was rather awkward. He had been identified as a key formative influence on Glam by one of Glam's key players; the front cover of *Transformer* had bestowed upon him an iconic visual identity (white face, black eye makeup, leather) which rolled over into live performance. The material he performed gave him at least some scope for moments of prepared theatre; in the mid-1970s he would use performances of the track 'Heroin' as background to a mimed fix. However, it would be wrong to say that Reed settled comfortably into the role of the 1970s rock frontman. Simon Frith and Angela McRobbie (2006) defined the archetypal behaviour of the male hard rock frontman as 'aggressive, dominating, and boastful, constantly [seeking] to remind the audience of their prowess, their control' (372). It is hard to argue that Reed comes anywhere near Frith and McRobbie's sexist alpha male; neither, however, is it possible to see him as gender-fluid in the mould of David Bowie, or as atavistic and self-immolating in the mould of Iggy Pop. What footage survives of Reed on stage in the 1970s shows a rather disconnected performer. In Huston, on the 1974 *Rock and Roll Animal* tour, Reed's entrance is halting. The moment should be one where a confident performer demonstrates his ownership of an event which is designed to place him at the centre of proceedings. The music signals a shift in the onstage power relationship; the opening jam ends with a sustained chord before the band launch into 'Sweet Jane''s chord sequence. Reed walks, head down, to the central microphone; he delivers the first line on the beat, but the second line is held back so far that it almost drops out of the rhythm of the song. Half-way through the first verse he starts to dance, awkwardly; for the rest of the track his performance strikes an odd balance between movements that do not seem to be cued by the music, and moments of stillness. The impression the performance conveys is that of a man who finds it difficult to accommodate himself to the performance modes required of the mid-1970s front man.

Reed's awkwardness as a performer was noted. Nick Kent, in 1973, wrote, 'Lou Reed, looking like a panda in ill-fitting leathers, lurched on in something akin to a swagger and a stagger … From then on, we were treated to Reed's clumsy but earnest attempts to carry himself off as a lead singer' (qtd. in Sounes 2015: 169). In part, as Sounes points out, this awkwardness was forced on Reed; he had stopped playing guitar on stage (partly because of the side effects of his amphetamine addiction). He had to adjust to a physical state on stage that was substantially different to the one he had adopted with the Velvets. As Deena Weinstein has noted, a singer that doesn't play an instrument is vulnerable, in a way that a guitarist, keyboard player or drummer is not. Other musicians might be able to fall back on a base level of technical competence; for a singer, however,

> [the] voice is part of the person, not a thing that can be carried, set up by others, or replaced by a better model. Like an athlete's body, the voice is vulnerable. It doesn't get played as much as it gets expressed, and its expression is influenced by the physical and mental condition of the person.
>
> (Weinstein 2004: 324)

Weinstein's point concerns the recorded voice, but it can be extended; a singer in live performance exercises a craft skill – the production of the voice to order at a specific point within the musical framework of a track is as much a matter of technical competence as fretting the right chord. However, the exercise of the singer's craft is largely invisible to an audience; what the audience sees is an individual whose physical and vocal response to the music are taken as clues to the artist's authentic inner self. In this context, Reed's halting performances in the 1970s were read as clear signs of his incipient disintegration, both as an artist and as a person.

Irony, comedy and *Live: Take No Prisoners*

However untethered Reed's life was during this period, there is an argument to be made that, in his case at least, the apparently simple equation between the singer's voice, the emotional temperature of the song and the audience's perception of both the singer and the song might not hold true. For one thing, there isn't the same differentiation between Reed's speaking voice and singing voice as one finds in other singers. David Bowie, for example, had a repertoire of singing voices that he would utilize as and when a particular song required. For Reed, the distinction between speaking voice and singing voice is so blurred as to be almost unnoticeable. In the performance of 'I'm Waiting for the Man' on *L:TNP*, Reed swings between the song's lyrics, new, improvised versions of those lyrics, fragments of monologue and aggressive repartee with audience members heckling him. Each one, though, is delivered in a tone which is very close to Reed's normal speaking voice. That voice itself does not display the same type of emotional investment in the material that we might expect of, say, Aretha Franklin. Rather, it carries all the marks of an ironic delivery (slow tempo, strong intonation, nasally inflected tone – see Zajaczkowska 2016).

Some of this is undoubtedly unconscious; New York accents are rather nasal, and Reed's problems with pitching help to explain a characteristic part of his vocal delivery in live performance. In practice, then, when Reed sings (as he does on 'Coney Island Baby') that he wants to play football for the coach, it is impossible to take him entirely seriously. We don't need to hear him trade the names of football stadia with the audience; the voice itself cues up a distance between the Reed incarnated in the lyrics and the Reed that sings. This doesn't mean that Reed lacks emotional investment in his material. However, it does mean that the listener is constantly aware that Reed seems to pull back from the emotional content of his material by framing it, marking it out as distinct from him, and, in some cases actively subverting it. Part of the oddness of *L:TNP* is that it gives us a singer whose relation to his material sounds as though it is fundamentally ironic. This irony is expressed in a way that elides the differences between apparently separate elements of live performance. For example, interaction with the audience between songs is as ironically overdetermined as the delivery of the songs themselves – but it is impossible to establish the extent to which the irony is a performative choice.

However, the implied irony of Reed's vocal delivery is part of a wider network of ironies that also help to structure the recording, and to give it a coherence which is not the normal coherence of a popular music event. It could be argued that Reed's delivery of the material, taken as a whole, constitutes a special case of the type of semantic inversion that usually constitutes irony. Zajaczkowska (2016) provides a useful summary of this point:

> Although irony can be expressed by various forms of language, such as hyperbole, rhetorical questions, or understatements (Gibbs 2000), most scholars define this form of figurative language as an utterance that is a semantic inversion of the literal (explicit) meaning and the intended (implicit) meaning (Anolli, et al. 2002). Barbe (1995) believes that one of the essential elements for comprehension and effective use of irony is the interlocutors' shared knowledge about the situational context. Additionally, irony detection is possible when speakers recognize the discrepancy between the literal and intended meaning.
>
> (2016: 279)

Irony is then a complex formation. It embraces incongruity, a knowledge of the particular ways that context shapes speech, and an ability to note a slippage in the speaker's discourse. In an event which is largely governed by a set of implicit rules, the second point is the most important; the context of a rock gig sets a framework against which the ironic content of a singer's discourse can most easily be judged. However it isn't a simple question of understanding the distance between word, delivery and meaning. As Deliens et al. note, the relation between ironic discourse and the comprehension of that discourse is itself based on a shifting set of interactions:

> while ironic tone of voice and/or ironic facial expression may be correctly discriminated, these cues are not necessarily efficient in a genuine process of irony comprehension. Arguably, successful social interactions do not reduce to tagging statements as literal or not (viz. discrimination), but require the identification of the speaker's discourse goals, and the selection of an appropriate reaction.
>
> (2018: 35–6)

The audience reads and re-reads the performer, as the performer reads and re-reads the audience; what is coded as ironic at one moment might not necessarily carry the same coding at another.

Reed had a long history of ironic interaction with audiences. As documented on the Velvet's *The Complete Matrix Tapes* (2015), when playing the club in San Francisco in November 1969, he introduced the band like this:

> Good evening. We're your local Velvet Underground. We're, uh, glad to see you. (Applause). Thank you. We're, ah, particularly glad on a serious day like today, that people could find it – y'know, a little time – to come out and just have some fun to some rock and roll. Because these are serious times, or I've been told they are. And, y'know, since they're serious, we felt impelled to do a very serious set. So this is going to be a very serious rock and roll set. I don't want any of you to

enjoy yourselves frivolously, because, ah, it'll run against national policy. Which rhymes, by the way, which is the way that poets are.

What is interesting about this and other examples of Reed's interaction with audiences is that, although the statement seems ironic, it is hard to identify the precise location of that irony. There are statements which comment ironically on the idea of rock musicians as the unacknowledged legislators of the 1960s ('we felt impelled to do a very serious set'). There are others that seem on the surface to be entirely sincere ('We're ... glad to see you'). There are some which could be read, from Reed's delivery, to be both a throwaway joke and an ironic deflation of Reed's own artistic status ('Which rhymes, by the way, which is the way that poets are'). Elsewhere, on the album *Live at Max's Kansas City* (1972), he introduces 'I'm Waiting for the Man' as '[a] tender folk song from the 1950s ... about love between man and subway'. In Texas in 1969, he introduces 'Femme Fatale' as 'a song about someone who was one, and has since been committed to an institution for being one, and will one day maybe open up a school to train others' (on *1969 Velvet Underground Live* [1974]).

His relation to his material in performance stands in contrast to that of one of Reed's avowed *bete noires*, Frank Zappa.[1] In Zappa's live work (and his practice of habitually taping shows allows us to track his development as a performer) everything is steeped in irony. Whether the announcements from the stage, the setting up of audience participation (or 'enforced recreation', as Zappa [1988] once memorably called it), the relation between the band and the audience and the relation between the band members, the interaction between musicological and performative complexity and the simplest possible riffs, at all points, Zappa satirizes the idea of the rock gig as both serious art and good-time gathering. This is not to deny the complex nature of Zappa's relation to the live event; but both he and the audiences that went to see him generally knew the performance would be in part comic, and that the comedy would derive from an ironic relation to the supposed seriousness of the rock gig.

Reed's relation to the form is far harder to place. He doesn't sit within Zappa's model (a thought that, perhaps, would please him, given how intensely he disliked Zappa); one of the strands of the performances caught on *L:TNP* is that of a man intensely concerned with the reception of his work. During 'Walk on the Wild Side', he names and shames rock critics that have given him bad reviews. However, neither is it a stirring defence of his work as art. The very act of moving away so decisively from a straight performance of canonical Lou Reed songs demonstrates that there is, at least, a certain distance between the Reed on tape and the figure of Reed the scribe of 1970s New York. Rather, the performance oscillates between these two poles, setting up an irresolvable tension between the idea of the singer as artist and the singer as sardonic commentator on his own work. This is a different version of Reed to the person whose work is discussed in Richard Witts' 2006 book on the Velvet Underground. According to Witts, one can assemble a typology of Reed's songs: they

1. observe and describe characters in situations:
2. use simple words to convey rich thoughts:

3. deal frankly with those people otherwise dispossessed of song:
4. carry a hint of the subconscious at play, of shrewd implications about personal identity and social anxieties;
5. possess a dry humour, finely balanced between satire and cynicism.

(Witts 2006: 43)

All of this adds up to the idea that Reed is a serious artist: a beat version of Richard Ford or Raymond Carver, perhaps, concerned not so much with the horrors of drug abuse but with the sociology of the addict. A contrasting image of Reed's work is offered by Bernardo Alexander Attias in 2016: for Attias, Reed and the Velvet Underground achieved their effects through a conscious negotiation with artifice. The experiences described in the songs were not conveyed directly to the audience; the band shaped those experiences, both through an accretion of teasing lyrical details and the employment of a compositional style that balanced conventional melodic and harmonic structures against moments of pure sonic disruption:

> That the Velvets' product was an artifice, a simulacrum of experience that they never had, is beside the point. The band's ability to construct meaning through this artifice is the point, as it is for all rock and roll. The Velvets' artistic self-consciousness allowed them the emotional distance to fairly represent images of a central paradox of human existence – the search for order in a chaotic world.
>
> (Attias 2016: 143)

The two Reeds – Witts' and Attias' – do not contradict each other entirely; there is considerable artifice in a Carver short story, and the relation between artifice and authentic expression is, as I have argued elsewhere (Pattie 2007), a complex, ambiguous one. However, arguably, neither the image of Reed the recorder nor Reed the artificer quite describes what is happening in *L:TNP*. Here, we have an artist who is set on disrupting any framework that could codify him (as in this segment of 'Sweet Jane' from the album):

> Now Jack, he's a banker/ and Jane, she's a clerk. Hey, clerk. Gimme good clerk. I give good clerk. Uh-huh. And both of them, man, they save their pennies, and their fucking nickels, and their dimes, and it builds up, they got a nest egg. Here comes the condominium. Oh, shit! (laughter, cheers). Hey, Miami!

As the band hold the main chord sequence, Reed delivers a vocal riff which takes the lyrics of the song as its starting point, but which spirals off into an expanded fantasy of Jackie's and Jane's life and their potential future. The recorded song suggests, very strongly, that their relationship is a bulwark protecting them against whatever happens in the rest of their lives. This version calls that into question, in two contrasting ways. First, Reed gets himself caught up in the potential connotations of the word 'clerk' (which he then uses as a substitute for head: a substitution that suggests, very strongly, that Jane prostitutes herself – either directly or by implication). Second, he expands the line about both money, a throwaway comment in the original song, into the description of a full-blown attempt to join the bourgeoisie. Far from being content with the bohemian life of New York, Jane and Jackie hanker after Florida, and a nice condo somewhere respectable. Don't listen to the lyrics, Reed seems to be saying; or, perhaps, listen to them, but don't accept them as the only story. The song might not mean what the song seems to mean.

A performance that works through the active subversion of meaning (rather than reportage or through consciously deployed artifice) is relatively rare in popular music; even rarer are performances that switch between subversion and engagement which fluctuate, from moment to moment, between strategies to keep the audience at a distance from the material and to involve them in the performance directly. This performance mode (which relies on keeping the audience in suspense as to both the overall direction of the performance and the way it will develop moment by moment) is more closely associated with another type of popular performance. A stand-up comic, it could be said, plays a complex game with an audience; the people watching have to be engaged in the performance; they have to want to follow the comic through his or her material, but only rarely does the comic simply rely on a slavish adherence to the material that has been prepared. Rather, the comic will more normally use the material as the basis for some type of extemporization in performance: a bit that goes well will be expanded, and a bit that doesn't will be discarded. The material of performance is both fixed and in flux (as opposed to the material in music performance, which tends to be far more stable), and a successful comic will become adept at blurring the distinction between what is set and what changes. What is more, his or her performance will rely on the audience's awareness that the material has been performed before, in other places.

Reed's performances, like those of a stand-up, oscillate between prepared material and spontaneity, a relation to the audience which is both combative and conspiratorial. However, a stand-up routine is arranged around a number of preset comic moments that will tend not to vary from night to night. Reed's delivery is, as far as I can tell, truly spontaneous, and on a par with other features of his live work (in particular his ability to improvise lyrics in performance). The fixed elements in his performance are provided not by Reed himself but by the musicians; Reed takes advantage of the repeating riffs, and as he does so, the musicians are stuck in a holding pattern until he finds his way back to the lyrics again. If stand-up is a complex game in which prepared material is both masked and revealed, then Reed's performance isn't simply the transposition of the stand-up format into the format of live music performance. It is too fluid, too aleatory, and it doesn't build to a climactic moment of performative release. Crucially, too, he delivers the monologues in the same nasal New York voice that he uses when he sings; monologues and vocal lines are, therefore, inflected in performance with the same irony. In both cases, the message is the same: don't listen to the monologues – or, listen to them, but don't accept them as a simple reflection of my attitude to this performance, to these songs or to my place in 1970s music. The jokes might not mean what you think they mean.

'Walk on the Wild Side': Performing irony

If Reed's performance in *L:TNP* doesn't entirely fit within the frameworks established either in the performance of popular music, or the framework of stand-up performance (in both cases because the operation of irony within the context of both frameworks cannot be clearly established), then what type of performance is it? To answer this question, I'd like to look at one particular song. 'Walk on the Wild Side', from the album *Transformer*, was Reed's first major hit: four minutes and twenty seconds long, the subject of a distinctive, spare arrangement by Mick Ronson and Bowie, the song reached the top 20 in the United States, and made it to number 10 in the UK. The song is an example of one of Reed's habitual lyrical techniques – distanced, dispassionate reportage, leaving the listener enough interpretive space to impute motives and emotions to the characters Reed sketches. The original version is scored for guitar, double bass, strings, drums (played with brushes) and female backing vocalists, whose interjections provide the song with the closest thing it has to a hookline. It builds a composite picture of Warhol's Factory through brief descriptions of its various alumni (Holly Woodlawn, Candy Darling, Joe Dellasandro, Jackie Curtis), each one scrabbling to find purchase in a city that offers little more than hustles, drugs and affectless sex.

On *L:TNP*, 'Walk on the Wild Side' is sixteen minutes and fifty-five seconds long. Two minutes of this is taken up by pre-song byplay with the audience. 'I just wanna have it quiet for a while', he tells them.

> I been here a week. You think that's an accomplishment? I think it's, you know, something you're sentenced to. And if you don't get that you get the Palladium with [unintelligible] (laughter). Two hours with fourteen thousand animals throwing beer cans at you for (voice trails off. Laughter, applause). Oh, but that's Rock and Roll.
>
> (Reed 1978)

When the main riff starts, it's greeted with whoops and applause. The drums build, the bass approximates the glissando of the studio version, but at the point where the vocals should come in, Reed instead provides a comment on the song's place in his canon. 'We know the riff, c'mon', he says. 'Eight measures of it.' Then, to the musicians: 'Don't show any passion. You show an emotion and I fire you.' This is, to say the least, unexpected. In the unfolding narrative of the rock gig, tracks like 'Walk on the Wild Side' would have a prescribed place; they'd come near the end of the performance, at the point at which the audience, having listened and responded to newer material, would be rewarded by performances of the tracks they associated most closely with the performer. The performer, on the other hand, would display their investment in the songs and the fans, using a song like this as a communal moment – a meeting place between the artist and those who have invested themselves in the work of the artist.

Reed does acknowledge the audience's familiarity with the song, but he does so ironically, and then he invokes the conventional emotional tone of such performances by negating them. To re-employ a point made earlier, Reed shows himself aware of the situational context of the performance; he knows how he should act at this point, and not only does he refuse to do so, he turns that refusal into an ironic performance of its own. He compounds the irony almost immediately: 'I am not sure that we did this song all week, right? It's not that I don't want to play your favourites; it's just, there are so many favourites to choose from (laughter).' He teases the audience with the song's first line, before breaking into a quick canter across a number of topics including smoking, gay sex and the fact that nothing – or presumably Nothing, as he converts the word from an absence to a culturally desirable state – is in style. The audience respond enthusiastically: 'Saturday night, man, what d'you want?' Reed asks them, before acknowledging the thing that keeps them engaged with the performance, the thing that provides, as much as anything can, a sure foundation on which the multiple ironies of the event can rest:

> Watch me turn into Lou Reed before your very eyes. I do Lou Reed better than anybody, so I thought I'd get in on it. (laughter, pause as the music continues). Enough attitude to kill every person in Jersey.

Once again, the effectiveness of the moment rests on a shared appreciation of the nature of the event. Reed understands that there is something artificial about the nature of this performance, as there is about any music performance. The performer does not present himself or herself to the audience unfiltered; what the audience responds to is a version of the person, not the person themselves. The audience's amused response to this shows that, in effect, they are in on the joke. However, Reed has already both acknowledged and dynamited this particular reading; before we reach this point, Reed has already told the audience that he's lonely, and that a cure for this loneliness is to stage debates between the various versions of himself ('Everybody gets bored with somebody sometime, except me, I'm lonely. Me and my several selves discuss it at night. Lou number one, Lou, Lou number 5. Hello. Is that you again …?'). As noted above, Reed begins 'Sweet Jane' by teasing the audience, daring them to discover who he is. This suggests that Reed doesn't believe that there is a definitive version of himself for the audience to discover; or that any definitive version will remain hidden from the audience, from the critics and, it might be inferred, from Reed himself.

Later in the performance, Reed fleshes out the brief character sketches in the verses. The Sugar Plum Fairy, he tells the audience, is

> a real terror, she was fired from the New Yorker for correcting Dorothy Parker's prose, can you imagine? For those of you who still read – what a snotty remark, I dunno. Anyway, she makes her living writing things for the Encyclopaedia Britannica. Five cents a word …. Last time I saw her she was doing the flower section in Africa … she said, what's a word that'll make this thing interesting. We call her Tiny Malice [a play on Edward Albee's, Tiny Alice].

(Reed 1978)

This story and the others Reed tells during the performance (about Joe Dellasandro, described by Reed as stupid; about leaving the Velvets, about meeting various celebrities – including Norman Mailer, who greeted him with the offer of a punch in the stomach – and about the process of writing the original song) are coded as ironic in several interlocking ways. First, as the above story demonstrates, the tales themselves come with their own weight of deflating editorial comment. Second, also as noted above, Reed's vocal tone provides enough contextual framing for the audience to assume his tales are ironically intended. Lastly, as in other performances captured on the album, the stretching of the material plays against the conventional framing of music in performance.

Partly, Reed here is trading on the particular relation the Velvets established to the political, cultural and social movements of the late 1960s. As Bannister argues, invoking Foucault's notion of the 'specific intellectual' (1988: 138), the band held themselves back from the idea that musicians had to operate as generational icons and spokespeople:

> The 'populism' of 1960s rock culture identified artists with their audiences, as speaking for 'youth' or specific ethnic groups. But the Velvets were under no obligation to advocate for anyone, and this granted them a degree of autonomy from the familiar dialectic of power/resistance. Rather theirs is the place of the 'specific intellectual' who surveys local sites where power emerges from practice.
> (2010: 166)

Bannister is right in arguing that the Velvets were more interested in local sites, rather than in broader social forces; but it is possible to refine his argument further, and to say that, in the Velvets' music, local sites were surveyed ironically, not simply as places where power emerged from practice but places in which various individuals find themselves unable to exercise that power. The narrator of 'Heroin' admits that 'he just doesn't know'; waiting for the man is an endless process; no dress, no attitude and no amount of preparation will fit the girl for all tomorrow's parties; even a murder, described in 'Sister Ray', is treated as something affectless. The bohemian freedoms of the 1960s, and the cultural ferment of New York, mean nothing to them; the wider situational context, known in this case to the singer and the listener, is something the characters in Reed's songs either ignore or are too caught up in the daily hustle to understand. His characters stand in an ironic relation to their time, and Reed, in performing the songs, stands in an ironic relation to his characters.

The performance of 'Walk on the Wild Side' extends this irony to the back story of the characters in the song and their real-life counterparts, to the music industry within which the track is produced and consumed, to the idea of music performance, to the celebrity networks in New York and to Reed's own history and mental state. The performance doesn't demonstrate, in Attias' phrase quoted earlier, a search for order in a chaotic world; rather, it demonstrates and describes a series of chaotic responses to a chaotic world. In the performance, the element that provides the fixed situational background against which the irony of the performance can be expressed is not in the words; rather, it is in the music. Reed, at this point in his career, could call on very competent, responsive musicians; the roughness of the Velvets had been replaced by the kind of band that could turn its hand to any form of popular music.

They provided the requisite codes of authentic investment in the performance of the tracks; the backing vocalists launched into chorus lines and fills like gospel singers; the saxophonist provided decorative flourishes; the bass and drums drove the tracks at a slightly faster pace than the studio originals; the guitar mixed power chords and fills, and on 'I Wanna Be Black' (from *Street Hassle*), an extemporized, overdriven solo. With Reed's voice removed, we could be listening to a very good, but standard, late 1970s ensemble. With Reed's voice added, even the passionate investment of the musicians is ironized, both through overt statements (such as the throwaway comment about not showing passion, quoted above) and through the more generalized tone of ironic detachment Reed cannot help but impart to his performances.

The band's skill is amply demonstrated during the performance of 'Walk on the Wild Side'. In contrast to the subdued recorded version, the song live is funky; the Rhodes piano provides an upbeat, rhythmic introduction, and the guitar adds accenting notes before moving into the main riff. The drums build up gradually over four bars; then, after a brief turnaround, they pick up a characteristic funk beat. The sax provides a melodic counterpoint to Reed's voice; the bass alternates between versions of the glissando that marks the original version and a more conventional funk baseline, locking in with the drums on the first beat of the bar. When Reed moves decisively away from the lyrics, the band settle into an extended jam on the two chords of the main riff. The adjective 'tight' is sometimes inappropriately applied to musical ensembles; it is relatively easy to remain rhythmically stable over the course of a three-minute song. To keep time and to provide the interlocking lines that funk requires, steadily, over fourteen minutes, as the lead vocalist veers unpredictably between lyrics and serio-comic extrapolation is rather less easy. And to do so with what can be read as performative enthusiasm (the beat doesn't slacken, the time-keeping is precise and the band are always prepared to support, accent and emphasize Reed's vocals) is the mark of musicians who understand that it is their job to display an authentic investment in the performance of live music.

And it is here, perhaps, that we reach the final irony; as noted above, an ironic reading of any type of discourse relies on an awareness of the context that frames the irony. Put simply, there has to be an unironic element somewhere within the framework of the performance. Rock gigs in the 1970s, as I have noted, moved increasingly to incorporate performative techniques drawn from theatre, but they did so, paradoxically, in a way that served to re-enforce the sense that performers were, in the midst of their performances, offering something authentic to the audience. Stand-up comedians rely on the existence of a series of stable meanings, accepted by the audience without much conscious thought. Even those artists that move between comic discourse and music performance point up, in their various ways, the existence of tropes that are supposed to be read authentically. However, as I have said, none of these frameworks fit Reed. There is no clear distinction between ironic and comic discourse and authentic investment; even when Reed is singing straight, the tone and timbre of his voice suggest disengagement and ironic distance. The element that enables an ironic reading of Reed's performances in *L:TNP* – the authentic grit around which the pearl of Reed's ironic performance coalesces – is the element that biographies of the artist tend to ignore. The musicians conform to the tropes of authentic performance throughout; they do not use their technique in the service of musical jokes, as Zappa's musicians do. They are there – on the beat, in sync, responsive, showing all the signs of emotional investment in their performances. Reed, in destabilizing the very structure of the music in which they invest themselves, effectively uses the band's performed authenticity as the foil for his irony; he also plays the audience in exactly the same way. Paradoxically, Reed makes the event work, not by adopting and adapting himself to the tropes of authentic rock performance but by maintaining a scrupulous distance from all of those tropes. Rather than binding the audience and band together into a temporary community, he denies the very possibility of such a community, even though everything the band does, and everything the audience does, suggests that community is on the point of formation. Everyone else in the performance event provides the discursive context against which an ironic reading can form. What we have isn't a comic destabilizing of a rock gig: what we have is an entirely conventional rock performance, rendered profoundly ironic because, in place of the invested central performer, we have Reed – an unpredictable, unfixed, unreadably ironic absence, right at the centre of the event.

Note

1   For example, when Reed played 'The Rainbow' in London in 1974, he gleefully told the Melody Maker's Charles Charlesworth, 'I enjoyed those shows I did in London at the Rainbow, but I kept thinking, Frank Zappa fell 17 feet down into that pit (Zappa was pushed offstage by a fan during a 1971 gig at the Rainbow). I hate Frank Zappa, and it made me so happy to think about that.'

References

Anolli, L., Infantino, M., and Ciceri, R. (2002), 'From "Blame by Praise" to "Praise by Blame": Analysis of Vocal Patterns in Ironic Communication', *International Journal of Psychology*, 37 (5): 266–76.

Attias, B. A. (2016), 'Authenticity and Artifice in Rock and Roll: "And I Guess That I Just Don't Care"', *Rock Music Studies*, 3 (2): 131–47.

Auslander, P. (2021), *In Concert: Performing Musical Persona*, Ann Arbor, MI: University of Michigan Press.

Bannister, M. (2010), '"I'm Set Free…"; The Velvet Underground, 1960s Counterculture, and Michel Foucault', *Popular Music and Society*, 33 (2): 163–78.

Barbe, K. (1995), *Irony in Context*, Amsterdam, The Netherlands: John Benjamins Publishing.

Charlesworth, C. (1974), 'Lou Reed: Man of Few Words', *Melody Maker*, 9 March. Available online: https://bit.ly/3r3IQ8p (accessed 15 December 2021).

Deliens, G., Antoniou, K., Clina E., Ostashchenkoa, E., and Kissine, M. (2018), 'Context, Facial Expression and Prosody in Irony Processing', *Journal of Memory and Language*, 99 (4): 35–48.

Double, O. (2007), 'Punk Rock as Popular Theatre', *New Theatre Quarterly*, 23 (1): 35–48.

Foucault, M. (1988), *Politics, Philosophy, Culture: Interviews and Other Writings, 1977–1984*, ed. L. D. Kritzman, New York: Routledge.
Frith, S. and McRobbie, A. (2006), 'Rock and Sexuality', in S. Frith and A. Goodwin (eds), *On Record: Rock, Pop and the Written Word*, 317–32, London: Routledge.
Gibbs, R. W. (2000), 'Irony in Talk among Friends', *Metaphor and Symbol*, 15: 5–27.
Pattie, D. (2007), *Rock Music in Performance*, London: Palgrave.
Sounes, H. (2015), *Notes from the Velvet Underground*, New York: Doubleday.
Weinstein, D. (2004), 'All Singers Are Dicks', *Popular Music and Society*, 27 (3): 323–34.
Witts, R. (2006), *The Velvet Underground*, Sheffield: Equinox Publishing.
Zajaczkowska, M. K. (2016), 'Influence of Voice Intonation on Understanding Irony by Polish-Speaking Preschool Children', *Psychology of Language and Communication*, 20 (3): 278–91.
Zappa, F. (1988), You Can't Do That On Stage Anymore Vol. 1, Rykodisc RCD 10081/82.

15

Portrait of the artist as Andy Warhol: Lou Reed and John Cale's *Songs for Drella*

Elizabeth Ann Lindau

Andy Warhol died unexpectedly in February 1987 while recovering from gall bladder surgery. Among the 2,000 mourners at the artist's memorial service at St. Patrick's Cathedral six weeks later were former Velvet Underground bandmates John Cale and Lou Reed. As is well known, the Velvets had been part of Warhol's 47th Street Factory from 1965 to 1967. Warhol featured them in the multimedia happenings he called the Exploding Plastic Inevitable, helped the band secure their first record contract with Verve and designed the iconic 'banana' cover of their self-titled debut release. At the time of Warhol's death, the band had long since disintegrated, and Reed and Cale, often regarded as its lead creative forces, had been estranged for nearly two decades.[1] But at the suggestion of artist Julian Schnabel, Cale and Reed put away their personal differences to collaborate on a memorial for their former producer and mentor. Cale and Reed gradually renewed their partnership following Warhol's memorial service. According to Cale, they began the project in a New York City rehearsal space by tape-recording their reminiscences of Warhol (Bockris and Cale 1999: 224). As Cale told Stephen Holden of the *New York Times*, 'it began as just the two of us having fun throwing around ideas ... Gradually it turned into songwriting. It was a great opportunity to pick up the threads of the Velvet Underground and draw our original ideas about arrangements and subject matter to a conclusion' (Holden 1989). That conclusion was *Songs for Drella* (1990), which went from multimedia stage show to acclaimed album release over the next three years. 'Drella', a portmanteau of Dracula and Cinderella, was a Factory nickname for Warhol that the artist reportedly disliked. Cale and Reed previewed a working version of the song cycle at the Arts at St. Ann's series in January 1989. Between 29 November and 3 December of the same year, they premiered the completed work in four sold-out performances at the Brooklyn Academy of Music (BAM).

The album version of *Drella* was recorded between December 1989 and January 1990 and released in April 1990 on Sire. Its fifteen songs tell Warhol's life story through a series of vignettes ordered roughly chronologically, chronicling his upbringing in Pittsburgh, his early work as a fashion illustrator, his forays into film-making with a motley crew of 'Superstars' and his withdrawal from his circle after one member of it nearly took his life. Sung by both Cale and Reed, the songs' lyrics are primarily in first person from Warhol's point of view. But this perspective is occasionally complicated when Reed takes over the narration or when the Velvet Underground themselves become characters in the drama. Cale discusses these slippages in his autobiography: 'When we were putting the thing together, we never quite clarified what our attitude was towards Andy speaking all the time. And that included the question of whether there should be any reference to the Velvet Underground. It's a good lyrical device to write from another person's point of view, but inevitably it was going to blur' (Bockris and Cale 1999: 224).

Drella is understood variously as a memorial album, a concept album, a musical biography or as a form of art therapy for Cale and Reed as they mourned their former mentor.[2] According to biographer Victor Bockris, 'the songs covered Warhol's life chronologically, mixing fact and fiction to portray the relationship between Warhol, Reed and Cale', and Reed reflected that the album would inaugurate a new genre he called 'Biorock' (Bockris and Malanga 2002: 208). In the album's liner notes, Cale declared *Drella* a 'tribute', while Reed described it as 'a brief musical look at the life of Andy Warhol [that] is entirely fictitious' (Reed and Cale 1990). Warhol's own artistic practice suggests yet another way of understanding and categorizing *Drella*: as portrait. The centuries-old visual art genre of portraiture depicts human subjects, often to preserve them beyond death. Warhol was arguably the most important portrait maker of the twentieth century, single-handedly reviving the démodé practice with his work in painting, film and photography. Portraiture is most often thought of as a genre of visual art or literature, but music has the capability to portray a human subject as well. This chapter considers *Drella* as a musical portrait of Andy Warhol, one whose effectiveness and complexity result from Cale and Reed's intimate knowledge of and identification with Warhol and from their ability to translate many of his innovations in portrait-making to music. Just as Warhol mixed photography and painting, or moving and still images to create his portraits, the album mixes fact and fiction, passages from Warhol's posthumously published diary with Reed's original poetry, portrait with self-portrait. *Songs for Drella* is a musical portrait of Warhol informed by the artist's own work in portraiture.

Defining the (musical) portrait

Portraits in painting, sculpture, engraving, photography or other visual media are distinguished by an attempt to depict and preserve a human subject (or on occasion, a group of subjects). In his book-length study of portraiture in the visual arts, Richard Brilliant (1991) offers this definition: 'Simply put, portraits are art works, intentionally made of living or once living people by artists, in a variety of media, and for an audience' (8). Traditionally, artists create these works in the physical presence of their subjects, who pose or sit for them. The subject's conscious pose and awareness of an unseen audience make them collaborators with the artist on their self-representation.

The resulting portrait, then, typically includes some aspect of the subject's physical appearance and has a quality of intimacy or communion between the two parties. Of course, not all artistic depictions of people created from life are necessarily portraits. In contrast to, say, Edgar Degas' anonymous dancers or washerwomen, the persons shown in a portrait are named individuals rather than general types. Historically, portraits were made of persons wealthy enough to commission them or important enough to be preserved for posterity. As philosopher Cynthia Freeland (2007) writes, 'Even the greatest artists of the Renaissance and modern periods worked on commission and at the pleasure of patrons. Portraits documented status, and artists were paid to reveal power, wealth, and authority' (97). In the twentieth century, artists became increasingly uneasy with working for hire and catering to the vanity or demands of their employers. Freeland uses the example of Henri Matisse, whose sitters were required to sign contracts stipulating that he had full artistic control of the product (97).

Perhaps more than any other artworks, portraits explore the relationship between identity and appearance, and arise from social interaction between artist, subject and viewer. Brilliant writes that we tend to think and speak of portraits as the people they represent. We judge them not as purely aesthetic objects but on their fidelity to their subjects (Brilliant 1991: 23-5; 62). In addition to physical likeness, portraits traditionally convey information about their subject's profession, social station and character. Theories of portraiture frequently discuss the artist's need to depict the subject's objectively visible features while alluding to invisible interior features. 'Historically, portrait artists have often sought to discover some central core of personhood as the proper object of their representation' (Brilliant 1991: 67). Freeland writes that portraiture resolves two potentially conflicting aims: the '*revelatory* aim' to accurately depict its subject and the '*creative* aim' to freely express the artist's stance on the portrait's subject. This first aim is already contradictory in itself: 'How can a subject, a person, ever be "revealed" in an image?' (Freeland 2007: 96-7). In the twentieth century, portraits became more likely to prioritize insight into the subject or artistic technique over accurate physical representation. Pablo Picasso obscured the faces of art dealers Ambroise Vollard and Daniel-Henry Kahnweiler with his cubist blocks, while Francis Picabia depicted the French artist Marie Laurencin as a schematic diagram of a machine.

If representational likeness is no longer essential to portraiture, then an abstract medium like music has the potential to depict human subjects. In his recent book *Musical Portraits*, Joshua Walden (2018) theorizes *musical* portraiture as a genre in addition to its more familiar visual and literary forms. Though music's inability to convey physical likeness would seem to put it at a disadvantage as a medium of portraiture, Walden argues that it can be particularly effective in capturing intangible properties of a person's character or essence. Both sound and image must resort to metaphor in order to depict these interior traits of the human subject. 'It is … precisely because identity is thought to reside beneath the surface, mapped onto but also hidden by the outward, visible aspect of the individual, that portraiture can operate without conveying a physical likeness at all' (9). Because music unfolds in time, it can outline a narrative or examine subjects at multiple points in their lives. In short, music can unlock entry to the invisible interiors visual portraits often sought to access.

Warhol as portrait artist

Though Warhol's images of celebrity women from the early 1960s are arguably his most familiar works, portraiture occupied him at every stage of his artistic career. Warhol's earliest work in portraiture began in his time as a fashion illustrator when he created advertisements and department store window displays. Warhol parlayed this commercial work drawing articles of clothing into depictions of people. Between 1955 and 1957 he drew a series of fanciful shoes and boots, naming them after celebrities he admired (e.g. James Dean, Truman Capote). These 'shoe portraits' garnered Warhol his first coverage in *Life* magazine (Warhol and Baume 1999: 100–9). By substituting a personal item for a person, Warhol tested portraiture's generic conventions. In the early 1960s, he continued to innovate by creating portraits based on widely available newspaper and magazine photographs. These served not merely as memory aids for hand-painted renderings but also as templates for the silk screens Warhol employed to further automate his work (Rosenblum 1999: 209). Warhol used this technique to produce the first of his famed Marilyn Monroe portraits following the actress's 1962 suicide. These silk screens establish techniques Warhol would use throughout his career as a portrait artist: garish and artificial colours, automation, multiplication and serialization. Brilliant argues that Warhol in some ways abdicates the portraitist's historical role as provider of psychological insight into the subject. *Marilyn Diptych* is actually more about celebrity and popular representation than it is about the actress (Brilliant also notes that 'Marilyn Monroe' was an alias). Warhol's technique obscures the subject; it distances us from her. 'Warhol's *Marilyn* is about image-making rather than portraiture because the work so clearly emphasizes the mechanism of popular representation in the modern age but not the person represented' (Brilliant 1991: 49). In contrast to traditional portrait artists, then, Warhol did not always interact with his subjects in the creation of their representations. During the 1960s – the most celebrated era of his work in portraiture – Warhol used familiar, mass-produced images rather than attempting to replicate a temporary pose or composite image that captures the subject.[3]

Warhol's prolific work in photography and film also continues the tradition of portraiture. Warhol acquired a Polaroid camera in the 1950s and used it to chronicle his activities and associates for the rest of his life. Between 1964 and 1966, he created nearly 500 films he called 'Screen Tests'. Screen Test subjects were instructed to remain still in front of a stationary camera, while close-up shots of their faces were recorded onto a single 100-foot reel of silent, black-and-white film. Critic and Warhol associate Henry Geldzahler, who sat for one of these hour-and-a-half-long endurance tests, later remarked that the resulting film had 'the quality of portraiture' (qtd. in *Andy Warhol* 1972), a movie designed to function more like a photograph or painting – to be looked at momentarily like a framed picture rather than watched from beginning to end. In fact, Warhol considered selling his screen tests as 'Living Portrait Boxes' (Warhol and Baume 1999: 88). Kenneth Goldsmith describes how Warhol's hybrid genre of portrait film eschewed typical experimental film-making techniques of the 1960s:

> The prevalent trend was the quick edit and jump cut, but Warhol did the opposite: he plunked the camera on a tripod and let it run ... and run ... and run ... There were no edits, no pans ... If you've seen his 3-minute screen tests, where the camera is fixed on a face, you can't but be persuaded by Warhol's point of view: they're among the most striking and gorgeous portraits ever made.
> (Goldsmith 2011: 145)

From the 1970s on, Warhol supported himself primarily as a portraitist for hire. In 1967, Geldzahler introduced Warhol to the Houston art manager Fred Hughes. Hughes began to manage Warhol's career the following year and remained in that role until the artist's untimely death two decades later. It was Hughes who introduced Warhol to wealthy socialites and celebrities, and who helped him secure lucrative portrait commissions. Warhol charged $25,000 for a forty-one-inch square portrait, and a fee of $15,000 for additional portraits using the same screen. Unlike the Marilyn portraits, these were created from a photograph taken by Warhol. Warhol freely admitted that these portraits were financially rather than artistically inspired (Geldzahler and Rosenblum 1993: 23–6). Their first complete exhibition was met with critical scorn, but more recent reconsiderations have argued that this distaste was for the wealthy and celebrated subjects of the portraits and the motivations behind them. In any case, portrait commissions occupied Warhol until the week he died. In his final entry of his posthumously published diary, he discussed a plan for bartering with trumpeter Miles Davis, whom he met at a fashion show: a portrait in exchange for ten minutes of music (Warhol 1989: 806).

Taking Warhol's likeness

While music alone cannot depict human physiognomy, the *Songs for Drella* project used images and descriptive text to give listeners a sense of Warhol's appearance. The 1989 BAM performances included slide projections of Warhol's art designed by the installation artist and set designer Jerome Sirlin. The entire multimedia show was captured in a film directed by Edward Lachman (*Songs for Drella* 1990). Within a week of these live appearances, Cale and Reed filmed the complete show, though this time without an audience. Warhol's artwork is intercut with footage of Reed and Cale performing to the empty theatre, and also projected on a screen behind them. This is one example of what Cale called 'picking up the threads of the Velvet Underground', returning to their early shows accompanying experimental films and enacting a more subdued version of the happenings organized by Warhol in the 1960s. The cover of the

Sire release repeats the themes of superimposed layers found in Warhol's art and in the album's narrative construction. A black-and-white photograph of Reed and Cale is superimposed on a black-on-black image of Warhol's face. All three men are shown as truncated torsos reminiscent of classical busts. Cale and Reed's expressions are neutral and unemotional, as is typical of subjects posing for formal portraits. Warhol's ghostly, barely perceptible face seems to loom above the two musicians. This part of the design hearkens back to the cover of the last album that Cale and Reed worked on together; *White Light/White Heat* (1968). That cover featured a photo of Warhol film actor Joe Spencer's tattooed arm taken by Factory photographer Billy Name. As it is on the cover of *Drella*, the image is nearly impossible to make out in most versions of the cover because of the black-on-black printing. Warhol himself used a similar tone-on-tone technique in a posthumous 1978 portrait of the art collector Norman Fisher. Rosenblum argues that this sombre colour palette was especially apt for a depiction of Fisher, who died of cancer at age thirty-nine (Rosenblum 1999: 213). Black on black was similarly appropriate for a Warhol memorial given the artist's unexpected and premature death.

In addition to its appearance as a ghostly background image on *Drella*'s cover, Warhol's physical likeness is a recurring theme in Reed's lyrics. Descriptions appear in album's opening tracks: 'Smalltown', which captures Warhol's youth in Pittsburgh and desire to escape to New York City, and 'Open House', which describes his early career in advertising and cultivation of an entourage through his studio's open-door policy. Reed's lyrics to both songs are narrated in first person and convey Warhol's lifelong struggle with body image. Biographers often link Warhol's negative physical self-perception to a childhood bout with Sydenham's chorea, or St. Vitus dance. This neurological disorder, which causes involuntary movements, kept Warhol home from school, a biographical detail alluded to in 'Open House'. He also suffered from chronic skin conditions that caused blotches to appear on his face. Indeed, his own later self-portraits were often overlaid with camouflage or other amorphous shapes that seem to either mirror or mask the flaws in his complexion. Reed's Drella details and expresses these hang-ups in some detail in 'Smalltown'. By 1953, Warhol had lost most of his hair, and resorted to wearing wigs (Koestenbaum 2001: 34). In 'Open House', Reed describes Warhol's silver-toned artificial hair as reminiscent of a watch from Tiffany's. Sirlin's slideshow in the staged BAM performance displays Billy Name's black-and-white photographs of Warhol, along with other Factory figures, during the performance of this song. The themes of Warhol's self-consciousness about his own appearance, enviousness of and fascination with people he found physically beautiful, and the relationship between appearance and inner character recur midway through the album. In 'Nobody but You', Reed as Drella wishes for a better chin, skin and nose. Another song in this vein is 'Faces and Names', a song whose title lists the two fundamental aspects of traditional portraiture. Warhol fantasizes about a world in which people's outward appearances, their faces and reputations, and their names are standardized to foster interaction without preconception or jealousy. In the song's lyrics Warhol perceives himself as an unexciting person behind a glamorous myth, usually disappointing those who meet him.

Warhol at work

When depicting another visual artist, it is common for a portraitist to imitate, represent or otherwise suggest the subject's own style or technique. Similarly, musical portraits of visual artists can fuse the subject with their working method, and draw parallels between the style of the artist and that of the composer (Walden 2018: 76). In several of the *Songs for Drella*, Cale and Reed's songwriting both describes and enacts Warhol's artistic practice. An example is *Drella*'s third track, 'Style It Takes', which musically depicts Warhol's artistic process of portrait making. It is the first song on the album sung by Cale, whose rather monotonous delivery seems to channel Warhol's famously affectless persona. Cale accompanies himself on piano in the BAM performances. On the album, he plays a similar keyboard part on synthesizer using a sustained string sound, and overdubs a viola descant. Reed adds to the texture with melodic finger-picked guitar lines. The song is structured in a standard thirty-two bar AABA form. One full iteration of the form is followed by a second chorus in which an outro replaces the final A phrase. Reed's lyrics name-check turning points in Warhol's art of the 1960s but also suggest his commissioned portraits of the 1970s and 1980s. Throughout the song, Cale-as-Warhol seems to be addressing patrons, sitters and subjects. The opening line establishes Warhol's transactional relationship with the addressee, effectively declaring that Warhol is not above profiting from the vanity of wealthy people. The portrait subject pays for Warhol's cachet, and Warhol feeds off of the subject's personal qualities and beauty: a mutually beneficial arrangement. The first B phrase directs an imaginary patron or sitter to participate in a Screen Test, and 'Drella' continually flatters his subject, telling them repeatedly how great they are. (As in the song, in interviews, Warhol typically described how great people were when asked his opinion [Goldsmith 2004: xv].) Cale's portrayal of Warhol through Reed's lyrics is complicated by the appearance of the Velvet Underground themselves in the final complete A phrase, with the fictional Warhol referencing the band's confrontational, grating sound. In the brief outro, Cale repeats variants on the title phrase, while Reed interjects speaking the monosyllabic titles of Warhol's erotic silent films of the early 1960s: *Kiss*, *Eat* and *Couch*.

'Style It Takes' references the Velvet Underground's early work musically as well as lyrically. The song's opening instrumental introduction is reminiscent of 'I'll Be Your Mirror', originally sung by Nico on the band's self-titled debut. Both 'Style' and 'Mirror' alternate between tonic and subdominant, with the harmony changing on the downbeat of each bar. Rhythmically, the gentle guitar melodies in the two songs are virtually identical. Given these musical similarities, it is tempting to draw comparisons between the two songs' lyrics. 'I'll Be Your Mirror' also has an unseen addressee who views their interior as grotesque. The song's first-person narrator claims to be capable of seeing that addressee's hidden beauty and reflecting it back to them. Thus, both 'Style' and 'Mirror' explore the relationship between interiors and exteriors, surface and depth, appearance and reality, beauty and ugliness. Both are about depending on another person for one's self-worth. One of the recurring phrases in 'Mirror', that mirrors reflect our real selves, might even serve as a kind of motto for the portrait artist.

Track four, 'Work', marks a shift in perspective in the *Drella* song cycle – it is the first of three songs told from Reed's rather than Warhol's point of view. As both lyrical narrator and vocalist, Reed describes his admiration for the older artist's discipline and work ethic, recalling advice that Warhol gave him as a young man. Again, the Velvet Underground's first album is referenced musically: Cale's piano accompaniment is rhythmically identical to that of 'All Tomorrow's Parties'. As I have argued elsewhere (2012: 21–69, 2015), the Velvets' hypnotic use of riffs and *ostinati* is a kind of musical analogue to Warhol's repetitious patterning. The song 'Images', which bisects the album, insists on the centrality of repetition and distancing to Warhol's work. The perspective has shifted back to Warhol, who describes his own repetitive aesthetic, with the same line itself repeated in the next two verses and again in the final coda. As vocalist, Reed's portrayal of a fictional Warhol seems in keeping with the song's title, as images are not real things but representations of them. Reed confirms this in the first verse when he sings that images are 'taken' from something else – a photograph or painting that is itself an image. These images are then replicated through mechanical processes of silk screening or film projection. Many of the images Warhol reproduced were portraits. Reed's lyrics briefly mention Warhol's altered copies of the iconic portrait of Mao Tse-Tung displayed at the Tian'anmen Gate in Beijing. Throughout 'Images', the duo's instrumental accompaniment parallels the lyrics' preoccupation with repetition, with Cale's relentless, oscillating viola accompaniment recalling 'The Black Angel's Death Song' from the Velvets' debut album.

'Forever Changed'

The second half of *Drella* documents the demise of the original Factory scene and Warhol's transformation from Pied Piper of New York City misfits to socialite. In 'Slip Away', aptly subtitled 'A Warning', Warhol, here portrayed by Reed, chafes against the suggestion that he should restrict entrance to the Factory for his own safety, worrying aloud that he will lose his inspiration if his workspace is no longer overrun by a bizarre cast of characters. Reed-as-Warhol also rejects the suggestion that he should exist in a state of fear, foreshadowing the subsequent track: 'I Believe'. 'I Believe' describes Valerie Solanas's 1968 attempt on Warhol's life. This horrific shooting marked a dramatic turning point for Warhol, who would live with the physical and psychological repercussions of the gunshot wounds he sustained for the rest of his life. But the 'I' in the title is not Warhol but Reed – it is the second of three songs told from the singer-songwriter's point of view. He expresses his desire for vengeance and payback in the shooting's immediate aftermath. Reed ends the song expressing his own guilt at not having visited Warhol in the hospital. Initially Reed portrays Warhol questioning why he didn't visit him in hospital, but by the song's outro, Warhol's voice seems to have reasserted itself as first-person narrator directly asking the same question. (Cale joins as backing vocalist on these words.) This song about the most pivotal moment in Warhol's life is more about Reed's reaction: his anger at Solanas, and his regret at having failed to comfort his mentor and friend. It also seems to conflate Reed's feelings of guilt from the late 1960s with the acrimony that developed between him and Warhol in the 1980s. Reed also expresses remorse in the album's final track, 'Hello It's Me', which is directed to Warhol. In one verse, he describes learning of the 1968 shooting, and in another, he sings that he regrets not spending more time with Warhol when he still could. This implies that Reed is talking to Warhol belatedly, only now that he has died. 'Hello It's Me' shows that one of the album's intended listeners is Warhol himself. Drella is both the subject and audience of this musical memorial portrait.

Drella's penultimate track, 'Forever Changed', sets to music the often-repeated assertion that Warhol was never the same after the attempted murder. Cale is lead vocalist here, and Warhol returns as first-person narrator. As in 'Style' and 'Work', the music is reminiscent of the Velvet Underground. The opening lyrical image of a train approaching a city paired with Cale's churning, insistent piano riff recall 'Train Round the Bend' from 1970's *Loaded*. 'Forever' discusses Warhol's international travels, and names several figures who supported him in his old age, including Geldzahler and 'superstar' Brigid Berlin. Drella also alludes to the negative critical reception of his work as a superficial portrait artist. At the song's conclusion, the tempo of Cale's piano riff slackens to suggest the train, and Warhol's life, gradually coming to a stop. In his autobiography, Cale wrote that the song felt equally applicable to his own life: 'I felt as if I was singing about myself as much as Andy. Specifically, my coming from Wales to New York and meeting members of the band' (Bockris and Cale 1999: 224).

'A Dream' and the *Diaries*

Warhol's diaries were posthumously published between Cale and Reed's workshop version of *Drella* at St. Ann's and the BAM performances. *The Andy Warhol Diaries* (1989) are a series of transcribed phone conversations with Warhol's long-time collaborator Pat Hackett.[4] This 800-page tome documents Warhol's life from 1976 to 1987 in intimate and mundane detail. He and Hackett spoke almost daily (excluding Saturdays and Sundays, though these were later recorded), and Warhol enumerated his activities and thoughts from the previous day: where he went, what he did and who he saw. Entries reveal his friendships with Bianca Jagger, Truman Capote, Jean-Michel Basquiat, heiress Catherine Guinness and fashion designer Roy Halston to name a few; his frequent visits to exclusive New York venues like 21 and Studio 54; and his work fulfilling portrait commissions and publishing *Interview*, the magazine he founded in 1969. In the *Diaries*, 'Society Andy' does not always appear in the most flattering light. They include his unvarnished assessments of people in his life – their artwork, appearance, body weight and intelligence. Adding to readers' exasperation, the book was first published without an index, forcing surviving friends and collaborators to pore over thousands of entries to learn what Warhol secretly thought of them.

Collectively, Cale, Reed and the Velvet Underground are mentioned roughly twenty-five times in the *Diaries*. Warhol's few remarks about Cale are uniformly positive, but his attitude towards Reed was more complex. Although diary entries from the 1970s mention the singer affectionately, Warhol's friendship with Reed sours by the book's conclusion. In the entry dated 10 March 1978, Warhol praised Reed's solo performance at the Bottom Line (albeit, in somewhat backhanded fashion by comparing it to inferior solo efforts):

> I was *(laughs) proud* of him. For once, finally, he's himself, he's not copying anybody. Finally he's got his own style. Now everything he does works, he dances better. Because when John Cale and Lou were the Velvets, they really had a style, but when Lou went solo he got bad and was copying people like Mick Jagger. But last night he did his song 'I Want to Be Black' – which never was good before but now it is.'[5]
>
> (116)

Four months later, Warhol admired Reed's new Christopher Street apartment after an impromptu visit, saying, 'oh, Lou's life is everything I want my life to be … and he's so sweet and so funny at the same time, so together, it's just incredible' (154). Warhol's opinion of Reed seems to have changed with the singer's marriage to Sylvia Morales in 1981. The Reeds apparently omitted Warhol from their wedding guest list, something that he mentioned to Hackett multiple times that year. He complained in the 29 March entry, 'oh, there was an article on Lou Reed in *People*. With his "British-born" wife. I still don't understand why I wasn't invited to the wedding. They had a big reception and everything' (368). Two weeks later, Warhol reported running into the couple on the street (he dismissed Sylvia Reed as 'nothing special') and asking Reed why he no longer called or visited (373). Judging by the diary, Reed and Warhol's relationship grew chillier as the 1980s wore on. Reed apparently snubbed Warhol at the 1984 MTV awards: 'Lou Reed sat in my row but never even looked over. I don't understand Lou, why he doesn't talk to me now' (599). By the diary's final mention of Reed in 1986, the two men seemed completely alienated from one another. On 20 September 1986, Warhol learned from Jane Holzer that Reed was shooting a video clip for MTV. (Holzer, a former Warhol 'superstar' from the Factory days, is the blonde woman in the pink dress in the video from the single 'The Original Wrapper' from *Mistrial*.) Hurt that he was not hired to participate, Warhol told Hackett, 'I hate Lou Reed more and more, I really do, because he's not giving us any video work' (759–60).

Reed seems to work through Warhol's complaints about him in 'A Dream', the album's longest and most narratively complex song, and the final addition to the *Drella* cycle. (It was composed between the workshop and the BAM versions as a response to the *Diaries* publication.) Unlike the formal, poetic song lyrics on the album's other tracks, 'A Dream' is structured in free prose as a fictional diary entry based in content and flavour on Hackett's transcriptions. Passages from the published *Diaries* are woven in as paraphrases and occasionally as verbatim quotations. Judith Peraino recently uncovered several archival demo tapes from the mid-1970s that show Reed using Warhol's words and character in his own lyrics. Reed recorded several songs reacting to the recently published book *The Philosophy of Andy Warhol: From A to B and Back Again* (1975). These songs, which Peraino dubs the 'Philosophy Songs', freely quote or react to the text in *The Philosophy*, another collaboration with Hackett. Peraino (2019) writes that 'while *Drella* bears no musical or lyrical resemblance to the "Philosophy Songs" beyond the use of Warhol as the first-person lyrical subject ... They do represent Reed's first large-scale attempt to write songs in Warhol's voice' (424, n. 59).

Cale recites Reed's text in 'A Dream', with the two accompanying the spoken-word monologue with echoing, arrhythmic interjections on piano and guitar. The track's sonic atmosphere is ethereal, in keeping with the text. The proximity of the *Diaries* publication and *Drella*'s complete live premiere at BAM prompted queries from reporters about the status of the men's relationship. Reed was, by all accounts, characteristically prickly when asked about this, growling at one reporter, 'I don't answer questions like that ... I don't want to get into my relationship with Warhol' (Leland 1989). Despite Reed's evasiveness, 'A Dream' was understood as a kind of collective therapy session. Reviewing the album for the *Washington Post*, Mark Jenkins wrote, 'Warhol's diaries, with explicit griping about Reed and Cale (and most everyone else), were published while this project was underway, and the duo decided to deal with their hostility by reading directly from them' (Jenkins 1990).

The song's premise and combination of real and fictional diary entries make 'A Dream' both intertextual and metadiegetic: intertextual because it draws loosely on material from Warhol's diary (itself complicated by Hackett as transcriber and mediator), metadiegetic because it has multiple narrative voices and levels. Cale portrays Warhol through Reed's adaptation of the diaries. Reed's text captures many of Warhol's verbal tics, such as his tendency to preface statements with the word 'gee'. But while Cale's delivery has something of Warhol's famously flat affect, it is not a Warhol impersonation. He maintains his characteristically low vocal register and does not suppress his Welsh accent. This is not a dramatic actor's portrayal of Warhol such as David Bowie's in the biopic *Basquiat* (1996) or Jared Harris' in *I Shot Andy Warhol* (1996). Thus, the track feels a bit like a reading from the *Diaries* (indeed, many commentators misheard it as such), with Cale retaining his identity as both the narrator and a character within the song. In addition, Reed's text contains nested narrative levels. The fictional Warhol seems to relate the previous day's activities as he did during his phone conversations with Hackett, who is implied as the addressee, but never explicitly mentioned. Within the diary entry, the fictional Warhol introduces a second narrative level when he begins to relate a nightmare. It begins with Warhol awakening in the middle of the night by his two pet Dachshunds. Already, the distinction between the two narrative realms is blurred – he is dreaming about having been asleep. In the dream, Warhol resolves to photograph the snow falling outside. He observes long-time friends Billy Name and Brigid Berlin beneath his staircase, which in the dream world has been transformed into a small meadow. Warhol calls to Name and Berlin, but they do not answer. The nightmare here is one of abandonment – throughout the dream Warhol's friends seem not to hear or know him. Warhol's entire telling of the dream is interrupted by asides and digressions, which seem to bring Warhol out of the dream and into the real world. He compares the dream world's imaginary meadow to a real park in the city, and this leads him to an idea for an *Interview* magazine feature ('maybe we should do an article on that in the magazine'). In other words, the fictional Warhol vividly remembers the thoughts that went through his head in his dream: internal monologue is nested within a dream told in a phone conversation.

Cale and Reed join Name and Berlin in Warhol's dream world. Here, fact and fiction are further blurred together as passages from the real Warhol's diary enter the fictional Warhol's dream. Reed's text paraphrases or quotes passages from the published diary that mention himself, Cale or their defunct rock band. Cale appears first, with the fictional Warhol commenting on Cale's healthy demeanour, and discussing their shared exercise regime.[6] With a slight note of disapproval, the fictional Warhol discusses an album cover commission from the singer, and how his black-and-white original design was colorized against his recommendation. (This album alluded to here is Cale's 1981 solo release *Honi Soit*.) Reed's prose seems modelled on the *Diaries* entry dated 30 October 1980: 'At the office John Cale came over, he wanted me to do an album cover for him. He's looking good. He had a girl with him. I signed all his old record covers' (339). The 'Dream' Warhol's discussion of Cale leads to another digression, this time about the Velvet Underground, with Warhol discussing the venues they played during their mutual association in the 1960s. Here again, Reed's fictional text is drawn from life. During a trip to San Francisco in February 1977, Warhol briefly mentions in the *Diaries* a gallery near Top of the Mark restaurant, remembering that it was 'where we used to stay with the Velvets' (26). In the 10 August 1982 entry, he reported,

> Wandered around the East Village and that made me feel weird ... I thought about the fifties when I lived on St. Mark's Place and then about the sixties when we ran the Dom discotheque there with the Velvets and Nico playing, and about going to all those psychedelic things at the Fillmore and eating at Ratner's delicatessen and everything. It was nostalgic.
>
> (457)

Warhol's musings in 'A Dream' move from these old haunts to the Velvets' debut album. From 1981 the *Diaries* show him trying to recoup some sort of financial benefit from the record, which had grown from obscurity to legend since its initial 1967 release. In the 3 August 1981 diary entry, Warhol reports entering a Fifth Avenue record store that happened to be piping in the record.

> I don't know if they saw me coming and then put it on quickly or if it was already on. It was so strange to hear Lou singing those songs and the music still sounds so good. It brought me back. Then they asked me to sign the album. It's still the original cover with the banana that you can peel the skin off. Does MGM keep reissuing it? I never got any money at all from that record.
>
> (398)

By 1985, Warhol was scheming about extracting money by selling the master tapes, monetizing old video footage of the band or encouraging a reunion. (Reed rejected the reunion idea while Warhol was still alive, much to the artist's disappointment.) In the entry for 25 April of that year, he complained, 'I mean, I just don't understand why I have never gotten a penny from that first Velvet Underground record. That record really sells and I was the producer! Shouldn't I get something? I mean, shouldn't I?' (645). Reed's text in 'A Dream' combines quotations and paraphrases from these two passages.

Reed himself is the final character to appear before the fictional Warhol in 'A Dream.' In this portion of the text, Reed seems to fixate on the *Diaries*' most negative statements about him. He lists the times when Warhol felt slighted by Reed: being left out of the wedding, the video filming and the MTV awards. Reed juxtaposes one of the earliest and most positive mentions of him in the Diaries – from 1978 – with the final and most bitter from 1986. He portrays Warhol as conflicted, feeling hatred for Reed but also pride on other occasions. Reed captured Warhol's sensitivity to abandonment and betrayal, and his own guilt at his callousness and neglect of his former mentor. On 'Hello It's Me', *Drella*'s concluding track, Reed drops the mask entirely and sings directly to Warhol about his regrets and resentments.

Aftermath

Much like the Velvets' albums, *Drella*'s release was a critical success and commercial flop. As one reviewer wrote while awarding it an A+ rating, 'Its uncompromising austerity ensures that it won't get much airplay' (Tremblay 1990). In his autobiography, Cale attributes at least part of the lacklustre sales to their failure to tour with the record. His reconciliation with Reed had been temporary. By the time their studio work on *Drella* was completed, the pair had decided never to work together again. However, the Cartier Foundation asked the pair to perform at a Warhol Exposition being organized in Paris. Because the exhibit featured a full room devoted to the Velvet Underground, all four band members were flown, all expenses paid, to France for the retrospective. Cale and Reed had agreed to perform some of *Drella* at the event and decided at the last moment to invite Sterling Morrison and Maureen Tucker onstage with them for a song. The result was an impromptu, unrehearsed, thirteen-minute rendition of 'Heroin' (Bockris and Malanga 2002: 210). The four members continued contributing to one another's solo efforts (e.g. Morrison backed Cale in a 1992 appearance on *The Tonight Show*), and the entire band started rehearsing their old material together the same year. Thus, *Songs for Drella* sowed the seeds of the Velvets' 1993 reunion tour of Europe, including the live album recorded over three nights at L'Olympia in Paris.

Conclusion

Portraits are compelling because they make absent people present. They preserve appearances and names for posterity. They let viewers in on the intimacy and physical proximity that existed between artist and subject. The artist's gaze at the subject is transferred to us as we observe the portrait. Portraits invite us to reflect on questions of identity and its relationship to outward appearance. Perhaps this is what drew Warhol to the genre of portraiture. The *Songs for Drella* project accomplishes for Warhol what Warhol's own portraits achieved in the media of painting, film and photography did for his subjects. Reed's lyrics help listeners visualize the artist's appearance. The project grants listeners psychological insight into Warhol, and shows how his outer shell affected his self-image (e.g. 'Faces and Names'). *Drella* analyses Warhol the artist as well as Warhol the person. Songs like 'Style It Takes', 'Work' and 'Images' show us Warhol at work, and enumerate the genres (e.g. screen tests) and techniques (e.g. multiplication, serialization) he employed. Sirlin's slide projections from the BAM performance linked images of Warhol's art with the songs, and hearkened back to Cale and Reed's original collaborations with the artist. Warhol's work in portraiture involved distancing, layering and unexpected uses and combinations of media: celebrity head shots reprinted in magazines and newspapers are silk-screened in multiples; posed photos become templates for silk screens; film becomes a medium of portraiture through stasis and temporal extension. *Drella* employs an unexpected medium – music – to create a portrait. Its nested narrative layers and adaptations of Warhol's own writing (especially in 'A Dream') seem analogous to the layers and adaptations found in Warhol's visual art. A contemporary review recognized Reed's work on the album as both portraiture and of self-portraiture: 'Here he goes beyond capturing his own experience – difficult enough – and gives us a complex portrait of a human being who also happened to be a pop star artist and a friend ... it says as much about Reed as it does about Drella' (Tremblay 1990).

Holly Solomon said of Warhol's portrait of her: 'I always think of the painting as my Warhol, before I think of it as my portrait' (Warhol and Baume 1999: 86). Geldzahler once asked the art critic Robert Rosenblum whether he saw Marilyn or Andy when looking at one of Warhol's portraits of Monroe. Rosenblum replied, 'I can think of two things at once.' It's difficult to look at a portrait by Warhol and see only its subject – we see both people at once. As Geldzahler writes, 'Andy and his subject matter remain identical in our minds' (Geldzahler and Rosenblum 1993: 13). An art patron desiring merely an accurate representation of their appearance would not commission a portrait from Andy Warhol. What those who paid for his work wanted was part of him, as Warhol was well aware. In the same way, *Drella* gives listeners more than a Warhol biography (though it functions quite well as such) – it is Warhol's life glimpsed through a Velvet Underground recording. The portraitist and portrait subject fuse, making it impossible to hear or see only one. For Cale and Reed, Warhol's life story is intertwined with theirs, making *Songs for Drella* a fusion of biography and autobiography, portrait and self-portrait.

Notes

1 Cale and Reed had interacted intermittently and performed live together over the years.
2 Maureen Tucker also paid tribute to Warhol on her debut solo album, *Life in Exile after Abdication* (1989) with the song 'Andy'. Reed's 'Dime Store Mystery' from

New York (1989) discusses Warhol's death less directly, though contains a reference to Warhol's funeral service.
3   While Warhol's depictions of Marilyn Monroe and Elizabeth Taylor are better known, Henry Geldzahler notes that the artist's earliest portraits featuring human visages were of men rather than glamorous women. The diptych of actor Troy Donahue, for example, predates the Monroe silkscreens. Noting that Donahue was widely rumoured to be gay, Geldzahler speculates that this and other portraits are in fact Warhol's idealized versions of himself, a strategy of displacing his own desire for the subject, or 'an act of sleight-of-hand to divert other people's curiosity about his own personal life' (Geldzahler and Rosenblum 1993: 18).
4   Hackett also co-authored his memoir *Popism*. Koestenbaum (2001) speculates that Warhol was an undiagnosed dyslexic, perhaps explaining the collaborative nature of many of his books.
5   The song Warhol references appears on Reed's solo record *Street Hassle* (1978). Its confrontational lyrics satirize white racist stereotypes of Black men.
6   Warhol worked out regularly with a personal trainer and encouraged Cale to join him when the singer was attempting to get sober in the 1980s (Bockris and Cale 1999: 214).

References

Bockris, V. and Cale, J. (1999), *What's Welsh for Zen? The Autobiography of John Cale*, London: Bloomsbury.
Bockris, V. and Malanga, G. (2002), *Up-Tight: The Story of the Velvet Underground*, 2nd edn, London: Omnibus.
Brilliant, R. (1991), *Portraiture*, Cambridge, MA: Harvard University Press.
Freeland, C. (2007), 'Portraits in Painting and Photography', *Philosophical Studies: An International Journal for Philosophy in the Analytic Tradition*, 135 (1): 95–109.
Geldzahler, H. and Rosenblum, R. (1993), *Andy Warhol: Portraits of the Seventies and Eighties*, New York: Thames and Hudson.
Goldsmith, K. (2004), *I'll Be Your Mirror: The Selected Andy Warhol Interviews: 1962-1987*, New York: Carroll & Graf.
Goldsmith, K. (2011), *Uncreative Writing: Managing Language in the Digital Age*, New York: Columbia University.
Holden, S. (1989), 'Recalling a Pop Artist and a Friend', *New York Times*, section c, 22.
Jenkins, M. (1990), 'Rock's Die-hard Death Songs: Reed & Cale's "Drella," Elias's "Requiem"', *The Washington Post*, 25 April, b07.
Koestenbaum, W. (2001), *Andy Warhol*, New York: Penguin.
Leland, J. (1989), 'Warhol and the Velvets songs for "Drella": Lou Reed and John Cale Pay Tribute to Their Late "Co-conspirator"', *Newsday*, 26 November, 11.
Lindau, E. (2012), '"Repetition without Tedium"? The Velvet Underground's Rock "n" Roll Minimalism', in 'Art Is Dead. Long Live Rock! Avant-Gardism and Rock Music, 1967–99', PhD diss, University of Virginia, Charlottesville.
Lindau, E. (2015), 'Review: The Velvet Underground 45th Anniversary Super Deluxe Editions', *Journal of the Society for American Music*, 9 (4): 517–21.

Peraino, J. A. (2019), 'I'll Be Your Mixtape: Lou Reed, Andy Warhol, and the Queer Intimacies of Cassettes', *Journal of Musicology*, 36 (4): 401–36.

Reed, L. (2008), *Pass Thru Fire: The Collected Lyrics*, Cambridge, MA: Da Capo.

Rosenblum, R. (1999), 'Andy Warhol: Court Painter to the 70s', in *On Modern American Art: Selected Essays*, 205–16, New York: Abrams.

Tremblay, M. (1990), 'Recent Releases: Lou Reed/John Cale: Songs for Drella (Sire/WEA)', *Calgary Herald*, 3 May, H5.

Walden, J. (2018), *Musical Portraits: The Composition of Identity in Contemporary and Experimental Music*, New York: Oxford University Press.

Warhol, A. (1975), *The Philosophy of Andy Warhol: From A to B and Back Again*, Orlando: Harcourt.

Warhol, A. (1989), *The Andy Warhol Diaries*, ed. P. Hackett, New York: Warner.

Warhol, A. and Baume, N. (1999), *About Face: Andy Warhol Portraits*, Hartford, CT: Wadsworth Atheneum.

16

The late musical voice: John Cale and Lou Reed in the twenty-first century

Sean Albiez

This chapter examines John Cale and Lou Reed's music and live performances in the twenty-first century and their recurrent attempts to move forward into new creative territory while simultaneously coming to terms with the overbearing legacy of the Velvet Underground and their own solo work. While Cale often speaks with regret about the Velvet Underground as a radical project that terminated in 1968 on his departure from the band, he has subsequently explored the progressive potential of balancing rock and the avant-garde in his solo releases, production work and collaborations. Reed was more equivocal and often less vocal in interviews on the subject of the Velvet Underground, but in the last thirteen years of his life, in his studio and live work, he likewise took on projects ranging across his rock, literary and avant-garde interests. In the twenty-first century both balanced this forward-looking creativity with a desire to remediate and curate their past musical selves, but in interviews in this period there is a marked anti-nostalgia and very little sentimentality concerning their earlier lives.

This study aims to build on the work of Richard Elliott's (2015) *The Late Voice: Time, Age and Experience in Popular Music*, which sought to 'connect age, experience and lateness with particular performers and performance traditions via the identification and analysis of "late voice" in singers and songwriters of mid- to late twentieth century popular music' (4). Although much can and has been said about Cale and Reed's vocal performances in their twenty-first-century work, this study shifts the focus from the voice to the *late musical voice*. That is, their late creative priorities and strategies within (though sometimes outside) music-making, and how these are represented to the public through their work and media interviews. In emphasizing their late musical voices and how they reflected on their work in this period, interviews and other media coverage from post-2000 will be the main sources used in the study. This is partly a response to Elliott's concern that in studying well-known artists such as Cale and Reed, 'the popular discourse' around an artist is 'saturated in cultural and historical context', and so it is therefore 'strategically necessary to remove that context and consider these artists and their work in our current context'. For this study, the 'current context' is admittedly broad, and much of the post-2000 media coverage 'contextually saturated', but by focusing on the narratives and critical thoughts of Cale and Reed published in this period, we can consider how their 'current' and retrospective commentary provided insights into their work in later life.

Don't look back

As Elliott (2015: 231) argues musical artists in later life are constantly confronted with the need to consider, assess and revise their earlier selves and ongoing creative identities on record and in performance. Audiences have expectations that the artist will honour their past while creating new music and might perhaps recapture aspects of their earlier selves in new releases. He also suggests that an artist is continually 'in dialogue with a younger self (and vice versa)' and they try to find ways of 'getting over, moving on from, mocking, admonishing or respecting' their creative pasts. In understanding the reflective stance of artists in this dialogue, it is important to consider the complexity of nostalgic engagement with these pasts. Boym (2001) suggests that rather than viewing nostalgia simply as a longing for past times, there are two potential ways of viewing an individual's nostalgic feelings – through *restorative* and *reflective* modes. In simple terms, restorative nostalgia aims to recapture and rebuild a past time, whereas reflective nostalgia concerns the emotive acts of remembrance, longing and loss (41). Boym further argues that '[n]ostalgia tantalizes us with its fundamental ambivalence; it is about the repetition of the unrepeatable, materialization of the immaterial' (xvii) and 'it is a yearning for a different time … [it] is a rebellion against the modern idea of time, the time of history and progress' (xv). If there is evidence of yearning in Cale and Reed's reflections on their pasts, Cale perhaps appears to look back to his Welsh heritage, but in no way wants to repeat it, and Reed has a nostalgia for the music of his youth. However, little else is obviously nostalgic in their engagement with their personal or recorded pasts. Reed's return to past works was through an audiophile obsession to perfect the sound of his album mixes, and Cale's aim is often to continually remediate and reimagine his earlier work, with little reverence shown to the past.

Perhaps Davis' (1979) notion of 'interpreted nostalgia' can help us to understand their perspective. Interpreted nostalgia 'moves beyond issues of the historical accuracy or felicity of the nostalgic claim on the past and, even as the reaction unfolds, questions and, potentially at least, renders problematic the very reaction itself' (24). This reflexive, critical stance appears closer to that taken by Cale and Reed than any simple sense of nostalgia as uncritical celebration of, or longing for, the past. Furthermore, Keightley and Pickering (2006: 935) argue it is wrong to look for a 'final or unitary definition' of nostalgia as it can contain popular notions of the term as well as those that are more complex and critical. They propose that by questioning the often positive connotations and multiplicity of meanings of the term, a more useful understanding arises. That is, nostalgia can be understood not as a simple desire to return to the past but as a way to 'recognize aspects of the past as the basis for renewal and satisfaction in the future. Nostalgia can then be seen … [as] … a means of taking one's bearings for the road ahead in the uncertainties of the present' (921). Keightley and Pickering (2012) also offer a nuanced understanding of how we continually construct and reconstruct our sense of identity and self, as we edit ourselves in the present from memories and experiences:

> the individual subject acts not only as an authorial self, continually scripting the story of a particular life, but also as a sort of editor-in-chief of the memories made to matter and cohere in the preferred version of who we think we are.
> (qtd. in Elliott 2015: 34)

Noting this and considering Cale and Reed's construction of a 'preferred version' of themselves, Moglen's work provides a way of understanding the complexity of our constructed identities as we age, and 'starts to see the potential for a non-linear model of ageing, one disarticulated from a rigid chronology and characterized, instead, by relations, moments, experience and memory' (Gardner 2020: 66). Even if Cale and Reed demonstrate ambivalence or distaste for the past in interviews, as with anybody else, their identity and musical voice are continually made and remade through fragmented and overlapping inner monologues and creative dialogues in the present. As Moglen (2008) outlines,

> Ageing … takes place across a lifetime that begins with conception and ends with death. It is a multiple, ambiguous, and contradictory process, which provides us – continuously and simultaneously – with images of past, present, lost, embodied, and imagined selves … It is possible to see … [the] ageing self as a dynamic multiplicity of innumerable selves: a compilation that is subject to endless, subterranean revision.
> (303–4)

Cale recognized this overlapping multiplicity when saying of the Velvet Underground, 'I can't turn my back on it … I can't deny that it was there. I'm not scouting for projects about my past, it's natural that I'm asked. You keep thinking it's over and guess what? It never is' (Hasted 1997). Baars (2012) underlines this by stating,

> Even if the time ahead is regarded as equally exciting or even more so, the past will remain important in shaping the future. Since we have become whoever we are, questions of identity will also concern the past; a past that is, however, never over or completed because the changes that are inherent in aging also change the perception of the past.
> (151)

The notion that the past is never over or completed is central to understanding Cale and Reed in the twenty-first century – always looking forward, sometimes sideways and, inevitably, reluctantly looking backwards. Both transformed their musical and creative voices while coming to terms with the drag of memory, sometimes revisiting older ideas in newer contexts or embarking on radical reinventions that were always, in part, a response to earlier inventions.

John Cale

In the period following the 1993 Velvet Underground reunion, Cale produced one solo rock album (*Walking on Locusts* 1996) but otherwise concentrated on composing a number of film scores, doing production work (with Siouxsie and the Banshees and Goya Dress), performing his own music and taking part in spoken word and film music performances. He contributed music to an opera about the life of Mata Hari, composed music for a Nico Ballet (released on CD as *Dance Music*), acted in the film *Rhinoceros Hunting in Budapest* and performed music to accompany Andy Warhol films with Sterling Morrison and Moe Tucker, released as *Eat/Kiss: Music for the Films of Andy Warhol* (but without Morrison, who died before the performance captured on the CD). His 1999 autobiography, *What's Welsh for Zen*, co-written with Victor Bockris, revealed many details about his life, career, personal and creative struggles and trauma as a child that complicated any nostalgia inherent in this excavation of his past. At the turn of the millennium, influenced by new studio digital technologies that he had encountered in his soundtrack work and other projects, he began recording material for solo releases. Cale recognized how new digital recording technologies afforded innovative compositional and sound design techniques to help him streamline and transform his studio practice. In 1999 Cale discussed his future musical plans to embrace new technologies but not fully bow to the norms of current music-making:

> I still want to twist pop out of shape. But ... I can't just hop, skip and jump around contemporary tastes. Loops are what people are interested in nowadays. My next album will have a lot of that ... but what I like about looping is not what everybody else likes. I really love drums that are slowed down, that's all I need.
>
> (Bockris and Cale: 265)

Cale's route into new music technologies was through his film score work 'that really helped drive the technology and the software and made me very familiar with it and I got fast at it and better at it. When it came the time to writing songs it seemed to be a piece of cake writing music' (qtd. in Heron 2008). This resulted in several releases that were influenced by currents in 1990s and early 2000s electronica and by artists such as Beck and the Beta Band, as well as the production sound of Hip Hop.

The importance of the digital audio workstation [DAW] (e.g. Pro Tools, Logic) for transforming Cale's production practice shouldn't be underestimated. DAWs afford complex editing, sound processing, sampling and compositional strategies that impact on music production in a number of ways. Central to DAW production is the fact that any recording, loop, sample or sonic fragment can be endlessly manipulated, layered and edited, drawing parallels to the way our sense of self is likewise constantly remade through similar processes. Discrete sound materials are forms of recorded memory, complete with environmental noise captured in the moments of creation. These sound memories are worked over, reversed, looped, cut and pasted much like our internal editing of memories and life narratives as outlined by Keightley and Pickering (2012).

In the mid-2000s Cale had specifically become drawn to Hip Hop as a form and to its production practices. In several interviews he spoke of Snoop Dog, Pharrell, Eminem, Lupe Fiasco, Kokane, Chingo Blingo, Not the 1s and Southern Hip Hop as particular favourites. He observed that 'what I've learned from Pharrell is that you really have, like, three or four elements in the song. There have been very successful epic productions, but the hip-hop guys, they have very little going on, and it's all in the angle of the work' (qtd. in Locker 2012). He also noted how he increasingly used an Akai MPC drum machine/sampler, an iconic standalone production instrument central to Hip Hop's history. After the Pro Tools, computer based *5 Tracks* e.p. and *HoboSapiens*, he used the MPC to generate grooves and beats as the foundation of songs created in the studio. When discussing his compositional process on the *Shifty Adventures in Nookie Wood* (2012) album, he stated,

> You pull out the MPC, you plug it in, and you see how far you get. And once you have a groove that works, then you start building the blocks – are you putting a synthesizer on there? Or are you putting on a real guitar? And even after you put on a real guitar, you screw around with it and use your software to make it sound like something entirely different.
>
> (qtd. in Deusner 2012)

In composing using sampling and samplers such as the MPC, Katz (2011) argues that 'composers who work with samples work directly with sound, thus becoming more like their counterparts in the visual and plastic arts … Sampling is a rich and complex practice, one that challenges our notions of originality, of borrowing, of craft, and even of composition itself' (157).

Across Cale's post-2000 solo studio albums, he worked alongside co-producers rooted in contemporary production practices such as Nick Franglen of Lemon Jelly, who had worked with Björk, Primal Scream and Hole, and Mike Petralia, who in this period collaborated with Beck, Ladytron and Peaches among others. These creative relationships enabled Cale to reposition his music in the present as well as question and develop his past practice: 'You get something out of other people by working with them, and in turn get something out of yourself you wouldn't have normally done … It's always a very revealing experience' (qtd. in Wray 2011). However, it is important to emphasize that in the 2000s, Cale didn't simply chase musical trends or disappear into avant-garde experimentation as Scott Walker and David Sylvian had done. Cale still retained an avant-rock, avant-pop desire to merge his popular music and avant-garde interests, keeping them in balance across his work. I will now briefly consider Cale's solo releases of new material in this period before moving on to discuss his rereleases and live performances up until the present.

5 Tracks (2003) to Lazy Days (2020)

The release of the *5 Tracks* e.p. (2003a) marked Cale's return to solo releases after *Walking on Locusts* (1996) and was a conscious attempt to bring his music 'back into the arena of writing and performing rock music' (Mitchell 2003: 196). There is little evidence of Cale's experimentalism on the *Locusts* album. It is smoothly produced and arranged with jazz and slide guitar embellishments, and an absence of avant-garde techniques either in the vocal performances or in the sonic environment. The *5 Tracks* e.p. capitalized on his newfound enthusiasm for experimentalism, with the first four tracks presenting us with soundscapes combining highly processed instruments and vocals, and sampled percussion and noise in multi-layered, accumulative productions. For example, the lazy drum and percussion loops, smooth and mellifluous guitar textures, delicate wordless female vocal performance and arpeggiated synthesizer of 'Verses' give way to industrial noise, with highly processed vocals that are sung and screamed in an incongruous middle eight section. 'Waiting for Blonde' samples ambient city and subway sounds, with a slowed drum loop, dub bass and dry and distorted vocals. A viola drone and barely comprehensible words float in the distance, processed as though through a walkie-talkie. 'Chums of Dumpty' combines glitchy, delicate drums followed by heavier sounds, wah-wah guitar and processed guitar chords, string and piano layers and indistinct vocals. 'E is Missing' blends acoustic guitar, strings, synthesizer, highly processed guitar sound, loops of noise and percussion, and heavy eq processing on Cale's vocal. Throughout the e.p. sound is treated as malleable and is processed through digital effects for textural interest, with little emphasis on what might be termed authentic or pure sound. As Cale observed, '[t]he thing I like about digital is that if you really want to, you can carve it' (qtd. in Doyle 2006). This approach would become a key technique in his following releases.

HoboSapiens (2003b) was described by *PopMatters* as 'dense and difficult for much of its running time, but the challenge comes from following the author through his many compositional twists ... Cale has always been strongest when he's subverting pop rather than ignoring it altogether' (PopMatters Staff 2004). The album was diverse, overflowing with ideas and production tweaks, and balanced accessible pop/rock ('Reading My Mind', 'Twilight Zone', 'Things' and 'Over Her Head') with more sonically adventurous material ('Look Horizon', 'Magritte' and 'Letter from Abroad'). Throughout the album Cale's previous multi-layered production approach, first developed on his arrangements and production for Nico, and explored on his 1983 album *Music for a New Society*, is presented in a disciplined, detailed and more complex manner, afforded by the precision, clarity and control of Pro Tools production.

Black Acetate (2005), produced in collaboration with Herb Graham Jr and Mickey Petralia, saw Cale reflecting on *HoboSapiens*, building on his sonic experimentalism but also encouraging studio play outside the computer environment: 'no matter how much I tried to deconstruct it, [HoboSapiens is] a creature of the studio ... So I changed my direction, I went into the funky side of things. The thing about [the] MPC popped up' (Hall 2005). Although Cale still created beats, employed sound design and layered sonic textures ('Brotherman', 'Satisfied', 'Hush', 'Gravel Drive', 'Wasteland', 'Mailman'), the album also has a number of rock songs with a deceptive band feel ('For a Ride', 'In a Flood', 'Perfect', 'Sold Motel') that recall Cale's music of the late 1970s as well as early 1990s grunge ('Woman', 'Turn the Lights On'). Cale said that the album 'was kind of a one-man-band issue ... we weren't doing ensemble playing, I was writing in the studio. We were working on making our own grooves'. However, he also found problems with the combinations of style and sound, noting that with the song 'Woman', in a live context 'it benefits from just having a good rock & roll band whack it out, rather than trying to do hip-hop' (Doyle 2006a). Reflecting on the diversity of style and sound on *Black Acetate*, Cale indicated how he liked 'finding new styles of expression, whether it's with lyrics or music. I like the new combinations ... That's the rubric generally. If I'm interested in what I'm doing then I think other people will be interested in it' (qtd. in Phillips 2006).

Cale's first release – *EP: Extra Playful* (2011a) – on Domino Records came after a period that included touring his *Paris 1919* (1973) album, and rather than reconnecting with the orchestral lushness of this release, he seemed to 'take a reactionary leap into the opposite direction, to further explore the deconstructed electronic productions and mechanized power pop' (Berman 2011) of *Black Acetate*. However, despite Cale's evident interest in creative studio play, he wanted to simply 'write better songs ... I mean as soon as I've finished with a song, it's over, and I've got to find another hook that I like, another groove that I like. There's lots out there. I need to grab them' (qtd. in Barry 2011). On what drives this quest for the next song, Cale stated, 'I still haven't found the perfect topic to take control of, the perfect balance of music and words. This is something I'm still looking for' (qtd. in Wray 2011). *EP: Extra Playful* capitalized on Cale's earlier innovations and lessons learned. Lucas (2011) identified the 'playful' pop direction of the first two songs 'Catastrofuk' and 'Whaddya Mean by That' that sounded 'more fun, excited and full of joie de vivre than anything else in Cale's extensive discography'. The following three tracks are viewed as a 'shift back towards Cale's experimental roots' combining jazz, gospel, spoken word vocals, drones, synthesizers and the sonic processing of vocals (specifically autotune) and instruments found in his previous twenty-first-century releases.

The album *Shifty Adventures in Nookie Wood* (2012) further explored the techniques of the *EP: Extra Playful* and was characterized by Deusner (2012) as '[a] pan-musical exploration of time and violence' that drew 'ideas and inspiration from seemingly every corner of the globe and every period in pop history' and tried 'to encapsulate the full breadth of Cale's storied career'. The album again saw Cale focusing on sound design. He indicated that 'there's a lot of software I can use to create strange noises, taking normal instruments and twisting them into something else', and on exploring the Akai MPC he said, 'I love the way hip-hop drives the funk by making the backbeat really lazy. On most digital drum machines there's a button that says "swing" on it and that gives you the amount of lateness or laziness on the backbeat.' He also revisited and integrated the viola drone as a key component of the album: 'I decided to go to town and use it as often as I can ... A lot of records use technology to make use of all sorts of noises – traffic, everything – but the viola can do that anyway without really telling you what it is. It's like a tapestry behind the song' (qtd. in Jonze 2012).

From 2012 Cale was involved in a number of projects, and there were reports in interviews of a forthcoming album, with sessions and songs completed. However, with the global Covid pandemic overtaking matters, plans were put on hold. Cale responded with the release of a single 'Lazy Day', commenting,

> [a]s a songwriter my truth is all tied-up in and through those songs that must wait a while longer. And then it occurred to me that I do have something for the moment … With the world careening out of its orbit I wanted to stop the lurch and enjoy a period where we can take our time and breathe our way back into a calmer world.
>
> (Domino Records 2020)

'Lazy Day' is an avant-pop song that drifts over a sluggish beat. The song sonically represents the locked-down landscape of 2020 where the world slammed on its brakes, and uses complex multi-layered, processed vocals in seemingly developing a humanistic, emotional commentary on events within the context of a meandering, listless song.

Sun Blindness Music, *Music for a New Society/M:FANS* and *Fragments of a Rainy Season*

While Cale was forging ahead in his music-making, subverting pop and experimenting with sound, three re-releases were valuable in affording a better understanding of Cale's 1960s avant-garde achievements (*Sun Blindness Music*), providing an opportunity to remediate and reconstruct a key solo album (*Music for a New Society/M:FANS*), and also to take a more traditional route in curating an expanded release of the live album *Fragments of a Rainy Season*.

Sun Blindness Music (2001) was the first time a wider public could experience Cale's innovative sound exploration from 1965 to 1968, where he experimented and improvised outside the context of the Velvet Underground. The first track 'Sun Blindness Music' is a forty-two-minute improvisation with a Vox electronic organ, creating drones from clusters of simultaneously played notes. Buckman (2001) noted that Cale created 'a dissonant wash of noise … with an escalating build of resonant, booming drones; other times, drones disintegrate into silence', and observed that '[u]nlike what most people perceive as minimalism, this opening track is propelled by momentous force, dynamism and sweat. It can be both mesmerizing and disconcerting'. Of the other two tracks, 'Summer Heat' is a distorted, riotous guitar track that Buckman suggests sounds 'more like pounding percussion than guitar strumming', and 'The Second Fortress' that 'borders on the popular conception of minimalist music, with repetitious ambient textures'. Collaborator Tony Conrad explained how he and Cale would get together and record on spare afternoons: 'We'd think, "That was excellent! What a fantastic recording! And then that's it …. there was no room within the culture at that time for this sound, so it was shut out' (qtd. in Pouncey 2001: 48). With the release of live Velvet Underground recordings in box sets and Deluxe Editions in the past two decades, it is possible to understand Cale's impact on the live sound of the band, but the emergence of these recordings provided deeper contextual and evidential insight into Cale's avant-garde interests at the time.

Music for a New Society/M:FANS (2016) was a re-release project that enabled Cale to revisit his former self, improvising in the studio in 1982 at a time of personal and creative despair and arduous self-reflection. Cale explained, 'I was trying to exorcise a lot of devils in my head … It really represents a tortured vigil of someone who's trying to struggle their way out' (qtd. in Temple 2016). Hoskyns (2016) argues that *Music for a New Society* 'falls into a category of Harrowing Interior Journey that includes Big Star's *Third*, Talk Talk's *Spirit of Eden* and Scott Walker's *Tilt*, along with … Nico's *Desertshore* [and] Lou Reed's *Berlin*.' Cale's work on the songs on the album was far from a sentimental nostalgic return. While the 1982 album was remastered, providing new clarity, Cale radically reworked and remediated the original music using new digital tools. Raymond (2016) suggests that 'whereas Music for a New Society has those wide open spaces that seemed unfillable in the 1980s, *M:FANS* imbues the air with something akin to menace. "Taking Your Life in Your Hands" is no longer a heart-rending song about frustration and dead ends, but is now a message from a ghost, a warning to the world.' Cale stated that it was the death of Lou Reed that partly influenced his critical and creative stance on the earlier material:

> Losing Lou [too painful to understand] forced me to upend the entire recording process and begin again … a different perspective – a new sense of urgency to tell a story from a completely opposite point of view – what was once sorrow, was now a form of rage. A fertile ground for exorcism of things gone wrong and the realization they are unchangeable. From sadness came the strength of fire.
> (Primary Talent 2016)

Again, this is not a fond revisitation of the past but a chance to exorcise the unchangeable as 'the basis for renewal and satisfaction in the future' (Keightley and Pickering 2006: 921). Cale's reflective and reflexive perspective makes 'nostalgia' as commonly understood an inadequate term to describe the cathartic but troubled process of working through past personal anguish.

On Cale's ongoing development of his late musical voice, Hermes (2016) suggested *M:FANS* represents 'the sound of a septuagenarian composer and rock dude using the past as a bridge to the present', describing 'Thoughtless Kind' as 'a goth-industrial ballad' with 'Cale's processed vocals split between mid-Seventies Bowie cybernetics and Auto-Tuned 21st century R&B'. The production aesthetic, a kind of 'inventive retrospection' (Petrusich 2017), is closely matched to Cale's work from the *5 Tracks* e.p. onwards but is also inflected by the radicalism and emotional distress of the original material from 1982.

The re-release of the live album *Fragments of a Rainy Season* on the other hand was a relatively straightforward affair, with a second album of outtakes included. Cale 'found a whole bunch of outtakes … There were other versions with string quartets, some with just strings, from different parts of the tour ... some of them were really, really good; especially the ones that benefitted from having real conceptual ground in them, and they sounded really rich and beautiful' (qtd. in Mullen 2016). What Cale described here was that in his live performances over the years, perhaps more so in the last two decades, he used the opportunity to transform his earlier and current music through new arrangements, new instruments and modes of staging and presentation: 'I think performances are fluid, and I think there are some things that you can put different emphasis on. Your tempos change, the mood of the night changes, and you find something new every time. It's like method acting through music' (qtd. in Mullen 2016).

Live performance

In November 2017 at the Brooklyn Music Academy (BAM), and March 2018 at the Barbican in London, Cale presented the show *John Cale (2018–1964): A Futurespective* on 9 and 10 March to mark his seventy-sixth year where he presented music from across his career. Cale said of the event that he would be 'doing old material in a new way, and stuff from the new album in a different way ... The shows will consist of a lot of different moments, anchored in the period when they were created, and redesigned for today's ideas' (Haider 2018). The title 'Futurespective' indicated Cale's intent not to wallow in past glories but to see what he could learn in the present by revisiting his past, and projecting his findings into the/his future – something, in fact, that he had been doing for some time in live performances and other projects. Alongside tours supporting his albums and festival work, Cale has explored diverse ways of curating and presenting his work – for example, a 1999 five-day mixed media event *Dead Agents* including performances, photography, film and book readings. More recently, in 2014 the *LOOP≫60Hz: Transmissions from the Drone Orchestra* event at the Barbican in London combined Cale's musical interest in the drone with Liam Young's drones that flew over the audience during the performance. But underpinning his live performances, as well as his studio work, is a desire to continually rethink and re-present his songs and music:

> I think what happened is that I used to switch it up so much, and take familiar material and twist it, that people got used to that. I used to warn them that those kinds of things would happen a lot, until they finally got to change their expectations for me ... it paid off in the end. Now people expect strange things.
>
> (qtd. in Marketos 2012)

In 2009 Cale and the composer Randall Woolf created new orchestral arrangements for his 1973 *Paris 1919* album and performed it live in Europe, the United States and Australia in 2010 and 2011, and in New York in 2013, with a live band and a new orchestra at each event. Cale commented that the concerts weren't an exercise in nostalgia: 'You're not doing it to recreate it, you're breathing new life into the songs' (qtd. in Wray 2011). However, when he worked on completing the original album in 1973, he realized that 'This is nostalgia, pure and simple: I'm writing about the stuff that I miss about Europe' (qtd. in Kozinn 2013). Revisiting a nostalgic work without a nostalgic intent raises interesting questions about the motivation and implications for Cale of these concerts as an anti-nostalgic engagement with emotive materials created by his younger self. Interestingly Cale also used the orchestra to reinvent recent studio tracks 'I Wanna Talk 2 U' and 'December Rains' in the second half of some of the concerts in a retreat from electronics into an earlier, more traditional style.

In 2008 Cale also began to curate live events celebrating the life and work of his friend and former bandmate Nico. Between 1967 and 1985 Cale worked on five of Nico's solo albums, feeling that her songs deserved to be performed rather than forgotten, with a number of musicians keen to take part. On the twentieth anniversary of her death in 2008, *Life along the Borderline: A Tribute to Nico* attracted performers including James Dean Bradfield of the Manic Street Preachers, Mark Linkous of Sparklehorse and Peter Murphy of Bauhaus. In 2013 at the BAM, Cale again curated the event with Kim Gordon of Sonic Youth, Joan as Police Woman, the Magnetic Fields, Meshell Ndegeocello, Peaches and Sharon Van Etten contributing. By organizing these events that – as in other Cale performances – revisited and reinvented Nico's music, Cale demonstrated his admiration for work that twenty years after Nico's death had gained a wider respect than in her lifetime.

Following the Nico tribute events, in 2017 Cale marked the fiftieth anniversary of the release of *The Velvet Underground and Nico* with guest artists in Paris, Liverpool and New York. At the BAM in November, Cale curated two performances of the album with Animal Collective, MGMT, Kurt Vile and Sky Ferreira among others on stage. In reflecting on his intentions for the shows, that also included music from *White Light/White Heat*, Cale said, 'I'm interested in changing the possibilities of all the Velvets' songs, even the instrumentation ... Though that's not really what I want to do for the anniversary, as I'm aware that people expect to hear things as they remember them – which isn't going to happen anyway ... I'm part of this situation and I'd like to show off and honor what we did back then' (qtd. in Amorosi 2017).

In live performance therefore it is clear Cale has other imperatives than in his forward-thinking studio practice. He balances his musical past, present and future, and simultaneously defeats audience expectations while appreciating the need to bring the audience with him on his creative journey. In the live performances of his solo work, and that of Nico and the Velvet Underground, he displays a complex reflective, reflexive and critical nostalgia. He does not aim to simply celebrate past achievements but intends to honour the past while recognizing the unfinished project that was the Velvet Underground and the 'unfinishable' nature of his songs that shift and mutate with each performance. This shifting process has also meant transposing his ideas beyond the confines of songwriting.

Wales, Dylan Thomas and *Dyddiau Du/Dark Days* at the *53rd Venice Biennale*

In Cale's autobiography *What's Welsh for Zen* (Bockris and Cale 1999), he outlined how in the latter part of the 1980s, tired of the grind of sustaining a career in rock music, he decided to return to his musical roots, noting that he was 'a classical composer, dishevelling my musical personality by dabbling in rock and roll' (218). He began to explore the potential of creating an opera based on Dylan Thomas's life, having previously drawn inspiration from the poet's work for 'A Child's Christmas in Wales' on *Paris 1919*. Cale observed,

> When you grow up in Wales, you can't skip Dylan Thomas. At school we were taught that he used his English the way other poets used their Welsh. In Welsh you can express a lot with only a few words. He was someone to identify with, a contrast to the strict Presbyterian community in Wales with his sense of humour – God knows he needed it.
>
> (218)

Cale struggled with the form of the work – eventually reconnecting with Brian Eno, who produced the project – and released *The Falklands Suite*, an orchestral arrangement of four of Thomas's poems, including 'Do Not Go Gentle into That Good Night'. Reflecting on the motivation for the work, in 2016 he stated, '[i]t was about finding a contact with Wales, finding a contact with me, finding a contact with myself as I remembered myself' (qtd. in Owen 2016). The project found him purposely looking over his shoulder to make sense of his past and how it wove its way through his present identity as an emigrant.

In 1998 the BBC documentary *John Cale* saw Cale return to the landscape of his childhood:

> Embraced once again by the warmth of the hills, the setting sun that shines on the church spire and flicks the tips of the gravestones, and by the warmth of the people, I felt a sense of wonder. Going home always gives me another lease on life; I am still fascinated by the emotional curve of my journey from Wales to New York and back again.
>
> (Bockris and Cale 1999: 269)

Cale has since returned to Wales on several occasions to take part in creative projects, including the 2001 documentary film *Beautiful Mistake* featuring Welsh bands Catatonia, Gorky's Zygotic Mynci and Super Furry Animals. In 2016 he appeared at the Festival of Voice in Cardiff, and after mishearing the question '[a]re you enjoying Wales', he responded, 'I certainly hope so. I feel like I'm rejoining every time I'm here' (qtd. in Moore 2016). This has led him to sustained reflection on his Welsh identity that, as in his perspective on his past solo music, was a complex form of critical and conflicted nostalgia: 'I'm now very sensitive to the idea that I have betrayed my heritage ... I wonder whether what I did has turned me into a traitor. If you reject something you grew up with, does that mean that you have the DNA structure of a traitor?' (qtd. in Vulliamy 2003).

In 2020 Cale stated that '[t]he further away Wales appears in my memory, the more complicated its images and demands become on my understanding of my past' (Davies 2020). On his thoughts on Wales captured in his autobiography, he commented, '[w]hen I think about some of the things that I wrote ... I've come up with a lot of different angles on what it meant. There's a lot of stuff that's gone on since then that can be addressed, but ... I'd rather do it through songs' (Barry 2011). In 2009 he had been asked by the Arts Council of Wales to represent his home country at the Venice Biennale of Art 2009, and through a multimedia installation he was able to revisit, investigate and represent these 'different angles' in exploring his difficult relationship with his past. Cale commented that it offered 'an occasion to address certain pernicious issues in my background that had lain dormant for so long. There are certain experiences uniquely suited to the exorcism of mixed media and I am grateful for this opportunity to address them' (Price 2008). Jones (2009) described the installation, *Dyddiau Du/ Dark Days*, as a 'confrontation with his heritage', with 'lucid and exact' images and 'extraordinary' audio in what is ultimately 'a filmed concept album' and 'a magnificent allegory of migration and loss, a poem of memory and distance.' For Holmes (2011) the artwork was an 'unlikely piece for any country to choose to represent itself on the international stage, saturated as it is with the repression, tedium and bleak hopelessness endemic in traditional Welsh society'. The installation consisted of five screens, twenty speakers and four sections presented over an hour. The audio was comprised of ambient sound effects, music and Cale's narration that reflected on his personal childhood trauma and desire to leave Wales. He is seen climbing steps in a slate quarry and visiting his (empty) childhood home in Garnant. Holmes indicates that '[t]he most disturbing section is "The Making of Unpretty" with 'images of Cale, bound and blindfolded, being waterboarded to the strains of Welsh choirs and rugby crowds. Painful to watch, it's a visceral and righteous indictment of the disabling attrition endured by the active mind in traditional Welsh culture.' Through this violent filmed performance, Cale again shows how creative sustenance can be gained from a critical review of difficult personal memories and experiences – that included tensions in his family home and sexual abuse outside it – complicating any simple 'longing for home' central to the usual understanding of nostalgia. Although traces of Cale's personal trauma can be mapped across his solo music, in the twenty-first century he perhaps confronted his Welsh childhood most effectively, starkly and convincingly through this multimedia artwork.

Lou Reed

In several biographies (Bockris 2014; Reed 2014; Levy 2016; DeCurtis 2017; Sounes 2015) and extensive music press and media coverage since the early 1970s, the early life, career as well as death of Lou Reed has been picked over and dissected in abundant detail. His mental health issues, treatment with electroconvulsive therapy, drug and alcohol addiction, sexuality and personal life provided him with many challenges, and like Cale, it was hardly surprising that he did not always look back on his earlier life and music with fond nostalgia. Although he often spoke of his music in its totality as a linear narrative or novel, it was the early chapters on the Velvet Underground that most music fans were consistently interested in, and that would haunt his later efforts to build on and escape his 1960s output. Time and again Reed felt that little critical respect was given to his solo career or his attempts to probe the boundaries of rock music through his 1973 concept album *Berlin* and 1975 noise album *Metal Machine Music*. After 1989's *New York* was well received, Reed spent the 1990s producing albums dealing with ageing, friendship and death (*Magic and Loss*, 1992) and hard-hitting songs about the joy and trauma of personal relationships and marriage (*Set the Twilight Reeling* [1995] and *Ecstasy* [2000]). *Ecstasy* at the beginning of the new millennium effectively marked the end of his solo career as a songwriter, leaving Reed disillusioned, but it also marked the beginning of a more expansive phase of artistic expression that had begun in 1992 after he met and eventually married avant-garde artist and musician Laurie Anderson. After 2000, Reed focused on merging his literary interests with music, returned to the avant-garde live guitar improvisations that he once explored alongside Cale in the Velvet Underground, published books of photography, worked hard on tidying and perfecting his recorded musical legacy, released electronic music and actively contributed to the rehabilitation of his once vilified albums *Berlin* and *Metal Machine Music*. Moving forward into new artistic territory in the albums *The Raven* and Metallica collaboration *Lulu*, Reed meanwhile looked backwards to recapture and re-present elements of his earlier career through which he could make sense of his present disenchantment.

Ecstasy

In a twentieth anniversary appreciation, Patrick Stickles (2020) incisively captures Reed's modus operandi in coming to terms with growing old as a rock musician, from *The Blue Mask* (1982) through to *Ecstasy*:

> A rock artist of a certain age must learn ... to recognize that working within a youth-obsessed idiom will not make youth endure ... the artist must turn inward, to assess their flaws and shortcomings without flinching or equivocating, to address the brutality both within and without, to become truly vulnerable ... For all intents and purposes, *Ecstasy* is his last word on the singer-songwriter archetype ... a fitting conclusion to rock's richest middle age.

The album focused on creating a live band aesthetic and shifted between reflective quietism and aggressive distorted guitar noise, between sensitive and thoughtful introspection and the sexually explicit and violent language that litters the songs, and between 'anger and the apology existing as a singular entity' (Stickles 2020). DeCurtis (2017) portrays *Ecstasy* as an album that explored the 'jealousy, boredom, dependence, lust for others ... that arise in nearly every long-term relationship' (403). Jeremy Reed (2014) argued, 'Not since the Velvets had he deviantly mined so decadent a library of obsessive emotional and sexual fetishes' (226). He further observed that the album and its predecessor *Set the Twilight Reeling* were 'the closest Reed ever got to evaluating his past ... Lou was prepared to strip something of his defensive layers in the interests of narrowing in on age ... [to] clarify and in the process open pathways to increased knowledge in the present' (231). In short, like Cale, Reed approached his past with a cold, critical and conflicted eye rather than yearning and wistfulness, with little sense of nostalgia.

In producing the album, Reed, in collaboration with his friend and production partner Hal Willner, aimed for sonic precision, presence and clarity in capturing the guitars and drums. In interviews over the years, Reed's audiophilia was sometimes viewed as a way to avoid subjects he didn't wish to confront, but they were sincerely held and drove his dissatisfaction with the way his music had been treated by record companies. In comparison to Cale's use of the twenty-first-century studio to digitally manipulate and mangle sound, Reed wished to capture living sound and performances in the best way he could. But these pure sounds would be peppered with extreme guitar distortion thanks to a number of effects pedals designed by Peter Cornish. However, the album received little critical or commercial interest. Reflecting on the album, Willner stated, 'To this day I have never worked harder on a record ... And it got a great reaction. And then nothing. Nothing. It freaked me out, and I think it broke his heart because he never really wrote another record after that' (qtd. in Decurtis 2017: 406).

The Raven and *Lulu*

In a 2000 interview with *Performing Songwriter*, Reed said, 'I think it's pathetic to put out only one record a year ... You could do ten a year, easy. I mean, it's nothing ... The hard thing is deciding what you want to do. Once you decide that, it's easy' (Zollo 2000). However, in the wake of the relative failure of *Ecstasy*, further work on solo albums seemed unattractive, so Reed broadened his artistic vision and directly took on the task of integrating literature and rock music.

The Raven was a recording project that grew out of *POEtry*, a rock-opera drawing from Edgar Allan Poe's writings, created by Reed and the playwright, producer and director Robert Wilson, and staged at the BAM in 2002. Williams (2003) viewed *The Raven* as an opportunity for Reed to stride 'fearlessly through and beyond his known territories, more than willing to risk ridicule and incomprehension in this latest expression of a lifelong ambition to escape the rock star's pigeonhole without actually denying its value'. The album was more experimental radio drama than rock album. It comprised readings by Steve Buscemi, Laurie Anderson, Fisher Stevens,

Elizabeth Ashley and Willem Dafoe, instrumental interludes, old and new songs sung by Reed, David Bowie, Kate and Anna McGarrigle and others, Reed's band and Ornette Coleman. Reed described the project not as a break with his past but as a continuum with it, stating that it was 'the culmination of everything I've ever done. All the ideas from all the other records, all of the ideas about sound, all the ideas about the way to record a voice and the way to use music under things, it's all in here' (Uhelszki 2003).

For the project Reed re-wrote Poe's work and commented that his aim was to 'free Poe up ... To just loosen it a bit and get it out of the book and take advantage of that amazing language ... not to mention that imagination' (Pareles 2001). Reed worked hard to update and modernize the language so it would speak more directly to twenty-first-century audiences. The rewriting process led him to identify closely with the theme of Poe's story *The Imp of the Perverse* – the urge to commit acts where '[w]e perpetrate them merely because we feel we should *not*. Beyond or behind this, there is no intelligible principle' (Poe [1935] 1986: 14). Reed felt this held a mirror to his past behaviour: 'I felt I was in league with the master. In that kind of psychology, that interest in the drives and the meaning of obsession and compulsion – in that realm Poe reigns supreme' (Pareles 2001). However, on release the two-hour double CD was met with confusion and opprobrium, with James (2003) commenting, '*The Raven* ... does nothing if not confirm that Reed is currently as clueless as his most spiteful detractors could suspect.' Jeremy Reed (2014) was more measured, arguing with some accuracy that 'like Scott Walker's later albums, *The Drift* and *Bish Bosh*, the self-indulgent lack of critical self-perception integral to their construction, makes *The Raven* ... a one-off listening experience' (238–9). Begrand (2003) defended the album identifying its form as like 'an old-fashioned radio drama experience ... [it is a] flawed, audacious, puzzling, maddening success'.

In 2011, Reed collaborated with Metallica on the album *Lulu*, with lyrics based on a story originally told across two plays by the early-twentieth-century German playwright Frank Wedekind: *Erdgeist* [Earth Spirit] and *Die Büchse der Pandora* [Pandora's Box].[1] Describing the motivation for the album, Reed said, 'The idea is the same as it's been for ever. What would happen if you could write like Tennessee Williams and put it in a long-form song?' (Helmore 2011), a theme he returned to incessantly in interviews – also citing Hubert Selby Jr and Delmore Schwarz. Lyrically the album was as explicit and challenging in its treatment of sexual and violent imagery as *Ecstasy* had been, but far darker and troubled. In describing *Lulu*, Reed said, 'I don't like the word rock opera, but I'm trying to write on that level that's reserved for plays still, or novels. I was trying to escape the simplistic form, and find a different kind of melodic form, but still rock' (Mccormick [2011] 2013). Like *The Raven*, *Metal Machine Music* and *Berlin*, the album attracted highly critical reviews but this response was not universal. Bowie for one was an admirer of *Lulu*, and Laurie Anderson reported that 'after Lou's death, David Bowie made a big point of saying to me, "Listen, this is Lou's greatest work. This is his masterpiece. Just wait, it will be like *Berlin*. It will take everyone a while to catch up"' (qtd. in Beaumont-Thomas 2015).

Metal Machine Music and Berlin

In 2000 when asked about his thoughts on *Metal Machine Music* and its lack of commercial appeal, Reed responded, 'I never tried to be voluntarily uncommercial ... I was convinced that *Metal Machine Music* would get its audience as it was the only album I could identify with at that time. As far as I remember, I have always only done what I wanted. I still love *Metal Machine Music*. I also love *Berlin*' (qtd. in Dax [2000] 2013). In the next few years Reed was given the opportunity to return to both albums, initially with suspicion, but eventually with enthusiasm, through the prompting of others.

In 2002 German saxophonist Ulrich Krieger, a member of the Zeitkratzer avant-classical ensemble in Berlin, created a form of transcription of *Metal Machine Music* for a performance of the work. When Reed heard an excerpt, he agreed to appear with Zeitkratzer in a *Metal Machine Music* performance in Berlin with the Asphodel label releasing a CD and DVD documenting the occasion in 2007. This experience reignited Reed's interest in his earlier work that soon led to him performing with Krieger, and adding electronic musician Sarth Calhoun, creating live improvisations influenced by but moving beyond the experimental approach of the original album. This provided a vehicle for Reed to reconnect with his experimental past and continue his renewed interest in guitar noise, evident on the track 'Fire Music' from *The Raven* and the Lou Reed's Metal Machine Trio album *The Creation of the Universe* (2008), documenting two performances in Los Angeles in October 2008.

Reed was prompted to revisit and tour *Berlin* by Susan Feldman of the Brooklyn performing arts venue St. Ann's Warehouse. Feldman had been crucial in the development of Reed and Cale's *Songs for Drella* project and *The Raven*, and approached Reed to stage *Berlin* in its original form (Gleason 2009). With Julian Schnabel directing, Reed performed the album at St Ann's in December 2006 with a choir, film projections and thirty musicians, and Jeremy Reed (2014: 242) described it as sounding 're-energised and apposite to the times, rather than maudlin and time-bound'. With the success of the event, performed over five nights, Reed gained confidence in opening the door on a once berated work, and toured the album successfully in Europe, Australia and the United States in 2007–8. The rehabilitation of his two most reviled albums (i.e. until *The Raven* and *Lulu* were released) in this period saw him enhancing and expanding his original vision for both rather than faithfully reproducing them. Like Cale, the intent was to transport older works into the present, to understand what they could mean in current contexts in remediated form.

Live improvisation

In January 2008, Reed, Laurie Anderson and John Zorn played together at two benefit shows at The Stone, a New York setting dedicated to experimental and avant-garde work. They performed again in 2009 in Antwerp at the Middleheim Jazz festival, with Longley (2009) describing the event as 'a divisive performance' with some audience members 'drifting off impatiently into the night', though most were said to be 'transfixed'. However, a later appearance at the Montreal International Jazz in July 2010 resulted in furious audience members booing the performance after paying $100 for tickets and seemingly expecting Lou Reed hits. As some loudly complained, Zorn responded with '[i]f you don't think it's music, then get the fuck outta here!' (Michaels 2010). In 2011 the Japan Society's *Concert for Japan* saw Reed, Anderson and Zorn perform again, demonstrating Reed's sustained commitment to free improvisation, despite mixed responses, at this late stage of his life and career. It also suggested how far Anderson's influence had afforded Reed the opportunity to branch out with confidence outside his comfort zone.

Curation – *NYC Man* and *Lou Reed: The RCA & Arista Album Collection*

In a 2000 interview Reed said of his eighteen-minute sustained guitar distortion-laden track 'Like a Possum' from *Ecstasy*

> I spent years of my life waiting for a technology that is so advanced that you can record and thus hear the sounds of an electric guitar the way it really sounds …. if you listen carefully to my new records, you will notice that they sound clear and clean … and powerful … I am willing to dedicate the time and to invest the money needed to achieve exactly that sound.

When listening to Velvet Underground recordings, Reed complained, 'I hear the lost frequencies, the irrecoverable musical shades and overtones … I only hear the mistakes, the missed opportunities, and the flaws' (Dax [2000] 2013). Sound mattered to Reed, and in the recorded documents of his studio work, he felt correctly that in the CD era his music had suffered from being manufactured from inferior master tapes. Despite interviewers dismissing these statements as 'hiding his heart behind the technobabble' (Hattenstone 2003), Reed worked hard in the 2000s to lift the veil of technical obfuscation that had settled over his music.

The two CD compilation *NYC Man* (2003) saw Reed curate studio and live versions of well-known and obscure tracks. In the CD liner notes, Hill (2003) described the process where Reed, acting as creative director, worked to construct a musical 'self-portrait' from tapes sourced from 'far-flung corporate vaults' representing his entire recorded output. New masters were created in a process of remembering and restoring: 'remembering background parts, guitar licks, the very feel of a track, that somehow got lost or muddled on the first trip to the pressing plant, and restoring these songs, as best as technologically possible, to a pristine form.' If there is any evidence of nostalgia in Reed's work, it occurs at the technological interface between himself and the traces of his recorded past in the moment of creative retrieval, in retrieving memories, something afforded him due to the extensive documentation of his efforts since the early 1960s. However, he was not satisfied with just creating masters in a new 'pristine form' and presenting them chronologically in a crowd-pleasing greatest hits format. As Hill (2003) indicates Reed purposely mixed 'distant past and near-present, live cuts and studio recordings, melodrama and tragicomedy, visceral rock and austere mood music', allowing the self-portrait to represent 'connections and consistencies among all his material'. This multi-layered and anti-chronological approach parallels the internal processes of memory construction in the present that we all consistently perform, representing who I am/we are now. Reed's 'authorial self' scripted the story of his musical life as an 'editor-in-chief of the memories made to matter and cohere in the preferred version' (Keightley and Pickering qtd. in Elliott 2015: 34) of who he felt he was at that time. *NYC Man* spoke more of his intention to establish a definitive 'preferred version' of his career achievements than observing commercial imperatives. The live album *Animal Serenade* (2004) was a counterpart to *NYC Man*, with a similar sifting, sorting and layering of memories in the live set and the arrangements. The first track on *NYC Man*, 'Who Am I? (Tripitena's Song)', a summary of the themes covered in *The Raven* project, sees Reed – or a character he performed – considering ageing, the time he has left, reminiscence, dashed hopes, spiritual questions and the power and tragedy of memory in a devastating reflection on the past. By 2013 Reed had the answers to many of these questions after a failing liver transplant, and after finalizing the remastering of *Lou Reed: The RCA & Arista Album Collection* box set in the months before his death.

The box set covered sixteen solo albums released between 1972 and 1986, and unlike *NYC Man*, Reed aimed to present the albums in the best form possible in their original format, with no extra tracks or alternate mixes (Roberts 2016). Despite his illness, Reed was present during much of the remastering process, working with Rob Santos, Hal Willner and the engineers Vlado Meller and Scott Hull at Masterdisk in New York. In 2016 Meller noted that 'the master tapes were of really good quality. I was totally shocked when I compared the original CDs to the tapes' presuming that 'second, or even third-generation masters were used to cut those original CDs', and that they were 'made specifically for vinyl, not for CDs'. Reed, confronted with the meticulous details found in the digital transfer of the tape masters, remarked, '"That's fucking amazing! It's unbelievable! What did you do?"', wrongly suspecting Meller had digitally enhanced the sound, as '[p]laying the original master, you could hear everything – the beautiful low end, the beautiful midrange, and the high end' (Mettler 2016). Reed heard all the finished masters before his death in October 2013 and cried with happiness at finally being able to hear his music as he intended it to be.

Hudson River Meditations

For the last thirty years of his life, Reed practised Chen Tai Chi on a daily basis. In the mid-2000s he experimented with a Minimoog Voyager synthesizer and a long field recording of Hudson River wind in composing ambient electronic music to help with this and other meditative practice.[2] He had become increasingly interested in electronic music technology after meeting Laurie Anderson and invested in a production rig similar to hers in the early 2000s that included an Access Virus synthesizer. He said that he composed the music for himself 'as an adjunct to meditation, Tai Chi, bodywork, and as music to play in the background of life – to replace the everyday cacophony with new and ordered sounds of an unpredictable nature. New sounds free from preconception' (Reed 2007). In some senses *Hudson River Meditations*, released in 2007, was the yang to *Metal Machine Music*'s yin, the calm in the eye of a noise storm – the Velvet Underground's third album compared to *White Light/White Heat*. Jeremy Reed (2014) described the effect of the music as 'islanding the individual from busy noise invasion by helping the mind create internalised silence, and a cut-off point from continuous thought associations' (243–4). Reed resisted the notion that the music was 'New Agey', stressing that Chen Tai Chi helped him become 'mentally and physically stronger', and when asked, he had little to say about the spiritual dimension of the practice (Reiss 2007).

The four tracks comprise two long pulsing, ebbing and flowing drone-based compositions, and two shorter pieces incorporating the field recording. In sound and feel it is closer to electronic music of the 1950s and 1960s than the complex sound experimentation evident in the work of ambient electronic experimentalists of the 2000s such as Christian Fennesz or Geir Jennsen. It is perhaps an aid to achieving a 'flow state', both for Reed and its listeners. In a flow state, often recognized as central to creative musical improvisation, there is intense, undistracted concentration on present activities, a feeling of control, a loss of a sense of self and a distortion of how time is experienced (Csikszentmihalyi 1996: 112–13). In *Hudson River Meditations*, the Metal Machine Trio and his performances with Zorn and Anderson, he appeared to be performatively attempting to hold back and transcend both time and himself. In doing so perhaps his sense of self expanded through these acts of forgetting in an attempt to step out of the constricting confines of 'Lou Reed' – as a musician and individual coming to terms with himself at the end of his life.

Conclusion

In considering the late musical voices of Cale and Reed in the twenty-first century, it is clear that both had no nostalgic desire to trade on past glories. Cale continually transforms his creative past into new forms on record and in live contexts, in a process perhaps best described as innovative 'futurespection' than 'inventive retrospection' (Petrusich 2017). Reed in his final years unsentimentally corrected the imperfections of his recorded past, revived his earlier failed projects and explored new creative territory while drawing from earlier intentions, inventions and innovations in his own work. Both critically, reflectively and reflexively recognized that even in attempts to escape it, the past inevitably shapes the future, and that it is 'never over or completed because the changes that are inherent in aging also change the perception of the past' (Baars 2012: 151). In different ways Cale and Reed found that in revisiting the past in their musical work, the retrieval of recorded memories and experiences altered their present perception of themselves and their creative possibilities. However, Cale's public discussion of emerging and changing perceptions of his work and identity should be compared with Reed's refusal to speak in any meaningful way about his private life. In interviews Reed focused on his current work and technological interests and largely shut down or ignored questions outside this. Nevertheless, Cale and Reed's complex and conflicted relationship with the past and nostalgia did not interfere with mapping future plans, developing strategies that encompassed aspects of their pasts in the development of their respective late musical voices in the twenty-first century.

Notes

1   This was a project instigated by Robert Wilson for a stage performance, but little of Reed's work was eventually used in the production in Berlin (DeCurtis 2017: 429).
2   Engineered, recorded and mixed by Hector Castillo alongside Reed and Willner, the album credits give special thanks to Ableton Live, making it likely this software was also used.

References

Amorosi, A. D. (2017), 'John Cale to Celebrate '*The Velvet Underground & Nico*'', *Variety*, 10 November. Available online: https://bit.ly/3ufblCj (accessed 22 November 2021).
Baars, J. (2012), 'Critical Turns of Aging, Narrative and Time', *International Journal of Ageing and Later Life*, 7 (2): 143–65.
Barry, R. (2011), 'A Will Of Iron: John Cale Interviewed', *The Quietus*, 11 October. Available online: https://bit.ly/3KLVUHe (accessed 22 November 2021).
Beaumont-Thomas, B. (2015), 'David Bowie: Lou Reed's Masterpiece Is Metallica Collaboration Lulu', *Guardian*, 20 April. Available online: https://bit.ly/3nZNNgx (accessed 22 November 2021).
Begrand, A. (2003), 'Lou Reed: The Raven [review]', *PopMatters*, 18 February. Available online: https://bit.ly/3G5hGlQ (accessed 22 November 2021).
Berman, S. (2011), 'John Cale – Extra Playful EP [review]', *Pitchfork*, 6 October. Available online: https://bit.ly/32uOhDQ (accessed 22 November 2021).
Bockris, V. (2014), *Transformer: The Complete Lou Reed Story*, London: Harper.
Bockris, V. and Cale, J. (1999), *What's Welsh for Zen: The Autobiography of John Cale*, London: Bloomsbury.
Boym, S. (2001), *The Future of Nostalgia*, New York: Basic Books.
Davis, F. (1979), *Yearning for Yesterday: A Sociology of Nostalgia*, New York: Free Press.
Buckman, L. (2001), 'John Cale – Sun Blindness Music [review]', *Pichfork*, 24 October. Available online: https://bit.ly/3KIX0Us (accessed 22 November 2021).
Csikszentmihalyi, M. (1996), *Flow and the Psychology of Discovery and Invention*, New York: HarperCollins.
Davies, D. M. (2020), 'On Making Music and Wales: John Cale and Kelly Lee Owens In Conversation', *AnOther*, 8 October. Available online: https://bit.ly/35o33gV (accessed 22 November 2021).

Dax, M. ([2000] 2013), 'From the Vaults: An Interview with Lou Reed', *Electronic Beats*, 28 October. Available online: https://bit.ly/3G03Z7U (accessed 22 November 2021).

DeCurtis, A. (2017), *Lou Reed: A Life*, London: John Murray.

Deusner, S. (2012), 'John Cale: I Wince at Each Velvet Underground Reissue', *Salon*, 11 October. Available online: https://bit.ly/3IBVAsN (accessed 22 November 2012).

Domino Records (2020), 'John Cale Returns with New Single & Video, "Lazy Day"', *Domino Records News*, 6 October. Available online: https://bit.ly/3fXkN4L (accessed 22 November 2021).

Doyle, T. (2006), 'John Cale – Artist/Producer', *Sound on Sound*, October 2006. Available online: https://bit.ly/3o133K7 (accessed 22 November 2021).

Elliott, R. (2015), *The Late Voice: Time, Age and Experience in Popular Music*, New York/London: Bloomsbury.

Gardner, A. (2020), *Ageing and Contemporary Female Musicians*, London: Routledge.

Gleason, H. (2009), 'Interview: Lou Reed', *American Songwriter*, January/February. Available online: https://bit.ly/3u10lrU (accessed 22 November 2021).

Haider, A. (2018), 'John Cale: A Futurespective', [article], *Barbican*. Available online: https://bit.ly/34aOmwQ (accessed 22 November 2021).

Hall, O. (2005), 'John Cale [interview]', *Perfect Sound Forever*, September. Available online: https://bit.ly/3KEDHM1 (accessed 22 November 2021).

Hasted, N. (1997), 'John Cale: Remembrance of Things Past', *Independent*, 28 June. Available online: https://bit.ly/3H245gB (accessed 22 November 2021).

Hattenstone, S. (2003), 'Interviewing Lou Reed: Not a Perfect Day', *The Guardian*, 19 May. Available online: https://bit.ly/3H2DH6a (accessed 22 November 2021).

Helmore, E. (2011), 'It has so much Rage': Metallica and Lou Reed Talk About Their New Album', *Guardian*, 20 October. Available online: https://bit.ly/3gdYvvT (accessed 22 November 2011).

Hermes, W. (2016), '*M:FANS/Music for a New Society* [review]', *Rolling Stone*, 27 January. Available online: https://bit.ly/3r2lH6w (accessed 22 November 2021).

Heron, C. (2008), 'John Cale Interview', *It Is Whatever* [blog]. Available online: https://bit.ly/3tWpRhR (accessed 22 November 2021).

Hill, M. (2003), 'NYC Man' [liner notes], Lou Reed, *NYC Man*, BMG 74321 98401 2.

Holmes, A. (2011), 'John Cale – *Dyddiau Du/Dark Days* (installation)' [review], *Freq*, 14 April. Available online: https://bit.ly/3IF4hm2 (accessed 22 November 2021).

Hoskyns, B. (2016), '"Danger: Depressing": John Cale's *Music for a New Society*', *Domino Records*, January. Available online: https://bit.ly/3G7TZJS (accessed 22 November 2021).

James, B. (2003), 'Lou Reed: *The Raven*' [review], *Pitchfork*, 5 February. Available online: https://bit.ly/33O31yp (accessed 22 November 2021).

Jones, J. (2009), 'From the Valleys to Venice [interview]', *Guardian*, 12 May. Available online: https://bit.ly/33TF2Od (accessed 22 November 2021).

Jonze, T. (2012), 'Interview – John Cale: 'I don't Want to End up in Pseud's Corner', *Guardian*, 26 September. Available online: https://bit.ly/3G2Gz1E (accessed 22 November 2021).

Katz, M. (2011), *Capturing Sound: How Technology Has Changed Music*, Oakland, CA: University of California Press.

Keightley, E. and Pickering, M. (2006), 'The Modalities of Nostalgia', *Current Sociology*, 54 (6): 919–41.

Keightley, E. and Pickering, M. (2012), *The Mnemonic Imagination: Remembering as Creative Practice*, New York: Palgrave Macmillan.
Kozinn, A. (2013), 'Q. AND A. – An Eclectic Rock Pioneer Traversing the Borderline', *New York Times*, 15 January, Section C, 1.
Levy, A. (2016), *Dirty Blvd.: The Life and Music of Lou Reed*, Chicago, IL: Chicago Review Press.
Locker, M. (2012), 'Turntable Interview: John Cale', *Stereogum*, 5 October. Available online: https://bit.ly/3Av94nk (accessed 22 November 2021).
Longley, M. ([2009] 2012), 'Lou Reed, John Zorn, Laurie Anderson – Live At Middelheim Park (2009) [review]', *Different Perspectives in My Room* [blog], 27 September. Available online: https://bit.ly/3qYFvHE (accessed 22 November 2021).
Lucas, D. (2011), 'John Cale – *Extra Playful*', *Drowned in Sound*, 14 September. Available online: https://bit.ly/347Bnwf (accessed 22 November 2021).
Marketos, C. (2012), 'Interview: John Cale Shares His Life Story', *Self-Titled*. Available online: https://bit.ly/3KGybZ3 (accessed 22 November 2021).
Mccormick, N. ([2011] 2013), 'Lou Reed and Metallica: The Interview', *The Telegraph*, 27 October. Available online: https://bit.ly/3tZMm5y (accessed 22 November 2021).
Mettler, M. (2016), 'Lou Reed's Digital Remasters Once Brought Him to Tears', *Digital Trends*, 16 December. Available online: https://bit.ly/3Azm4s1 (accessed 22 November 2021).
Michaels, S. (2010), 'Lou Reed Booed in Canada for Free-Improv Set', *Guardian*, 5 July. Available online: https://bit.ly/3rMUxQc (accessed 22 November 2021).
Mitchell, T. (2003), *Sedition and Alchemy: A Biography of John Cale*, London: Peter Owen.
Moglen, H. (2008), 'Ageing and Transageing: Transgenerational Hauntings of the Self', *Studies in Gender and Sexuality*, 9 (4): 297–311.
Moore, D. (2016), 'John Cale, Festival of Voice, Cardiff [review]', *The Arts Desk*, 4 June. Available online: https://bit.ly/3FVJ2ux (accessed 22 November 2021).
Mullen, M. (2016), 'John Cale Tears Up His Past', *Interview*, 5 December. Available online: https://bit.ly/3H261FT (accessed 22 November 2021).
Owen, K. (2016), 'Velvet Underground's John Cale' [interview], *Buzz*, 1 June. Available online: https://bit.ly/3u0meYu (accessed 22 November 2021).
Pareles, J. (2001), 'Lou Reed, the Tell-Tale Rocker', *New York Times*, 25 November, Section 2, 1.
Pareles, J. (2013), 'Droning, Rocking, Leading and Paying Tribute to a Dead Collaborator', *New York Times*, 21 January, Section C, 3.
Petrusich, A. (2017), 'John Cale's Inventive Retrospection', *The New Yorker*, 22 January. Available online: https://bit.ly/3fTkBnb (accessed 22 November 2021).
Phillips, A. (2006), 'Of Anger and Twitching: An Interview with John Cale', *PopMatters*, 9 January. Available online: https://bit.ly/3IFkojU (accessed 22 November 2021).
Poe, E. A. ([1935] 1986), *Poe's Tales of Mystery and Imagination*, London: Octopus.
PopMatters Staff (2004), 'John Cale: HoboSapiens', [review]. *PopMatters*, 6 September. Available online: https://bit.ly/3H9dt24 (accessed 22 November 2021).
Pouncey, E. (2001), 'Inside the Dream Syndicate', *The Wire*, 206, April, 43–8.
Price, K. (2008), 'John Cale: From Velvet to Venice', *Wales Online*, 12 December. Available online: https://bit.ly/3fUJBu7 (accessed 22 November 2021).
Primary Talent (2016), 'John Cale: *Music for a New Society/M:FANS*' [press release], Available online: https://bit.ly/3G4Iqmq (accessed 22 November 2021).

Raymond, G. (2016), 'Album: *Music for a New Society* [review]', *Wales Arts Review*, 6 April. Available online: https://bit.ly/3KJ2vCs (accessed 22 November 2021).

Reed, J. (2014), *Waiting for the Man: The Life and Music of Lou Reed*, London: Omnibus.

Reed, L. (2007), 'Liner Notes', Lou Reed, *Hudson River Meditations*, Sounds True M1117D.

Reiss, V. (2007), 'Lou Reed Meditating on the Wild Side', *Beliefnet*, 7 June. Available online: https://bit.ly/3AFh6KE (accessed 22 November 2021).

Roberts, R. (2016), 'Producer Hal Willner Discusses Lou Reed and Their Work on the Late Artist's New Boxed Set', *Los Angeles Times*, 17 October. Available online: https://lat.ms/3nXy69R (accessed 22 November 2021).

Sounes, H. (2015), *Notes from the Velvet Underground: The Life of Lou Reed*, London: Doubleday.

Stickles, P. (2020), '*Ecstasy* Turns 20', *Stereogum*, 2 April. Available online: https://bit.ly/3FUZhrS (accessed 22 November 2021).

Temple, L. (2016), 'John Cale [interview]', *Issue*, January. Available online: https://bit.ly/3GXqaN8 (accessed 22 November 2021).

Uhelszki, J. (2003), '10 Questions for Lou Reed', *Mojo*, February. Available online: https://bit.ly/3tWgpew (accessed 22 November 2021).

Vulliamy, E. (2003), 'Velvet Goldmine', *Guardian*, 23 May. Available online: https://bit.ly/3fX5edj (accessed 22 November 2021).

Williams, R. (2003), 'Lou Reed: *The Raven* [review]', *Guardian*, 17 January. Available online: https://bit.ly/3Auydid (accessed 22 November 2021).

Wray, D. D. (2011), 'John Cale interview.' *Loud and Quiet*, Issue 30. 11 July. Available online: https://bit.ly/3rMcSNf (accessed 22 November 2021).

Zollo, P. (2000), 'Lou Reed [interview]', *Performing Songwriter*, July/August. Available online: https://bit.ly/3fVHlCK (accessed 22 November 2021).

Discography – The Velvet Underground and Solo Works

The discography features studio, compilation and live releases by The Velvet Underground, solo and collaborative releases and other record appearances by John Cale, Sterling Morrison, Nico, Lou Reed, Maureen Tucker and Doug Yule that are referenced in this collection.

The Velvet Underground

Studio albums:

The Velvet Underground and Nico (1967), Verve V-5008.
1. Sunday Morning / 2. I'm Waiting for the Man / 3. Femme Fatale / 4. Venus In Furs / 5. Run Run Run / 6. All Tomorrow's Parties / 7. Heroin / 8. There She Goes Again / 9. I'll Be Your Mirror / 10. The Black Angel's Death Song / 11. European Son.

White Light/White Heat (1968), Verve V6-5046.
1. White Light/White Heat / 2. The Gift / 3. Lady Godiva's Operation / 4. There She Comes Now / 5. I Heard Her Call My Name / 6. Sister Ray.

The Velvet Underground (1969), MGM SE4617.
1. Candy Says / 2. What Goes On / 3. Some Kinda Love / 4. Pale Blue Eyes / 5. Jesus / 6. Beginning to See the Light / 7. I'm Set Free / 8. That's the Story of My Life / 9. The Murder Mystery / 10. After Hours.

Loaded (1970), Cotillion SD 9034.
1. Who Loves the Sun / 2. Sweet Jane / 3. Rock & Roll / 4. Cool It Down / 5. New Age / 6. Head Held High / 7. Lonesome Cowboy Bill / 8. I Found A Reason / 9. Train Round the Bend / 10. Oh! Sweet Nuthin'.

Squeeze (1972), Polydor 2383 180.
1. Little Jack / 2. Crash / 3. Caroline / 4. Mean Old Man / 5. Dopey Joe / 6. Wordless / 7. She'll Make You Cry / 8. Friends / 9. Send No Letter / 10. Jack & Jane / 11. Louise.
Compilations:

VU (1985), 823 721-1 Y-1.
1. I Can't Stand It / 2. Stephanie Says / 3. She's My Best Friend / 4. Lisa Says / 5. Ocean / 6. Foggy Notion / 7. Temptation inside Your Heart / 8. One of These Days / 9. Andy's Chest / 10. I'm Sticking with You.

Another View (1986), Verve 829 405-1 Y-1.
1. We're Gonna Have a Real Good Time Together / 2. I'm Gonna Move Right In / 3. Hey Mr. Rain (version 1) / 4. Ride into the Sun / 5. Coney Island Steeplechase / 6. Guess I'm Falling in Love (instrumental version) / 7. Hey Mr. Rain (version 2) / 8. Ferryboat Bill / 9. Rock and Roll.

Peel Slowly and See [box set] (1995), Polydor 314 527 887-2.
[CD1] 1965: 1. Venus in Furs (demo) / 2. Prominent Men (demo) / 3. Heroin (demo) / 4. I'm Waiting for the Man (demo) / 5. Wrap Your Troubles in Dreams (demo) / 6. All Tomorrow's Parties (demo).

[CD2] 1966–67: 1. All Tomorrow's Parties (single version) / 2. Sunday Morning / 3. I'm Waiting for the Man / 4. Femme Fatale / 5. Venus In Furs / 6. Run Run Run / 7. All Tomorrow's Parties / 8. Heroin / 9. There She Goes Again / 10. I'll Be Your Mirror / 11. The Black Angel's Death Song / 12. European Son / 13. Melody Laughter (live) / 14. It Was a Pleasure Then / 15. Chelsea Girls.

[CD3] 1967–68: 1. There Is No Reason (demo) / 2. Sheltered Life (demo) / 3. It's All Right (The Way That You Live) (demo) / 4. I'm Not Too Sorry (Now That You're Gone) (demo) / 5. Here She Comes Now (demo) / 6. Guess I'm Falling in Love (live) / 7. Booker T. (live) / 8. White Light/White Heat / 9. The Gift / 10. Lady Godiva's Operation / 11. Here She Comes Now / 12. I Heard Her Call My Name / 13. Sister Ray / 14. Stephanie Says/ 15. Temptation Inside Your Heart / 16. Hey Mr. Rain (version one).

[CD4] 1968–69: 1. What Goes On (live) / 2. Candy Says / 3. What Goes On / 4. Some Kinda Love / 5. Pale Blue Eyes / 6. Jesus / 7. Beginning to See the Light / 8. I'm Set Free / 9. That's the Story of My Life / 10. The Murder Mystery / 11. After Hours / 12. Foggy Notion / 13. I Can't Stand It / 14. I'm Sticking with You / 15. One Of These Days / 16. Lisa Says / 17. It's Just Too Much (live) / 18. Countess from Hong Kong (demo).

[CD5] 1970: 1. Who Loves the Sun / 2. Sweet Jane (full length version) / 3. Rock and Roll / 4. Cool It Down / 5. New Age (full length version) / 6. Head Held High / 7. Lonesome Cowboy Bill / 8. I Found a Reason / 9. Train Round the Bend / 10. Oh! Sweet Nuthin' / 11. Satellite of Love / 12. Walk and Talk / 13. Oh Gin / 14. Sad Song / 15. Ocean / 16. Ride into the Sun / 17. Some Kinda Love (live) / 18. I'll Be Your Mirror (live) / 19. I Love You.

Live albums:

Live at Max's Kansas City (1972), Cotillion SD 9500.
1969 Velvet Underground Live with Lou Reed (1974), Mercury SRM-2-7504.

Live MCMXCIII (1993), Sire 9362-45464-2.
Bootleg Series Volume 1: The Quine Tapes (2001), Polydor 314 589 067-2.
Final V.U. 1971–1973 (2001), Captain Trip CTCD-350-353.
The Complete Matrix Tapes (2015), Universal Music Enterprises B0023 955-02.

John Cale

Studio albums:

Vintage Violence (1970), Columbia CS 1037.
[with Terry Riley] *Church of Anthrax* (1971), Columbia C 30131.
The Academy in Peril (1971), Reprise MS 2079.
Paris 1919 (1973), Reprise MS 2131.
Fear (1974), Island ILPS 9301.
Slow Dazzle (1975), Island ILPS 9317.
Helen of Troy (1975), Island ILPS 9291.
Honi Soit (1981), A&M SP-4849.
Music for a New Society (1982), Island/ZE 204 951.
Caribbean Sunset (1984), Island/ZE ILPS 7024.
Artificial Intelligence (1985), Beggars Banquet BEGA 68.
Words for the Dying (1989), Opal 9 26024-2.
[with Lou Reed] *Songs for Drella* (1990), Sire 7599-26140-2.
[with Brian Eno] *Wrong Way Up* (1990), Opal 7599-26421-1.
[with Bob Neuwirth] *Last Day on Earth* (1994), MCA MCD 11037.
Walking on Locusts (1996), Hannibal HNCD 1395.
HoboSapiens (2003), EMI 5939092.
Black Acetate (2005), EMI 0946 3 39182 2 1.
Shifty Adventures in Nookie Wood (2012), Double Six DS047CD.
M:FANS/Music for a New Society (2016), Double Six DS108LP.

E.P.s:

Animal Justice (1977), Illegal IL003.
5 Tracks (2003), EMI CDEM621.
EP: Extra Playful (2011), Double Six DS046CD.

Compilations:

Guts (1977), Island ILPS 9459.
The Island Years [2xCD] (1996), Island 524 235-2.
New York In The 1960s [3 x CD] (2006), Table Of The Elements Fr 87.
  [CD1] *Sun Blindness Music*; [CD2] *Inside the Dream Syndicate Volume II: Dream Interpretation*; [CD3] *Inside The Dream Syndicate Volume III: Stainless Gamelan.*

Conflict and Catalysis: Productions and Arrangements 1966–2006 (2012), Big Beat CDWIKD 299.

Live albums:

[with Kevin Ayers, Brian Eno and Nico] *June 1, 1974* (1974), Island ILPS 9291.
Sabotage/Live (1979), Spy SP 004.
Comes Alive (1984), ZE 206 531.
Circus Live (2007), EMI 00946 377944 2 5.
Fragments of a Rainy Season ([1992] 2016), Domino REWIGCD107X.
[with Lou Reed and Nico] *Le Bataclan '72* (2017), Grey Scale GSGZ036CD.

Film soundtrack releases and other compositions:

Antártida [soundtrack] (1995), Les Disques Du Crépuscule TWI 1008.
Eat/Kiss: Music for The Films of Andy Warhol (1997), Hannibal HNCD 1407.
Dance Music (Nico, The Ballet) (1998), Detour 3984-22122-2.
Le Vent De La Nuit [soundtrack] (1999), Crépuscule France TWI 1083.
The Unknown [soundtrack] (1999), Les Disques Du Crépuscule TWI 1023.
Saint-Cyr [soundtrack] (2000), Virgin 849545 2.

Sterling Morrison (post-Velvet Underground appearances on record)

Cale, J. (1995), *Antártida* [soundtrack], Crepuscule 0630118962.
Cale, J. (2002), *Stainless Gamelan*, Table of The Elements Hg 80.
Luna (1994), *Bewitched*, Elektra 61617–2.
Shotgun Rationale (1993), *Rollercoaster*, Vince Lombardy Highschool Vince 014.
Tucker, M. (1991), *I Spent a Week There the Other Night*, New Rose 273.
Tucker, M. (1992), *Oh No, They're Recording This Show*, New Rose 422 418.
Tucker, M. (1994), *Dogs Under Stress*, New Rose 422 492.

Nico

Studio albums:

Chelsea Girl (1967), Verve V-5032.
The Marble Index (1968), Elektra EKS-74029.
Desertshore (1970), Reprise RS 6424.
The End… (1974), Island ILPS 9311.
Drama of Exile (version 1) (1981), Aura AUL 715.

The Drama of Exile (version 2) (1983), Invisible C 3813.
[with The Faction] *Camera Obscura* (1985), Beggars Banquet BEGA 63.

Compilations:

The Classic Years (1998), Chronicles 314 565 185-2.
Innocent & Vain – An Introduction to Nico (2002), Polydor 589 421-2.
The Frozen Borderline 1968-1970 (2007), Elektra 8122-74885-2.

Live albums:

[with Kevin Ayers, John Cale and Brian Eno] *June 1, 1974* (1974), Island ILPS 9291.
Behind the Iron Curtain (1986), Dojo DOJO LP 27.
Heroine (1994), Anagram CDMGRAM 85.
Nico's Last Concert 'Fata Morgana' (1994), SPV Recordings SPV CD 084-96202.
Reims Cathedral – December 13th, 1974 (2012), Cleopatra CLP 9430.
[with John Cale and Lou Reed] *Le Bataclan '72* (2017), Grey Scale GSGZ036CD.

Lou Reed

Studio albums:

Lou Reed (1972), RCA Victor LSP-4701.
Transformer (1972), RCA Victor LSP-4807.
Berlin (1973), RCA Victor APL1-0207.
Sally Can't Dance (1974), RCA CPL1-0611.
Metal Machine Music (1975), RCA Victor CPL2-1101.
Coney Island Baby (1975), RCA APL1-0915.
Rock and Roll Heart (1976), Arista AL 4100.
Street Hassle (1978), Arista AB 4169.
The Bells (1979), Arista AB 4229.
Growing Up in Public (1980), Arista AL 9522.
The Blue Mask (1982), RCA Victor AFL1-4221.
Legendary Hearts (1983), RCA Victor AFL1-4568.
New Sensations (1984), RCA Victor AFL1-4998.
Mistrial (1986), RCA PL87190.
New York (1989), Sire 9 25829-2.
[with John Cale] *Songs for Drella* (1990), Sire W2 26140.
Magic and Loss (1992), Sire 7599-26662-1.
Set the Twilight Reeling (1996), Warner Bros 9362 46159-1.
Ecstasy (2000), Reprise 9 47425-2.

The Raven (2003), Sire 48372-2.
Hudson River Wind Meditations (2007), Sounds True M1117D.
[with Metallica] *Lulu* (2011), Warner Bros 529084-2.

Compilations:

Rock and Roll Diary 1967–1980 (1980), Arista A2L 8603.
A Rock & Roll Life (1989), Sire PRO-CD-3358.
Between Thought and Expression (The Lou Reed Anthology) (1992), RCA PD90621.
NYC Man (2003), BMG 74321 98401 2.
The RCA & Arista Album Collection [17 x CD box set] (2016), Sony Music 88843038032.

Live albums:

Rock 'n' Roll Animal (1974), RCA Victor APL1-0472.
Lou Reed: Live (1975), RCA Victor APL1-0959.
Lou Reed Live – Take No Prisoners (1978), Arista AL 8502.
Perfect Night in London (1998), Reprise 9 46917-2.
Animal Serenade (2004), Reprise 48678-2.
[with Zeitkratzer] *Metal Machine Music* (2007), Asphodel ASP 3002.
[Lou Reed's Metal Machine Trio] *The Creation of the Universe* (2008), Sister Ray Recordings IFPI L533.
Berlin: Live at St. Ann's Warehouse (2008), Matador OLE 849-1.
[with Laurie Anderson and John Zorn] *The Stone: Issue Three* (2008), Tzadik TZ 0004.
[with John Cale and Nico] *Le Bataclan '72* (2017), Grey Scale GSGZ036CD.

Maureen Tucker

Studio albums:

Playin' Possum (1982), Trash TLP-1001.
Life in Exile after Abdication (1989), 50 Skidillion Watts MOE 7-1.
I Spent a Week There the Other Night (1991), New Rose rose 273.
Dogs Under Stress (1993), New Rose 422492.

E.P.s:

Moejadkatebarry (1987), 50 Skidillion Watts MOE 1.
Grl-Grup (1997), Lakeshore Drive LSD CD2001.

Compilation:

I Feel So Far Away: Anthology 1974–1998 (2012), Sundazed Music CD 11201.

Live albums:

Oh No, They're Recording This Show (1992), New Rose 422418.
Moe Rocks Terrastock: Live in Seattle 11/05/2000 (2002), Captain Trip CTCD-400.

Appearances:

[Drums and vocals] Magnet (1997), *Don't Be a Penguin*, PC Music PC 0003.
[Drums and vocals] The Kropotkins (2000), *Five Points Crawl*, Mulatta mul 003.
[Drums] The Raveonette's (2005), *Pretty in Black*, Columbia 519426 2.

Doug Yule (post-Velvet Underground appearances on record)

American Flyer (1976), *American Flyer*, United Artists UA-LA650-G.
American Flyer (1977), *Spirit of a Woman*, United Artists UA-LA720-G.
Red Dog (2009), *Hard Times*, Olddog 0409.
Red Dog (2011), *Nine-Tail Cat*, Old Dog 0411.

Other discographical and musical work references

Ayers, K. (1973), *Bananamour*, Harvest SHVL 807.
Ayers, K. (1974), *The Confessions of Dr. Dream and Other Stories*, Island ILPS 9263.
Apple, F. (2020), *Fetch the Bolt Cutters*, Epic 19439774432.
Arctic Monkeys (2013), *AM*, Domino WIGCD317.
Babatunde, O. (1960), *Drums of Passion*, Columbia CL 1412.
Baker, C. (1954), 'My Funny Valentine', *Chet Baker Sings*, Pacific Jazz PJLP-11.
The Band (1968), *Music from Big Pink*, Capitol SKAO 2955.
The Beatles (1965), 'Michelle' and 'Girl', *Rubber Soul*, Parlophone PMC 1267.
The Beatles (1967), *Sgt. Pepper's Lonely Hearts Club Band*, Parlophone PMC 7027.
The Beatles (1968), *The Beatles* [The White Album], Apple PCSO-7067-8.
Berio, L. ([1964]1971), 'Black Is the Colour of My True Love's Hair', 'I Wonder as I Wander', *Epifanie And Folk Songs*, RCA Red Seal LSC-3189.
Bowie, D. (1971), 'Andy Warhol', 'Queen Bitch' and 'Song for Bob Dylan', *Hunky Dory*, RCA Victor SF 8244.
Bowie, D. (1972), 'Rock "N" Roll Suicide', *The Rise and Fall of Ziggy Stardust and the Spiders from Mars*, RCA Victor SF 8287.
Bowie, D. (1973), 'Time', *Aladdin Sane*, RCA Victor RS 1001.
Bowie, D. (1976), *Station to Station*, RCA Victor APL1 1327.

Bowie, D. (1977a), *Low*, RCA Victor PL 12030.
Bowie, D. (1977b), *"Heroes"*, RCA Victor PL 12522.
Bowie, D. (1995), *1. Outside (The Nathan Adler Diaries: A Hyper Cycle)*, BMG 74321303392.
Bragg, B. (1990), 'I Dreamed I Saw Phil Ochs Last Night', *The Internationale*, DRO 3D-0736.
Brel, J. (1967), 'Fils De…', *Jacques Brel 67*, Barclay 80 334 S.
The Byrds (1968), *Sweetheart of the Rodeo*, Columbia CS 9670.
Cale, J. (1970), 'Charlemagne', 'Amsterdam', 'Ghost Story', *Vintage Violence*, Columbia CS 1037.
Cale, J. (1972), 'Brahms', 'Legs Larry at Television Centre', 'The Academy In Peril', 'Faust', 'King Harry', *The Academy in Peril*, Reprise MS 2079.
Cale, J. (1973), 'Child's Christmas in Wales', 'Hanky Panky Nohow', 'The Endless Plain of Fortune', 'Andalucía', 'Paris 1919', 'Graham Greene', 'Half Past France', 'Antarctica Starts Here', *Paris 1919*, Reprise MS 2131.
Cale, J. (1974), 'Fear Is a Man's Best Friend', 'Buffalo Ballet', 'Ship Of Fools', 'Gun', *Fear*, Island ILPS 9301.
Cale, J. (1979), 'Mercenaries (Ready for War)', 'Dr. Mudd', 'Walkin' The Dog', *Sabotage/Live*, Spy SP 004.
Cale, J. (1996), *Walking on Locusts*, Hannibal HNCD 1395.
Cale, J. (2001), 'Sun Blindness Music', 'Summer Heat', 'The Second Fortress', *Sun Blindness Music*, Table of The Elements Re 75.
Cale, J. (2003a), 'Verses', 'Waiting for Blonde', 'Chums of Dumpty (We All Are)', 'E is Missing', *5 Tracks*, EMI CDEM621.
Cale, J. (2003b), 'Letter from Abroad', 'Look Horizon', 'Magritte', 'Over Her Head', 'Reading My Mind', 'Things', 'Twilight Zone', *HoboSapiens*, EMI 5939092.
Cale, J. (2005), 'Brotherman', 'For a Ride', 'Gravel Drive', 'Hush', 'In a Flood', 'Mailman', 'Perfect', 'Satisfied', 'Turn the Lights On', 'Sold Motel', 'Wasteland', 'Woman', *Black Acetate*, EMI 0946 3 39182 2 1.
Cale, J. (2011a), 'Catastrofuk', 'Whaddya Mean by That', *EP: Extra Playful*, Double Six DS046CD.
Cale, J. (2020), 'Lazy Day' [single], Double Six DS151D.
Cale, J. and Riley, T. (1971), 'The Hall of Mirrors in the Palace at Versailles', 'The Soul Of Patrick Lee', 'Ides Of March', *Church of Anthrax*, Columbia C 30131.
Cherry, D. (1967), *Symphony for Improvisers*, Blue Note 7243 5 63823 2 9.
Cochran, E. (1959), 'Somethin' Else' [single], Liberty F-55203.
Collins, J. (1967), 'Sisters of Mercy', 'Hey, That's No Way to Say Goodbye', *Wildflowers*, Elektra EKS-74012.
The Deviants (1968), 'I'm Coming Home', *Ptooff!*, Underground Impresarios IMP 1.
The Doors (1967), 'The End', *The Doors*, Elektra EKL-4007.
Downliners Sect (1966), *The Rock Sect's In*, Columbia SX 6028.
Drake, N. (1972), *Bryter Layter*, Island ILPS 9134.
Dylan, B. (1964), *The Times They Are A-Changin'*, Columbia CL 2105.
Dylan, B. (1965), *Bringing It All Back Home*, Columbia CS 9128.

Dylan, B. (1965), 'Like a Rolling Stone' and 'Ballad of a Thin Man', *Highway 61 Revisited*, Columbia CL 2389.
Dylan, B. (1965), 'Positively 4th Street' [single], Columbia 4-43389.
Eno, B. (1973), *Here Come The Warm Jets*, Island ILPS 9268.
Eno, B. (1982), *Ambient 4: On Land*, Editions EG EGED 20.
Fairport Convention (1968), 'Who Knows Where the Time Goes', *Unhalfbricking*, Island ILPS 9102.
Faithfull, M. (1964), 'As Tears Go By' [single], Decca F.11923.
Fallersleben, A. H. H. von (and Haydn, J.) (1841), 'Das Lied Der Deutschen'.
Foxx, J. (1981), 'Europe after the Rain' [single], Metal Beat VS 393.
Fripp and Eno (1973), *No Pussyfooting*, Island HELP 16.
Joy Division (1981), 'Sister Ray', *Still*, Factory FACT 40.
Kraftwerk (1970), 'Von Himmel Hoch', *Kraftwerk*, Philips 6305 058.
Kraftwerk (1981), 'Computer Love'/'The Model' [single], EMI 12 EMI 5207.
Lennon, J. and Ono, Y. (1968), *Unfinished Music No. 1. Two Virgins*, Apple SAPCOR 2.
Lewis, J. (2005), 'Williamsburg Will Oldham Horror', *City and Eastern Songs*, Rough Trade RTRADCD237.
Luna (1994), *Bewitched*, Elektra 61617-2.
Magazine (1978), 'Shot By Both Sides' [single], Virgin VS 200.
Mahler, G. (1905), 'Wenn dein Mütterlein', *Kindertotenlieder* [song cycle], 29 January.
McKenzie, S. (1967), 'San Francisco (Be Sure to Wear Flowers in Your Hair)' [single], Ode ZS7-103.
The Modern Lovers (1976), *The Modern Lovers*, Home of The Hits HH-1910.
The Mothers of Invention (1968), *We're Only in It for the Money*, Verve V6-5045.
Nico (1965), 'I'm Not Sayin''/'The Last Mile' [single], Immediate IM 003.
Nico (1967), 'The Fairest of the Seasons', 'These Days', 'Winter Song', *Chelsea Girl*, Verve V-5032.
Nico ([1968] 1991), 'Ari's Song', 'Evening of Light', 'Frozen Warnings', 'Julius Caesar (Memento Hodie)', 'Nibelungen', 'No One Is There', 'Roses in the Snow', *The Marble Index* [extended], Elektra 7559-61098-2.
Nico (1970), 'Abschied', 'Afraid', 'Janitor of Lunacy', 'My Only Child', 'Mütterlein', 'The Falconer', *Desertshore*, Reprise RS 6424.
Nico (1974), 'Das Lied Der Deutschen', 'Innocent and Vain', 'It Has Not Taken Long', 'Secret Side', 'We've Got the Gold', 'You Forget to Answer', *The End*, Island ILPS 931.
Nico (1981), '60-40', 'Henry Hudson', 'Heroes', 'I'm Waiting for the Man', 'Orly Flight', *Drama of Exile*, Aura AUL 715.
PiL (1979), *Metal Box*, Virgin METAL 1.
Reed, L. (1972), 'Perfect Day', 'Vicious', *Transformer*, RCA Victor LSP-4807.
Reed, L. (1972), 'Walk on the Wild Side' [single], RCA Victor RCA 2303.
Reed, L. (1973), 'Lady Day', 'Men of Good Fortune', 'Caroline Says I', 'Caroline Says II', 'The Kids', 'The Bed', 'Sad Song', *Berlin*, RCA Victor APL1-0207.
Reed, L. (1978), 'Street Hassle', *Street Hassle*, Arista AB 4169.

Reed, L. (1978), *Live: Take No Prisoners*, Arista AL 8502.
Reed, L. (2000), 'Mystic Child', 'Tatters', 'Like a Possum', *Ecstasy*, Reprise 9 47425-2.
Reed, L. (2003), 'Fire Music', *The Raven*, Sire 48372-2.
Reed, L. (2003), 'Who Am I? (Tripitena's Song)', *NYC Man*, BMG 74321 98401 2.
Reed, L. and Cale, J. (1990), 'Smalltown', 'Open House', 'Style It Takes', 'Work', 'Faces and Names', 'Images', 'Slip Away (A Warning)', 'I Believe', 'Nobody But You', 'A Dream', 'Forever Changed', 'Hello It's Me', *Songs for Drella* [CD], Sire 7599-26140-2.
The Riats (1967), 'Run, Run, Run'/'Sunday Morning' [single], Omega 35.796.
Richman, J. [and The Modern Lovers] (n.d.), *Songs of Remembrance 1970–1973* [CD bootleg].
Richman, J. [and The Modern Lovers] (1976), *Jonathan Richman & The Modern Lovers*, Beserkley BZ-0048.
Richman, J. (1985), 'Chewing Gum Wrapper' and 'Vincent Van Gogh', *Rockin' and Romance*, Twin/Tone TTR 8558.
Richman, J. (1988), 'When Harpo Played His Harp', *Modern Lovers' 88*, Demon FIEND 106.
Richman, J. (1991), 'Monologue About Bermuda', *Having a Party with Jonathan Richman*, Rounder ROUNDER CD 9026.
Richman, J. (1992), 'Velvet Underground', *I, Jonathan*, Rounder CD 9036.
Richman, J. (2004), 'Salvador Dali', *Not So Much to Be Loved As to Love*, Sanctuary SANCD 290.
Richman, J. (2008), 'No One Was Like Vermeer', *Because Her Beauty Is Raw and Wild*, Vapor 2-453180.
Richman, J. (2010), 'My Affected Accent', *O Moon Queen of Night on Earth*, Vapor VPR2-526072.
Richman, J. (2015), 'Keith'/'They Showed Me the Door to Bohemia' [single], Blue Arrow BAR 002.
Riley, T. (1969), *A Rainbow in Curved Air*, Columbia Masterworks MS7315.
The Riot Squad (2013), *Toy Soldier e.p.*, Acid Jazz AJX329S.
R.E.M. (1986), 'Femme Fatale', 'Superman' [12" single], I.R.S. IRMT 128.
The Rolling Stones (1968), 'Stray Cat Blues', *Beggars Banquet*, Decca LK 4955.
The Rolling Stones (1971), *Sticky Fingers*, Rolling Stones Records COC 59100.
The Rolling Stones (1972), *Exile on Main St.*, Rolling Stones Records COC 69100.
Roxy Music (1972), *Roxy Music*, Island ILPS 9200.
Roxy Music (1973), *For Your Pleasure*, Island ILPS 9232.
Roxy Music (1973), 'Song for Europe', *Stranded*, Island ILPS 9252.
Saint Etienne (2012), 'Over the Border', *Words and Music*, Heavenly HVNLP 92CD.
The Savage Rose (1970), *Your Daily Gift*, Gregar GG-103.
Schubert, F. (1824), *String Quartet No. 14 in D minor, D 810* [aka *Death and the Maiden*].
Sex Pistols (1977), 'Holidays in the Sun' [single], Virgin VS 191.
Sex Pistols (1979), 'Something Else' [single], Virgin VS 240.
Siouxsie and the Banshees (1979), 'Mittageisen' [single], Polydor 2059 151.

Stockhausen, K. (1969), *Hymnen*, Deutsche Grammophon 139 421/22.
Stockhausen, K. (1970), *Stimmung*, Deutsche Grammophon 2561 043.
Television Personalities (2006), 'Velvet Underground', *My Dark Places*, Domino WIGLP 166.
Thompson, R. (2015), 'Guitar Heroes', *Still*, Proper PRPLP131.
Ultravox (1981), 'Vienna' [single], Chrysalis CHS 2481.
Various Artists (2021), *I'll Be Your Mirror – A Tribute to The Velvet Underground & Nico*, Verve B0033527-01.
The Velvet Underground (1966), 'Noise', *The East Village Other*, ESP Disk 1034.
The Velvet Underground (1973), *Squeeze*, Polydor 2383 180.
Visage (1980), 'Fade to Grey' [single], Polydor POSPX 194.
Wagner, R. (1845), 'Overture', *Tannhäuser* WWV 70.
Waits, T. (1983), *Swordfishtrombones*, Island 7 90095-1.
The Walker Brothers (1978), *Nite Flights*, GTO GTLP 033.
Weezer (1994), 'In the Garage', *Weezer*, DGC DGCD-24629.
Wire (1977), *Pink Flag*, Harvest SHSP 4076.
Zappa, F. (1988), *You Can't Do That on Stage Anymore Vol. 1*, Rykodisc RCD 10081/82.

Film, television and radio references

Andy Warhol (1972), [Film] Dirs. Kim Evans and Lana Jokel, USA: Michael Blackwood Productions.
Andy Warhol's Exploding Plastic Inevitable with The Velvet Underground and Nico (1966), [Film], Dir. Ronald Nameth, USA.
Antártida (1995), [Film] Dir. Manuel Huerga, Spain: Sogetel, Canal+ España, and Iberoamericana Films.
Ari and Mario (1966), [Film] Dir. Andy Warhol, USA.
Beautiful Mistake (2000), [Film] Dir. Marc Evans, Wales, UK: Merlin Films.
The Big Lebowski (1998) [Film] Dir. Joel and Ethan Coen, USA: Polygram/Working Title.
Cabaret (1972), [Film] Dir. Bob Fosse, USA: Allied Artists/ABC/Feuer and Martin.
Couch (1964), [Film] Dir. Andy Warhol, USA.
David Bowie: Finding Fame (2019), [TV Programme] BBC2 [UK], 9 February.
Eat (1963) [Films] Dir. Andy Warhol, USA.
Empire (1964), [Film] Dir. Andy Warhol, USA.
En Effeuillant la Marguerite (1956), [Film] Dir. Marc Allégret, France: Films EGE/Hoche Productions.
**** (Four Stars) (1967), [Film] Dir. Andy Warhol, USA.
Hedy (1966), [Film] Dir. Andy Warhol, USA.
Henry Geldzahler (1964), [Film] Dir. Andy Warhol, USA.
I, A Man (1967), [Film] Dir. Andy Warhol, USA.
Imitation of Christ (1967), [Film] Dir. Andy Warhol, USA.
John Cale (1998) [Film documentary] Dir. James Marsh, UK: NVC Arts and BBC Wales.

Kiss (1963) [Films] Dir. Andy Warhol, USA.
La Cicatrice Intérieure (1972), [Film] Dir. Philippe Garrel, France.
La Dolce Vita (1960), [Film] Dir. Federico Fellini, France/Italy: Riama/Cinecittà/ Pathé Consortium.
Les Hautes Solitudes (1974), [Film] Dir. Philippe Garrel, France.
Lou Reed's Berlin (2007), [Film of live performance – DVD] Dir. Julian Schnabel, USA: Fortissimo Films/Artificial Eye.
Nico Icon (1995), [Film] Dir. Susanne Ofteringer, Germany: Edition Salzgeber.
Nico/Antoine (1966), [Film] Dir. Andy Warhol, USA.
Sleep (1963), [Film] Dir. Andy Warhol, USA.
Songs for Drella (1990), [Film] Dir. Ed Lachman, USA: Warner Reprise.
Strip-tease (1963), [Film] Dir. Jacques Poitrenaud, France/Italy: Lambor Films/ Champs Elysee Productions/Variety Film.
Take Me to the Plaza (2003) [Film] Dir. Miles Montalbano, USA: Vapor.
The Chelsea Girls (1966), [Film] Dir. Andy Warhol, USA.
The Closet (1966), [Film] Dir. Andy Warhol, USA.
The Royal Tenenbaums (2001), [Film] Dir. Wes Anderson, USA: Touchstone.
The Seventh Seal (1957), [Film] Dir. Ingmar Bergman, Sweden: Svensk Filmindustri.
The Velvet Underground (2021), [Documentary Film] Dir. Todd Haynes, USA: PolyGram Entertainment, Verve Label Group, Killer Films and Motto Pictures.
The Velvet Underground and Nico: A Symphony of Sound (1966), [Film] Dir. Andy Warhol, USA.
The Velvet Underground in Boston (1967), [Film] Dir. Andy Warhol, USA.
13 Most Beautiful... Songs for Andy Warhol's Screen Tests (2009), [Film DVD] Dir. Andy Warhol, [Music – Dean and Britta], USA: Plexifilms 034.
Un Ange Passe, [Film] Dir. Phillippe Garrel, France: Philippe Garrel.
Une Femme est une Femme (1961), [Film] Dir. Jean-Luc Godard, France/Italy: Euro International Films/Rom Paris Films.
Venus in Furs (1965), [Film] Dir. Piero Heliczer, USA.
Wax! Crackle! Pop! (2014), [Radio programme] *Radio Valencia*, 3 March. Available online: https://bit.ly/3HfFsNe (accessed 2 December 2021).
Wholly Communion (1965), [Film] Dir. Peter Whitehead, UK: Lorrimer Films.
Zwischen Gestern und Morgen (1947), [Film], Dir. Harald Braun, Neue Deutsche Filmgesellschaft.

Index

'3 Orchestral Pieces' 137
5 Tracks 257, 258, 261
13 Most Beautiful: Songs for Andy Warhol's Screen Tests 63–4
14 Hour Technicolor Dream 37, 42, 46
120 Days of Sodom 98
1969 Velvet Underground Live 12, 228

'Abschied' 135, 186, 189
Academy in Peril, The 137
'Academy in Peril, The' 137
Adventures of Augie March, The 105, 109
Adventures of Huckleberry Finn, The 98, 105, 106, 108
'After Hours' 10, 22, 142 (note)
'Afraid' 135
Against Nature 98
Agitation Free 124, 173, 183
Albin, Shelley 69
'All That Is My Own' 135
'All Tomorrow's Parties' 19, 57, 86–7, 117, 122, 132, 244
Ambient 4: On Land 218
Amis, Martin 2
Amon Düül 124
'Amsterdam' 137
'Andalucía' 8
Anderson, Laurie 198, 266, 267, 268, 269, 270, 272
Anderson, Wes 127 (note)
'Andy Warhol' 147
Andy Warhol Diaries, The 245–9
Andy Warhol's Exploding Plastic Inevitable with The Velvet Underground and Nico 197
Andy Warhol's Velvet Underground and Nico 197
Animal Serenade 271
Anohni 162
Animal Collective 263
Another View (album) 8

'Antarctica Starts Here' 138
Antonioni, Michelangelo 153
'Ari's Song' 119–20, 192 (note)
Arnold, PP 36
Arrabal, Fernando 69
Arts Lab, The 37, 42
Ash Ra Tempel 124
Ashley, Elizabeth 268
Ayers, Kevin 124, 174, 179, 182
Ayler, Albert 37

Baader, Andreas 136, 190–1
'Baby's on Fire' 180
'Baby What You Want Me to Do' 139
Baez, Joan 39
Baker, Chet 116–17
'Ballad of a Thin Man' 20
Bananamour 179
Bangs, Lester 2, 40, 79, 122, 145, 154, 198–9, 202
Barrett, Syd 38, 121
Bauhaus 141, 263
Bauhaus, The 184, 187
Beatles 17, 20–3, 25, 28, 35, 39, 41, 43, 58, 84, 121, 142 (note), 147, 179, 199
Beatles, The 22, 199
Beautiful Mistake 264
Beck 256, 257
Beckett, Samuel 70, 78
'Bed, The' 140, 167
Beefheart, Captain 43
Bellow, Saul 105
Beloved 108
Berlin 13, 119, 124, 133, 137, 139, 140, 173–94, 269, 273 (note)
'Berlin' 139, 140, 166
Berlin (album) 13, 49 (note), 79, 102, 139–40, 161–71, 261, 266, 268, 269
Berlin, Brigid 126, 245, 247
Beta Band, The 256
Better Books 31, 39, 40, 43, 48

Beuys, Joseph 183
Big Star 261
Birthday Party, The 91
Bish Bosh 268
Black Acetate 258, 259
Black Angels 92
'Black Angel's Death Song, The' 40, 87, 92, 244
Blow Up 153
Blue Mask, The 266
Bolan, Marc 43, 212
Book of the Courtier, The 99
Borges, Jorge Luis 102
Bowie, David 2, 5, 13, 36, 37, 41, 89, 90, 91, 136, 140, 141, 142 (note), 145–57, 161, 162, 170, 191, 211, 218, 219 (note), 224, 225, 226, 231, 247, 261, 268
Bradfield, James Dean 263
Bragg, Billy 210
Braxton, Anthony 202
Brecht, Bertold; Brechtian 3, 115, 134, 193 (note)
Brecht, George 173
Brel, Jacques 137, 139, 142 (note), 154
'Brotherman' 258
Brothers Karamazov, The 104
Brown, Pete 44
Browne, Jackson 8, 117, 175
Bruckner, Anton 137
Bryars, Gavin 176
Bryter Later 177
Buckley, Tim 175
'Buffalo Ballet' 138, 180, 186
Bukowski, Charles 162
Burroughs, William S. 38, 67, 68, 74, 76, 79–80, 81 (note), 97–8, 100, 103, 105, 123
Buscemi, Steve 267
Butterfield, Paul 20, 45
'Buzz, Buzz, Buzz' 149
Byrds, The 7, 21, 177

Café Bizarre 34, 40, 53
Cage, John 4, 5, 17, 19, 34, 36, 173, 178
Calloway, Cab 99
Can 124, 136, 141, 179
Canned Heat 20
Capote, Truman 240
Caravan 124
Cardew, Cornelius 36, 44, 173, 178
'Caroline Says I' 140
'Caroline Says II' 139, 140, 163, 167–70
Carver, Raymond 162, 229
Castiglione, Baldesar 100
'Catastrofuk' 259
Catatonia 264
Catcher in the Rye, The 24
Cave, Nick 91
Chandler, Raymond 79, 104
'Charlemagne' 137
Chelsea Girl 134, 174, 176
Chelsea Girls 42, 54
Cherry, Don 123, 202
'Chewing Gum Wrapper' 216
'Child's Christmas in Wales, A' 138, 185, 264
Chingo Blingo 257
'Chums of Dumpty' 258
Church of Anthrax 137, 176
City of Night 67, 68, 74, 75, 76–7, 79, 81 (note)
Clash, The 224
Cobain, Kurt 211
Cocteau Twins 92
Cohen, Leonard 117, 120, 137, 163
Cole, Lloyd 91
Coleman, Ornette 68, 117, 202, 268
Collins, Judy 120, 121
Coltrane, John 202–3
Coney Island Baby 224
'Coney Island Baby' 226
Confessions of Dr Dream and Other Stories, The 179
Conrad, Tony 33, 34, 40, 58, 203, 260
'Conversation Piece' 151
Corso, Gregory 33
Counterculture, The 2, 3, 17, 18–19, 20, 23, 24, 26, 27, 28, 31–46, 68, 71, 136, 148, 154, 155, 182, 190, 194 (note), 199
Cowboy Junkies 91
Crawdaddy 79, 124
Creation, The 42
Creation of the Universe, The 269

Cream 20, 25
Creem 81 (note), 118, 122, 124
Cure, The 91, 141
Cygnet Committee 151

Dafoe, Willem 268
'Das Lied Der Deutschen' 136, 174, 180–4, 187, 188–91, 192, 193 (note), 194 (note)
Davies, Ray 41
Davis, Miles 241
Dean, James 240
'Decadence' 179
'December Rains' 263
Degas, Edgar 239
Delafield, Daryl 34
Delillo, Don 109
de Maria, Walter 33, 58
Denny, Sandy 122
Depeche Mode 141
Desertshore 118, 122, 123, 134–5, 175, 177, 180, 181, 186, 261
Dietrich, Marlene 47, 119, 127 (note), 132
'Dirty Boulevard' 109
'Do Angels Need Haircuts?' 77
'Do Not Go Gentle into That Good Night' 264
'Dr. Mudd' 141
Doctorow, E.L. 109
Dogs under Stress (album) 8, 11
Dom, The 34, 45, 60, 61, 175, 248
Donovan 38, 39, 57
Don Quixote 97–8
Doors, The 20, 21, 23, 124, 175, 188
Dos Passos, John 104, 105, 108
Dostoevsky, Fyodor 73, 104
Drake, Nick 121, 177
Drama of Exile 113, 141
'Dream, A' 245–9, 250
'In Dreams Begin Responsibilities' 104
Drift, The 268
'Driving Me Backwards' 180
Drums of Passion (album) 10
Dvořák, Antonin 177
Dyddiau Du/Dark Days 265
Dylan, Bob 3, 19–20, 35, 36, 39, 43, 57, 63, 80 (note), 116, 117, 147, 163, 211

'E is Missing' 258
Eat/Kiss: Music for the Films of Andy Warhol 256
Echo and the Bunnymen 91
Ecstasy 163, 266–7, 268, 270
'Eight Miles High' 21
Emerson, Keith 224
Eminem 257
Empire (film) 55
End, The 124, 136, 174, 180–2, 184, 186
'End, The' 124, 180–2, 188
Eno, Brian 2, 6, 13, 46, 91, 124, 136, 139, 141, 146, 157 (notes), 173, 174, 178–94, 218, 264
EP: Extra Playful 259
Epstein, Brian 36, 41, 42, 43, 44
Europe, European 131–42
'Europe after the Rain' 141
'European Son' 22, 43, 87, 132
Evergreen Review 68, 71, 73, 74, 75, 76, 77, 78, 79
Exploding Plastic Inevitable 4, 8, 23, 34–5, 44, 45, 54, 55, 59, 60–4, 78, 146, 197, 237
Ezrin, Bob 161, 162, 166

'Faces and Names' 242, 250
Factory, The 3–5, 31, 33, 34, 39, 41, 42, 47–8, 53–4, 56–7, 60, 61, 99, 115, 117, 135, 137, 147, 148, 151, 153, 155, 174, 197, 231, 237, 242, 244, 246
'Fade to Grey' 141
Fahey, John 39
Fairport Convention 121, 122–3
Faithfull, Marianne 39, 40
'Falconer, The' 135, 137, 186
Falklands Suite, The 264
Fall, The 141, 218
Falling Spikes, The 33–4, 49 (note)
Farren, Mick 38, 41, 46, 151, 152
Faust (band) 136, 141, 179
'Faust' 137
Fear 138, 179–80, 185
'Fear is a Man's Best Friend' 138, 186–7
Feldman, Morton 4, 173
Feldman, Susan 269
Fellini, Federico 4, 114

'Femme Fatale' 46, 86, 92, 113, 115, 132, 137, 138, 228
Ferlinghetti, Lawrence 39, 43
Ferreira, Sky 263
Ferry, Bryan 178
Fields, Danny 47, 61, 121
'In a Flood' 259
Floh de Cologne 189
Fluxus 3–5, 121, 187
'Foggy Notion' 7, 100, 101
Fontaines D.C 93
Ford, Richard 229
'Forever Changed' 245
Foxx, John 141
Fragments of a Rainy Season 260, 261–2
Franglen, Nick 257
Free Jazz 202
Fripp, Robert 179
'Frozen Warnings' 134, 186
Fugs, The 17, 34, 36, 37, 38, 44, 150

Gainsbourg, Serge 115, 121
Galaxie 500 63
'In the Garage' 210
Garrel, Philippe 124, 174, 175
Gaye, Marvin 22
Genesis 176
Genet, Jean 70, 74, 79, 150, 211
'Ghost Story' 137
'Gift, The' 69, 85, 88, 101, 102
'Gimme Shelter' 212
Ginsberg, Allen 33–5, 36, 37, 39, 43, 44, 47, 67, 68, 80 (note)
Glam 5, 83, 133, 150, 154–5, 161, 224
Glass, Philip 39, 134, 173
Godard, Jean-Luc 115
Godard, Vic 156
Gong 176
'Good Night' 22
Gordon, Kim 263
Gorky's Zygotic Mynci 264
Gothic, Gothicism 24, 88, 125, 132, 133, 135, 136, 137, 138–9
'Graham Greene' 138
Grateful Dead 2, 25
'Gravel Drive' 258
Gravity's Rainbow 108

Grove Press 67–81
'Guitar Heroes' 210
'Gun' 138, 180
Guthrie, Arlo 22

'Hall of Mirrors at the Palace at Versailles, The' 137
'Halloween Parade' 109
'Hanky Panky Nohow' 138
Hardin, Tim 117
'Have I the Right?' 22
Haynes, Todd 6, 12, 64, 92
'Heartbreak Hotel' 138, 180
Helen of Troy 139
Heliczer, Kate 33, 35, 40, 43, 44, 45
Heliczer, Piero 33, 34
'Hello It's Me' 245, 249
Hendrix, Jimi 36, 43, 189, 193–4 (note), 204, 211
'Henry Hudson' 141
Here Come the Warm Jets 179, 191
'Here She Comes Now' 88
Herman's Hermits 35
Heroes 140, 191
'Heroes' 141
'Heroin' 3, 6, 10, 21, 23, 25, 40, 46, 67, 83, 87, 92, 99, 101, 149, 164, 212, 213, 219 (note), 225, 233, 249
Hippie(s) 2, 3, 5, 17, 19, 24, 27, 28
'Hitch Hike' 22
HoboSapiens 257, 258
Hoenig, Michael 173
Hole 257
'Holidays in the Sun' 140
Hollies, The 35
Holzer, Baby Jane 39, 54, 58, 246
Honeycombs, The 22
Honi Soit 141, 248
Hopkins, John ('Hoppy') 31, 33, 35, 43
Horovitz Michael 43
Horses 191
'Howl' 67, 68
Hudson River Meditations 271–2
Hunky Dory 147, 156, 211
'Hush' 258
Huysmans, J.K. 98
Hymnen 183, 184

'I Believe' 244
'I Heard Her Call My Name' 89, 204
'I Wanna Be Black' 101, 108, 234, 246
'I Wanna Talk 2 U' 263
'Ides of March' 137
I'll Be Your Mirror' 46, 57, 69, 87, 92, 243
I'll Be Your Mirror: A Tribute to The Velvet Underground and Nico 92
'I'm Coming Home' 41
'I Dreamed I Saw Phil Ochs Last Night' 210
'I'm Not Sayin' 47, 58, 115, 116, 117
'I'm Sticking with You' 10, 216
'I'm Waiting for The Man' 1, 40, 76, 86, 101, 132, 141, 145, 147, 149–53, 155, 157 (note), 186, 213, 226, 228
'Images' 244, 250
Impressions, The 22
Incredible String Band 121
Indie 92, 127
'Innocent and Vain' 136, 181, 187
International Times 37–8, 39, 41, 42, 44, 45, 46, 148
Ionesco, Eugene 70
I Spent a Week There the Other Night (album) 8, 11
'It Has Not Taken Long' 136, 180, 181
'It Was a Pleasure Then' 175
Ives, Charles 177

Jackson, Shirley 102
Jane's Addiction 91
'Janitor of Lunacy' 123, 134, 186
Jagger, Mick 40, 47, 246
Jefferson Airplane 2, 20, 21, 23, 28
Jenner, Pete 41
Jesus and Mary Chain, The 89, 91, 156
'Jeweller, The' 139
Joan as Police Woman 263
John Cale (2018-1964): A Futurespective 262
'John Milton' 177
John's Children 42
Jonathan Richman and The Modern Lovers 214, 215, 216
Jones, Brian 4, 47, 48, 57, 134
Joy Division 89, 91, 92, 141

Joyce, James 102
'Julius Caesar (Memento Hodie)' 121, 123, 134, 137
June 1, 1974 124, 174, 179–80, 185
Jung, Carl 73, 84, 89–90, 93
Junkie 105

Kahlo, Frida 211
'Keith' 211, 212
Kerouac, Jack 33, 80 (note)
Khan, Salamat Ali 173
Khan, Ustad Vilayat 173
'Kids, The' 139, 140, 167
'Kill Your Sons' 106
'King Harry' 137
King Princess 93
Kinks, The 35, 36, 41, 133, 156, 214
Kiss (film) 9, 60, 243
Kiss 210
Knef, Hildegard 119, 132
Kokane 257
Kraftwerk 141, 179, 187
Kupferberg, Tuli 37, 39, 44

La Dolce Vita 4, 114
Lady Chatterley's Lover 67, 74
'Lady Day' 140, 167
'Lady Godiva's Operation' 88, 105, 132
Last Exit to Brooklyn 67, 68, 76–7, 79, 80 (note), 81 (note), 103
'Last Great American Whale, The' 109
'Laughing Gnome, The' 149
Lawrence, D.H. 67, 74, 80
'Lazy Day' 260
'Le Petit Chevalier' 176
'Leaving It Up to You' 139
Led Zeppelin 47, 133, 153
'Legs Larry at Television Centre' 137
Lennon, John 43, 199
'Letter from Abroad' 258
Life along the Borderline: A Tribute to Nico 263
Life in Exile after Abdication (album) 8, 10
Lightfoot, Gordon 47, 58
'Like a Possum' 270
'Like a Rolling Stone' 23
Linkous, Mark 263

'Little Toy Soldier' 150, 151
Live at Max's Kansas City (album) 11, 12, 61, 228
Live: Take No Prisoners (album) 13, 99, 223–35
Loaded (album) 6, 7, 10, 11, 12, 21, 27, 103, 146, 223, 245
Lobel, Elektrah 34
Lonely Woman Quarterly 68, 70, 71–4, 76, 80 (note)
'Look Horizon' 258
'Loop' 204
LOOP>>60Hz: Transmissions from the Drone Orchestra 262
Los Angeles 3, 61, 62, 74, 137, 153, 157 (note), 177
'Lottery, The' 1–2
Lou Reed: The RCA & Arista Album Collection 271
Lou Reed Live 161, 224
Lou Reed's Berlin 162
Love Supreme, A 202
Low 140
'Lucy in the Sky with Diamonds' 21
Lulu 266, 268, 269
Lupe Fiasco 257
Lustig, Jo 180, 192

M Train 211
Maclise, Angus 5, 9, 33, 40
Madame Bovary 74, 97, 99
Magazine 140
Magic and Loss 266
Magma 176
Magnetic Fields, The 263
'Magritte' 258
Mahler, Gustav 118, 135, 136, 137
'Mailman' 258
'Making of Unpretty, The' 265
Malanga, Gerald 33, 34, 36, 37, 39, 42, 44, 45, 47, 48, 53, 59, 60, 61, 147
Manic Street Preachers 263
Manzanera, Phil 136, 179–80, 181
Marble Index, The 118–19, 120–1, 122, 123, 127, 133, 175, 176, 181, 186
March Violets 141
Marquis de Sade, The 38, 73, 98
Massive Attack 91

Matisse, Henri 239
McCartney, Paul 43, 45
McGarrigle, Kate and Anna 268
McLuhan, Marshall 62–3, 201, 204
Meinhof, Ulrike 136, 190–1
Mekas, Jonas 34, 59, 62
'Melody Laughter' 200
Melody Maker (music press) 25, 42, 45, 120, 126, 146, 178, 180, 203, 235 (note)
'Men of Good Fortune' 139
'Mercenaries (Ready for War)' 141
Metal Box 141
Metal Machine Music (album) 13, 107, 197–206, 266, 269, 272
Metal Machine Trio, The 269, 272
'Metal Postcard [Mittageisen]' 140
Metallica 266, 268
MGMT 263
Miles, Barry 36–45
Miller, Henry 67, 72, 74, 80
Mistrial 246
Mitchell Adrian 43
Moby-Dick 108, 109
'Model, The' 141
Modern Lovers, The 177, 209–19
MoeJadKateBarry (ep) 10
'Monologue about Bermuda' 218
Monroe, Marilyn 240, 241, 250, 251 (note)
Montez, Mario 33
'Moonage Daydream' 155
Moore, Thurston 93
Morales, Sylvia 246
Morrison, Toni 108
Morrissey, Paul 35, 36, 42, 53–4, 113, 121, 127 (note)
Morrison, Jim 21, 116, 175
Mott the Hoople 162
'Murder Mystery, The' 10, 22
Murphy, Peter 263
Murray, Pauline 141
Music for a New Society 258
Music for a New Society/M:FANS 260, 261
Musique concrete 149, 204
'Mütterlein' 135, 186, 188, 189
'My Affected Accent' 218
My Bloody Valentine 92
'My Funny Valentine' 116–17

'My Maria' 139
'My Only Child' 135, 175
'Mystic Child' 163

Naked Lunch 67, 74, 76, 79, 80 (note), 105, 123
Name, Billy 5, 242, 247
Nameth, Ronald 197
Napier-Bell, Simon 35, 36, 153
'Never Get Emotionally Involved with Man, Woman, Beast or Child' 41
New Order 91
New York 1–6, 7, 8, 10, 20, 31–48, 54, 56–7, 60, 69, 74–5, 77, 91, 98, 100, 108, 132, 137, 146–8, 151, 153, 155–6, 162, 173, 175–7, 190, 193 (note), 197, 203, 213, 219 (note), 223, 226, 228, 230, 233, 237, 242, 244–5, 262, 263, 264, 266, 269, 271
New York (album) 8, 108–9
Newley, Anthony 150, 151
Ndegeocello, Meshell 263
Nico Icon 113
NME (New Musical Express) 40, 117, 118, 124, 125, 126, 180
'No One Is There' 133, 186
'No One Was Like Vermeer' 211, 212
No Pussyfooting 179
'Nobody but You' 242
'Noise' 37, 201
Not the 1s 257
Nova Express 79, 161
Nuttall Jeff 39, 44
NYC Man 270–1

Ofteringer, Suzanne 113, 117, 118, 125
O'Hara, Frank 73, 80
'Oh Jim' 139
Oh No, They're Recording This Show (album) 8
Oldfield, Mike 180
Oldham, Andrew Loog 47, 116
Oliveros, Pauline 173
Ono, Yoko 43, 127 (note), 199
'Open House' 242
Orange Juice 125
'The Original Wrapper' 246
'Orly Flight' 141

'Ostrich, The' 33, 58
'Over the Border' 210
'Over Her Head' 258

Page, Jimmy 47, 153
'Pale Blue Eyes' 7, 11, 69, 99
Paris 1919 137–8, 139, 177, 179, 259, 262, 264
'Paris 1919' 138
Pass Thru Fire 99
Patten, Brian 44
Peaches 257
Peel, John 8, 41, 43, 46, 148, 155, 176
'Penny Lane' 147
'Perfect' 259
'Perfect Day' 164
Petralia, Mike 257, 258
Pharrell 257
Picabia, Francis 239
Picasso, Pablo 239
Pink Floyd 17, 38, 40, 42–5, 224
Pitt, Ken 35, 39, 41, 42, 147, 152
Plath, Sylvia 125, 211
Playin' Possum (album) 10
'Please Mr Gravedigger' 149, 151
Poe, Edgar Allan 73, 79, 109 (note), 267–8
Poitrenaud, Jacques 114–15
Pop, Iggy 5, 93, 116, 117, 147, 156, 162, 219 (note), 225
Pop Art 3, 55, 58, 59, 79, 145, 148, 154–7, 197, 217
Popol Vuh 179
Portsmouth Sinfonia 178
'Positively Fourth Street' 23
Pretty Things, The 38, 41, 42, 154
Primal Scream 257
Proby, PJ 36
Procul Harum 124, 177
Primitives, The 33, 58
'Prominent Men' 19, 41
Psychedelia 18, 23, 28, 147
Post-punk 83, 90, 92, 124, 138, 140, 141
Ptooff! 41
Public Image 141
Punk 4, 8, 11, 17, 20, 28 (note), 83, 89, 90, 92, 122, 124, 125, 126, 131, 140, 145, 152, 162, 192, 217, 224

'Quarter Ahead, A' 74, 75, 76, 81 (note)
'Queen Bitch' 146, 147, 155

Rachel Papers, The 2
Radiohead 91
Ragtime 109
Rainbow in Curved Air, A 176
Raven, The 73, 226, 267–8, 269, 271
'Reading My Mind' 258
Rechy, John 67, 68, 74–5, 76–7, 81 (note), 97, 100, 105, 108
Record Mirror 43, 47, 113, 116, 118, 126, 177
Reich, Steve 173
R.E.M. 92
'Revolution 9' 22, 199
Richards, Keith 211, 212, 219 (note)
Richman, Jonathan 13, 209–19
'For a Ride' 259
Riley, Terry 121, 137, 173, 176, 203
Rimbaud, Arthur 211
Ritchie, Adam 34, 35, 38, 44
'Roadrunner' 214, 215, 218
'Rock and Roll' 12, 20, 27, 168
Rock and Roll Animal (album) 161, 198, 224, 225
Rolling Stone (magazine) 79, 108, 135, 161–2
Rolling Stones 4, 20, 23, 27, 35, 40, 45, 47, 48, 58, 116, 134, 156
Romanticism 24, 132, 133–6, 140, 141, 154
'Roses in the Snow' 121
Roundhouse 42
Rosset, Barney 67, 70
Rotten, Johnny 224
Roxy Music 6, 124, 136, 142 (note), 174, 177, 178–9, 185
Roxy Music 178
Royal Tenenbaums, The 127 (note)
Rubin, Barbara 34, 39, 43, 53, 59
'Run Run Run' 86, 150, 214
'Russian Roulette' 141

Sabotage/Live 140
'Sad Song' 140, 162, 167, 169
Saint Etienne 210
St. Vincent 93

Sally Can't Dance 161, 224
'Salvador Dali' 211
San Francisco 2, 3, 23, 61, 68, 175, 228, 248
'San Francisco (Be Sure to Wear Some Flowers in Your Hair)' 23
'Satisfied' 258
Saunders, Pharoah 37
Schaeffer, Pierre 204
Schenker, Henrich 84–5, 90, 93
Schnabel, Julian 162, 237, 269
Schnitzler, Conrad 183
Schubert, Franz 134, 135
Schwartz, Delmore 3, 69, 79, 105, 206
'Screen Tests' 53–64, 240, 241, 250
'Second Fortress, The' 260
'Secret Side' 136
Sedgwick, Edie 39, 47, 54
Selby, Hubert Jr. 38, 67, 68, 74, 79, 80 (notes), 98, 100, 103, 104, 268
Set the Twilight Reeling 266, 267
Sex Pistols 20, 140, 145
Sgt. Pepper's Lonely Hearts Club Band (album) 20, 21, 22, 154
Shakespeare, William 123, 217
Shepp, Archie 44
Shifty Adventures in Nookie Wood 257, 259
'Ship of Fools' 138
Shostakovich, Dimitri 135, 137
'Shot By Both Sides' 140
'Silly Boy Blue' 150
Simon & Garfunkel 151
Simone, Nina 116, 117, 118
Simple Minds 91
Siouxsie and the Banshees 140, 141, 256
'Sister Ray' 3, 41, 68, 89, 92, 98, 100, 101, 103–4, 132, 200, 202, 203, 209, 216, 218, 233
'Silver Treetop School for Boys' 150
'Sixty/Forty' 113
Skids, The 141
Sleep (film) 55, 60
'Slip Away (A Warning)' 244
Slow Dazzle 138
'Smalltown' 242
Smith, Patti 116, 140, 141, 191, 211
Smiths, The 91

Snoop Dog 257
Social Deviants, The 41, 42, 46, 152
Soft Cell 141
Solanas, Valeria 126, 244
'Sold Motel' 259
'Song for Bob Dylan' 147, 211
Songs for Drella (album) 13, 237–50, 269
Songs of Remembrance 213
Sonic Youth 10, 218, 219 (notes), 263
Sounds 118, 214
Spandau Ballet 141
Sparklehorse 263
Spirit of Eden 261
Springsteen, Bruce 212, 219 (note)
Squeeze (album) 11, 12, 26, 146
'Star Spangled Banner, The' 189, 193–4, 204
'Starman' 155
Stevens, Fisher 268
Stipe, Michael 93
Stockhausen, Karlheinz 36, 121, 134, 135, 136, 183, 184, 187
Story of O, The 75
Street Hassle 79, 224, 234, 251 (note)
'Street Hassle' 166
Strip-tease 114–16, 125
'Strip-Tease' 115, 121, 125, 127 (note)
Strokes, The 91
'Style It Takes' 243, 250
Styles, Harry 211
Styrene, Poly 141
'Subway Sect' 156
'Sudden Death' 139
'Suffragette City' 155
'Summer Heat' 260
Sun Blindness Music 260
'Sun Blindness Music' 260–1
Sun Ra 37
'Sunday Morning' 1, 46, 86, 150, 163, 168
Super Furry Animals 264
Swados, Lincoln 71–3, 80 (note)
'Sweet Jane' 12, 84, 155, 223, 225, 229
Sweetheart of the Rodeo (album) 21
Swordfishtrombones 163
'Sylvia Said' 138
Sylvian, David 257
Symphony for Improvisers 123

Syracuse 10 71, 76
Syracuse University 3, 67, 69–73, 75, 76, 80 (note), 107

'Taking Your Life in Your Hands' 261
Talk Talk 261
Talking Heads 91, 218
Tangerine Dream 124, 173, 179, 183, 184, 192 (note)
Tarkovsky Andréi 211
'Tatters' 163
Taylor, Cecil 69, 202
Taylor, Vince 38
'As Tears Go By' 116
Television (band) 91
Television Personalities 211
Ten Years After 176
Theatre of Eternal Music 33, 35, 121
'There She Goes Again' 22, 87, 150
'These Days' 122, 127 (note)
'They Showed Me the Door to Bohemia' 218
'Things' 258
Third 261
Thomas, Dylan 185, 264
Thompson, Richard 210
Between Thought and Expression 97, 100
'Thoughtless Kind' 261
Throbbing Gristle 141
Tilt 261
Times They are A'Changin', The 19
Tommy (album) 20
Tomorrow 42
Ton Steine Scherben 189
Townshend, Pete 45
Traffic 20
'Train Round the Bend' 245
Transformer 147, 156, 161, 162, 170, 214, 224, 231
Trocchi, Alexander 43
Tropic of Cancer 67, 72, 74
'Turn the Lights On' 259
Twain, Mark 98
'Twilight Zone' 258

UFO Club 31, 43, 44, 48
Ultravox 141

Ulysses 74
Underworld 109
Une Femme est Une Femme 115
Unfinished Music No. 1 199
Up-Tight 4, 59–60, 61, 63
U.S.A. 104, 105, 108

'Valley of the Kings' 181, 192 (note)
Van Etten, Sharon 93
Van Ronk, Dave 22
'Velvet Underground' 209, 210, 211, 215, 218
Velvet Underground, The (album) 6, 10, 12, 22, 102, 103, 109, 272
Velvet Underground, The (documentary) 6, 64
Velvet Underground: The Complete Matrix Tapes, The (album) 12, 227
Velvet Underground & Nico, The (album) 6, 21, 32, 41, 45, 48, 53, 60, 67, 79, 83, 86–7, 93, 101 (note), 103, 145–6, 147, 151, 174, 204, 219 (note)
Velvet Underground: Peel Slowly and See, The (album) 12, 19, 41
'Venus in Furs' 17, 19, 34, 40, 46, 61, 78, 86, 87, 150, 151
Venus in Furs (film) 34, 40
Venus in Furs (novel) 104
'Verses' 258
'Vicious' 156, 168
'Vienna' 141
Vile, Kurt 263
Village Voice, The 35, 38, 41, 44, 62, 77, 148
'Vincent Van Gogh' 211
Vines, The 91
Vintage Violence 133, 176, 177
Violent Femmes, The 91
Visage 141
Visconti, Tony 161
'Von Himmel Hoch' 187
VU (album) 8, 10, 12, 92

'Waiting for Blonde' 258
Waits, Tom 163
'Walk on the Wild Side' 228, 231–5
Walker Brothers, The 36

Walker, Scott 142 (note), 154, 257, 261, 268
'Walkin' the Dog' 141
Walking on Locusts 256, 258
Wallenstein 124
Warhol, Andy: 2–6, 8, 9, 13, 20, 23, 27, 31, 33–7, 39–42, 44, 45, 47, 48, 49 (notes), 53–64, 78, 79, 114, 117, 126, 127 (notes), 135, 145–9, 151, 153–5, 175, 197, 200, 204, 206, 213, 231, 237–51, 256
Warlocks, The 33
'Wasteland' 258
Waters, Roger 38
Wedding Present, The 91
Wedekind, Frank 268
Weezer 210
We're Only in It for the Money (album) 2
Wesker, Arnold 42
'We've Got the Gold' 136, 181, 192 (note)
'Whaddya Mean by That' 259
'And What, Little Boy, Will You Trade for Your Horse?' 73, 74–7
What's Welsh for Zen 256, 264
'When Harpo Played His Harp' 211
White Album, The 22, 199
White Light/White Heat (album) 46, 79, 88–9, 204, 206, 209, 242, 272
'White Light/White Heat' 88, 132, 147, 155, 156, 157
Who, The 36, 133, 153
'Who Am I? (Tripitena's Song)' 271
'Who Knows Where the Time Goes' 122
'Why Don't You Smile Now' 149
Wilson, Robert 273 (note)
Wilson, Tom 39, 48, 175
Winehouse, Amy 211
Wire 140, 141
Wolff, Christian 173
'Woman' 259
Woodstock 189–90
Wordsworth, William 123, 127
'Work' 244, 245, 250
Wornorov, Mary 60–1
'Wrap Your Troubles in Dreams' 40
Wyatt, Robert 180

X for Henry Flynt 173

Yardbirds, The 35, 42, 152–3, 204
Yo La Tengo 218
Yoshihide, Otomo 198
'You Forget to Answer' 136, 181
Young, La Monte 3, 5, 6, 33, 34, 35, 49 (note), 121, 173, 176, 186, 203
Young, Neil 186
For Your Pleasure 178

'You're Driving Me Insane' 149
Yule, Billy 26
Yule, Doug 6, 7, 10, 11–13, 26, 27, 42, 146, 219 (note)

Zappa, Frank: 2, 7, 17, 21, 39, 45, 150, 228, 234
Zeitkratzer 205, 269
Ziggy Stardust 145–57
Zorn, John 269–70

www.ingramcontent.com/pod-product-compliance
Lightning Source LLC
Chambersburg PA
CBHW052152300426
44115CB00011B/1628